NCIDENTS THAT GAVE AMERICA THE MOTOR CAR

Birth of a Giant

The Men and Incidents that Gave America the Motorcar

Birth of a Giant

The Men and Incidents That Gave America the Motorcar

Richard Crabb

Chilton Book Company

Philadelphia   New York   London

Dedication

To Herbert R. Lewis

Who worked with both
Buffalo Bill Cody and Alfred Sloan, Jr.
—from horses to horsepower

Foreword

This book developed from a strange question asked me at lunch one day by Roy Porter of Evanston, an editor of many, notable, non-fiction books. Without preliminary remarks, Roy asked, "How would you like to meet a man who worked for both Buffalo Bill Cody and Alfred Sloan?"

This is how I met Herbert R. Lewis who worked with Sloan both before and after Sloan joined General Motors. Lewis, who like his friends Dave Buick, Billy Durant and Louis Chevrolet did not keep his General Motors stock, lives with his wife, Lila, in a Chicago suburb. I met Lewis almost every week for several hours over a period of more than two years. In this time, I was able to develop the feeling of personal acquaintance with every man who had made an important contribution to the motorcar, from Duryea to Chrysler, except for Jonathan Maxwell and James W. Packard. Lewis had never met either of them.

In the course of these interviews, Lewis made several thousand feet of tape recordings of his motorcar experiences and recollections that began in 1908, the year that the Ford Motor Company introduced the "Model-T" and Durant founded General Motors. During this period, Lewis also placed in my hands enough letters, pictures and mementos to fill four standard filing cabinets. They included such things as the formal notification of the $72,000 General Motors cash- and stock-bonus awarded him (on Sloan's recommendation), in 1920, for unusual service to the corporation.

Meanwhile, I was becoming familiar with the important books, and magazine and newspaper accounts dealing with the subject. I was meeting others, also, who had firsthand recollections to contribute. For example, I had an extended visit and tape interview with Howard Crawford of Detroit. Crawford reported for work only days before the opening of the Buick plant that Durant built on the Old Hamilton Farm at the north end of Flint.

By this time, I had become convinced that here was an opportunity to make a solid addition to the literature of the motorcar. I realized that no account existed which described the important achievements, step by step from the beginning, that contributed to the automobile as we know it today.

Before I began writing the manuscript, I went to California to talk with Allan Nevins. I grew up in western Illinois not far from the Camp Point farm where Dr. Nevins was born and grew to manhood. What an opportunity it was to consult with this man, one of the foremost living historians of the English-speaking nations!

Done in collaboration with Frank E. Hill, Nevins's three volumes on Henry Ford and the first sixty years of the Ford Motor Company are the most comprehensive yet done on the rise of the motorcar. The volumes constitute a history of American industry for the first half of this century projected against the major developments of the previous two hundred years.

In addition, Nevins speaks from a personal acquaintance with many of those who had decisive roles in developing the motorcar. Here is an example of his personal observations: "Sloan was a humble man. I often saw him, and occasionally joined him for dinner, at the Century Club in New York. What a shame it is there is not a car named for him. He deserves much more recognition than he has received."

Then, I began writing. As each chapter was developed, I sent it to an authority on the work of the particular individual involved. The Duryea chapters went to Donald M. Macaulay of Longmeadow, Massachusetts. Judge Macaulay, now the senior judge of the Superior Court of Massachusetts, was Frank Duryea's advisor and legal counsel during the last fifty years of Duryea's life. Judge Macaulay knew, better than anyone living today, the man who built the first successful self-propelled vehicle in the United States.

As has often been the case, Judge Macaulay did more than check the manuscript for accuracy. He responded with additional information that has enriched the book. For instance, for years it has been said and written that the booklet published in 1903 by the Olds Motor Works of Lansing describing the Curved-Dash Oldsmobile was the first publication of its kind in the United States. But—in the private papers of Frank Duryea, placed with Judge Macaulay by the family after Duryea's death, there is an impressive brochure published in 1898. Printed in black and gold, it presents pictures of various body styles of the Duryea. This is, perhaps, the only surviving copy. Its value is the greater because a few years before his death in 1967 (Duryea outlived most of the founders), Frank Duryea had been so thoughtful as to identify, in his own handwriting, the men appearing in the pictures.

The chapters dealing with the career of Ransom E. Olds were read by his daughter, Gladys Olds Anderson, and by his grandson, R. E. Olds Anderson. When the Olds Motor Works was established in Detroit, Ransom E. Olds moved his family from Lansing, but it had not been possible before to establish the date. The first draft of the manuscript acknowledged this. Mrs. Anderson unlocked the matter when she recalled, "We were in Detroit on December 31, 1899. I remember Father got all of us children out of bed just before midnight, explaining that we would not have the chance ever again to see a new century born and he didn't want us to miss it. We saw the old century out in our home in Detroit."

Mrs. Wilfred Leland, wife of Wilfred Leland and daughter-in-law of Henry M. Leland, read the entire manuscript. Her own book, "Master of Precision—Henry M. Leland," was published in 1966. In reviewing this manuscript, she not only had the advantage of having lived through the events, but also of having reduced them to a book very recently. To Mrs. Leland, special appreciation.

At the suggestion of Dr. Nevins, the chapters dealing with Ford matters went to Owen Bombard with whom Nevins and Hill worked closely in the preparation of their exhaustive work.

Clarence Young of Flint, Michigan, an authority on the early years of Buick development in that city, reviewed the chapters dealing with William C. Durant and the Buick Motor Company. Young is at work on a biography of Durant. There is now no adequate source of information about this man who played such a vast role in the development of General Motors.

Dr. and Mrs. Ray Billington were consulted on the Dodge chapters. Both of the Billingtons grew up in Detroit where Mrs. Billington's father represented car component manufacturers. He sold such large orders to the Ford Motor Company that, as Mrs. Billington reports, "We always drove Ford cars." Mrs. Billington was a guest at the wedding of Delphine, daughter of Mr. and Mrs. Horace Dodge, and still has a piece of the wedding cake.

The account of the first motorcar trip from Detroit to New York City, undertaken by Roy D. Chapin, was reviewed by his son, Roy D. Chapin, Jr., Chairman of the Board of The American Motors Corporation. Mr. Chapin also provided the picture of his father and the Curved-Dash Oldsmobile taken in New York at the end of the historic trip.

James V. Fletcher, Director of Editorial Services for the Chrysler Corporation, reviewed the manuscript dealing with Chrysler development and bringing Dodge into the Chrysler Corporation.

The account of the Thomas Flyer's victory in the 1908 New York-to-Paris-Race and its re-enactment in 1968, contains information not previously published. Special credit is due Roy Nagle, Niagara frontier historian, of Buffalo, New York.

For the remarkable pictures of the early Oldsmobile and Ransom E. Olds, taken more than sixty years ago, I am indebted to Dean William Combs of Michigan State University. Dean Combs is in charge of organizing, for the University, the personal papers and mementos of Ransom E. Olds that, at the beginning, filled more than eight hundred filing boxes.

My wife, Rachel, has taken much time away from her tasks as a University of Illinois home economist to help with important field research and interviews.

Marlene Bennett of Wheaton, Illinois, has performed the almost endless and vital tasks of the processing editor.

To Mrs. Vera Dehring of Arlington Heights a special kind of thanks. She suggested nearly seventy-five different titles, including "A Giant Is Born," the final title being merely a derivative of her thinking.

Of the many persons who read one or more of the numerous versions of the developing manuscript, there are seven to whom special appreciation is due. As in all of my serious writing efforts, my mother, Mrs. C. R. Crabb, of Macomb, who edits the family newspapers, has made many useful suggestions. Hulin Cross and George Campbell of the Waukegan Antique Car Club have been most helpful in confirming, and sometimes correcting, names, dates and facts.

Frank and Ethel Kolerus of Mount Prospect have, from the beginning, provided a sensitive sounding board for the evaluation of material. James Hall of Palatine, public school administrator, and Mrs. Beth Hamilton, analyst for International Minerals Corporation in Skokie, have been of great help in their respective fields.

To all concerned, I am greatly indebted.

RICHARD CRABB

Wheaton, Illinois

Contents

Part One

The
Horseless Carriage
Era

1

In the Beginning:
The Duryea

The 20th of September brought a pleasant, late-summer day to southern New England. In Springfield, Massachusetts, a young tool-maker and bicycle shop mechanic from Illinois scanned the morning sky and concluded there would be no rain that day. He had an unusual and exciting task before him. He would need good weather. The year was 1893.

This was the moment he had hoped for, through nearly two years of unrelenting labor. He had worked, almost alone, on the second floor of the Russell Machine Shop at 47 Taylor Street in the Springfield business district—worked alone to avert the possibility of having his ideas stolen and patented by another. He had labored every day, except Sunday, and sometimes right on through the night. He had continued to work even when he was ill with typhoid fever, until he was unable to rise from his bed for a month during which he fought for his life.

At about nine that morning, twenty-three-year-old J. Frank Duryea opened the doors of the horse barn. There stood what appeared, at first glance, to be a smart-looking buggy. It was the type to be found in most of the thousands of barns and carriage houses back of the homes of upper middle class families in New England

and much of the rest of the United States. But there was something very different about this buggy. Insofar as Duryea and his three companions knew, there was no other carriage like it, anywhere. This was a horseless buggy. Duryea had just thrown open the barn doors with the intention of giving his new self-propelled vehicle its first road test.

His older brother, Charles, a bicycle manufacturer in Peoria, Illinois, had conceived the idea—not all at once, but over a period of six or seven years. Charles was capable of such thinking, especially about machines and transportation. Since his boyhood on a farm at Canton, west of Peoria, Charles had been predicting that, one day, men would use a machine to fly across the Atlantic Ocean. A lot of people thought Charles was strange, but his younger brother idolized him. Charles had designed the horseless carriage, supervised the making of the drawings, secured financial backing in Springfield, and engaged his brother, Frank (already an expert machinist), to build the self-propelled vehicle.

On the previous afternoon, the revolutionary vehicle had been brought down from the second floor of the Russell machine shop. To maintain secrecy and to avoid possible scorn of the townspeople, Duryea had concealed his horseless buggy behind the Russell building until nightfall. After dark, he had used a horse to pull the vehicle through the business district to the horse and buggy barn on the west edge of Springfield where the test could be made on little-used Spruce and Florence Streets. With a horse hitched in its accustomed place in front of the buggy, and in the darkness, no one noticed anything unusual.

The four men taking part in the test pushed the horseless buggy into the street. With Duryea, were Howard Bemis, trusted friend who had been helpful during the construction of the vehicle, Rudolph MacPhee of the *Springfield Evening Union* (who had already written the first comprehensive account of a horseless carriage powered by an internal combustion engine to be printed in an American newspaper) and Erwin F. Markham of Springfield, who had financed the building of the motorized buggy.

Duryea climbed into the right side of the buggy seat. A tiller, an adaptation of a bicycle handle bar, extended up from the front axle to steer the vehicle. On the tiller was a lever for adjusting the amount of gasoline feeding into the motor. The tiller was used to change gears, also.

Duryea quickly checked his instruments and, with a forward

By 1905, Leland's engineers were using the single-cylinder
horseless carriage to support a glass-enclosed body.
This is Leland and the first Cadillac sedan. He used
it as his personal car for years, and the sedan is now
in the Detroit Historical Museum.

motion of his arm, signaled to his associates to begin pushing. The men began moving the carriage forward. By the time they had moved 50 feet, they were in a slow run. Duryea made some adjustments with the lever.

Suddenly, there was a loud noise, almost like the firing of a shotgun. From the small, single-cylinder motor, housed under the buggy seat, smoke poured out as though the vehicle were on fire. The men stopped pushing and the horseless carriage moved forward on its own, continuing down Spruce Street for 200 feet until Duryea attempted to drive over a 6-inch earth curbing where the horseless carriage stalled because of slippage in the friction-type transmission. Years after, Duryea delighted to point out to acquaintances (including his long-time friend, Judge Donald M. Macaulay, still living), the Spruce Street curb that had ended his first horseless carriage trip. Nonetheless, the career of the American motorcar had begun.

Although Frank Duryea was not aware of it, his horseless carriage was not the first self-propelled road vehicle to be built. In 1875, Dr. J. M. Carhart of Racine, Wisconsin had developed a steam-powered car. That summer, he had driven two hundred miles, from Green Bay to Madison, and averaged nearly 20 miles an hour over unpaved roads. The same year, a German inventor and scientist, Siegfried Marcus, completed his second motor wagon; his first was built fifteen years earlier. The second Marcus motor wagon, powered by an improved type of internal combustion gas engine, worked so well that friends offered him the financial backing to market the car. However, Marcus concluded that it would not be economically practical to manufacture his car.

The Carhart and Marcus self-propelled vehicles were typical of a large number that had been built both in the United States and Europe during the Nineteenth Century. The Marcus motor wagon, in several respects superior to the first Duryea horseless carriage, established an important fact. Young Frank Duryea had never heard of either Carhart or Marcus, or their remarkable road vehicles. Charles and Frank Duryea believed, at this time, that they were the first persons in the world to plan, design and build an internal combustion engine for a self-propelled road vehicle.

Coincidentally, another young man, only a short distance from Duryea, was at work on a horseless carriage powered by an internal combustion engine. He was Percy Maxim, son of the man who invented the Maxim gun. Percy Maxim was working at the Pope Bicycle Works, in Hartford, Connecticut, only 35 miles to the south.

A graduate in engineering, Maxim had experimented earlier with a steam engine on a three-wheeled vehicle. In developing a small internal combustion engine, he concluded that gasoline for fuel was a better power source. Maxim had made considerable progress. However, Colonel Albert A. Pope suggested that he produce an *electrically-powered* car, instead. The first Pope electric was sold in the summer of 1895.

Later, Maxim observed, "I am amazed that so many of us began work so nearly at the same time, and without the slightest notion that others were working on the problem. In 1892, when I began my work on a mechanical road vehicle, I suppose there were fifty persons in the United States working on the same idea." It has been estimated that three hundred Americans were at work before the turn of the century on some type of self-propelled road vehicle. Most of them were attempting to place mechanical power in a buggy as a means of replacing the horse. This experimental work was most intensive in the prairie states, along the Great Lakes and in southern New England.

In the fall of 1893, when Duryea took his first ride through the streets of Springfield, some of the others intensively at work were twenty-nine-year-old Ransom E. Olds of Lansing, Michigan; thirty-six-year-old Elwood G. Haynes of Kokomo, Indiana; thirty-three-year-old Alexander Winton of Cleveland, Ohio; twenty-eight-year-old Percy Maxim of Hartford, Connecticut and thirty-year-old Henry Ford, as well as twenty-five-year-old Charles King of Detroit, Michigan. Not one of them had advanced to the point of a public demonstration and, for the most part, it would be several years before they did.

No one in this group knew of the existence of any of the others. The men who made possible the American motorcar started on their work from isolated positions and did not have the advantage or stimulation of one another's ideas. Miraculously, without a centralizing force, this absorption with the development of a self-propelled road vehicle in the 1890s began assuming the proportions of a movement.

The motorcar, and the momentous results that stemmed from it, were a direct outgrowth of the American spirit, resourcefulness and determination to smash the age-old barriers of transportation and communication. Technologically, the generation living in the United States in 1890 was the most advanced the world had known up to that time.

Americans, in 1890, had introduced the greatest revolution in

7

communication and transportation in recorded history. They had advanced the transmission of information from approximately *15 miles* in an *hour* (or as fast as a horse could run) to *185,000 miles* in a *second* with Samuel B. Morse's telegraph!

Only twenty-nine years before, messages first flashed from New York to San Francisco as Western Union linemen hastily welded the wires together on the main street of Salt Lake City to complete the first transcontinental telegraph. In 1866, messages were moving directly from New York to London via the first trans-Atlantic cable. In 1869, Americans completed the first railroad to cross North America or any other continent. The decade of the 1880s introduced Alexander Graham Bell's telephone and Thomas Alva Edison's incandescent electric light.

A prediction of American creativeness and a show of confidence in Man's mastery of the untried are found in a youthful pronouncement of Charles Duryea. In his high school graduation thesis, Duryea revealed a keen interest in the transportation of the future. His subject was "Transportation Other Than Rails." His paper was written twenty years before the Wright brothers completed the first airplane flight at Kitty Hawk, North Carolina. Yet, young Duryea predicted that the day would come when men would use a flying machine to cross the Atlantic Ocean in half a day. He lived to see his prediction come true.

Charles and Frank Duryea are examples of the men of that era and of more recent generations from farms and small towns of the Middle West who have prominently figured in the rise of the United States to a position of world leadership in many fields during the past century. Commenting on the Duryeas, and others such as Haynes, Chrysler, Ford, Jeffery, Winton, Kettering, Nash, Olds, Packard and the Dodge brothers who made the American motorcar possible, historian Allan Nevins says they are "... examples of the midwest man, trained to hard work and endowed by their parents with the intellectual, educational, religious and ethical lights—the old faiths and traditions—that shed a benign radiance over life in the Middle West and a hope that amounted to a vision of future grandeur."

Charles and Frank Duryea grew up in western Illinois. There was a difference of some years in their ages and, in a large measure, this accounted for the historic work they did on early motorcars. Charles Edgar Duryea was born on the Duryea farm between Canton and

Signature cover of first motorcar publication in U. S.
Frank Duryea first accomplished what thousands of
Americans had dreamed of doing—reducing the
ponderous steam and gasoline engines of the period to
one small enough to be mounted in a buggy to replace
the horse. Identification in Duryea's own hand.

Duryea Motor Wagon Company

GEORGE HENRY HEWITT, President.
DAVID ALLEN REED, Treasurer.
J. F. DURYEA, Mechanical Engineer.

837 State Street
Springfield, Mass., U. S. A.

*Right to left are
George H. Hewitt, David Allen Reed and J. Frank Duryea,
officials of America's first gasoline automobile company*

Peoria, December 15, 1861, the year the Civil War began. J. Frank Duryea was born in Wyoming, Illinois, in 1869.

Charles was always intensely interested in transportation. Shortly after he married, at the age of twenty-two, he moved to Peoria to work in a bicycle shop. The younger brother, Frank, fourteen, had shown a special interest in tools and mechanical work. Since Frank was able to help at the bicycle shop, he moved to Peoria to live in his brother's home, and to finish his schooling.

Almost from the time he entered the bicycle business, Charles talked of developing a small motor and mounting it on a bicycle. This interest was stimulated by a trip to Columbus, Ohio in 1886. At the Ohio State Fair he saw a motor designed to be used on a tricycle built by a Dayton, Ohio, mechanic, H. K. Shanck. The Shanck motor was big "as a heating stove," Duryea said. But, he began thinking of building a small internal combustion engine that could be mounted on a bicycle or buggy.

Charles Duryea did well in the bicycle business. By 1890, he had designed and built the "Duryea Sylph Bicycle." With some Peoria associates, he formed a new firm to manufacture bicycles. Until the financing was arranged and a building completed, Duryea contracted to have the bicycle built, first in Hopewell, New Jersey, and later in Springfield, Massachusetts. Frank, then twenty years old, moved east with his brother. By now an outstanding craftsman in working with wood and metal, Frank accepted a job as a toolmaker at the Ames Manufacturing Company in Chicopee, a city just north of Springfield.

Perhaps Charles Duryea's supervisory work in Springfield gave him time to design his self-propelled road vehicle. At any rate, he began intensive work early in 1891, five years after he had seen the Shanck motor in Ohio. His first efforts were directed toward creating an internal combustion engine that would be small, light in weight, yet powerful enough to move a buggy or wagon. No such motor existed in the United States; and, as the work of the Duryea brothers would prove, a motor with the performance they had in mind did not exist in any other country.

Charles Duryea's design work continued through 1891. By late winter, 1892, he was ready to begin building his horseless carriage. At this point, Charles made an important decision. He decided to move boldly. As a man with a business and a young family, Duryea knew that he could not give undivided time to building the horseless buggy. He had the good judgment to know that, if the new idea were to succeed, a capable mechanic would be needed to devote his entire time to building the vehicle. Charles decided to seek financial backing so there would be money to buy materials and to pay a mechanic to handle the construction work.

Charles Duryea had a particular mechanic in mind. He wanted his young brother, Frank, to do the work. He had trained Frank from boyhood in the mechanical arts, and considered him an outstanding young craftsman. He knew, too, that no one else could be counted on to take such an intense interest in the work. Frank had helped him plan the vehicle, and, in fact, had worked out the design for some of the important parts in the motor.

In March, 1892, Charles Duryea solved his financial problems by selling a 10 percent interest in the manufacturing rights to Erwin F. Markham of Springfield for $1,000. Markham's money made possible the first successful motorcar in the United States. It represented a very large investment to Markham, an investment from which, unfortunately, he received no financial reward. He did earn the distinction of becoming the first major investor in the United States to risk his money on a self-propelled road vehicle. He gained the satisfaction of knowing that his action contributed directly to the greatest development of his lifetime.

Charles bought a used buggy that was in exceptionally good condition. He rented working space on the second floor of the Russell Manufacturing Company in Springfield and moved the buggy to the Russell building. Actual work began on the 4th of April, 1892, and for seven months Frank worked full time on the project and Charles worked as much as he could. The work progressed. During the last months of that year, Charles and Frank Duryea and their financial backer, Markham, dared to hope they might demonstrate their vehicle early in the new year.

But it was not to be. In September of 1892, even before the motor was built, Charles Duryea moved back to Peoria to begin manufacturing his bicycles. Frank remained in Springfield to finish building the horseless carriage. The work progressed well but, in October, perhaps as a result of long hours of work, Frank Duryea became seriously ill. He was living at the Patrick boarding house on Front Street and friends nursed him there day and night for several days. One was David H. Nesbitt, who had attended the same Sunday School class at the Chicopee Methodist Church and who had become well acquainted with the young man from Illinois.

"I went to the house where he was boarding," explained Nesbitt, "and stayed up with him several nights all night until his illness was determined to be typhoid fever. After we knew that he had typhoid fever, I brought Frank to the hospital with the help of my brother-in-law, Samuel Craig, and Craig's buggy."

Frank Duryea recovered slowly, and after he left the hospital returned to his family in Illinois. It was January before he was able to return to Springfield and resume work on the horseless carriage.

Frank Duryea and Markham still hoped to see the vehicle in operation before summer. But, unsolved mechanical troubles developed. The motor was a constant problem. There was no one to consult, no printed source to check. Duryea had to figure it out himself. He would build a part that would not function and then rebuild it again and again until it would work. During this trying time, Duryea lived with his friend Nesbitt who became deeply concerned about the young man's health. In recalling these months, in 1893 and 1894, Nesbitt reported:

"While this car was struggling through the birth pangs of invention, guided by the brain and hand of Frank Duryea, he lived with me in Chicopee. No other can speak with greater knowledge of its ins and outs, the heartaches and the sacrifices made by Frank that an automobile could be possible.

"I remember all the discouraging factors. I remember when the small capital was exhausted. I remember Frank being chased to bed at 2 in the morning, not once but dozens of times, as he sat up scheming and planning. ...Yes I knew what the boy went through!"

By the end of June, Duryea had all the parts assembled and was moving the vehicle, under its own power, across the big second floor of the Russell plant. But each shop test revealed new flaws.

About mid-July, Frank Duryea admitted to Markham what he had suspected for some time. He had concluded that the free-piston type of engine could not deliver enough power to propel a buggy. The motor had to be scrapped. It was a discouraging moment, seeing so much work and expensive materials wasted, but Duryea did not consider giving up. Instead, he told Markham that he would contribute his services to building an entirely new type of motor if Markham would pay for the materials. Markham agreed, although his first investment of $1,000 had come to nothing.

In the next two months Duryea designed and built an entirely new motor that used the four-cycle principle and was water-cooled. He also built a new electric ignition system, a spray carburetor, a muffler and a framework that supported both the engine and transmission.

By the middle of September, Frank Duryea had the new parts installed and performance was greatly improved. At last, he was ready to take the vehicle out for a road demonstration! On September 19th, the motorized buggy was lowered to street level and the first public demonstration took place the following day.

The first newspaper account of an American-built, gasoline-powered self-propelled road vehicle appeared in the *Springfield* (Massachusetts) *Evening Union,* September 16th, 1893, four days before the first demonstration of the Duryea car. Staff writer Rudolph MacPhee wrote the account after talking with Frank Duryea and his backer.

"Rudy" MacPhee, a young reporter, was beginning a distinguished lifetime of work in the editorial rooms of the *Evening Union,* and, except for his journalism, little would have been known of the early Duryea vehicles. His frequent articles followed closely the historic work Duryea and Markham did in Springfield in 1893 and 1894. His was an assignment of considerably greater importance than keeping the *Union's* readers informed of developments on his beat. It has been said that the motorcar in the United States would not have been possible without the aid of an aggressive press. MacPhee's articles illustrate this contribution.

In the article appearing before the first demonstration, MacPhee's first sentence revealed not only the intent of Duryea and Markham, but also the public mood regarding a new form of road transportation.

"A new motor carriage, which, if the preliminary tests prove successful, as expected, will revolutionize the mode of travel on highways, and do away with the horse as a means of transportation is being made in this city," MacPhee wrote.

That Duryea had convinced MacPhee that the revolutionary new vehicle would run was established in the next sentence: "It is quite probable that within a short time one may be able to see an ordinary carriage, in almost every respect, running along the streets or climbing country hills without visible means of propulsion."

MacPhee attended the demonstration. While it was successful, Duryea, Markham and MacPhee had hoped for a better performance. The *Union's* account in the September 22nd issue was short. It stated that the first street demonstration was successful, but that there was more work to be done before the vehicle could be considered dependable. The motor and the transmission had disappointed Duryea and his companions. It lacked the power to move

13

the carriage except under favorable road conditions. The horseless carriage did not have the power to go "up a country hill," as MacPhee's first story had promised.

The September 20th demonstration was chiefly important for the effect it had on Frank Duryea. With his horseless carriage back in the barn that evening, he had reached two conclusions. Riding down the street without a horse was an exciting experience; and, he was sure that he knew how to build an even *better* horseless carriage.

Frank moved quickly. The next day he had his machine back at the Russell Machine Shop. For nearly two months he worked on the engine and the transmission. The transmission presented difficult problems. Finally, the substitution of leather for rubber on the friction areas helped.

On November 9th, Duryea made his second road test. The *Evening Union* reported the results in its November 10th issue: "The gasoline wagon on which Mr. J. F. Duryea (C. E. Duryea's brother) and E. F. Markham have been at work for some time was given a second test yesterday afternoon. The test was made to determine the value of a leather friction surface for propelling the wagon that has been substituted in place of the rubber surface used in the former test. The wagon worked quite satisfactorily, but there was a short delay on account of the friction surface wearing smooth, but this was remedied by wetting the leather belts."

Frank Duryea was encouraged by the improved performance. He took his motorcar back to the Russell shop and worked on it another ten days, then made his third public demonstration. This time he was so confident that he let his friend at the Russell shop do the driving. MacPhee reported the result in the November 19th issue of the *Evening Union*: "Residents of the vicinity of Florence Street flocked to the windows yesterday afternoon astonished to see gliding by in the roadway a common top carriage with no shafts and no horse attached. This vehicle is operated by gasoline and is the invention of Mr. Erwin Markham and J. F. Duryea. It has been previously described in the *Union*. . . . The vehicle, which was operated by Mr. Bemis, started from the corner of Hancock Avenue and Spruce Street. . . ."

Duryea was pleased with the progress demonstrated in the November test, but there was much more that he could do to make it better. The horseless carriage was not yet good enough to market. He went back to the Russell building and worked for two more months,

First American-made 4-passenger horseless carriage,
promoting new vehicle's use in law enforcement.
Car shows influence of older vehicles, the bicycle and
the buggy. Motor was mounted under front seat.

developing many refinements. He reworked and added so much that he really had a new vehicle. He had increased engine power and added a new-type of clutch and transmission, along with many other improvements. The sturdier carriage-type wheels were substituted for the lighter bicycle wheels used on the first car. The tires were of rubber cushion material with much more shock absorbing capacity. The steering was improved. All of the machinery, including the power drive to the rear wheels, was enclosed so that general appearance was better. Duryea's new clutch and transmission provided for two speeds forward, a reverse and a neutral postion.

By noon on Thursday, January 18, 1894, Duryea was sure that, before the end of the day, his new horseless carriage would be ready to road-test. Duryea used a different approach to the initial road test of his second car. There was no secreting the vehicle until nightfall. There was no use of a horse after dark to pull the carriage to the edge of town. It was nearly 9 o'clock in the evening before the car was moved to the ground floor. Shortly after, Duryea cranked the motor, climbed into the driver's seat and drove off. He spent an hour driving around Springfield.

The next day, January 19th, the *Evening Union* reported the unveiling of the second Duryea horseless buggy with this account:

"Last night the new motor carriage...was successfully tested by J. Frank Duryea, the designer and constructor. About 9 o'clock the start was made, the route taken lying through Summer and Magazine Streets, across to the Watershops and down Maple Street, the carriage doing all the grades encountered with ease, and developing a speed of about ten miles an hour .....Mr. Duryea regards the trip as fully proving the practical efficacy of the invention, and nothing remains now but to perfect the details."

This is the Duryea horseless carriage that is on display in the Smithsonian Institution in Washington, D.C.

Frank Duryea now reported to his brother, Charles, in Peoria, and to Markham, that he believed the present machine had been improved to its limit. It ran dependably; however, Duryea did not think its engine, improved as it was, could ever provide enough power. He said he was sure that, by starting all over, he could build a better gas-powered buggy which could be manufactured and marketed.

Markham had come to the end of his slender savings and could not go on. Charles Duryea was unable to finance the building of a second vehicle. Frank Duryea, for all his remarkable work, was out of a job. He could go back to his old job at the Ames Company in Chicopee, but he still wanted more than anything else to go on building a better horseless carriage. Two months passed. In March, Frank Duryea reached an understanding with H. W. Clapp under which, for an interest in the marketing rights, Clapp would provide the money to build the new Duryea car. Under the agreement, Duryea was to build the pilot model of the machine that would be put on the market. The agreement also provided for repaying Markham and Charles Duryea funds they had invested in the first Duryea.

This motorcar was built at the Stacy Machine Shop in Springfield where more space was available. By April, 1894, the new model was ready to test. Frank first designed a two-cylinder, two-cycle motor, but later changed it to a four-cycle, the two cylinders having 4-inch bore and 4½-inch stroke. Of the new motorcar's design generally, Frank Duryea reported:

"The car was a new design throughout. Instead of using a ready-built body, as had been done before, I designed a body with a width of thirty-three inches and a depth, at the rear, of eighteen inches. The only flooring was under the feet of the driver and passenger. Under this floor was placed the water tank from which water was circulated through the engine jackets by a water pump operated by an eccentric on the engine shaft.

"The interior framing of this body was especially designed for the purpose of forming supports for the motor and transmission. The rear part of the body was covered behind the seat, and in this cover were ventilators maintaining a supply of fresh air to the motor. A slot was provided in the rear panel near the left side, to give clearance for a large sprocket on the rear axle. The front wheels were thirty-eight inches in diameter and the rear wheels forty-six inches. The wheels were equipped with cushion tires which, three months later, were removed and two-inch pneumatic tires were substituted.

"The engine was placed in the rear end of the body. A governor mounted in the flywheel operated upon the intake valves so as to maintain, normally, a constant speed, but this speed could be manually controlled from the seat by the pressure of a rod on the governor springs. The cylinder heads being close to the right side of the body, at which point a small door or panel served to cover them, could be opened to expose the combustion chambers carrying the electric ignition device."

The "motor-wagon," as the Duryea Brothers called this new vehicle, was road-tested during the spring of the year. It performed satisfactorily, but called for improvements which could be made. Road-tests led to changing from a two-cycle to a four-cycle. Frank continued to send Charles, sometimes daily, communications on developments. On February 19th, he wrote, "Motor all right—can run right up to 700 (rpm)—looks elegant. Am casing gears." Reports of March 21st and 28th record that the new motor-wagon was complete and that it was being painted.

On April 25th, Frank reported a major success. "Everyone is pleased with wagon. She takes Pearl Street and Maple Street (hilly streets in Springfield) on second speed, six or seven miles an hour, anyway. She will run anything that can be found on the road. We had out a Philadelphia man yesterday and fascinated him." Again on April 29th: "The wagon continues to run well. No trouble to keep it in order at all now. Is a surprise to all. Pleases all that see it."

Problems were discussed in a May 20th letter· "We have had a tough experience with those cushion tires. They are no good," and the letter goes on to explain that the new pneumatics are being purchased from the Hartford Rubber Works at Hartford, Connecticut, and will be installed as soon as possible. Soon after, "Examined motor Saturday and found it in excellent condition. Wagon has done probably 6 or 7 hundred miles, and motor shows no signs of wear. Believe with proper care they will out-wear the wagon. No trouble to keep it in order—fill up oilers and gasoline and go ahead."

On June 10th, Frank wrote his brother again reporting that pneumatic tires had been put on the motor-wagon. He added: "Everybody pleased with it (wagon) and Clapp is getting actual orders every day. An order received this A.M. says, 'Book me for two carriages to be delivered at earliest date—kindly inform me what number my orders are and when you think you will be able to deliver.' Some of the orders state that they do not care how much the wagon costs—send it and draw on our bank. There is no doubt that the orders are genuine."

In July, Charles came from Peoria to discuss with Clapp the matter of organizing a company to manufacture and market the Duryea Motor-wagon. This is how Frank Duryea reported on the founding of the first organization in the United States to manufacture a motor-car: "... A group of local capitalists were favorably impressed and employed a Mr. Slater, a steam-engine expert from Connecticut to examine the car and submit a report. In the course of his investigation, he requested a ride to Westfield, Massachusetts and return—a distance of eighteen miles. The road was difficult, deep in sand and hilly. The car made the round trip without any trouble, and a glowing report from Mr. Slater brought capital sufficient to assure the formation of the Duryea Motor Wagon Company."

Frank drove Slater to Westfield, since Charles did not know how to drive. Charles stayed in Springfield a few days after the company was established and learned to master the Duryea.

While Frank Duryea was hard at work on his second car, the Duryea's first competitor was introduced in Indiana. The Haynes horseless carriage was successfully demonstrated in July, 1894.

Elwood C. Haynes was typical of the driving force that was causing the self-propelled road vehicle to spring up in scores of places throughout the United States. Like the Duryea brothers, Haynes did not know that anyone else in the United States was building a horseless carriage.

In 1892, Haynes covered a rural district, centering around Kokomo in central Indiana, for a utility company. He saw his time being wasted by riding in a buggy pulled by a horse. He thought that a small internal combustion engine could be developed and installed in his buggy so that he could make two or three times as many calls in a day as he could with a horse. Haynes took his problem to the machine shop in Kokomo, Indiana, run by the Apperson brothers, Edgar and Elmer.

Haynes worked with the Appersons and they began building their horseless carriage in the fall of 1893, about the same time that Frank Duryea was demonstrating his first successful self-propelled vehicle. Haynes and the Appersons were so sure their motorcar would work that they scheduled its first public exhibition as a part of Kokomo's 1894 July Fourth parade. They invited the famous Indiana poet, James Whitcomb Riley, to be the first passenger. Everything worked out well in the Kokomo parade and, as a result, Haynes and the Appersons also found themselves pioneers of the American motorcar business. The Apperson "Jack Rabbit," built several years later, became one of the magic names in early motorcar annals. Both the Apperson and Haynes cars remained in production until the mid-1920s.

It is interesting to observe the difference between Haynes and the other early developers of the American motorcar. Haynes was a brilliant engineer. He held degrees from Worcester Polytechnic Institute and Johns Hopkins University. He could read German, and was undoubtedly aware of the beginning work on self-propelled road vehicles created by such men as Karl Benz and Gottlieb Daimler.

Before he became interested in developing a motorcar, he had worked out the process for making carbon steel. In 1888, he invented the vapor thermostat. Nevertheless, his first car did not prove to be superior to the Duryea made the same year.

The vehicles that laid the foundation for the motorcar industry in the United States were built for the most part by more-or-less untaught, self-trained mechanics, like the Duryeas, Olds and Ford.

2

The Great Chicago Race
—and Duryea Again

In the fall of 1895, as the time approached for the manufacture of the first self-propelled vehicles in Springfield, Massachusetts, an event occurred that brought fame to the Duryea and moved the United States into the era of the motorcar. Early in the year, Herman H. Kohlsaat, publisher of the *Chicago Times-Herald,* decided that his newspaper would sponsor the first race in the United States for horseless carriages.

Kohlsaat did not have to support his Chicago horseless carriage race entirely on faith. Three years earlier, in the fall of 1892, there appeared in the Chicago business district an electric motorcar built by William Morrison of Des Moines, Iowa. Morrison is generally credited with having built, in 1891, the first successful electric car in the United States. Police had to clear the way for the vehicle, so eager were the crowds to see the electric car.

Chicago was a logical place for the new era to begin. Only two years before, the city had held the World's Fair of 1893, known as the Columbian Exposition, celebrating the 400th anniversary of the first voyage of Columbus to the New World. Of the major cities, Chicago was the fastest growing. It was already the transportation center of the country, the place where the great railroads of the West and East met to exchange passengers and cargoes.

Kohlsaat was a forward-looking and aggressive leader in Chicago. He had made a comfortable fortune in the bakery business, and was now engaged in what he regarded a form of public service, the publishing of the *Chicago Times-Herald,* a daily newspaper.

Kohlsaat had read, with keen interest, reports from France and Germany of the new, self-propelled road vehicles being made in those countries, and of the competitions taking place from time to time, especially in France. He sensed that this new self-propelled vehicle could make a highly important contribution to the already fast developing economy of the United States, especially of Chicago and the Midwest where the land was level and the distances great. He knew of very little being done in the United States with the new vehicle, although he was aware that some work was going on in a few places such as Springfield and Kokomo.

Kohlsaat sought to hold a sort of a congress of self-propelled road vehicles in Chicago that would bring together the best of the work being done on both sides of the Atlantic. He decided that a contest with liberal prizes would be the best way to bring this about.

Early in 1895, he announced that the *Times-Herald* would sponsor the first race in the United States for self-propelled road vehicles with a total of $5,000 in prizes of which $2,000 would be awarded to the winner. He modelled the event after the big Paris-to-Rouen race with a study of all competing machines after the event was over. Kohlsaat announced that the race in Chicago would begin on the World's Fair grounds in Jackson Park, continue north to Milwaukee, and return. One of the World's Fair buildings would provide a place in which to hold the after-race examination of vehicles.

The Chicago race announcement got wide publicity in newspapers throughout the United States and, within a month, Kohlsaat had made a discovery of the greatest importance. His newspaper had received not five, not twenty-five, not fifty, but approximately *sixty* letters and telegrams from men in the United States who wanted to enter a machine in the Chicago Race. Eventually the number of persons interested in taking part increased to nearly one hundred. Kohlsaat's judgment of the future importance of the motorcar had been promptly confirmed, and he began talking to other civic leaders about making Chicago the center of a new industry.

The inquiries and entries received by Kohlsaat revealed several things that were previously unknown. There was already in existence a widespread, strictly local experimentation with a self-propelled road vehicle in the United States. Most of the interest was in

In 1908, the Royal
Automobile Club of
England tested three,
single-cylinder
Cadillacs; took them
apart, exchanged the
pieces and found
them so perfectly
standardized that the
reassembled horseless
carriages performed as
well after as before.
Cadillac and Leland
were awarded the
Dewar Trophy
for automotive
engineering
achievement. Here
Leland's grandson,
Wilfred Leland, Jr., is
pictured in the trophy.

a broad band extending from St. Louis to Boston. Most of the inventors knew nothing of the work of others in this country or in Europe. Finally, the communications indicated that most of these experimenters had already been working on their machines in spare time, from two to three years. Some said they needed an event such as the Chicago Race to provide an incentive to get their vehicles completed. Most of them did not indicate a great interest in marketing their machines, although the response from Frank Duryea in Massachusetts and Elwood Haynes in Indiana were definite exceptions.

More than half who wanted to enter said they could not complete their machines in time, and hoped the *Times-Herald* would postpone the race until later in the year. Kohlsaat, realizing the value of attracting as many entries as possible, immediately considered delaying the contest until Labor Day. Soon he decided even that date would be too early, and settled upon Saturday, November 2nd, perhaps the last week when balmy Indian Summer weather might still prevail.

On November 2nd, only two of the nearly eighty drivers entered appeared in Chicago with their motorcars. They were Frank Duryea of Springfield and Oscar Mueller of Decatur, Illinois. Mueller was driving a Benz belonging to his father, owner of a Decatur Machine Shop. The elder Mueller had modified the German car to increase its power and speed. Unbelievably, most of the other eighty who wished to compete pleaded that if Kohlsaat would once more postpone the race until the end of the month, and run it in Thanksgiving Day, November 28th, they would have their machines ready. All this became apparent only on the day before the planned contest.

This put Kohlsaat in a difficult and embarrassing position. He had been under increasing, competitive fire from other Chicago newspapers ever since he had been unable to hold the race on July 4th. With the ridicule that was sure to follow another postponement, he feared the public would lose all interest in the matter. In addition, he had a crowd to face in Jackson Park at the appointed hour of 8:30 when the race was to begin.

Kohlsaat talked with Duryea and Mueller. He would make another postponement if the two drivers would agree to stage an exhibition for the benefit of the people who would assemble along the race route the next day. They should not attempt to run all the way to Milwaukee, Kohlsaat assured them. The exhibition would be only from Jackson Park to Waukegan, Illinois, a round trip of about 90 miles. The drivers were willing and the competition between the

Duryea and the Mueller-Benz took place in good weather on November 2nd. It was the first public motor-car competition ever to take place in the western hemisphere.

Charles Duryea rode with his brother, Frank, and Mueller had Charles Reed and S. F. Gilmore as passengers. The lighter Duryea, also having the advantage of carrying two passengers rather than three, quickly moved out in front of the heavier Benz. Mueller had tire trouble that delayed him, but the Duryea's driving chain broke, forcing Duryea to stop and do a repair job. Duryea had regained the advantage when an accident occurred that forced his motor wagon out of competition. At Prairie View, between Chicago and Evanston, a farmer, his team and wagon were at a crossroad, ready to cross, when the Duryea approached. Suddenly the team lunged across the Chicago-Evanston road an instant before the Duryea reached the intersection. In an effort to avoid a collision, Frank turned his motor wagon off the road and smashed into the ditch with such force that the motor wagon's differential housing was smashed. Without competition, the Benz completed the course, averaging about 10 miles an hour, a rate of speed beyond the reach of horse-drawn carriages.

Ironically, the Duryea brothers had their motor wagon pulled back to the railroad station by a horse. It was a discouraging moment. Frank was undecided as to whether he could afford to return for the race twenty-six days later, a race which might be postponed again, anyway. He really could not make plans until he got the motor wagon back to Springfield and determined how much damage had been done. There was one encouraging note. Oscar Mueller, with his Benz, while not pushed by a competitor, was anxious to make an impressive record on the Waukegan run. He had averaged only 10 miles an hour. If the motor wagon could be quickly and fully restored, Duryea knew that under the same conditions he could average at least 14 to 15 miles an hour, possibly even better. Frank Duryea sensed that his motor wagon might be able to win the $2,000 in the Times-Herald Race.

Back in Springfield, Duryea found that the broken housing was easily mended and within a few days he was driving daily on the streets of Springfield. After reviewing the developments in Chicago on November 2nd, the directors of the Duryea Motor Wagon decided to send not only Frank Duryea and his motor wagon to the Thanksgiving Day Race, but also the President, George H. Hewitt, and director, T. W. Leete.

They arrived the morning before Thanksgiving in threatening

25

weather. Seventy-nine of the ninety-two drivers who wanted to participate were on hand. Some of them, including Charles King (who would soon demonstrate the first motorcar to be built in Detroit), came without their cars.

Early in the evening snow began to fall, but Publisher Kohlsaat promptly ruled that the contest would be run, regardless of the weather. During the night, however, the snow thickened and the wind whipped in off Lake Michigan so that by daylight, Thanksgiving morning, 4 to 6 inches of snow had fallen, from Chicago to Milwaukee. In numerous places, the wind had piled up drifts to the depth of 2 or 3 feet. The judges kept in touch with the drivers during the night. Faced with such a storm, only eleven of the seventy-nine who had come were willing to risk their machines.

Kohlsaat announced that, in view of the storm, the race course would be reduced to a round trip from Chicago to Evanston, a distance of about 55 miles. Five of the eleven drivers willing to race were unable to reach Jackson Park, including the Haynes-Apperson from Kokomo which broke down in the heavy snow. Max Hertel of Chicago collapsed his steering gear when his car hit a snow drift on the way to the park. The weather weeded out the weak ones before the race could even begin.

At the appointed hour of 8:30 a.m., six of the contestants were waiting to start at the Midway Amphitheater on the World's Fair grounds. Two were electric cars whose appearance was more or less ceremonial, since, in the heavy snow, their batteries would run out of power long before the 55-mile course could be completed. The four gasoline vehicles included the Duryea Motor Wagon, the Mueller-Benz and two other Benz cars imported directly from Germany. One of these was entered by the R. H. Macy store in New York, hopeful of beginning regular sale of the Benz in Chicago after the race. The other Benz was entered by the De LaVergne Refrigeration Company of New York.

Each vehicle was assigned an umpire and no one else could ride with the driver. Charles H. King of Detroit was named umpire for the Mueller-Benz. Duryea was not as fortunate in the umpire draw. He got the ponderous, but capable, newspaper writer, Arthur W. White, of Toronto. White weighed a third as much as the Duryea Motor Wagon whose weight without passengers or fuel was 750 pounds, lightest of any of the competing cars. Since time lapse would determine the winner, the vehicles left one at a time, but in quick succession.

26

Charles Duryea had arrived from Peoria the day before the race to join his brother and the officials of the Duryea Motor Wagon Company. He rented a team and sleigh so that they could follow the motor wagon in the early stages of the race.

Frank Duryea and Umpire White left the starting line at 8:55. Before getting out of Chicago, the motor wagon rammed into heavy snow and snapped its steering mechanism. Duryea made a repair in fifty-five minutes during which time the Macy-Benz passed him. The Duryea had a considerable advantage in the open and, on the approaches to Evanston, the Springfield motor wagon passed the Macy-Benz. Shortly after, the Macy-Benz crashed into a hack that failed to yield the right of way. The Macy-Benz was restored to running order, but was not able to finish the race. The two electrics did not reach Evanston. Shortly after Frank Duryea made the turn around at Evanston he met the Mueller-Benz and, later, the third Benz.

On the trip back, the Duryea motor quit on Chicago's Diversey Avenue near Clark Street. The mechanism that supplied electricity to the two cylinders had burned out. Again Frank Duryea effected a repair, but the delay amounted to nearly fifty minutes. While none of the other cars passed him during this interval, Duryea and White could not be sure they had not followed an alternate route and passed them. It was dark by the time they got to Ashland Avenue on the way to Jackson Park. They had passed only one sleigh between 5 and 6 o'clock.

At 7:18 p.m., Duryea and White crossed the starting line, and Judge John Lundy stepped forward to proclaim that the Duryea Motor Wagon had established a world's record for a 55-mile course. Only one other entry had finished, and that was the Mueller-Benz which arrived an hour and a half later at 8:57 p.m. Umpire King had been forced to drive much of the route back from Evanston. Under the extreme tension and fatigue, Oscar Mueller had fainted in mid afternoon and was unable to resume driving. King had driven in the big race, even though he had failed to have his own car ready.

Reporter White's official account detailed the story of the Thanksgiving Day contest:

"We left the starting point at 8:55 and ran without a stop to the corner of Erie and Rush Streets. Here we broke our steering gear, running over a high crossing covered with snow. A wait of fifty-five minutes ensued. From this point to Evanston, we ran without a stop, arriving there at 12:35 o'clock. On the return we were delayed four minutes at Chicago

Avenue, Evanston, by a sleigh that tipped over in the street. Continuing, we got into the wrong road on account of the absence of a sign at Lawrence Avenue and Clark Street. We ran down Clark to Diversey Street before discovering our mistake. Then we went up to Diversey to Lincoln Avenue, and on Lincoln Avenue to Roscoe Street where we resumed the correct route. I estimated the extra distance travelled at two miles, approximate. While on Diversey near Clark we broke our "sparker" and spent fifty-five minutes repairing it. At 3:10 we resumed the journey. We were delayed fifteen minutes at Drake Avenue and Central Park Boulevard to adjust the machinery and refuel. Numerous slight delays of a minute or so I have not mentioned.

"Three and one-half gallons of gasoline, and nineteen gallons of water were consumed. No power outside the vehicle was used. I estimate that enough power was used to run the motor 120 miles over smooth roads. We finished at 7:18, and ran back to Sixteenth Street with our power. Our correct time was seven hours and fifty-three minutes. We covered a distance of 54.36 miles—averaging a little more than seven miles per hour."

From the day of the race in Chicago, there could be no question that the threat of the motorcar to the horse era was real. The Duryea and the Benz had accomplished a feat in the transporting of two passengers that would have been impossible in a horse and buggy. Even the stagecoaches, using heavy equipment and horses in relays, could not move passengers 55 miles in ten and one-half hours through heavy snow, mud and winter weather.

The great race also made it clear that the most important part of the motorcar was its motor. The Duryea won because Frank Duryea's four-cycle, two-cylinder motor proved to be superior, under the severe weather conditions, to the electric, steam, and to other internal combustion engines in the Chicago race. Closely related was the fact that the Duryea was the lightest of the six vehicles in the race.

More significant than all else, the Chicago race provided the first indication that an independent American motorcar industry could be developed. It was expected that the European cars would dominate the event. R. H. Macy Company of New York, with its European rights to the Benz, sent its car to the Chicago race with the obvious objective of interesting some Chicago retailer in becoming a distributor. Work on internal combustion engines and motorcars had been going on in Europe at least a decade longer than in the United States. Anticipating that Europe would become the great manufacturing center for motorcars, European producers of the Daimler, Benz and others had begun selling American rights as early as 1888.

The triumph of the light Duryea horseless carriage over the heavier Benz, blunted the effort of European cars to take over the American market. Frank Duryea's extensive road-testing on the sandy unpaved roads along the Connecticut River bottoms in New England had paid a handsome dividend! The Benz motor, built to move the heavier car on Europe's paved roads, did not have the stamina to operate in the snow and ice encountered in the Chicago race.

Another important contribution of the 1895 Chicago race was that it brought into focus the large amount of work being done on self-propelled vehicles in the United States, from the Missouri River east to New England. Until the last week in November, 1895, the three men, Duryea, Haynes and Pope, who had developed pilot horseless carriages, had believed they were the first of their breed.

Even when Frank Duryea and Elwood G. Haynes met at the race in Chicago, Haynes could not believe that the Duryea had been demonstrated in 1893, almost a year before the first public demonstration of the Haynes. Haynes refused, until the day of his death in 1925, to accept that fact. Haynes cars were produced for thirty years and the Haynes advertisements always carried the statement, "The Haynes Is America's First Car."

Quickly the news of the great test of self-propelled vehicles at Chicago was carried across the nation and to Europe, by newspapers, magazines and word-of-mouth. Both the United Press and Associated Press sent reporters to cover the event, and their stories appeared the following day all the way from California to Paris and Berlin. The scores of experimenters at work in the United States suddenly ceased working in isolation and became something of a fraternity. The convictions of these men in the future of the self-propelled road vehicle were strengthened. They ceased to be concidered "a little crazy" by their neighbors.

The Chicago race also revealed that the people of the Midwest were as intensely interested in a horseless buggy as the people of New York, London and Paris. The *Chicago Times-Herald,* pardonably enthusiastic about the success of its historic race, predicted that, in five years, there would be five motorcars on the streets for every horse-drawn vehicle. It did happen, but it took almost twenty years.

The Chicago race brought immediate fame to the Duryeas. When the Barnum and Bailey Circus opened in New York on April 2nd, 1896, the "Duryea Motor Wagon" was featured in the parade. The publicity was well-timed. In February, 1896, less than three months after the Chicago race, the Duryea Motor Wagon Company produced its first cars for sale. The machine was exhibited at the Mechanics Fair in Boston, February 20th to 24th.

These were the first multiple sales of a motorcar made in the United States. Of them, Frank Duryea later reported: "At that time (during the Boston show) I demonstrated the car to many, including George H. Morrill, Jr., of Norwood (Massachusetts). Mr. Morrill was, I believe, our first buyer, and Mr. Warren also ordered a car. All sales that year were to New England people."

May 30th, 1896, proved to be one of the happiest days in the lives of Charles and Frank Duryea. It was the only time they appeared together in a horseless carriage contest. In some respects, it was a rematch of the Chicago race held six months before. John Brisben Walker of New York and his publication, *Cosmopolitan Magazine,* offered even larger prizes for a horseless buggy race from the New York City Hall to Ardsley-on-the-Hudson and return. The distance was less than the Chicago race, and the condition of the route was greatly improved. There was no snow and a part of the route was paved. Again, the only real competition for the Duryea was the Benz. In this contest the Benz had a much better advantage, the route conditions being favorable to the heavier vehicle. As evidence that the Duryea was now in production, four Duryeas were entered. Frank and Charles drove the newest Duryeas, just out of the shop.

The New York race proved to be a romp for the Duryea brothers. The leading Benz competitor failed to finish. Frank Duryea came in first and Charles was second. The first prize was $3,000.

The race in New York set the stage for the Duryea's greatest triumph. But before that event took place in November, an important new American motorcar was introduced. It was the Winton, made in Cleveland, Ohio.

Alexander Winton was reared near the sea in Scotland and became a steamship engineer. He migrated to the United States in 1880. By the time he was thirty, he was in the bicycle business in Cleveland. Winton built his first motorcar in 1896 in his bicycle factory. In September, he drove it in public for the first time. The trip was a drive from the Winton Cycle Company factory to Cleveland Square, a distance of five miles. The car performed perfectly.

The Winton was more than a horseless buggy. Its body clearly indicated that Winton had seen the Benz... although it had important features that were new both in the United States and Europe. The first Winton possessed an excellent power plant, a two-cylinder internal combustion engine with a 5-inch bore and electrical ignition, similar to but larger than the Duryea motor. Because of its increased power, the Winton provided for five passengers, and could carry six if the driver did not object to being crowded. The three passengers seated in the rear, entered from the rear and faced the rear. Winton called it an "Omnibus."

In March, 1897, Winton formed the Winton Motor Carriage Company. One of his first efforts was to build a small fleet of six omnibuses to start a bus service in Cleveland. But, there were so many damage suits from owners of horse-drawn vehicles that the project had to be cancelled.

In the summer of 1897, Winton personally made the first Cleveland-to-New York trip in a motorcar, an 800-mile excursion that required ten days. Winton left Cleveland on Wednesday, July 29th, and arrived in New York on Saturday, August 7th. His route took him through Rochester, Syracuse, Utica and Albany. His driving time was 78 hours and 43 minutes. Winton's general description of the roads between towns was a single word: "outrageous."

Winton was the first to change the tiller to a steering wheel. He developed the first practical storage battery. He was one of the first to move the power plant from under the car and install it in front of the passengers. Two or three motorcars made the change the same year, but the idea was original with Winton. In 1905, Winton introduced an eight-cylinder motorcar.

Winton was an energetic, resourceful and highly emotional man. His associates said they could always tell whether his mood was high or low by the way he handled his hat. When elated, he often tossed his hat into the air. When in a fit of temper, he would throw his hat on the floor and jump on it. He found criticism difficult to take, even from customers.

Once an irate customer pulled a Winton through the streets of Detroit behind a team and wagon with a sign attached: "This is the only way to drive a Winton." Quickly, Alexander Winton arranged to cover the same route, pulling behind his Winton car, a farm wagon with a lone jackass aboard, and a sign which stated, "This is the only living creature unable to drive a Winton."

On another occasion, a Winton customer from nearby Warren, Ohio, visited Winton's Cleveland office to discuss improvements he thought could be made in the vehicle. The Scotsman lost his temper, and yelled: "All right, if you don't like the car, and you know so much, why don't you make a car of your own?" He was addressing a young manufacturer of electrical supplies, James W. Packard, who

31

went home and built his first Packard. It became one of the great motorcars of the world for more than half a century.

Alexander Winton built powerful and attractive automobiles for wealthy families. Often these cars were made to order. But Winton's most important contribution was his effect upon others. He challenged Packard to build his own car. He raced against Henry Ford and helped Ford get parts for his racing cars.

Using the Chicago and New York prize money for labor and parts, the Duryea Motor Wagon factory in Springfield was a busy place during 1896. The Duryea was the only American-made motorcar in production. (The first machines to be sold by Haynes and Winton did not become available until 1897.) Frank Duryea supervised the production. All the Duryea cars were custom made. The idea of mass assembly of such a complicated piece of machinery had not yet been seriously considered. Before the end of the year, seventeen Duryeas had been produced and sold.

In the fall, Frank Duryea left for England with two of his newest Duryeas to take part in the London-to-Brighton race. The distance was about the same as the 55-mile Chicago race. This outstanding European event took place November 14th, 1896, to celebrate the repeal of the restrictive laws in England which prevented the English from taking a serious interest in developing self-propelled road vehicles. Such restrictive laws were first passed by Parliament as early as 1830. In 1865, the "red flag" law was passed. It specified that a man carrying a red flag must walk ahead of any self-propelled vehicle on the English highways.

More than forty motorcars were entered in the big London race, most of them from Germany and France. Just as in the races in Chicago and New York, there were electric-, steam- and gasoline-powered vehicles. Entered, and favored to win, was the Panhard & Levassor motorcar which had run fourth in the Paris-to-Rouen race in 1894, and had won the Paris-to-Bordeaux 727-mile race in 1895. The London-to-Brighton race brought together the foremost motorcars in the world.

The race operated under rules different from those used in the Chicago and New York contests. There were no umpires with the drivers. The cars were lined up at the starting point, and they all left together at the referee's signal. The first car to reach the finish line would win.

The American Duryea, perhaps because it was a relatively unknown entry in the race, was placed at the end of the great procession of cars as they roared away from the starting point. Frank Duryea soon realized that his little car had the speed to win, if he could overcome the handicaps of the poor starting position and the dust. Soon another hazard was added as some of the cars, especially the steam and electric vehicles, began to stall. The stalled vehicles caused accidents that could take an otherwise sound machine out of the race. For nearly 20 miles, Frank Duryea used his speed advantage to thread his way past competitors and avoid pileups that became more and more common as the race proceeded.

Finally, the Duryea pulled up even with the leaders. The hazards of late starting, dust and the danger of accidents were suddenly gone. The Duryea took the lead before the turn around at Brighton. It continued to gain until it was out of sight of any other car in the race. Frank Duryea drove across the finish line and waited a full hour for the second car to reach the finish. The European observers found it hard to believe. The American Duryea had taken on the world's best—and won so decisively there was almost no contest!

H. J. Lawson, a London bicycle distributor, realizing the impact of the Duryea victory, approached Frank Duryea immediately and said that he and his associates wished to buy the European rights for distribution of the Duryea motorcar. After consultations, Lawson offered 40,000 pounds (about $250,000) provided the transaction could be closed quickly, so they could take advantage of the impact of the Duryea victory in the London-to-Brighton race. It was an electrifying moment.

The opportunity was greater than the ability of the Duryea Motor Wagon Company to respond. Charles Duryea, whose approval was needed, was in Illinois, and other officials were in Massachusetts. Even reaching them by cable was difficult and took time. Although Frank Duryea had been largely responsible for the Duryea's existence and success, he was not one of the principals in the firm. The company already had under consideration an offer from a New Jersey firm for American rights. It is likely that Charles Duryea and the directors in Springfield never understood the magnitude of the Lawson offer, or its implications for the Duryea motorcar. In any event, the deadline for action slipped away and no understanding with Lawson and his associates ever was concluded. The opportunity for Springfield, Massachusetts, to become the hub of the new motorcar industry flickered and shortly died.

After the victory in England, the Duryea Motor Wagon Company sold the rights to the Duryea "Buggyaut," the name under which

Frank Duryea entered his famous vehicle in the Chicago race and all those that followed. The purchase was completed with the Canda Manufacturing Company of Carteret, New Jersey, before the end of 1896, for $25,000.

Officials of Canda dealt with Charles Duryea. Charles was never able to appreciate how decisive were the contributions of his brother. Discussions with the New Jersey firm began after Charles Duryea appeared in the Memorial Day race in New York. As a result, Canda officials made it part of the understanding that Charles Duryea would move to New Jersey and work with them as a consultant for one year. No effort was made to secure the services of Frank whose experience and capabilities would have been many times more valuable to the concern. Canda produced a few motorcars in 1900 and 1901, and then wrote off its losses and retired from the business.

After the sale of the Duryea motorcar, Frank was immediately engaged by the Stevens Arms Company of Springfield, Massachusetts, to direct that company's efforts to develop and produce an automobile. The result was an outstanding motorcar that came into production in 1902 and continued to be produced through 1924. It was known as the Stevens-Duryea. The Stevens-Duryea cars were also manufactured in Coventry, England, for sale in European countries.

Frank Duryea was the chief engineer until 1915, when he sold his stock in the firm and moved to Madison, Connecticut. Financially independent the rest of his life, his only luxury was a remarkable workshop in which he busied himself working on especially intricate and difficult mechanical problems that occurred to him or were brought to him by his friends. He maintained close contacts with the important figures in the expanding motorcar industry of the United States.

Charles Duryea returned to Peoria in the fall of 1897. He established a little machine shop in the barn at the back of the Duryea home at 208 Barker Street. There he developed the first effective three-cylinder motor in the United States. In 1898, he tested it extensively on the Peoria streets, especially on the steep hills in the west section of the city where the campus of Bradley University is now located. Later, a university building was named "Duryea Hall" in his honor.

Charles Duryea and his associates attempted to manufacture the new three-cylinder car in the Peoria area, adding Peoria to the growing list of candidates for the role of America's "motor city." A building in Peoria Heights, (near the present Duryea Avenue) was outfitted. About 20 motorcars were produced there. Financial backing did not prove to be available in Peoria for large-scale operations. The factory and the support were available in Reading, Pennsylvania, and Charles Duryea moved his operations there. His three-cylinder Duryea car was produced for years. Duryea took great pride in the fact that his three-cylinder motor could climb the toughest hills in Pennsylvania in "high gear."

Before 1900, and, in part, as a result of the achievements of the Duryea Motor Wagon, New England made another bid to take over leadership in the young motorcar industry. Colonel Albert Pope, a trusted officer on General U. S. Grant's staff in the final stages of the Civil War, had gradually converted his bicycle factory to motorcar production. He began this conversion when Hiram Percy Maxim joined his staff in 1892. After the Chicago race, the Duryea brothers discussed joining forces with Pope and making the Duryea Buggyaut available for manufacture in Pope's Hartford facilities. But Albert Pope could not believe that the noisy, smelly, internal combustion engine would prove to be an important power plant for the motorcar. Nonetheless, Pope believed that the automobile was destined to replace the horse. The quiet, odorless, steam and electric cars would be favored by the customers, Pope contended. He constantly expanded his production of steam and electric motorcars until, in 1899, his Hartford plants out-produced all other American manufacturers combined.

That year, 4,172 motorcars were produced in the United States. Pope produced 2,092 steam, electric and gasoline vehicles. Nearly 40 percent of the cars made, that year, were steam-powered. Pope produced 1,191 of the 1,661 steam cars made in the United States in 1899. Pope produced 734 of the 1,575 electric motorcars made, but only 171 of the 936 gasoline motorcars manufactured.

Had Colonel Albert Pope seen as much future in the gasoline engine as he did in steam, Hartford, Connecticut, might well have become the "motor city" of the United States. Pope had the necessary financial connections, the skilled workmen, the factory facilities and contact with the market. For lack of proper judgment, largely that of a single man, Hartford did not become a permanent part of the most important new industry to rise in the United States during this century.

The Pope achievement in automobile production was historic, not only in this country, but also throughout the world. No European

35

manufacturer achieved a production of 2,000 automobiles in 1899!

In addition to the Pope cars, other automobilies produced in the United States in 1899 were: Sturges Electric, J. B. West's Gasoline Vehicle, Electric Wagon, Electrobat, Haynes, Hertel, Hill's Loco-motor, Howard Gasoline Wagon, Hall Gasoline Trap, Electric De-livery Wagon, Cross Steam Carriage, Columbia Motor Carriage, Barrows Motor Vehicle, Anthony's Electric Runabout, Elliott's Motor Carriage, Erie & Sturgis Gasoline Carriage, Whitney Steam Wagon, Stanley Steamer, Reeves' Motor Carriage, Morgan's Motor Carriage, Gasoline Motor Carriage, Wood's Electric, Waverly Elec-tric, Waltham Steam Vehicle, Stearns Steam Car, Altham, Brown's Touring Cart, Clapp's Motor Carriage, Langan's Motor Carriage, Jones Steam Car, Kennedy Electric Carriage, Lewis Motor Carriage, Marsh, Oakman, Rae Electric Car, American Electric Autocar, Wood's Motor Car, Baker Electric, Wisconsin, United States Motor Vehicle, Chicago, Eastman Electric, Grout, St. Louis, Overman, Ohio, Mobile, Hasbrouck, Henley, Holyoke, Jackson, Kensington, Locomobile Steamer, Leach and Lane Steamer. Most of these pro-ducers turned out fewer than 25 cars; none of them produced more than 200. Pope made more cars than all of them together.

The greatest of all American motorcars in the years before 1900 was the tough, little Duryea "Buggyaut." This is true, not because it was the first to be driven in public, but because of what the vehicle achieved in the seven years following its first successful runs in 1893 and 1894. The car stands as a lasting tribute to J. Frank Duryea.

That slight, modest, young man took the plans for a self-propelled buggy drawn by his brother, Charles, and set to work building a complex machine no prototype of which he had ever seen. He re-designed many of the vital parts, not once, but many times. Twice, he reworked and improved the original single-cylinder motor. On the second model, he developed an entirely new two-cylinder motor, incorporating the four-cycle principle. His two-cylinder motor was the outstanding motorcar engine of its time.

Refusing to stop with building the Duryea Buggyaut, Frank Duryea became the first American to prove a motorcar's worth in public exhibition. He took his car from Chicago to London to take part in demonstrations to prove that his horseless buggy was practical and dependable, and to a degree not yet achieved even by European automobiles. He met every challenger and took the measure of every opponent.

For seven years, the Duryea "Buggyaut" was the outstanding

motorcar in the United States. Only one other car was ever able to match that Duryea record, the "Model-T" Ford.

The great contribution of Frank Duryea and his rugged vehicle was the shield from European competition provided for the infant motorcar industry in the United States. The little Duryea that humbled the cars from Europe in three great races, and many lesser ones, single-handedly forestalled, for several years, a European take-over of the American market. The Duryea provided the time needed for the American industry to establish its leadership.

Stevens-Duryea cars are to be found in a number of museums throughout the world. The original Duryea conceived by Charles and built by Frank Duryea, which, in 1893 and 1894, proved the potential of the motorcar in the United States, looks exactly as it did that evening in January of 1894, when Frank Duryea turned its crank, got into the seat and drove with confidence and ease up and down the streets of Springfield. The Smithsonian Institution's inscription reads:

> "Duryea Automobile, 1893-94. Built by the Duryea brothers,
> Charles E. and J. Frank, at Springfield, Massachusetts.....
> It has a one-cylinder, four-stroke, four-horsepower, water-
> cooled, gasoline engine with make-and-break electric ignition.
> Up-and-down movement of the steering tiller shifts the gears
> to give two forward speeds and reverse. Weight about 750
> pounds."

3

Olds Leads the Way

The idea of a self-propelled road vehicle that could replace horse-drawn transportation quickly became a matter of widespread public interest in the United States, something that did not happen in any other country. The Chicago race in the fall of 1895 destroyed the curtain of isolation behind which scores of Americans were already seriously experimenting with a horseless carriage or wagon. The Chicago event encouraged the farm-shop and town machine-shop mechanics to accelerate their work so that results came quickly in the country's most populated area, from St. Louis to Boston.

Just one year after the Thanksgiving Day Chicago race in 1895, 8 horseless carriages, including the Duryea, Pope, and Haynes, were being marketed. By 1899, more than 50 self-propelled vehicles were available for purchase. In the year 1900, almost another 50 motorcars, mostly steam- and electric-powered, made their entry into the United States market.

There were other notable developments in 1900. The United States Army began its first use of motorcars for non-combat use. They were electric-powered. The United States Post Office began its first use of self-propelled road vehicles to collect mail. In the fall of 1900, more than fifty thousand people paid admission to enter Madison Square

Garden in New York City to attend the first automobile show in the United States. About half of the American firms making motorcars exhibited the largest collection of horseless carriages ever assembled —300 in all. The cars ranged in price from $280 to $4,000.

Within six years after Duryea's first successful demonstration, the motorcar had established a permanent bridgehead. In Chicago, Mrs. John Howell Phillips was the first woman to be issued a permit to drive a motorcar in the United States. Also in 1900, electric cab, delivery and ambulance service began in New York and Boston. Freelan O. Stanley went to the top of New Hampshire's Mount Washington in his Stanley Steamer, and John Brisben Walker drove his steam car to the top of Pikes Peak. A Riker electric won the 50-mile race on Long Island. Pope proclaimed that his Columbia was the first car to mount the engine in front of the passengers. Brooklyn buyers of Haynes cars were being promised delivery from the factory in Kokomo, Indiana, in twenty-one days.

Public interest in the motorcar was rising rapidly, and the infant industry was struggling to respond. As a result of the Duryea brothers split-up, the outstanding motorcar in the United States was not in production. Hartford, Connecticut, was the center of car manufacturing.

Two-thirds of the vehicles made by the approximately one hundred United States firms producing cars in 1900 were powered by steam or electricity. Women preferred steam and electric cars, especially the quiet electrics which started with the pressing of a button and created no exhaust vapor or odor. The electric cars' shortcomings were high cost and limited driving range. On battery power, they could travel only a little more than 50 miles.

In open competition, both in the United States and in Europe, the gasoline-powered vehicles were proving superior in range, power, speed and durability, but they were noisy and belched out clouds of ill-smelling smoke. The only important motorcars being manufactured west of the Appalachians were the Haynes in Kokomo and the Winton in Cleveland. Although they were superior models, they were larger than the cars made in the East. The Haynes and Winton were mostly custom-made, and were priced at a level which restricted their market to wealthy families and commercial users.

European producers were aggressively probing for control of the American market. The better-looking and more comfortable European cars were the Benz, Panhard & Levassor and the Daimler. In 1899, a new model of the Panhard & Levassor won the 1,428 mile

39

Tour-de-France race. In September of 1900, American sportsman, William K. Vanderbilt, drove a Daimler to victory on the Quidneck Park track at Newport, Rhode Island. He covered the 5 miles in eight minutes and fifty-three and one-half seconds. Wealthy families along the East Coast were buying the European automobiles.

European producers considered it but a matter of time until they would take over the quality automobile market in the United States. As early as 1888, Daimler had secured United States patents on his car. By 1890, Benz had appointed distributors in the United States.

In 1900, the United States motorcar industry was without the power to prevent this European takeover. The future was not on the side of Colonel Pope and the New England carmakers. They were committed to steam- and electric-power. The New Englanders had the plants, the workmen and the market, but they lacked the car.

A thirty-six-year-old midwestern businessman, hardly known outside the central Michigan town of Lansing, would, within a remarkably short time, change this. Son of an Ohio blacksmith, he was a quiet-spoken, pleasant man, more like a Sunday school teacher than the giant who was to move the automotive industry beyond the reach of foreign car competition. This man was Ransom E. Olds.

It was no accident that Ransom E. Olds became the pivotal personality in switching the center of the motorcar industry from the East Coast to the Midwest and providing new and larger shape for its future. Unlike many of the early motorcar principals, Olds was no part-time innovator. In 1900, Ransom E. Olds was one of the country's leading authorities on the internal combustion engine, its design, manufacture and marketing. Power was his business and had been for nearly twenty years.

In the early 1880s, Olds, still in his teens, was convinced that horses could be replaced by mechanical power. He helped his father design, build and sell the first Olds gasoline engine. In 1887, when he was twenty-three, he built his first horseless carriage, a three-wheeled, steam-powered vehicle. He soon built another, so dependable that he sold it to the Times Company in Bombay, India. It was the first American motorcar sold for export.

In 1895, he entered the nation's first motorcar race in Chicago, but could not complete his car in time to compete. He exhibited and demonstrated his first gasoline-powered car early in 1896. He directed the building of a factory in Detroit to make automobiles at a time when Ford, Cadillac, Buick, Dodge, Chevrolet, Lincoln and Chrysler were no more than men's names.

Ransom E. Olds (left) and Frank G. Clark of Lansing,
Michigan, and their wives in the 1897 horseless
carriage built by Olds and now exhibited in the
Smithsonian Institution in Washington, D.C. Olds had
started building steam-powered horseless carriages
ten years earlier.

In 1864, Ransom E. Olds was born to Mr. and Mrs. Pliny Olds in Geneva, forty miles east of Cleveland, Ohio. Pliny Olds was the village blacksmith for sixteen years. Since Geneva was a small rural town, with many horses to be shod and plenty of farm equipment to be repaired, the blacksmith shop was a center of business activity. From 1870 to 1874, he was employed at the Variety Iron Works in Cleveland, but he found he preferred having his own business and for a short time the family farmed near Parma, Ohio. In 1880, Pliny traded the farm for a house and some other property in Lansing, Michigan.

Ransom was sixteen when the Olds family moved to Lansing, Michigan, and he finished his schooling there. The change represented a great step forward for Pliny Olds. He established a small machine shop on the bank of the Grand River in Lansing. There Ransom learned to work in machine shop precision.

The new shop brought Ransom Olds into close contact with the gasoline engines then in use. These were large, stationary engines, for use on lake craft, power units for producing electricity, pumping water or doing heavy farm work. The steam-powered threshing machine was the only self-propelled vehicle, aside from the railroad engine. From time to time, Pliny Olds and his son worked on the threshers.

Soon after he took over the machine business in Lansing, Pliny Olds was aware that an opportunity existed to design, produce and market gasoline engines. He was constantly repairing European engines, such as the "Otto" made in Germany. Replacement parts were not available in Michigan.

The elder Olds and his son recognized the advantage of developing a new engine, perhaps several of them, for different uses. There would be income from the production of the motors, as well as from maintenance. But most important, he could offer his customers better service.

Ransom had an important part in this undertaking. From boyhood he had always had what his father called an obsession with motors of any kind. When he was only eighteen, he had built his first steam engine. Before he was twenty he had built a gasoline engine. The engines were small and had remarkable power for their size as compared with the engines then in use.

The first Olds gasoline engines were sold in 1885, the year Ransom was twenty-one. Shortly, there were Olds gasoline engines for marine, factory and farm use. At first they were sold only in Michigan.

Eventually, they were marketed from coast to coast across the United States. Ransom assumed an important responsibility for the building and selling of the gasoline engines made in the Olds machine shop.

Not long after the building of gasoline motors began, Pliny Olds made his son a half-owner in the River Street Machine Shop. The young man was soon to be married and his father knew he would need additional income. Further, it was understood that Ransom would, in due time, acquire the remaining interest. As a result, at twenty-one, young Olds began accumulating the experience of operating a successful business. Ransom E. Olds had completed his apprenticeship.

Ransom Olds began thinking about putting a motor in a buggy or wagon to replace the horse, perhaps as early as the time he spent on the Olds farm in Ohio. His earliest intensive work was done on steam engines. He was thinking in terms of reducing the size of a steam thresher power plant to the point that it could be installed in a buggy or wagon and still have enough power to drive the vehicle. His first steam engines were too small to provide power for a buggy. They were built merely to prove to himself that small motors could be dependable.

When he was twenty, he decided to undertake the building of a motorcar. Two years later, in 1886, he completed and began using his first self-propelled road vehicle. It was a three-wheeler with a steam engine. Olds used it around Lansing, and even drove it to neighboring towns, seven years before Frank Duryea demonstrated his first horseless buggy.

Only months before Olds completed his first steam car, Karl Benz and Gottlieb Daimler in Germany demonstrated their first self-propelled road vehicles. In some respects, Olds's first motorcar was more dependable and useful than those of the Europeans, although Benz and Daimler used internal combustion engines. Olds was not aware of the horseless carriage work going on in Europe or anywhere else; the Germans were not aware that Ransom Olds had put into use a successful self-propelled road vehicle in the United States.

The two Germans and Olds were working in complete independence of each other with the same idea. They were all demonstrating that it was possible to reduce the massive engines then in use (largely to move railroad trains or lakecraft and ships) to a size that could be used on a road vehicle. Any priority enjoyed by the Europeans was to be found in their better communications. For some years, it did not occur to Olds that what he was doing would be of interest

43

to even the newspapers of the United States or the scientific journals. The Europeans, in their more tightly-knit surroundings, promptly attracted public attention and publicity.

By 1893, Ransom Olds had taken two steps which had much to do with his motorcar career. He had concluded that it would be less difficult to adapt the internal combustion engine for use in a self-propelled road vehicle than it would be to adapt the steam engine, and he had started to work developing a small gasoline motor.

Further, he and his father had agreed that the demand for their stationary gasoline engines had grown to the point where they could no longer make them merely as a sideline in the machine shop. They would have to set up a new company whose business it would be to concentrate on making the gas engine. This required more capital than they alone had to invest. Accordingly, they organized the new firm in 1893 with two well-to-do men who supplied new capital. They were Edward W. Sparrow of Lansing and Samuel L. Smith of Detroit. Both Sparrow and Smith had made fortunes in Michigan lumbering. The firm was given the name "P. F. Olds & Son." Pliny Olds was president, and his son was both secretary and treasurer.

The horseless carriage developments going on elsewhere had, by this time, become known to Olds. He knew about Carhart's steam car, built in Wisconsin a decade before he built his first horseless carriage. He read the *Scientific American Magazine* which covered the European developments in self-propelled road vehicles. He was not only a reader of the magazine but also a contributor. In the May 21st issue of 1892, the magazine published a quotation from Olds which concerned his earlier steam cars. The article revealed how far his thinking had advanced on the potential of the horseless carriage. "It never kicks or bites, never tires on long runs and never sweats in hot weather. It does not require care in the stable and only eats while on the road."

Before the *Chicago Times-Herald* announced, in 1895, the first motorcar race in the United States, Olds had completed designs for his new motorcar with a gasoline engine. The idea of entering the race appealed to him. He knew the value of the publicity.

He intended to take part in the Chicago race and began serious work on building his new gas-powered motorcar. But his other business responsibilities prevented daily work on it. In the end, while the new motor was ready for the race, the carriage and power linkage could not be completed in time. Olds went to the race without his car.

Henry Ford's first horseless carriage. This vehicle
originally driven June 4th, 1896. Ford's first two
companies failed and first Ford car was not sold until
July 15th, 1903.

The Chicago race made a great impression on Olds. After he had completed his car six months later, Olds told friends, "I am thoroughly convinced that had we placed our vehicle in the *Times-Herald* contest at Chicago we could have captured the first prize easily."

The Chicago race confirmed most of the conclusions he had already reached. Steam and electric cars could not compete with gas engine-powered vehicles. The race indicated that the European cars, which had gotten most of the pre-race publicity, were no match for the American-made Duryea motor. The horseless carriage had clearly done what no horse-drawn vehicle could have accomplished. The crowds that witnessed the race indicated that people in the cities, who perhaps needed new transportation opportunities the least, were intensely interested in the horseless carriage.

After the Chicago race, Olds moved quickly to complete his new car. By the end of December, the vehicle was finished and tested on blocks in the limited space of the Olds machine shop. By this time, severe winter weather had begun. The people of Lansing did not see the new Olds horseless carriage until the spring of 1896. Like the first Duryea, the Olds car closely resembled a buggy. It had high carriage-type wheels with 1½-inch, solid rubber tires. The motor was mounted on the frame, underneath the seat.

The stationary gasoline engine business of the firm increased in a spectacular manner for four years. Although Ransom Olds was increasingly interested in building horseless carriages, the demands of the stationary engine business prevented him from doing so on a regular basis. In the summer of 1897, Pliny Olds, who was soon to be seventy years old, retired to San Diego, California, to live.

His son knew, now that, just as they previously found it impossible to make stationary gasoline engines as a sideline in the machine shop, it was going to be impossible to make motorcars as a sideline to the production of stationary gasoline engines. He knew also, that more working capital would be required to produce motorcars.

On a warm Saturday afternoon, the 21st of August 1897, a new firm, the "Olds Motor Vehicle Company," was organized at a meeting held in Edward W. Sparrow's office in Lansing. Sparrow was elected president, Ransom E. Olds was named general manager, and Samuel L. Smith became an important stockholder in the firm capitalized at $50,000. The secretary recorded at the first meeting, on the 21st of August, that the "manager was authorized to build one

As motors became more powerful, the horseless
carriages became larger with such features as tops
becoming standard, but with steering wheels still on the
right side. Dr. George H. Ripley of Kenosha, Wisconsin,
is at the wheel of his Rambler on a fall
hunting expedition in 1908.

carriage in as nearly perfect manner as possible and complete it at the earliest possible moment."

The vehicle was built before the end of the year. It was the only motorcar made by the Olds Motor Vehicle Company. Olds's new car was a considerable advance over the one built following the Chicago race. It seated four passengers, had smaller wheels and a number of other new features. Designed by one of the country's leading designers of gasoline engines, and built by shop craftsmen accustomed to working with motors, the car performed well from the first time Olds drove it.

This is the vehicle that is on display in the Smithsonian Institution in Washington, D.C. With a magnificent use of poetic license, the vehicle is described by the Smithsonian as "the first Oldsmobile." The Royal Academy in France would not give status to the word, "Automobile," for another two years, and the term, "Oldsmobile," was not developed for a year after that.

Olds knew that he now had a car which could be sold in quantity. From his experience with producing gasoline engines, he was keenly aware that the selling price could be reduced if a production rate of as many as ten cars a week could be achieved. Olds planned to produce the motors, and most of the components in his own plant. Before the Olds Motor Vehicle Company was more than a few months old, however, he was forced to conclude that it was too small an organization, and lacked the capital to support such a volume of production.

In the early weeks of 1899, Ransom Olds clearly saw an important motorcar industry developing in the United States. Later, he reflected about this period:

"The gasoline engines were our bread-and-butter business, and most people thought the car was just a toy, but *I KNEW THAT THE CAR WAS THE BIG VENTURE.*"

Olds knew that still another company with a vastly greater capitalization would be required to develop, produce and market cars. Amazingly, the money soon became available to him, and not from one source alone. He would have preferred to have had the new capital come from investors right in Lansing, and he talked to President Sparrow and his other associates about it. But Lansing, although the state capital, was a town of considerably fewer than 15,000 population. There just was not enough investment capital to sustain the project. After all, no other firm in Michigan was making horseless

The Olds Motor Works introduced its Curved Dash
Oldsmobile in 1901 into an era of horse-drawn vehicles
and dirt roads and streets that, after rains, often
looked like this.

carriages, and none in the United States that could yet point to any financial success.

The chief reason that Olds had money available to him in Detroit was that he was head of a highly successful stationary gasoline engine manufacturing business. At thirty-five, he had been successful for a decade in a succession of ever growing businesses. John T. Holmes and John M. Nicol of Detroit came to Lansing and offered to put more than $400,000 in cash into a new firm that would absorb the present Olds companies and reward Olds adequately. Olds turned the offer down. If necessary to move from Lansing, he thought it would be wise to establish the new organization in the New York area where the greatest market for horseless carriages would be found. He had an offer from New Jersey that would put the factory in Newark. He went to New York and New Jersey to investigate the offer but declined it because he did not think the backers there were sufficiently interested.

After Olds returned, Holmes and Nicol renewed their offer to establish the new business in Detroit. By this time, Olds was willing to move. When his present associate, Samuel L. Smith, who lived in Detroit, learned this, he offered to put up the necessary capital in order that his sons might have a business to come into when they were through college.

Shortly after, the Olds Motor Works, with headquarters in Detroit, was formed. The new firm was capitalized at $500,000. The corporate charter which became effective May 8th, 1899, revealed the confidence that Smith had in Olds and in his existing business in stationary motors. It is clear that Smith felt that the new firm would succeed, regardless of the fortunes of the Olds horseless carriage. The charter stated that the objective of the new organization was "the manufacture and sale of all kinds of machinery, engines, motors, carriages and all kinds of appliances therewith." Fifty thousand shares of stock were authorized with a par value of $10.00. Of the 20,000 shares initially sold, S. L. Smith held 19,970. Olds and two Lansing friends held ten shares, each. After Olds brought his Lansing companies into the new organization, he received an additional 10,000 shares of company stock.

Since there was no building available in Detroit which could be adapted for efficient production of motorcars, Smith suggested that a factory be built. The new plant of the Olds Motor Works was erected on a 4½ acre site on Jefferson Avenue East, near the present

John Maxwell, a 1901 tester for the Oldsmobile,
later developed his own car and, in the 1920s,
became one of the originators of the Chrysler.

Belle Isle Bridge. Begun in the spring of 1900, the factory was completed in the fall.

The Olds Motor Works factory was the first of the kind to be built in the United States, the motorcars made in the east having been manufactured in existing plants. Not only the decision to build, but also the nature of the factory represented a new kind of attitude and determination not present in earlier efforts to produce cars in the United States. The plant was developed as a small manufacturing complex with a total of four buildings. The main building to house the assembly and machine shops was an imposing structure, 300 feet long, 70 feet wide and 2 stories high. The foundry was 140 feet long and 70 feet wide. The blacksmith shop, a building for the final processing and grinding of moving parts, was 100 feet long and 31 feet wide. The structure housing the offices and display room with some provision for storage was another impressive structure, 170 feet long, erected in two tiers, each 50 feet wide.

With the completion of the Jefferson Avenue plant, office operations and all work on motorcars were transferred from Lansing. The Olds Motor Vehicle Company was phased out of existence early in 1900, but the original Olds company established to make stationary engines continued to operate in Lansing.

Ransom Olds did not wait for the completion of the new factory to begin work. In 1899, and most of 1900, the intensive engineering work and building of cars were pushed vigorously in Lansing. In all, eleven pilot cars of different types were built, largely with the spring sales season of 1900 in mind. The cars developed included some electric vehicles, demonstrating how extensively Olds was probing for the kind of vehicle that would attract buyers. Interest was limited in the new vehicles, which were heavier and more expensive than the first little horseless carriages Olds had built in 1897. While a number of cars were made, and sold, in 1900, no mother lode of customer enthusiasm was uncovered. The stationary engine business continued to be good, but the motorcar department had lost $80,000, eating up most of the firm's working capital. The future was anything but bright. As the year passed, and since the heavier motorcar, gasoline or electric, had not attracted buyers, Olds thought about adding to the family of cars to be offered in the spring of 1901, a light and less expensive car. This would be more like the first two that he had built.

On a Monday morning early in the fall of 1900, Olds discussed the matter with Horace F. Loomis, a graduate engineer, one of the men who had been important in developing new models. Loomis explained later that Olds had his ideas completely formulated.

"What we want to build," Olds explained to Loomis, "is a small, low-down runabout that will have a shop cost of around $300 and will sell for $650."

The Curved Dash Oldsmobile was the result. It was to become the most important horseless carriage ever built, but not until after a period of travail during which the life of the Olds Motor Works hung in the balance.

Loomis and his men built a pilot car. It was an exciting project from the first, even for the workmen. They tested it in the fall, before a transmission had been developed, by putting a man in the driver's seat, pushing the vehicle to start it and shutting off the engine to stop it. When Olds and Loomis completed the new planetary transmission (providing two speeds forward and one reverse), everyone around the plant used the "Curved Dash" because the spunky little car was so much fun to drive.

The Curved Dash had a single-cylinder, water-cooled, four-cycle, horizontal engine positioned at the rear. A single chain carried the engine's power the short distance to the center of the rear axle where a differential gear was located. The body was mounted so that it was only 2 feet above the ground, having a seat for two in front and a box for the engine and some space behind. It was steered by means of a tiller that came up from the floor and was curved to give the passengers all possible leg room. Small bicycle-type wheels with wire spokes were used.

The most distinctive feature was a curved dash similar to those on sleighs and toboggans. This gave the small vehicle a sporty touch and a personality all its own among horseless carriages.

Business in general did increase during the winter and cars were being produced for spring delivery. However, there were few orders for the Curved Dash model since the pilot car had scarcely been seen by anyone outside the organization. An uncertain feeling existed even within the organization, about the little horseless carriage. It was an interesting machine, sort of a mascot to the larger Oldsmobile cars, but perhaps too small and too light to be placed on the market. Although it was not Ransom Olds's view, there was a tendency for his associates to look upon the Curved Dash as a big toy.

All this suddenly changed, early in the afternoon of Saturday, March 9th, 1901, when fire quickly destroyed most of the Olds Motor Works in spite of the fact that the factory was dispersed in several buildings. The fire started on the first floor of the main building and spread so rapidly that workmen had to jump from the windows of the top floor to keep from being trapped. Fortunately, because it was Saturday afternoon, only a few of the three hundred workmen were in the plant. The conductor on an east-bound Jefferson Avenue streetcar saw the fire just as it started. When he came back sixteen minutes later, the walls of the main building had already tumbled. The cause of the fire was never fully established, but it appeared that a gasoline explosion had caused the flames to rush ᵗhrough the first floor of the main building in a matter of minutes.

Olds could not be reached the day of the fire. With his family, he was on a train bringing him from California where he had been on his first visit to his parents since they moved to San Diego. He arrived in Detroit the next morning, and was on the streetcar going to his home when he got the first news of the fire. He chanced to see the headlines of the Detroit newspaper being read by the man in the seat in front of him and learned that the new factory of the Olds Motor Works, and most of its contents, had been destroyed.

Olds rushed to the scene. He found that the Olds Motor Works plant had been extensively burned, and that the buildings of Detroit Stove Works and Peninsula Iron Company had been severely damaged, too. W. M. Murray, manager of the motorcar department, gave Olds a firsthand report:

"There were twenty or more machines, almost ready for the market, that are totally destroyed . . . one machine was saved and that is the one that the company has been running (the Curved Dash). The department was stocked with all parts for the machines, and we were running a full force of men assembling them."

A timekeeper, Jimmy Brady (later to become Mayor James J. Brady of Detroit), was still working in the office when the fire alarm was sounded. He ran to the car department in an effort to save some of the machines. There was no one else in the department to help him. The Curved Dash was standing not too far from the door. Even though the smoke and heat were intense, he was able to push it out of the building, but, when he turned to go back for other cars, flames filled the doorway.

Olds went home to struggle with the problem. He spent the night studying ways in which to save the business. They had saved the pilot car of the Curved Dash and the big foundry building had escaped the fire almost unharmed. The season for selling horseless

First famous Americans to make regular use of the
motorcar included President Theodore Roosevelt,
President William Howard Taft, Mark Twain and
Buffalo Bill Cody. Here, in Milwaukee, William
Jennings Bryan, riding 1907 Jeffery-built car is greeting
George W. Peck, former Wisconsin governor and
author of "Peck's Bad Boy."

carriages was already starting. After cutting through the shock and sifting out these three basic facts in the crisis situation, Olds came to his decision. He told his associates the next morning, "After the sleepless night, I decided to discard all our former plans and build the little one-cylinder runabout. I was convinced that if success was to be achieved it must be through a more simple machine."

It was a miracle, he told them, that the Curved Dash runabout had been saved. There was a market for a small car that could sell for only a little more than the cost of a good team and carriage. He went on to map a course of immediate action.

Rebuilding the plant would begin at once. The big foundry would be converted into a general purpose area, and foundry work would be contracted for on the outside. The company could expand operations in its Lansing plant and look for additional space there until the Detroit factory could be rebuilt. In the course of a few hours, Olds committed the last of the firm's working capital to put the Curved Dash runabout into production, immediately. He admitted later, "I risked everything on the little car."

Almost immediately help came from friends in Lansing. A group of businessmen, anxious to keep as much of Ransom Olds's horseless carriage business in Lansing as possible, saw an opportunity to be helpful and, at the same time, advance the interest of the Lansing community. They arranged immediately to take over the former fairgrounds in Lansing and use the buildings for temporary quarters for some departments of the Olds Motor Works. As it turned out, the Olds Motor Works never left the fairgrounds with its racetrack and excellent location. Before the emergency was over, arrangements had been made to acquire the property. In 1905, the entire Olds Motor Works operation was moved to Lansing, and the land is a part of the great industrial complex which produces Oldsmobiles there to this day.

Ransom Olds was especially pleased to have the racetrack as a testing area for new cars and for proving experimental vehicles. The old racetrack became the first automobile proving grounds in the United States. For years, while most firms continued to do their testing and proving work on public highways around the towns in which their factories were located, Oldsmobiles were tested on their own racetrack.

Olds's leadership in the critical period after the fire was magnificent. Shuttling back and forth between Detroit and Lansing, he worked long days and, sometimes, all night. Overwork finally caught up with him, and his doctor sent him to the hospital, a very sick man. Exactly thirty days from the time of the fire, some of the plant men brought a new Oldsmobile to the hospital so that the head of the firm could rejoice with them. Ransom Olds was soon well.

By late May, Curved Dash Oldsmobiles were being produced at a rate of two or three a week. It was a slow process for the man who had planned on producing at least a car per day. The motor had been improved and weighed but 120 pounds, but the car was, like the Duryea before it, strictly a horseless carriage. It was without a top, lights or fenders. The car was not intended for use at night nor in severe weather. The motor was mounted under the seat and steering was done with a tiller.

The loss of the factory did have its one unexpected benefit. The news of the fire, and assurance that production would soon be resumed, was potent publicity. Thousands who were completely unaware of the Oldsmobile suddenly knew of the motorcar, greatly expanding public interest in a new form of transportation. The appearance of the first Curved Dash Oldsmobile on the streets of Detroit, Cleveland, Lansing, Battle Creek, Chicago and other midwestern cities, created additional interest.

As June slipped by, a miracle began to unfold. Inquiries and orders from people wanting to own a horseless carriage were beginning to accumulate. Some were accompanied by cash payments. The Curved Dash Oldsmobile was catching on.

By August, there were so many unfilled orders that Olds made a bold move. By now he knew that even the production of a car per day would not be adequate to meet the demand. The Olds Motor Works was in the position of being able to sell many more cars than it could produce. He knew that he needed a means of quickly increasing production before public interest in the new car cooled. With the limitations imposed by the loss of the factory, the complex parts, such as the motors and transmissions, could not be produced by the Olds Motor Works for more than 5 cars per day. 15 to 20 motors and transmissions, per day, were needed. However, if these components were built under contract in another machine shop, they could be shipped to Lansing or Detroit for assembling.

Olds went to see Henry M. Leland. Leland was head of the Leland & Faulconer Company, the foremost machine shop in Detroit, perhaps in the entire country. Leland assured Olds that his shop could make the small motors. Tooling would take time, but he was sure Leland & Faulconer could, within weeks, begin delivery of 10 to 20 motors a day. Leland agreed to produce 2,000 Oldsmobile motors. At the time, only 200 Oldsmobiles had been produced.

The Olds-Leland agreement was the first large component order from a motorcar manufacturer in the United States placed with an outside supplier. The agreement established a precedent that was soon adopted by the industry as a lasting practice. The component supplier contract became a means, just as it was for the Olds Motor Works in the beginning, of tapping new sources of materials, trained men, management experience and financial strength, so that producers of motorcars could quickly increase production on short notice.

After reaching an understanding with Leland & Faulconer, Olds approached a smaller machine shop in Detroit to supply his transmission needs. The shop was operated by two brothers, John and Horace Dodge. They agreed to supply the Olds Motor Works with 2,000 transmissions.

October 20th to November 20th, 1901, stands as a most important period in the early motorcar industry. By this time, it was evident that something was problematical in the New England industry that even the Haynes-Apperson and Winton cars in the Midwest could not solve. For three years, the motorcar in the United States had followed the European trend of catering to the limited market of wealthy families and commercial users.

Olds had completed arrangements for a record production of his new Curved Dash Oldsmobile runabout. Olds brazenly predicted that he planned to produce and sell 4,000 Oldsmobiles the following year. This was equal to the total car production in the United States for the year before. Many people in Lansing and Detroit thought Olds would destroy the business through overexpansion and said so, some of them to his face.

Olds had solved his production problems; he was ready to turn his attention to selling cars. Marketing had been his responsibility for years in the stationary gasoline engine business. He knew it would be necessary to expand the market for his car. To do this, he must secure customers, not from the wealthy and commercial users alone but from professional men, farmers, merchants and people, generally.

This thinking of Ransom Olds represented a new concept in the marketing of the new kind of vehicle. Pope, and the other producers of the motorcar in New England and New York State, had generally accepted the European attitude that the self-propelled road vehicle was for sportsmen, the wealthy and businesses. Winton and Haynes

This fire had a big role in shaping the United States
motorcar industry of today. On March 10th, 1901,
just as the new Olds factory was beginning to produce
cars, it caught fire. Of several models that had been
developed, only one was saved, the small Curved Dash
Oldsmobile. To stave off financial disaster, the company
concentrated all of its efforts on the little car that was
considered a sort of mascot. A years later the "Merry
Oldsmobile" had become the most popular car
ever built in the country.

did nothing to change the pattern. This was the concept that Henry Ford, with Olds's example before him, was to develop to the point of making the replacement of the family horse his primary objective.

Late in October, Olds had a meeting with his young associate, Roy D. Chapin, who he had known since Chapin was a small boy in Lansing. Now twenty-one, Chapin had dropped out of the University of Michigan the year before when Olds gave him a wide range of assignments to carry out, among them plant photographer, gear grinder, car tester. Olds now had the most exciting job yet for the young man.

Olds began by recalling that, two years earlier, Alexander Winton of Cleveland had gotten a lot of publicity for his car by making the first trip from Cleveland to New York City in a self-propelled vehicle. No such direct trip had yet been made from Detroit to New York City in a horseless carriage. The second national automobile show would be opening in New York in ten days. Olds pointed out what an advantage it would be for the new Oldsmobile if Chapin would take one right out of the factory and drive it to New York City in time for the show.

"For one thing," said Olds, "it would let everyone know there is now an automobile being made in Detroit."

Only Chapin would make the trip, so there would be more opportunity to carry spare parts. He would have the advantage of being able to make repairs and install parts himself at any blacksmith shop, or right on the road, if necessary. He would carry extra tires, the parts for the motor most likely to wear under such constant driving, transmission parts and drive chains. Many of the items were small and took little space, such as the motor head gaskets. On long hills, gaskets were likely to blow out on the single-cylinder motor.

Chapin would immediately select an Oldsmobile from those being finished in the plant. He and John Maxwell would test the car thoroughly. Maxwell was the chief tester for Oldsmobile and had worked on the first cars made at the Apperson Machine Shop in Kokomo for Elwood Haynes. Later, he designed his own car, the Maxwell, predecessor of the Plymouth.

The start of the New York trip was to take place as early in the following week as possible. The automobile show would open on November 2nd, the following Saturday. Chapin's route would be east out of Detroit across southern Canada to the point where the Niagara River empties into Lake Erie. He would cross over into New York State and continue directly east along the Lake Erie shore to Rochester. From there, he would turn southeast into Syracuse and Albany. From Albany he would drive directly south along the Hudson River into New York City. He would meet Olds at the Waldorf Astoria Hotel.

Olds and Chapin speculated on how long it would take to make the trip. October had been generally dry. They had reason to expect a minimum of muddy roads. By the railroad, over the same general route, the distance was about 750 miles. The route a motorcar would have to take probably would be 800 miles, possibly more. Chapin was sure he could make the trip in five or six days, driving during daylight only.

Preparations proceeded during the week with no problems. Chapin and Maxwell were pleased with the performance of the car they had selected for the long trip. Installed on the Oldsmobile was a new Jones speedometer, the first to be used on any motorcar.

Chapin left Detroit the last Tuesday in October, but he didn't get a very early start. By the time he crossed into Canada and drove to Leamington on the north shore of Lake Erie (a distance of only fifty miles), he decided to stop for the night rather than face a considerable amount of driving after dark before getting to the next town of any size.

Wednesday, the 30th, was a beautiful October day in southern Canada. It was hardly light when Chapin drove east out of Leamington. The lake shore road was in excellent condition, and Chapin was soon aware that the was maintaining the highest sustained speed in his entire experience as a test driver. There were times when his new speedometer registered 30-to-35 miles an hour, a speed which until now had been associated only with railroad trains.

All morning the Curved Dash Oldsmobile made excellent progress. Before noon Chapin was in London, the halfway point between Detroit and Hamilton on the westernmost tip of Lake Ontario. Chapin was sure he could make it all the way to Lake Ontario before dark. By noon he had already driven three times the distance a good team of horses could have pulled a buggy in an entire day.

Chapin found a country store where he bought gasoline, then skirted London and headed for Brantford, 75 miles to the east on the way to Lake Ontario. He was in Brantford by three o'clock in the afternoon, and almost immediately resumed his trip toward St. Catherine's, fifty miles further east and almost to the high bridge over the Niagara River that would put him back into the United States. By the time it was dark, he could see the lights of St.

Catherine's in the distance. Even though his two carriage lamps provided little light, and were not intended for use during night country driving, he decided to attempt the trip into St. Catherine's.

Ten minutes later he wished he had not, as his car rammed into a large stone at the foot of a hill and came to an abrupt stop. Chapin started the engine and found that the car would still run, although steering was extremely difficult. When he arrived in St. Catherine's, he discovered that the front axle had been severely bent. He straightened it as best he could. The steering was still difficult, but with extra effort he could get almost normal operation from the vehicle. It was a narrow escape at the end of an unprecedented day. Chapin had driven 278 miles. He had driven one-third of the distance to New York in one day.

Roy Chapin had become the first person in the United States to drive a motorcar, cross country, and cover more than 275 miles in one day. There were times when he was driving on little more than farm roads used by cattle and horses. His progress was so astonishing that when Ransom Olds received Chapin's telegram, giving his location for the night, he was sure the Canadian telegraph operator had made a mistake. Chapin's drive across Canada that day ranks with Frank Duryea's winning of the 1895 Chicago race in the snow.

The next day, Thursday, the 31st, slowed by fatigue and the details of reentering the United States, Chapin traveled only about 150 miles. He serviced the Oldsmobile carefully when he got to Rochester, New York.

On Friday, November 1st, Chapin turned away from Lake Ontario and headed southeast toward Syracuse. Although there had been some rain, he drove the 75 miles by noon. There, he learned the rains had been so heavy in the hills between Syracuse and Albany that driving a horseless carriage over the route was impossible. He went from livery stable to livery stable, but the report was the same. He talked to freight wagon drivers who had just come over the route and they told him there was not a chance of making it.

It was noon and as Chapin went into a small restaurant, it appeared that Ransom Olds's proposal of a quick trip by horseless carriage from Detroit to New York City had ended in failure. Moments later, Chapin had an electrifying thought. The famous Erie Canal, with its mule towpath, ran directly from Syracuse to Troy on the Hudson River, just north of Albany. The towpath had to be level and barges moved every day, regardless of the weather,

Roy D. Chapin drove this Curved Dash Oldsmobile
from Detroit to New York in seven and one-half days,
arriving at the old Waldorf Astoria Hotel November 5th
during the week of the second New York Automobile
Show. Ransom Olds received an order for one thousand
cars, more than were owned in New York City at
that time. The order made Detroit the leading
motorcar city in the country for the first time.

except when the canal was frozen in winter. Chapin wondered, why couldn't he drive his car over the towpath to Albany?

He rushed back to the livery stable to make inquiry. The wagon drivers shook their heads. The towpath was government property, and trespassers had been jailed. They admitted that, in emergencies, doctors had driven the towpath to reach critically ill patients.

That was good enough for Chapin. For him, this was certainly an emergency. Fifteen minutes later he drove onto the towpath and gazed on an amazing sight. Here was an all-weather road that stretched out of sight along the canal. Even though he encountered brief rain storms during the afternoon, there was little mud on the road and the Oldsmobile could maintain its regular speed.

He drove a considerable distance before meeting a barge with its mule teams. The mule driver couldn't have been more shocked if he had encountered a visitor from another world! Chapin stopped his car at the edge of the towpath to let the mules pass, but the animals were so frightened they would not pull the barge past the parked horseless carriage. Finally, the mule driver ordered him to start the car and move past the terrified mules, driving next to the canal lest the mules jump into the water.

When no barges were in sight, Chapin was able to drive the car at top speed. By evening, he had reached St. Johnsville, only 50 miles from Albany on the Hudson. Chapin had driven 145 miles since he left Rochester and was within 200 miles of New York City. The car had given a flawless performance over nearly 650 miles, since leaving Detroit four days earlier. Chapin had the prospect of being in New York City by Sunday.

On Saturday, Chapin reached Albany, turned south and drove the 25 miles to Hudson. He arrived by late afternoon and went immediately to the express office to pick up a new front axle. The part had been shipped from Detroit following Chapin's accident outside St. Catherine's, Canada. He took his car to a machine shop and had the bent axle replaced. It was a great relief to have the steering restored to normal. On Saturday night, Chapin was 100 miles from the Waldorf Astoria Hotel in New York City. He expected to be in New York the next afternoon.

It was not to be so. The first 50 miles of the trip on Sunday morning were uneventful. Soon after noon, noises developed in the Oldsmobile transmission. As the difficulty increased, Chapin just managed to get the car into the town of Peekskill under its own

First sight of its kind! This 1902 state fair parade through the streets of Lansing was led by a "quarter of a mile" of Curved Dash Oldsmobiles. Note how the street is lined with horse-drawn vehicles.

power. He was 45 miles north of New York City. He knew that nothing less than a rebuilding of the transmission would enable the car to take the road again. The repair job took him all day Monday. Chapin talked to Olds by telephone Monday night to report that the car had been repaired and he would drive to New York the following morning.

Chapin was up early Tuesday morning. He was in New York City by 9:30 a.m. While driving down Fifth Avenue, only blocks from the Waldorf Astoria, he had his second accident of the trip.

A man stepped in front of the Oldsmobile. Chapin applied the brake and swerved to miss the pedestrian but his car skidded out of control. The left rear wheel crashed into the stone curbing. Several of the wire spokes were snapped and the wheel frame was bent. It took forty-five minutes to repair the damage sufficiently to permit the car to continue. He then drove on to the Waldorf Astoria. Roy D. Chapin had completed the longest motorcar trip made in the United States up to that time.

Chapin arrived at the hotel with greasy hands and clothing. The doorman took him to be a mechanic and made him go to the rear of the hotel, park his car and enter through the service entrance.

Olds had already arrived at the Waldorf lobby. For an hour he paced up and down, anxiously waiting for Chapin's arrival. He had several guests waiting to meet the first man to drive a horseless carriage from Detroit to New York in one week—actually seven and one-half days total elapsed time.

Even before changing his clothes, Chapin sent a telegram to the Olds Motor Works office in Detroit. It read, "Arrived here at eleven in good order. Total distance eight hundred twenty miles. Time seven one-half days. Average 14 miles per hour. Used 30 gallons gasoline 80 gallons water. Roy D. Chapin, New York City."

The Curved Dash Oldsmobile was serviced, washed and polished Tuesday afternoon and placed on exhibit at the automobile show the next day, Wednesday the 6th. The New York Tribune, in its November 7th issue, took notice of the fact in the following item:

"Another new machine reached the Garden (Madison Square Garden) yesterday for which the owner claims an interesting record. It arrived in the city Tuesday ... The automobile is of the gasoline sort, and was driven from Detroit to this city in seven and one-half days. The machine weighs eight hundred pounds, and on the trip covered 820 miles and consumed thirty gallons of gasoline. The route was through Canada, crossing to the United States over the suspension bridge just below Niagara Falls. The owner says his experience has showed that the lightweight automobiles are well adapted to such tours."

When Olds asked Chapin what he would remember longest about the journey, he replied: "The way the mule team drivers swore when they encountered our Oldsmobile on the Erie Canal towpath. Mr. Olds, the profanity of the men in our factory just can't begin to match that of the Erie Canal mule drivers."

Roy Chapin never forgot his experience on the Erie Canal towpath. He became a powerful advocate of building better roads and highways in the United States. Some of his most effective efforts in behalf of better highways came during the years he served as Secretary of Commerce in the cabinet of President Herbert Hoover.

4

From Maine to California

The pendulum was swinging to gasoline-powered cars. The presence of Henry B. Joy, wealthy Detroit manufacturer, at the New York Automobile Show of 1901 was additional proof. Among his enterprises, Joy, too, was making gas engines for marine use. When the Olds factory was built in Detroit, Joy decided to enter the new horseless carriage business. Since there was no other motorcar company in Detroit for him to buy out, except Oldsmobile, he went to the New York Automobile Show to look over the cars. His brother-in-law, Truman Newberry, also a man of means, accompanied him.

Told that Locomobile was perhaps the most advanced car made in the east, Joy and Newberry went to the Locomobile agency. The salesman showed them the steam car. While Joy and Newberry waited for the boiler to heat and provide steam, the pressure gauge exploded within 36 inches of Newberry's head. Both Detroit men were showered with hot water, bringing to an abrupt end their interest in a steam Locomobile.

Minutes later, they stopped at another car agency in front of which were two parked cars. While the men were looking at the cars, a fire engine roared past with smoke belching from the stack, and drawn by three powerful horses on the deadrun. Two car salesmen dashed from the agency, spun the cranks momentarily to start the gasoline engines, jumped into the cars and were off chasing the fire engine.

Joy and Newberry were impressed. They entered the agency and learned that the cars they had seen move quickly into action were built by James W. Packard of Warren, Ohio. Only three Packards had been brought to the New York Automobile Show, the agency man told Joy, and two of the three had already been sold to William Rockefeller, brother of John D.

Joy paid $1,500 in cash for the remaining Packard and had it shipped to Detroit. He liked the car and soon made a trip to Ohio to see Packard. On behalf of a group of nine Detroit investors, Joy bought the rights to the Packard motorcar. The Packard Motor Company of Detroit, Michigan, was organized and produced quality cars for more than half a century. The new Packard factory was built in Detroit in 1904, the first motorcar factory to be designed by the young architect, Louis Kahn. His factories for production of cars would eventually dot Detroit and extend around the world.

Another event, as important as the giant strides of Ransom Olds, took place in 1901. Almost completely across the United States from Detroit, on a farm near Beaumont, Texas, the famous oil gusher, Spindletop, was brought in. It possessed such enormous output that it almost doubled the country's production of petroleum. An almost inexhaustible supply of inexpensive fuel had been discovered for the motorcar.

As the New York show closed, Olds was moving toward another historic achievement. Before the automobile show opened, he had arranged with A. G. Spalding & Company, the sporting goods firm, to represent the Olds Motor Works in the New York area. It was the understanding that the first order would be for 100 cars. During the show the Spalding representative came to Olds and explained that the Spalding board of directors wished to withdraw from the agreement since they could not see the possibility of selling 100 cars when there were only about 1,000 motorcars operating in the city at the time. Olds agreed to cancel the agreement, provided the Spalding sign at the Olds exhibit be allowed to remain for the rest of the show.

Before the show was over, Olds was grateful for the Spalding move. Ray M. Owen, who had been highly successful in selling Oldsmobiles in Cleveland, was attending the New York Show. Late in the week, he came to Olds and asked if he might have the New

York territory. Olds said that he would be pleased to have Owen become the New York distributor, providing he thought he could sell 500 cars in the coming year. Owen and his financial backer, Roy Rainey from Cleveland, were confident they could sell that many cars in the New York area during 1902.

Later, Rainey and Owen invited Olds to their room at the Waldorf Astoria to work out an agreement. Olds began the conference by saying, "It isn't my business but I would like to see you two put this thing over in a big way. I would like to see you make this order for a thousand cars. Then the public would drop its jaw and take notice." A thousand it was. Owen and Rainey soon made the Curved Dash Oldsmobile the best known motorcar in the city. Before long, Chauncey Depew, president of the New York Central Railroad, bought a Curved Dash Olds for his personal use. Depew permitted Owen to have a photograph made of him with the little car, and after that many wealthy families in the East owned Oldsmobiles.

Ransom E. Olds, an unknown in the motorcar business, had literally driven his saucy, little Curved Dash Oldsmobile into New York City, met the European and New England competition head-on, and come away with the trophy! The era of large scale production of the low-priced motorcar in America had begun.

The impact of the Owen order for 1,000 Oldsmobiles produced astonishing results. In the following year, the contract led to the Olds Motor Works becoming the leading producer of gasoline-engine-powered motorcars in the United States. In fifteen months, Detroit, a city that produced no cars at all, became the city that turned out *more* motorcars than any other city on either continent, a position it has never surrendered.

The days immediately following Olds's return from the New York Show were exciting. Associates, bankers and friends in Lansing and Detroit wanted to hear firsthand reports of the historic trip.

Olds was surprised, and at times astounded, by the new opportunities. As news of the crosscountry run spread, orders followed. A lesser man might have lost his way. Instead, the Lansing businessman turned all his energies into putting a solid foundation under his Olds Motor Works.

Henry Leland and the Dodge Brothers agreed to increase their commitment for production of motors and transmissions. Because of sales, Olds found he could make better terms for money at banks. He could also hire the best workmen and secure additional suppliers. Some of the very men who were suddenly ready to do business with

Olds were the same men who had said, ninety days earlier, he was nothing more than a promoter and a dreamer.

Ransom E. Olds was the first to experience the tremendous power generated by the American motorcar business. His production of Oldsmobiles moved from one record to another. The creator of the Oldsmobile soon discovered that those who could chart and soundly direct the course of such a business were men apart. The one-time boy blacksmith from Geneva, Ohio, never was poor again.

As the first motors from Leland & Faulconer, and transmissions from the Dodge Brothers Machine Shop, became available, supplementing those already being made at the Olds factory, production was increased to 25 cars a day. In 1901, the year fire destroyed everything but the prototype for the runabout, production had totaled 425 cars. Only Pope had produced more.

But the real Ransom Olds miracle came in his efforts in market expansion—the developing of new customers. The news of Oldsmobile's Detroit-to-New York run and of the single order for "trainloads of cars" swept the country. Thousands of people who had never before taken the horseless carriage seriously suddenly realized that the greatest transition in the history of transportation had begun.

Through his spectacular arrival at the New York Automobile Show, Olds had generated enough new demand for all the cars his Olds Motor Works could produce in a year or more. This was a new achievement in the motorcar industry, and it set the stage for an entirely unprecedented development—mass marketing of an expensive and complex product. Until this time, mass marketing had been limited to inexpensive and relatively simple items, such as kerosene lamps, razors or common pins.

Immediately, businessmen from all over the country began contacting the Olds Motor Works. They wanted to become distributors or dealers for the "Curved Dash Horseless Carriage." Distributors resold to dealers in towns throughout an area. Dealers sold cars directly to customers, usually in a single town. Most of these men had no previous experience with motor cars. Some had not seen or ridden in them. They reflected the expanding interest in the self-propelled road vehicle. From the fall of 1901, and throughout the winter to follow, new dealers placed orders for future delivery, often with substantial advance payments to assure delivery dates.

As a result, Olds was able to reaffirm boldly, even before the new year began, that, in 1902, the Olds Motor Works would "sell 4,000 motorcars in the coming year."

"This will be four times as many automobiles as any firm in Europe has made in a year and twice as many as any American firm has ever produced. We will be producing in a week what most plants produce in a year," Olds explained.

Ransom E. Olds made good his prediction for 1902. The Olds Motor Works did secure orders for 4,000 motorcars. But a tenfold increase in production in a single year proved to be more than even the Olds genius could deliver. The firm began the year with a production of 5 or 6 Oldsmobiles a day, and production climbed steadily. By spring, the firm was producing 50 cars per week. Later in the year, production rose from 70 to 80 cars a week. By the year's end, 3,299 Oldsmobiles had been produced and sold.

Working in the Olds Motor Works plant in the months that followed became something of a crusade. The men in the Oldsmobile assembly plant, and even the suppliers, were aware that the Pope feat of producing 2,000 cars in Hartford, Connecticut, during 1899, was the world car-production record to beat. When the 2,000th Oldsmobile was produced in Lansing that fall of 1902, the workmen took up a collection. They engaged a jeweler who took a twenty-dollar gold piece and hammered it into a watch chain pendant in the shape of a miniature Curved Dash Oldsmobile. The workmen presented it to Ransom E. Olds. Before his death in 1950, Olds gave it to R. E. Olds Anderson of East Lansing, Michigan, his grandson, who today counts the small watch charm one of his most prized possessions.

Ransom Olds had touched off a market expansion for the horseless carriage that would soak up the output of the factories of competitors, as well as his own. For those who were ready with a dependable motorcar, the opportunity was almost as great as it was in Detroit. This was proved by the experience of Thomas B. Jeffery and his Thomas B. Jeffery Company of Kenosha, Wisconsin.

Jeffery had invented the clincher rim for bicycle tires ten years before. His firm made the Rambler Bicycle, perhaps the leading competitor to the Columbia Bicycle manufactured by Pope in Hartford, Connecticut. The rims were quickly adapted for use on motorcars. Jeffery saw the importance of the horseless carriage and completed the development of his vehicle, similar to the Oldsmobile, early in 1901. Jeffery produced about 100 of his Ramblers in 1901. With Olds unable to fill all orders, the Kenosha firm's production in 1902 skyrocketed to 1,500 cars.

Jeffery's Rambler became the direct ancestor of today's Rambler-

American. Except for the Oldsmobile, the Rambler name has been used at the same point of manufacture for a longer period of time than that of any other United States motorcar.

The motorcar leadership moved from southern New England and the East Coast to the Midwest in 1902. The total production of cars that year was 9,000. Midwest firms produced nearly 5,000 cars. The two firms, Olds in Detroit and Jeffery in Kenosha, accounted for 4,000 cars. The Haynes, the Winton, the Apperson, the Packard, Pope-Toledo, the Akron, Pierce Arrow, the Buffalo, the Milwaukee, White Steamer, the Chicago, the Ohio, the Wisconsin and the St. Louis in the Midwest accounted for the remainder. The eastern United States had lost the opportunity to become the base for the largest new industry to be developed in the United States during the twentieth century.

The heart of the Oldsmobile success was its motor. Ransom Olds had become the first man to develop a gasoline engine superior to the Frank Duryea motor. The Olds motor was a few pounds lighter, mostly as a result of having one cylinder rather than two, and had superior carburetion and ignition features. Ransom Olds would entrust decisions to associates about any part of his cars, but, when it came to his first love, the motor, he insisted on having the final word. Largely because of his emotional attachment to the motor, Olds missed one of the great opportunities of his life.

In the early weeks of 1902, one of the most important meetings held in the early years of the motorcar took place at the Olds Motor Works in Detroit. Henry Leland called on Ransom E. Olds. The difference between the men was mountainous. Leland, nearly sixty years old, was one of the great machinists of the period. He was a tall, graying man who would not permit even close associates to smoke or swear in his presence. Olds was thirty-eight, and at the peak of his electrifying, unprecedented career with horseless carriages. The smallish, handsome man, never without his heavy-rimmed glasses, made friends everywhere. The chances of these two men failing to agree on any constructive matter seemed remote, particularly since the austere Leland was on an errand of friendship.

Leland and his machinists had been making the small, single-cylinder Oldsmobile motor for several months. Leland was grateful for the Olds Motor Works contract and wished to show his appreciation.

Henry Leland and his men had made some surprising discoveries. Leland & Faulconer had discovered that by making several

73

important, yet simple, modifications in the Olds motor, they could more than double its power. Amazingly, the changes actually reduced the cost of producing the motor. The most important improvement stemmed directly from the genius of the Leland & Faulconer machine shop. By stepping up the machining tolerance from one one-hundredth of an inch to one one-thousandth, Leland increased the horsepower from 4.5 to 7.0. By enlarging valves, the horsepower could be increased to 10.25, two and one-half times the power of the motors being produced at the Olds Motor Works. Alanson Brush, who later designed the Brush Runabout, was the young engineer in charge of this work for Leland & Faulconer.

Their meeting started pleasantly. Leland explained his discovery. He offered, at no increase in cost, to make either the more closely-machined motor, capable of raising the horsepower by 75 percent, or the modified motor that would deliver 10.25 horsepower. Leland was offering more than an improved motor. He was, in effect, offering to pool his engineering resources with the Olds Motor Works. Leland had no other loyalties in the new horseless carriage business. He planned no car of his own. He wanted to help his customer, the Olds Motor Works, to prosper. The Olds Motor Works turned the offer down. Leland and his associates were hurt and "dismayed by the refusal...." Though Leland did not know it at the time, the way had been opened to a vast, new opportunity for Leland in horseless carriages; one that would give new shape to the motor-car business.

Although more orders were coming in than could be filled, Ransom Olds moved relentlessly to keep his motorcar in the news. He knew, above everything else, that the market must be lengthened and broadened. The Olds Motor Works would need several thousand customers annually, for years to come. Even taking into account the indefatigable Alexander Winton, nobody (to this time) had worked as hard as Olds at the job of finding new customers and expanding the market for the new motorcar.

In 1902, only months after Chapin's Detroit-to-New York run, an Oldsmobile won the trophy in the first 100 mile, non-stop endurance race held in the United States. Between 1902 and 1904, Milford M. Weigle drove an Oldsmobile to three gold medals, twelve silver cups and several world records for speed. The races were held on racetracks which were used for horse racing.

Alexander Winton, Henry Ford, Louis Chevrolet and other well-known early drivers were competing in the same events. For Oldsmobile, there was an important difference, and no one knew this better than Ransom E. Olds. Oldsmobile had a car on the market and public attention could be turned directly into car sales. Soon Oldsmobile had twenty-six regional dealer distributors, and the Olds became the first car to be sold from Maine to California.

In the summer of 1902, another incident of importance occurred at the Olds Motor Works plant. Early in the year, Chapin, accompanied by an Oldsmobile engineer, was returning to the Olds plant from a conference at the Wilson Body Plant of Detroit. When they had driven about a mile from the Wilson plant, the steering mechanism spring broke and Chapin was unable to steer the car. They were still a long way from the Olds Motor Works. Chapin's associate said there was a small machine shop less than a mile away where he was sure a mechanic could be found to fix the spring.

Chapin was skeptical, but had no alternative. The two men drove the car, stopping frequently to kick the front wheels back into the position that would enable the vehicle to move forward. Later Chapin described the incident.

"I was willing to be shown, but I must confess I did not feel much enthusiasm when I saw this mechanic's shop which was nothing more than a lean-to at 81 Park Place. We went in and found a slender man in blue overalls who came out to see what was wrong with our car. As soon as he went to work, I saw that he was unquestionably an expert mechanic. Quickly, he bolted a plate on our broken spring and soon had us on our way. As we left the shop, my companion waved and called out, 'Much obliged, Henry'."

It was Chapin's first meeting with Henry Ford. During the summer of 1902, Ford visited the Olds Motor Works several times. He often remained a long while, and asked penetrating questions.

In 1903, Oldsmobile set a world record by traveling 5 miles in six minutes. Everytime the new motorcar racing addicts gathered, there was talk of a motorcar that could travel a mile a minute. Only the railroad engine had been able to transport people at that pace. Most racing drivers were sure a speed of 60 miles-an-hour was attainable.

Before the middle of the year, Oldsmobile had done it. H. T. Thomas, later to produce the "Thomas Flyer," became the first American to drive a mile in less than one minute. He used the same Oldsmobile that earlier in the year had set the world record. The car was equipped with a motor made by Leland & Faulconer. In the fall, the same car was used to win the famed European race, the Tour-de-France.

In 1903, the Olds Motor Works, between its Detroit and Lansing shops, turned out 4,000 Oldsmobiles. This was double the number made by any other company that year and accounted for well over one-third of the 11,235 motorcars sold in the United States.

In 1904, motorcar production in the United States doubled, moving up to 22,134 automobiles. The Olds Motor Works produced 5,000 cars that year, 20 percent of the nation's total. In 1905, the last year in which the firm's full attention was given to production of the horseless carriage, Oldsmobile accounted for more than one-fourth of an even larger total of cars produced. The Olds Motor Works produced 6,500 Oldsmobiles, an average of 125 cars a week. National production for 1905 was 24,250 cars.

The feat that attracted the most public attention to Oldsmobile came in 1905. Two Oldsmobiles took first and second places in the transcontinental race from New York to the Lewis and Clark Exposition at Portland, Oregon. The cars left New York on May 8th, 1905. The Oldsmobile, driven by Dwight B. Huss of Lansing, Michigan, with the durable and experienced Weigle as his assistant, was in Portland, forty-four days later. The second Oldsmobile, driven by T. R. McGargle and following a somewhat different route, arrived soon after.

The winning Oldsmobiles were seen by a third of a million spectators enroute. In 1931, Huss drove the same Oldsmobile, equipped exactly as it was in 1905, over the same route to the cheers of ten million people.

No man had ever before encountered the need to produce, sell and service so many automobiles. Olds faced a wide range of problems. Solutions he devised have become standard throughout the motorcar industry. Under his direction, the first "assembly line" procedure for the motorcar was developed. Assembly stations were established on the floor "in a line." Beginning with the chassis, components were brought to the station until the car was complete.

With concern for the business side of the enterprise, Olds greatly simplified the financing. He established a policy of full cash payment at the time cars were delivered to the dealer. The Olds Motor Works inaugurated the publishing of a sales manual for dealers and a magazine for Oldsmobile users. The firm was the first to bring dealers to Detroit for a national convention.

Roy Chapin, at the age of twenty-four, was named sales manager. He was the first to devote his entire energies to sales in the new industry. Olds and Chapin developed the concept that to support mass marketing the manufacturer must assume the responsibility for creating public interest and the demand for its product.

To create new customers and to increase the satisfaction of present users, Oldsmobile became the first motorcar to be regularly promoted through national advertising. The firm appealed directly to women by placing the first motorcar advertisement in *"The Ladies Home Journal."*

Under the headline, "The Best Thing On Wheels," the advertisement claimed, "The ideal vehicle for shopping and calling—equally suitable for a pleasant afternoon drive or an extended tour. It is built to run and does it. Operated entirely from the seat by a single lever —always under instant control...."

The Oldsmobile people became the first to take a major interest in customer satisfaction. Olds induced Howard Coffin, an accomplished engineer, to leave his post at the University of Michigan and join the Olds Motor Works. He, thus, was the first professional engineer to join a motorcar firm in the United States.

Chapin and Coffin conceived for Oldsmobile the first comprehensive instruction book for car buyers, something which soon became universal. In the 1905 edition of the Oldsmobile instruction book, a list of "Don'ts" appeared to which Olds himself obviously gave some attention. The following indicates how little the public yet knew about the motorcar:

"Don't take anybody's word for it that your tanks have plenty of gasoline and water and your oil cup plenty of oil. They may be guessing.

"Don't do anything to your motor without knowing just what you are doing.

"Don't imagine that your motor runs well on equal parts of water and gasoline. It's a mistake.

"Don't make 'improvements' without writing the factory. We know all about many of those improvements and can advise you.

"Don't think your motor is losing power when clutch bands need tightening or something is out of adjustment.

"Don't drive your 'Oldsmobile' 100 miles the first day. You wouldn't drive a green horse 10 miles until you were acquainted with him. Do you know more about a gasoline motor than you do about a horse?

"Don't delude yourself into thinking we are building these motors like a barber's razor—'just to sell'. We couldn't have sold one in a thousand years, and much less 5,000 in one year, if it hadn't been demonstrated to be a practical success.

"Don't confess you are less intelligent than thousands of people who are driving Oldsmobiles. We make the only motor that 'motes'."

77

In 1903, Ransom Olds laid plans to sell Oldsmobiles in a number of European countries. This was the first concerted effort to sell American cars abroad. That year, agents for the Oldsmobile were established in England, France, Germany and Russia. The first Oldsmobiles were exported to Europe early in 1904. The Olds Motor Works set the pattern in the export of cars which prevailed until after World War II. American cars were sold abroad in tremendous numbers. Like the original Oldsmobile, they were less expensive and required less service than the automobilies made in Europe.

Strangely, the Curved Dash Oldsmobile appealed to the wealthy, as well as to the professional and business people in Europe. The Queen of England, the famed English sportsman, Sir Thomas Lipton, the Krupp Family in Germany and the Queen of Italy owned and used the little car. Twenty-five years later, an effort was made to buy the single-cylinder Oldsmobile from the Krupp family for an American Museum. The car was still in use, and the Krupps declined to sell it.

Ransom Olds's horseless carriage became an American institution. Only two motorcars have achieved this distinction—the Oldsmobile and Henry Ford's "Model T." Proof of the immortality of the Curved Dash Oldsmobile came from an unexpected quarter. Gus Edwards, the leading songwriter of the period collaborated with Vincent Bryan in writing "My Merry Oldsmobile." The song became so popular that, "Come along with me, Lucille, in my merry Oldsmobile," became a phrase of the language. The popularity of the song has continued, decade after decade, and has become part of the Americana of best loved melodies.

With "My Merry Oldsmobile" leading the way like a spirited band at the head of a mighty parade, the Oldsmobile has become one of the few motorcars to continue in production to this day. Several thousand motorcars have been introduced and discontinued since the Curved Dash Oldsmobile captured the fancy of the nation.

* * *

A struggle for power had developed within the Olds Motor Works. The mild-mannered Olds was not constituted to face unreasonable opposition within his organization. Ever since those days, twenty years before, when he began working with his father, Olds had faced hard work and great risks, and had experienced many kinds

Norval Hawkins and his men sold three-quarters
of a million "Model-T" Fords in 1916. No other firm
had yet sold 100,000 cars. Most Fords sold were the
touring car, but there was great demand for this sedan
with its single center door. There was no self-starter,
no battery, and a magneto (generating unit) fed electric
current directly to the sparkplugs and headlights.

of adversity, but he had never been in a position of having to debate his judgment with his associates.

There had been no difficulties with Samuel L. Smith in the management of the Olds Motors Works. Both were reasonable men, and, in addition, a fondness existed between them that amounted almost to a father-son relationship. The Detroit millionaire had taken great risks with Ransom Olds and was proud of what they had accomplished together. But, times were changing at the Olds Motor Works. Smith was becoming less active due to his age and health. His sons, Frederick and Angus, were taking a more aggressive role in the business.

The Smith sons looked with scorn on the small horseless carriage. They wanted the Oldsmobile to become a big car, like the Winton and the custom-made European cars displayed at the automobile shows. These were the cars the wealthy friends of the Smiths were driving. The records established by the Oldsmobile, both in open competition and in sales, blanketed the opposition but could not eliminate it. Olds failed to convince the young shareholders that the path to success and wealth in the motorcar business was to be found in the production of a light, rugged and inexpensive car that most people could afford.

The question of producing a big car came up again and again during 1903. Each time, Olds would point out that the company had made a $1,200 to $1,500 car during its first year of operation in 1900. The firm had also lost $80,000, and almost destroyed the business. Olds explained that it was the Curved Dash Oldsmobile that had saved the business from failure. By concentrating on the mass production of a single model, the Olds Motor Works had become the leading producer of motorcars in the world. It had orders on hand assuring, at least, another full year of record production. "The Olds Motor Works," Olds often explained, "is the only one in existence that provides work for its employees the year around."

Soon after the 1904 Detroit Automobile Show, held early in February, Olds saw that he was headed toward a showdown with the Smith family for control of the business. Olds proposed that either he buy out the Smith interest or let the Smiths buy him out. In the end, the Smiths bought the Olds interest.

In June, without advance notice, Ransom E. Olds resigned as general manager of the Olds Motor Works. He was forty years old. A few days later, Olds cleaned out his desk at the Olds Motor Works in Detroit and went home to Lansing to take a "long vacation." In the five years between 1899 and 1904, he had set the foundation of a new industry that, in the next quarter century, would become the largest in the United States.

The motorcar industry, brought into existence by Ransom E. Olds, was strictly an American concept. The work of Olds was, at no point, supplemented or supported to any important degree by the efforts of anyone either in the United States or Europe. Ransom Olds is as entitled to the right of discovery for his first cars as is Whitney for the cotton gin, Morse for the telegraph, or Bell for the telephone. Later, speaking in the presence of his contemporaries, he confided:

"Even as a boy, engines were the one thing I could never get out of my head. In my father's machine shop the work mostly consisted of repairing, but I wanted to develop and make our own engines. It seemed to me there was a great need for small engines to speed up the work people wanted to do, and most of all, to mount in a buggy so there could be a horseless carriage. At first I worked with steam engines. Gradually we worked out plans for small steam engines and a boiler of one or two horsepower which could be operated by an ordinary (kerosene) stove burner. But there was so much deposit in the river water that the small boilers soon filled up with mud and were not satisfactory. Next, I invented a gasoline motor which was the first manufactured in the United States to use gasoline directly in the cylinder.

"We made this engine as high as twelve to eighteen horsepower. These engines sold so well that we had to enlarge our machine shop and finally build a new factory. But I never lost sight of, or faith in, my idea of using gasoline for locomotion. I spent every spare minute tinkering with engines and experimenting with different forms of combustion. That little gasoline engine I had invented sold so well that it finally pulled us out of debt and we could hire more help. This gave me more leisure time to work on a car."

In those years, the destiny of the American motorcar rested in his hands. Olds, and the men he gathered around him, had devised and put into use radical, new methods of production, marketing and customer service. The concentration of raw materials; the appointment of suppliers to make even the most complex components; the production assembly-line; the testing; the development of an engineering staff to improve performance; the establishment of local franchise dealers; appointment of foreign distributors; the intensive use of advertising to support mass marketing; distribution of repair parts; instructions to buyers and customer service—all were introduced by the Olds Motor Works during these historic years. Refined and advanced, these are the procedures in use throughout the American motorcar industry to this day.

While the years of Olds's indispensable contribution were over, there is much more to his story.

He returned to Lansing in 1904, just as school was out for the summer. The Olds children were at an age to enjoy an outing in northern Michigan, something the family had not been able to do during the hectic years. They had just begun their vacation in the north when Olds received a telegram. It was from his longtime friend and financier, Edward W. Sparrow, asking him to return to Lansing at once.

On returning, Olds learned that his success had overrun his hometown. A group of friends, many of them the very men who had turned down his requests for financial backing five years before, were now making their own proposal. They were ready to organize a half-million dollar company to manufacture a new Olds car. Under the plan, Olds would be given controlling interest, so there would not be a recurrence of the management problems encountered at the Olds Motor Works. Olds signed the agreement, and immediately added to his holdings another quarter of a million dollars. Such was the magic of the name of the man behind the "Merry Oldsmobile."

Ground was broken for the new factory within a month. Mrs. Olds stayed with the children in northern Michigan and Olds remained in Lansing to begin work on the new car. On October 15th, he was driving the first pilot model on the streets of Lansing. The new motorcar was not a competitor with the Oldsmobile. Olds did not want to get involved in a marketing struggle with the car he created earlier. The new Olds car was larger, heavier and made to sell for $1,000. It was not a luxury car. It was a forerunner of the intermediate motorcar.

There was one, unsolved problem with the new car. It, as yet, had no name. Some of his associates wanted to name it the "Olds." But Ransom Olds did not want to create confusion between such a name and the Oldsmobile. Everyone was happy when REO (his initials) was proposed.

Olds steadfastly refused to recruit men for REO from among his former associates. Gradually, however, some of his most valuable earlier co-workers and others who had distinguished themselves in the business, requested the opportunity to join Olds in Lansing.

The new firm prospered to such an extent that Olds became one of the wealthiest men in the United States. The firm endures to this day, although, in recent years, it has produced trucks, rather than motorcars.

By one of the strangest strokes of fate, both of the names created by Olds have stood, side-by-side, for more than six decades in his hometown of Lansing.

Few American industrialists have enjoyed the fruits of their labors for so long or so fully as did Ransom E. Olds. From the first, he was not deeply involved in the day-to-day operations of REO. He lived in Lansing until his death almost half a century later. He enjoyed a respect that was above factionalism or partisanship. He took a keen interest in the affairs of his community and state. His counsel was often sought. His advice was positive, and offered with an open look to the future. For decades, there was great power in such phrases as, "Mr. Olds would be interested in knowing this."; "This is something dear to Mr. Olds' heart."; "Why don't you see Mr. Olds about this?"

Ransom E. Olds became a legend in his own time. More than any other man he stands as the father of the American motorcar. He had earned the admiration of the automotive industry; the people of Michigan and his neighbors in Lansing, many of whom knew him as a boy working in his father's small machine shop with its dirt floor, on the banks of the Grand River.

5

"Mr. Whitney" Moves to Detroit

Two men drove their 1901 Curved Dash Oldsmobile up to a horse hitching-post, in Detroit, near the Cass Avenue entrance to the Henry Ford Company. The younger man was at the tiller. The older man, with an austere manner and the features of a Greek god, was one of the great machinists in the United States. Together they entered the building and went immediately into conference with the company's directors.

The motorcar firm had been organized by four wealthy citizens of Detroit less than a year before, November 30th, 1901, with Henry Ford as chief engineer. Misunderstanding developed and Ford left the company four months later. Now in August, the directors were meeting to close out the business. The two visitors, who had just arrived, had in their possession an independent appraisal of the firm's machinery and materials. But they also had with them something more—a proposal.

"I have done what you asked me to do," the older man said. "But gentlemen I believe you are making a great mistake in going out of business." As he spoke he placed on the table before them an internal combustion motor so small that he could handle it without difficulty. "I have brought you a motor which we worked out at Leland &

84

Faulconer. It has three times the power of the Olds motor. . . . I can make these motors for you at less cost than I make the others for Olds. . . ."

The directors of the Henry Ford Company had just been offered the most powerful motor of its kind in existence. They accepted the offer at face value. It had been made by Henry M. Leland.

A few days later the directors of the Henry Ford Company met again. They were ready to dissolve the company formed around Henry Ford, and found another with Henry Leland and his remarkable motor as its hub. One problem remained to be resolved. What name would the new horseless carriage be given? The most logical name would be, the "Leland." Perhaps, because one well-known business in Detroit already had the Leland name, Henry Leland suggested that the new motorcar be named in honor of the French explorer of the city, Antoine de la Mothe Cadillac. A few minutes later the directors unanimously voted to establish the Cadillac Automobile Company. The date was August 27th, 1902.

Fifty-four days later, on October 20th, the firm that had been producing Henry Ford cars when the year began, completed its first Cadillac horseless carriage. The new, self-propelled road vehicle actually was built in the Leland-Faulconer plant. It performed perfectly from the beginning. By the end of the year, three Cadillacs had been built. On January 17th, 1903, two of them were in New York City for the opening of the third New York Automobile Show.

The response of the public was even more spectacular than that created by Ransom E. Olds' Curved Dash Oldsmobile at the second New York Show held fourteen months earlier in November, 1901. Olds had sold one thousand horseless carriages to a dealer without financial guarantees. By the end of the show on January 24th, Cadillac's new sales manager, William A. Metzger, had taken orders for more than one thousand of the unbuilt Cadillacs, all with substantial down payments. In a brief seven days, buyers had placed a firm foundation under the Cadillac Company whose owners had planned to get out of the motorcar business only four and one-half months before.

These four one-half months were equally historic for Henry Leland, already an important figure in American industry. The overwhelming acceptance of the small, single-cylinder Cadillac came as a sixtieth birthday present to Leland, already at an age when most of his contemporaries were retired or planning to retire. For Leland, it was the beginning of a new career that extended over two decades.

Leland created both of America's first quality cars, Cadillac and Lincoln. He became one of the five men chiefly responsible for making Detroit the Motor City. Like Ransom E. Olds, William C. Durant, John and Horace Dodge and Henry Ford, Leland provided an indispensable element in the rapid development of the motorcar in the United States.

It is important to consider the life and career of Henry Leland before he took his first ride in a self-propelled road vehicle. More than the experiences of any of the other founders of the motorcar, Leland's career explains how the infant industry of the United States defied the practices and traditions of Europe's much older industrial establishment and produced a miracle that has affected the entire world in the short span of seventy-five years.

Against the background of the old industrial establishment, Eli Whitney worked out an idea that has changed man's mode of life more rapidly than any discovery since the dawn of civilization.

Whitney's new concept for a new machine occurred to him at his work bench as he whittled from wood parts. If special machines could be developed to make identical parts, such as he was laboriously whittling, how simple it would be to have an unlimited supply of any type of complex equipment needed by men. The idea was so impractical that most men would have discarded it as being idiotic, but Whitney could not push even such a fantastic theory from his mind.

In a remarkably short time, less than a year, Whitney concluded that his idea was something that could be achieved. He thought the idea through with such care that he knew perfectly what the virtues and the limiting factors would be. It was at this point that he wrote to a friend, "I have worked a kind of a program so that I might produce some sort of a machine in large lots. I would have to know ahead that there would be some great demand for it. Else it would not pay to make the (machine) tools."

The idea that was to bring about such a radical change in man's lot had been set free.

In a short period of time, the mind of Eli Whitney had created a radically new method of producing manufactured goods. In doing so, he opened the way for an entire series of new industries, including the machine tool business, the manufacturing of component parts, and mass marketing, to mention a few.

In 1798, Whitney, the Yankee mechanical wizard, who five years before had invented and, within ten days, built the first successful cotton gin, grappled with another problem. The army of the United States and the state militia, were in need of more guns than could be produced by handcraft methods. There simply were not enough skilled craftsmen to supply the American army with guns. Guns not only were in short supply, but also were expensive to make.

In 1798, the one machine, for which there existed enough demand to justify Whitney's going to the expense of making machine tools, was the army rifle. His factory, just outside New Haven, did the first "tooling up" job in history and accomplished a previously unheard-of feat of producing 10,000 rifles of superior quality in a short time.

For a century after Whitney's epochal work, the pattern of acceptance was similar to that which has greeted a great many other discoveries. Fortunately, there was some immediate use of the new manufacturing procedures in New England and a lasting and growing impact was made on the manufacturers of guns and, ultimately, other arms. Within fifty years, other manufacturers in the area took up Whitney's standardization and New England, as a result, became the foremost manufacturing center in the Western Hemisphere. By 1890, the radical new methods were beginning to spread to other parts of the United States.

However, as the 1900s began, most production of complicated machines throughout the world was still being done by hand craftsmen. Ships, railroad engines, stagecoaches and wagons were custom-built, one at a time. Repairs, also, had to be made by craftsmen.

The earliest Duryea and Haynes horseless carriages were largely custom-built. This was true of the first cars built by Ransom E. Olds. Even when Olds shifted over to making the small, Curved Dash car in record numbers, his men were still grinding down gears and hand-fitting the moving parts. Only limited production and limited performance could be achieved in motorcars built by such methods.

Then came the adoption of the Whitney technique of interchangeable parts and rapid assembly by the makers of motorcars in Michigan. The impact struck with such force and rapidity that in the short period of twenty-five years the lives of millions of people in the United States were completely changed, and this revolutionary change began spreading to other parts of the world. The development of the truck, the tractor, the tank, the airplane and an almost endless list of other machines were merely further application of the Whitney-inspired atmosphere of change.

During this period, the capacity of the United States for industrial productivity overtook and surpassed that of any other country. For the first time in this country, unlimited mobility, upon which both social and economic opportunities rest, and which until now had always been reserved for the wealthy, suddenly became available to a majority of the people of a large nation. The heart of this development was the new economic force unleashed in the United States, community by community and state by state, by the motorcar.

Limited handwork was still necessary, even in the Whitney factory. This was because the tools and equipment available at that time did not permit the making of parts to the fine tolerances that are necessary for complete interchangeability. The best gauges of measurement in Whitney's time could only register a uniformity of one-thirty second of an inch. Half a century passed before the vernier caliper, capable of measuring thousandths of an inch, was developed.

Henry Leland, whose life overlapped the lives of the millions of Americans who are now forty years old, was born February 16th, 1843, on a Barton, Vermont, farm only twenty-five miles from the Canadian border. Eli Whitney had died only eighteen years before Leland was born. The United States had been in existence only half a century. The boy was given the name, Henry Martyn Leland, in honor of a noted English missionary to India, indicating the nature of the deeply religious family background into which he was born. This largely explains why Henry Leland read the Bible and offered prayer with his men during work breaks at the Cadillac plant. Not far across Detroit, free beer was dispensed to the men at the Dodge factory.

Due to the stern life of early, rural New England, young Henry was accustomed to doing regular chores by the time he was six. The family moved to a farm at Worcester, Massachusetts. At eleven, Henry, already tall as a man, was working in a Worcester factory where heavy shoes were made for slaves on southern plantations.

Leland revealed his inventiveness at this first job, devising a special system that enabled him to earn up to $1.50 a day when the most skilled worker earned $1.75. When he was fourteen, he went to work in a wheel factory.

Then, a major development occurred in his life. The Leland family attended the Second Adventist Church of which the Reverend Mr. Jerald was pastor. Jerald recognized that the boy possessed unusual ability and he persuaded the superintendent of the Crompton Works to make the sixteen-year-old youth an apprentice-machinist. The Crompton Works handled more precision work than most of the numerous small factories in the Worcester community. The firm made power looms for the rapidly growing New England textile industry. With some misgivings about giving up the good wages he was earning and accepting an apprentice wage of fifty cents a day, in addition to working ten hours a day, six days a week, Henry Leland became an apprentice-machinist.

Fortunately, he soon realized the advantages and began to enjoy the work. He advanced rapidly as a machinist and, in due time, became one of the youngest master mechanics in New England.

There were other unrelated, but important, developments during young Leland's apprentice period. For the first time, he began reading books, other than the Bible. In this way, he learned about the contributions of Eli Whitney, Thomas Jefferson, Robert Fulton and other men who were outstanding in the early years of the United States. Also, he made the acquaintance of Ellen Hull, whom he met at church. She became one of the great influences of his life.

Only seventeen when the Civil War began, Henry schemed with his older brother, Edson, to enlist. They planned to go to the recruiting station together. He was more than six feet tall, and sure the army would not question his age. If questions were raised, his brother could vouch for him. Knowing that their mother was opposed to Henry going to war, they secretly went to the recruiting office to join the Union army. When they arrived, the Leland boys found that their mother had already been there to record Henry's proper age, preventing him from going to war with Edson.

However, Leland soon found a way to be of service to his country in wartime. The firm for which he was working accepted an important government contract to make lathes used in the manufacture of gun stocks at federal armories. The manufacture of the machine tools to produce such lathes required the highest degree of precision known in the tool-making industry. So expert was Henry Leland, he was entrusted with the vital assignment. It was an important moment in his life when Army officers arrived from the Springfield Armory (in existence from Revolutionary War days), and inspected and approved his work.

About that time, the family was notified of the death of his brother, Edson. Although his firm offered him higher wages in an effort to induce him to stay, the grief-stricken Leland went to the U. S. Armory at Springfield to make Union rifles, at lower wages. He remained there until Lee surrendered to Grant at Appomattox.

In Springfield, Massachusetts, one of the moments of which he remained forever proud occurred on November 8th, 1864, Then, old enough to vote for the first time, he cast his ballot for his idol, Abraham Lincoln. Five and one-half decades later he was to name a motorcar, declared by himself to be "the finest car of which I am capable," in honor of the Civil War president.

With the war over, work at the Springfield Armory ended abruptly. The day after the armory closed, Leland took the train 20 miles down the Connecticut River to Hartford, and began work immediately at the Colt plant, home of the already famed Colt revolver.

Just as he had done in Springfield, he read the Bible each noon during his lunch hour and, as before, he soon had a group around him to hear the reading of the Scriptures. The tall, pleasant young man was already exhibiting the leadership qualities that enabled him to play a decisive role in establishing the motorcar industry.

All during the long war, Leland and Ellen Hull had corresponded. She had been in school most of the time studying to become a school teacher. Their devotion had grown and they were engaged by the time the war ended. When she completed her college course and returned to Worcester, Leland ended his work with firearms in the Colt factory and returned to Worcester to be near Ellen.

A year later, September 25th, 1867, Henry and Ellen were married and established their home in Worcester. The next five years constituted the period of great adjustment for Henry Leland, a time when great happiness and struggle with seemingly endless problems were often woven into the fabric of a single day. They were the years when their two children, a daughter, Gertrude, and a son, Wilfred, were born. They were also years of financial struggle. Leland moved from one job after another in the Worcester area in an effort to increase his meager income. At one time he was a policeman. These, also, were the years when he took an active role in community affairs for the first time in his life, further revealing his capacity for leadership. He even served as tongue man on Rapid No. 2 Volunteer Fire Company in the Worcester Fire Department.

On July 1st, 1872, Henry Leland began an eighteen-year association with the Brown & Sharpe Company of Providence, Rhode Island, the foremost machine toolmaker in the United States. He had the good fortune to be with the firm the last four years the founder, Joseph R. Brown, was still active. Brown had grasped the full significance of the new concept of interchangeable parts and systematic assembly of complex machines. He was regarded as the outstanding precisionist in New England's highly advanced industry. The mantle of Whitney was on his shoulders.

At times the impetuous younger man found it difficult to get along with the aging genius who developed and made calipers capable of dividing an inch into one thousand equal and exact parts. By the time Leland left Brown & Sharpe, he was one of the few men in the world who could produce machine parts to such fine tolerances.

After working in all departments of the new Brown & Sharpe factory, built the same year he joined the firm, and getting to know most of its three hundred employees, Leland's big break into a leadership role came. He was made head of the screw-machine department, a small but vital unit in the Brown & Sharpe operation. It marked the first time that the determined and, at times, explosive young man in his early thirties had been recognized as more than a master mechanic. His new role would allow him to teach his machinist magic to others, and provide the opportunity to explore new ways to use the Whitney concept of interchangeability and assembly.

There were only six machines in the department when Leland took over. He improved some of the machines and discarded others. He increased the jobs that could be done by screw-machines until there were sixty-six machines in the department. He was placed in charge of other departments and, finally, in 1878, he was made head of Brown & Sharpe's largest and most important division, the sewing-machine department. In six years, he had become Brown & Sharpe's leader in production management.

Despite his rapid rise, Brown & Sharpe associates found Leland a man of sharp contrasts. Generally, a fair man who went out of his way to accommodate others, Leland could be temperamental, unreasonable and unyielding. An example of this occurred after he had become a department head. What began as a head-on clash with his management, ironically, led to an important invention. It, also, provided a clue to Leland's future.

Leland's department was given an order to make a quantity of horse hair clippers. With memories of cold Vermont winters, Leland thought it inhuman to clip horses' hair in cold weather, and he flatly refused to have his men make the clippers. After a time, management convinced him that the horse hair clippers were going to be made, anyway, and Brown & Sharpe might just as well handle the business.

Satisfied, Leland made a study of the production of the clippers. The product his department turned out was so superior that a barber who used a pair on his horses came to see Leland about developing a clipper that could be used to cut human hair.

In a short while, Leland developed a clipper that pleased the barber, but not Leland. He continued to improve the hair clipper until at length he applied for, and received, a patent as the inventor of the first barber's clipper. After Brown & Sharpe began manufacturing the barber clippers, sales came in from all over the world. Brown & Sharpe organized a special production unit that produced up to three hundred clippers a day.

Strangely, although the production of barber clippers proved to be highly profitable to Brown & Sharpe, Leland's reward was small. Leland later explained it as, "a thank you, and fifty cents a day more in my pay envelope." He added, "That was one of the times when I thought I ought to quit making other men rich and go to work for myself."

Earlier, there were times when Leland had thought about going into business for himself. His farm background, which had called for the use of many skills and independent thinking, was sufficient reason for him to probe the possibilities of setting up his own machine shop business. With a family to support, he could not raise enough capital to start a business of his own. Nonetheless, the idea continued to appeal to him.

In 1883, when he had been with Brown & Sharpe nearly twelve years, Leland almost lost his life in a battle with typhoid fever. Even when he recovered, the doctors agreed that he could not continue in indoor factory work.

Out of respect to this man who had contributed so much to the firm, Brown & Sharpe created a new job for him. The organization had traveling representatives contacting major manufacturers of metal products in the New England, New York and Pennsylvania areas, but they had no regular representation in other parts of the country. The rising importance of major midwest cities in manufacturing offered Brown & Sharpe an additional market. Leland was appointed its traveling representative from Pittsburgh west. In the next six years, Leland traveled as far west as St. Louis, Milwaukee and Chicago, as well as to all the important cities in Ohio, Michigan, Indiana and Illinois.

Leland found it hard to be away from his family. The Leland family ties had always been close, especially between Leland and his son, Wilfred. Leland wrote frequent letters home. Often he directed them to Wilfred. In one of his letters from Chicago, he wrote, "I have had thee much in mind these days of our separation and have often wondered what you and sister and Mama were doing at that particular time.... I shall be in Milwaukee next Sunday I expect, and shall from there feel that every move brings me nearer home."

Leland's relationship with his son amounted to more than a father's devotion. There was a growing sense of respect for and dependence on his only son. Wilfred reciprocated in the respect and trust his father extended to him and soon took over many of the responsibilities as head of the house when his father was away for long periods. In time, he handled the family budget and paid the family bills. Ellen's health had deteriorated under long years of caring for her family, and teaching to supplement the family income. Wilfred was also working, doing odd jobs for a doctor near the Leland home in Providence. He became increasingly interested in studying medicine.

Despite his displeasure over being away from home, Leland found that his new job opened up important, new opportunities for him. He soon acquired an understanding of the manufacturing being done in the Midwest. While much of the factory work was, to him, primitive, he was greatly impressed with the driving spirit of the midwestern people. Everywhere he traveled, there was growth. Not only were there new businesses, and new factories, but also new towns. There was some growth in the eastern United States, but nothing like the expansion taking place in the Midwest. Chicago and Detroit, especially, impressed Leland. They were growing more rapidly than even the other expanding cities in the area.

Not long after he started traveling in the West, Leland began to see an opportunity to achieve his lifelong dream of having a business of his own. There was need, in a number of midwestern cities, for a Brown & Sharpe type of enterprise.

From his contacts with owners and managers of new businesses throughout the area, he also discovered a means of establishing his own business without having to invest funds of his own; money which he did not have. Soon he knew, intimately, heads of many successful midwest businesses, whose initial investment of capital came from sharing ownership with men who had money to invest. By 1889, Leland had narrowed down the list of cities in which he preferred to locate his own machine shop and had begun to look for financial backers.

The lightning struck in Detroit. Leland had met Charles A. Strelinger soon after he began traveling the Midwest. Strelinger, for years, had sold machine tools in Detroit and throughout the area, including some made by Brown & Sharpe. He had become wealthy selling bicycles that then were coming into general use for the first time. In 1885, Strelinger had founded his own toolmaking and machine shop business under the name, Charles A. Strelinger & Company. The business had done well. Strelinger convinced Leland that there was ample business for several more new machine shops to serve the rapidly growing Detroit industry and the factories in the smaller towns nearby, such as Jackson, Lansing and Flint.

Strelinger also solved Leland's need for financial backing. He introduced the representative of Brown & Sharpe to Robert C. Faulconer of Alpena, Michigan. Faulconer had made a comfortable fortune in lumber. He was looking for an investment opportunity.

Leland talked over his plans carefully with members of his family, particularly with his son. Wilfred was then at Brown University taking a preparatory course for medicine. Leland talked to his son about the possibility of giving up his dream of being a doctor and coming into the new family business.

On September 19th, 1890, Henry Leland's dream of having his own business became a reality. The new machine shop and toolmaking firm of Leland, Faulconer & Norton opened for business with a dozen employees on the fourth floor of the Strelinger Building at the corner of Bates and Congress Streets. The new business was capitalized at $50,000. Faulconer supplied $40,000 of the capital. Leland's important interest was based on his personal contribution to the business and upon his investment of $3,600 of which $2,000 was loaned him by Lucian Sharpe of Brown & Sharpe. Charles F. Norton, a highly capable machine designer for years at Brown & Sharpe, joined the new business in Detroit and had a small stock holding, as did Charles Strelinger. The first officers were Faulconer, president; Leland, vice-president and manager; Strelinger, secretary.

Detroit, in 1890, was a city of just over 200,000 population. The city was a highly-congested area along the Detroit River flowing from Lake Huron into Lake Erie. The two new architectual wonders of Detroit were the first 10-story building in its business district and the new Belle Isle Bridge that connected Detroit with Belle Isle Park, spanning a branch of the Detroit River. No motorcar had yet been seen on the streets of Detroit. David J. Buick was an important citizen of the city, but he was still a decade away from building a car. He was in the business of manufacturing bathtubs, a business that led him to discover the first effective method for fixing porcelain on metal. Nor was Henry Ford in Detroit. He was still farming near the small town of Dearborn, west of the city.

As soon as the founding of Leland & Faulconer was assured,

Leland made another effort to get Wilfred to leave his medical course at Brown University and join the new business. Finally, when Leland proposed that his son come and be with the firm during its first crucial year, Wilfred agreed. He arrived in Detroit on his twenty-first birthday, November 7th, 1890. Wilfred was no novice in the machine shop. He had worked at Brown & Sharpe in the summers between school terms.

By the end of the year, Wilfred had assumed important duties. He realized how much his father needed him as a trusted associate. So, instead of returning to Providence to resume his study of medicine, he went back to Brown & Sharpe for additional training as a precision machinist. In time, he, too, could machine to one thousandth of an inch. Wilfred's first assignment on returning to Detroit was to take charge of the gear-cutting department where he began training other men in the art of precision manufacturing of interchangeable parts.

In the motorcar's first years, a number of family teams made important contributions, but none exceeded those made by Henry and Wilfred Leland. The varying abilities of the two Lelands meshed perfectly. They lived and worked in a spirit of compatibility. Both men found an inner pleasure in according the other credit for achievement. They generally spoke of their work in terms of "our," "we," and "us."

For Henry Leland, the Leland family and the coming age of the motorcar in the United States, Wilfred's decision to give up his career in medicine was of the greatest importance. It was a difficult decision, since his entry into the field of medicine also held great promise. He had inherited the keen sensitivity of his mother, Ellen Hull Leland, something that is often the difference between mere success and greatness in a doctor. But, this same sensitivity also suited him well for his role as the chief associate of his gifted, but strong-willed father. Wilfred administered to his aging father much as he would have to a patient. It was a difficult role for the younger man, but one which unquestionably added many years to Henry Leland's remarkable career. And, in so doing, Wilfred Leland became one of that select group of men who had a major hand in shaping the future of the American motorcar industry.

Success was immediate at the new firm of Leland, Faulconer & Norton. In contrast to the dozen men employed when the firm opened in early fall, by the year's end there were sixty. This was significant beyond the success of the new firm. It meant that the first of many men who would follow at Leland & Faulconer were being trained in the new art and skills of precision manufacturing. They were being made the sons of Eli Whitney to whom the accuracy required for interchangeability of parts was a way of life.

Many a man, trained under the stern eye of Henry Leland, went on to an important career in other organizations. One of them was Horace Dodge, ultimately the production wizard of the Dodge Brothers machine shop. The roots that made Detroit the Motor City were in great measure nurtured at Leland & Faulconer.

Although Henry Leland had a highly successful business of his own, he remained tremendously proud of his association with Brown & Sharpe. His men often got weary of hearing Leland's continuous praise of Brown & Sharpe achievement in the field of precision work with metals. One of his associates insisted that, at the close of a prayer, Leland unconsciously substituted the reference "Brown & Sharpe" for "Amen."

Before long, the performance of Leland's firm in Detroit rivaled even that of Brown & Sharpe. Inventors of many new machines called on the firm to work out the difficulties of manufacturing. In this way, the firm's craftsmen acquired experience making the first of such unlike machines as typewriters, chicken feeders and pencil sharpeners.

By 1893, the business had completely outgrown the space available at the Strelinger Building in downtown Detroit. The Lelands designed and built a new factory on the east side of the city, on Trombly Avenue. The following year Norton left the firm and the name was changed to "Leland & Faulconer." In 1895, its was necessary to increase the capitalization to $70,000, and a year later to $100,000. Under a new agreement, Henry Leland was given 10 percent of the profits, an arrangement that soon enabled him to become debt free and to buy additional Leland & Faulconer stock.

Faulconer found it difficult to increase his large holdings to permit the firm to have just Leland and himself as principal stockholders. Leland looked to Joseph Boyer of St. Louis, whom he had befriended during his traveling days for Brown & Sharpe, and interested him in loaning Faulconer $40,000. The contact focused Boyer's attention on Detroit, and he moved his own firm to the city in 1904. The firm became the Burroughs Adding Machine Company and soon developed into one of Detroit's most important manufacturing enterprises.

In 1896, Leland & Faulconer added a grey-iron foundry that soon made the firm one of the most important machine shops in the

United States. Leland insisted on building the foundry at the Leland & Faulconer location because of the impossibility of obtaining closely-machined castings outside New England. Even in New England, only Brown & Sharpe was able to produce the precision castings required by the new customers of Leland & Faulconer. Leland's skill at designing machines with complete interchangeability of parts placed his demands, particularly for machined castings, beyond the reach of midwestern foundries. The grey-iron foundry on Trombly Street was the first in the West to equal the machined castings produced at Brown & Sharpe.

Success in the new foundry did not come easily. Even the men who had been especially trained could not develop the superb quality sought by the vigorous, white-haired Leland. He alone saw the possibilities, clearly. His confidence in his own ability, and his innate stubbornness, would not permit him to settle for less than his new concept of perfection. Each day he stormed through the new foundry inspecting the day's castings. As a final act, he lifted them and fairly flung them on the floor. If they did not break, they had stood his test. There were days when half the castings lay shattered on the foundry floor.

His men said his standards were too high for any foundry to meet; higher than any other foundry in existence, including the one at Brown & Sharpe. The old man was unyielding. In desperation, some of the men who had been with Leland & Faulconer from the beginning took an unprecedented step. They went over Leland's head and appealed directly to Mr. Faulconer. When the kindly Faulconer interceded in behalf of the foundry leaders, Leland replied with a manifesto that was to become the hallmark of the yet unborn motorcar industry in the United States.

> "There always was and there always will be a conflict between 'good' and 'good enough', and in opening up a new business or a new department one can count upon meeting this resistance to high standard of workmanship. It is easy to get (worker) cooperation for mediocre work, but one must sweat blood for a chance to produce a superior product."

In the end, Henry Leland had his way, and soon there were no broken castings on the foundry floor. Horace Dodge witnessed the struggle. Henry Ford, who was just beginning work on his first car in the barn behind his home, heard about it, especially the way it had ended. Every important machinist in Detroit heard about what was going on at Leland & Faulconer's new foundry. Most important, the manufacturers learned about the new kind of quality being built into the machined castings at Leland & Faulconer. They began paying premiums, often up to three times the going rate, for a prompt delivery of Leland & Faulconer castings, the ones that were accurate to one thousandth of an inch and that didn't break, even if they were inadvertently dropped on the floor during assembly.

At about the same time, Leland worked out a new technique for grinding case-hardened gears for the chainless bicycle so they could perform well and be completely interchangeable. It opened up important new opportunities in bicycle manufacture. The foundry success and new techniques in case-hardening of gears led to new opportunities for Leland & Faulconer in the manufacturing of both bicycles and internal combustion engines, important predecessors of the motorcar.

Leland had become experienced in the building of stationary internal combustion motors for boats while with Brown & Sharpe. From that time, he was convinced that the internal combustion engine would be adapted to many uses. It came as no surprise or puzzle to him when Ransom Olds approached Leland & Faulconer to build the small, single-cylinder internal combustion motor for the Curved Dash Oldsmobile. What a day that was, in 1901, when Olds brought the foremost horseless carriage motor in the United States and placed its manufacture in the hands of the nation's foremost machinist! Something of historic significance virtually *had* to follow.

6

Leland's Cadillac

From the very first, the Cadillac represented a new high standard of performance for the horseless carriage. Its single cylinder motor was the first that could be relied upon to start dependably and easily. The car maintained its power in a period when it was expected that the motorcar engine could be temperamental, "with a personality all its own."

The motors, also made for the Curved Dash Oldsmobile by Leland & Faulconer, were dependable and easy to start, something that was interestingly demonstrated by the Leland family in its family horseless carriage. In 1901, even before Leland & Faulconer began making Oldsmobile motors, the Lelands bought their first motorcar. Ransom Olds, personally, delivered the Curved Dash Olds to the Leland home in Detroit.

Olds drove the horseless carriage up to the curbstone, turned off the motor and went in to pay his respects to the Leland family. He explained the operation of their new motorcar and pointed out some opportunities that would now be theirs as a result of having shifted to the entirely new kind of transportation. He may even have recited his own little free-verse ditty, "It never kicks or bites, never tires on long runs, and never sweats in hot weather."

After the explanations, and with the entire Leland family out in the street to see their new horseless carriage off on its first run, Mr. Olds cranked the Oldsmobile a considerable time, without results. Wilfred, who was present, described the situation, "Mr. Olds worked quite awhile cranking it, muttering something about each car having an individuality of its own. But after we began making motors for him, father took the individuality out of them." Leland replaced the original motor with one of those made by Leland & Faulconer. Then, as Wilfred explained, "After our own little Oldsmobile was properly equipped, it acted in quite an exemplary fashion."

In the year following the 1903 New York Automobile Show (at which the "little one lunger" Cadillac was introduced), 1,895 of the horseless carriages were delivered. Known as the "Model-A," the small car had the important features of the Curved Dash Oldsmobile and the other small cars offered to the public that year, plus the remarkable dependability made possible by superior manufacturing.

The driver sat in the right seat with a steering wheel in front of him, rather than a tiller used on the Olds and other horseless carriages. The small, air-cooled Leland & Faulconer motor was located under the front seat with a hand-crank on the side next to the driver.

The car had two patent leather guards or "fenders," almost exactly the same type of equipment found on the most expensive buggies and surries. There was no running board, no top, no lights or horn. For an extra charge, heavy brass kerosene lamps, of the kind to be found on the finest horse-drawn equipment, and a hand-operated bulb horn were available.

From the beginning, each Cadillac carried the coat of arms of its famous namesake, the French explorer and founder of Detroit. The emblem is used to this day.

There were many far-reaching engineering advancements. This was not surprising, since the car was the first to be designed by a staff or team of engineers, one of the most competent groups of engineers ever assembled up to that time. Cadillac was the product of many men's minds, directed by the foremost machinist of his time.

The car consisted of a chassis, on which were mounted a motor and a body, each easily attached or detached. The motor was mounted in the middle of the chassis, providing unusual balance. Only six bolts fastened the body to the chassis. Taking a leaf directly out of Leland & Faulconer experience with the making of large stationary internal combustion engines for marine use, even in the small Cadillac motor, the crankshaft was large. The bearings sup-

Leading the state fair parade was this Curved Dash Olds
driven by Ransom E. Olds's ten-year-old daughter,
Gladys, with her younger sister, Ethel, as the passenger.

porting it were large and the motor housing was designed so that worn bearings could be changed without removing the crankshaft. These were refinements no other carmaker had yet contemplated. As Leland said, "Our cars are made to run, not to sell."

But his remark did not mean that Leland was unaware of the vital role selling must take in any major success. The proposal to hire William E. Metzger as Cadillac's first sales manager probably was made originally by director, William H. Murphy, but the Lelands, both Henry and Wilfred, regarded the appointment of Metzger as an important additional thrust for the new enterprise.

The irrepressible Metzger had cut his sales teeth in Detroit as a bicycle salesman. He immediately understood the potential of the horseless carriage. In 1898, he established the first motorcar agency in Detroit. He sold several early cars including the Winton, Haynes and Oldsmobile. He was one of the sponsors of the historic race in Detroit at which Henry Ford drove his own car to victory.

The combination of Leland's engineering and Metzger's sales-magic resulted in Cadillac registering a more thunderous success in its first year than had been won by any other early motorcar to this time, including the Oldsmobile. But, that the Oldsmobile achievement preceded the Cadillac effort and lighted the way must be recognized.

Metzger knew before he was appointed Cadillac's advertising and sales manager that the little horseless carriage had the most outstanding single-cylinder motor ever developed. As an Oldsmobile salesman he knew what a difference it meant to get an Olds with a Leland & Faulconer-built motor. He was aware that Leland had offered Ransom Olds a much more powerful motor and that the Cadillac had that improved motor. It was this knowledge that was the basis of Metzger's startling success that included a dealer organization stretching from Maine to Colorado. Dealers began delivering orders, accompanied by cash, before Cadillac was able to produce cars.

The advertisement which Metzger placed in leading newspapers and magazines immediately after the New York Show indicated his supreme confidence in Cadillac's future. The advertisement began with quotes attributed to the new dealers appointed at the New York Show. "The Cadillac's a Cinch," "Best I Ever Saw" and "Don't See How They Can Do It For The Money," the headline read. No doubt the new dealers did make such remarks, but not until after they had been under the hypnotic spell of William E. Metzger who knew that the Leland & Faulconer motor would make him an honest salesman.

The extent of the new car's success was found in the signature which included the names and addresses of twenty-one Cadillac dealers. There were two in New York (New York City and Buffalo); a record four in Ohio (Cleveland, Cincinnati, Columbus and Dayton); two in New Jersey; two in Michigan; one each in Maine, Massachusetts, Rhode Island, Pennsylvania, Washington, D. C., Georgia, Indiana, Illinois, Minnesota, North Dakota and Colorado. The advertisement was signed "William E. Metzger, Sales Manager," with the Metzger name in type as large as Detroit, and well it might have been.

Nor did Metzger neglect the publicity stunts so common in the introduction of early motorcars. The first of these took place before the New York Show, and Metzger had the picture with him in New York City as proof.

Shortly after the first Cadillacs had been produced in the fall of 1902, Alanson Brush (who later built his own famous Brush runabout) drove the car in a major publicity stunt. He drove the "Model-A" up the steep steps of the Wayne County Court House on Cadillac Square in Detroit to the cheers of several thousand persons.

On February 9th, the *Free Press* carried a story as a followup to the New York Automobile Show. The account stated that, based on its achievements, the Cadillac had to be regarded as the most versatile at the New York Show. The new Cadillac had, the item reported, pulled a 5-ton truck loaded with railroad iron up a 4 percent grade after a two-cylinder car (undoubtedly a Duryea) had failed to move the load at all.

Two months later, on April 3rd, 1904, as soon as the winter weather had moderated, the *Detroit Free Press* carried a picture and story on its sports page (motorcar news, then, generally appeared on sports pages) of the little Cadillac moving up Detroit's Shelby Hill with sixteen persons aboard.

By working furiously, Metzger established forty-eight Cadillac agencies by September of 1903, placing a new Cadillac dealer in major cities from New York to San Francisco. As a result, Cadillac delivered all of the more than 1,000 cars sold at the New York Show, and sold all the vehicles which the company's Detroit plant on Cass Avenue could produce.

Until the year was over no one knew how many Cadillacs could be made. The facilities of the Murphy Company on Cass Avenue were inadequate to the task of building so many cars, even though the motors were produced ready for assembly at Leland & Faulconer.

New buildings had to be erected and equipped. It was a year of frantic effort by the production men.

One year after the New York Show, Cadillac had produced and sold more cars during the twelve-month period than any firm, except the Olds Motor Vehicle Company, whose operations were already beginning to be moved from Detroit to Lansing. As a result of the Olds move to Lansing, completed in 1905, Cadillac became Detroit's first permanent, and now oldest, producer of motorcars.

As 1904 began, things were going so well that Metzger had visions of overtaking Oldsmobile in the new year and becoming the foremost producer in the United States. But it was not to be.

The Leland & Faulconer contract to produce motors for Cadillac had been made for but one year. Despite the favorable developments, some of the major investors and directors were not convinced that the Leland & Faulconer motor was as good as it could be. In addition, they thought Cadillac was paying too much for the power unit.

Aware that there was controversy among the directors, and fearing that the Cadillac contract might not be renewed, Henry Leland took steps to protect Leland & Faulconer from a sudden loss in business. Shortly before the March director's meeting, at which a decision affecting production for the following year was to be made, he took a trip through Ohio and Indiana. Leland called on three firms making horse-drawn vehicles and explained the company position. The firms were the Columbus Buggy Company at Columbus, Ohio, Parry Brothers Company and Studebaker Brothers in Indianapolis and South Bend, Indiana.

All of the firms were interested in securing rights to the Leland & Faulconer motor and entering the new self-propelled road vehicle business. The officials at Studebaker were particularly interested. They made a firm offer to buy 3,000 Leland & Faulconer motors in the coming year at $15.00 per motor more than Leland & Faulconer was being paid by Cadillac. As soon as Leland had returned home, Studebaker sent one of its principals to the Leland & Faulconer plant to press its interest in securing the contract. Leland acknowledged that the additional $45,000 offered on a production of 3,000 motors was tempting, but he pointed out that Cadillac had the right to renew the contract, hence there could be no understanding with Studebaker until Cadillac failed to renew.

In the Cadillac director's meeting, those who opposed renewal of the Leland & Faulconer contract pressed their contention vigorously. The two most important stockholders, William H. Murphy and

Open-road contests had a big role in proving the capabilities of the motorcar during the horseless carriage era. One of the most famous was the New York to Paris Race of 1908. George Schuster (left) was the winner, driving this 1907 Thomas Flyer made in Buffalo. At ninety-five, Schuster still lives in Buffalo and took part in 1968 ceremonies celebrating the famous race.

Lem W. Bowen, were in Europe. The noisy directors' session reached a point where Leland told the directors that he considered the Leland & Faulconer relationship with Cadillac terminated and left the room in anger.

As Leland left the building, Clarence A. Black, one of the original directors, asked Leland to return to the meeting on the assurance that an arrangement would be worked out. A new contract for Leland & Faulconer motors was soon completed. Had Black not moved to save the situation, how things might have changed! Armed with the Leland & Faulconer motor, Studebaker might easily have made its hometown of South Bend, Indiana, the motor city. Without the Leland & Faulconer motor, the Studebaker brothers introduced their first car later in 1904, advertising the firm as, "Wagonmakers and Blacksmiths." Studebaker built cars for more than half a century.

Within a month, another crisis developed. On April 13th, 1904, when production had reached the level of 50 cars a day, fire destroyed much of the expanded Cadillac plant on Cass Avenue. Spreading out of the rivet department where varnish and gasoline caused explosions, the flames moved into a part of the main factory and a part of a large addition, not yet in use. A great amount of material and parts was destroyed, but 2,000 engines from Leland & Faulconer and 500 completed cars were stored in a warehouse across the street and were saved. Dealers were asked to hold all orders for thirty days. By June, the six hundred employees of the firm were back on the production lines.

Production climbed during the summer, and that fact made the supplier problem worse. Hundreds of parts were on order from suppliers and inability to obtain delivery on any one of them prevented cars from being shipped. There was constant pressure on Leland & Faulconer to take over the production of more parts. Early in the fall, circumstances reached the point where the directors, Murphy and Bowen, went to the Lelands and insisted that they take over the entire management of Cadillac. The alternative, the directors claimed, was to dissolve the business.

An arrangement was worked out by which the Lelands took over the management. They agreed to spend a part of each working day in the Cadillac plant. The new arrangement went into effect December 26th, 1904. Work did not begin at the Cadillac plant the next day until a "Model-B" Cadillac arrived bringing both Lelands and Ernest Sweet, the Leland & Faulconer engineer. Both the elder Leland and Sweet wore beards. One of the workmen couldn't resist the temptation and shouted to his confederates, "Well, boys, our troubles are all over now. Here comes the Father the Son and the Holy Ghost." Insofar as Cadillac was concerned, the first part of the remark proved to be remarkably accurate.

Soon after, a reorganization was completed, under which both the Cadillac Automobile Company and Leland & Faulconer were absorbed by the new firm, the Cadillac Motor Car Company, capitalized at $1,500,000 with the assets of Leland & Faulconer valued at $500,000, Cadillac at $1,000,000. The new firm had one thousand employees. Henry Leland took over responsibility for production, while Wilfred took charge of sales and the office work and personally wrote all checks. Each Leland was paid $750.00 a month, and jointly assigned 5 percent of the profits, annually.

The effects were soon evident in production. In the year between the spring of 1904 (after the fire damage had been overcome), until May, 1905, production climbed to 3,863 cars. On August 1st, 1905, the firm produced the eight thousandth Cadillac, including a small number of the new "Model 30," a full-sized car with a four-cylinder engine.

Henry Leland and his engineers were also working on completely glass-enclosed cars. Leland had one custom-built, using the little, single-cylinder "Model B." The Leland family used it for years. This first sedan stands 7 feet, 4 inches high. There was such public interest in the car which offered so much protection from the weather that it was put into production, and sold for $1,200. In 1954, the original Leland personal car was driven through Detroit at 17 miles an hour, propelled by its original Leland & Faulconer motor, to the Detroit Historical Museum where it is now on exhibit.

While Cadillac eventually sold nearly 70,000 of its larger "Model 30s" before it was replaced by later models, it was the topless, one-cylinder runabout that made Cadillac a famous name in motorcars, both in the United States and in Europe. This was accomplished in a period when there were no service stations or garages, other than blacksmith shops, whose workmen had little or no experience in repairing cars.

In his memoirs, "Horses to Horsepower," Herb Lewis describes his first ride in a motorcar in the Platte Valley of his native Nebraska. It was in a Cadillac in the summer of 1907. The former cowboy and horseman who worked for Buffalo Bill Cody on the Cody ranch at North Platte had gone to Aurora in eastern Nebraska to visit his family. He was invited to take a trip in a horseless carriage from

Aurora to Giltner, 15 miles away. He made the trip with Josh Isaman, an insurance man, and George Wanek, president of the Aurora bank. It was a trip that, in good weather, required five to seven hours in a horse and buggy. They left from the bank at 9:00 in the morning in Isaman's "Model B" Cadillac. Lewis sat in the rear seat, entering the car from a step at the back.

It was a nice day in June. Farmers working in the fields with horses were often overcome with shock at the sight and sound of the strange and noisy contraption moving along the road. The Cadillac's chain drive created a high, shrill noise when the car was driven at full speed. Despite Isaman's efforts to avoid driving near horses, the team of one farmer, still some distance from the road, was so frightened it bolted, turned over the corn cultivator and ran half a mile to the farmstead dragging the implement behind.

Even with the delay, Isaman, Wanek and Lewis rode into Giltner shortly after 11 o'clock. Isaman and Wanek had business appointments at lunch. They agreed to meet at 2 p.m. to begin the trip back to Aurora. As the men left Giltner, an afternoon thunderstorm was approaching. They had driven only 3 or 4 miles when the storm hit. Since their horseless carriage had no top, Isaman drove under an oak tree that provided shelter. The rain continued for fifteen minutes and left the dirt road in a muddy condition. They decided to wait another thirty minutes for the road to dry. Isaman had bought a few bottles of iced beer in Giltner so the time passed pleasantly for the men stranded, temporarily, by the thunderstorm.

About 3 o'clock, Isaman cranked the car and the trip back to Aurora was resumed. They had traveled only a few miles when they passed a "knight of the road" with his possessions in a bundle tied to a stick carried over his shoulder. The itinerant visibly was alarmed even before the Cadillac caught up to him. Since there was room for a fourth passenger, Isaman stopped and offered the man a ride. The tramp, pale with fright, kept right on walking, and protested, "You ain't goin' get me in that speed buggy." Isaman, a big friendly sort of man, tried to reassure the tramp by offering him a bottle of beer with, "Even if you won't ride with us, have a bottle of beer, my friend." The hobo was so unnerved he walked on without a reply.

Despite the delay caused by the rain, Isaman, Wanek and Lewis were back in Aurora at 5 p.m. They had left at 9:00 in the morning, gone to Giltner, transacted important business and returned to

David D. Buick,
Eugene C. Richards
and Walter DeMarr
developed the first Buick
engines in Detroit, and
together invented the
valve-in head motor now
used, almost universally,
in motorcars of the
United States. Buick sold
his company to the Flint
Wagon Works of Flint,
Michigan. William C.
Durant quickly made it
one of the country's
great cars.

Aurora by 5:00 in the afternoon in time to have their evening meal with their families.

It would, at best, have been a dawn-to-dark trip with a horse and buggy. In addition, they would have had the horse to unhitch, the harness to put away and the horse to water and feed. In all probability, without the car, the trip would not have been made. Already on the plains of Nebraska, the small Cadillac had extended the daily opportunities for business and pleasure from the approximately 5 miles practical with horse-and-buggy to, at least, 50 miles.

It was the dependability of the Cadillac that kept Isaman using the little car for years. The Leland & Faulconer motor cranked so easily and so dependably that even Mrs. Isaman used the car regularly in Aurora. At times she visited nearby towns, trips that for the most part she would not have taken in a horse and buggy. Such was the nature of the new opportunity brought to rural America by the horseless carriage.

One February day in 1903, Frederick S. Bennett was reading the *Cycle and Automobile Trade Journal* in his London place of business. He came upon the first advertisement of the Cadillac Automobile Company since the car's great success at the New York Automobile Show. Although Bennett worked for a London automobile agency, he had not heard of Cadillac before. He was greatly impressed by the long list of dealers and the claims made for the Cadillac in the advertisement.

Bennett was so impressed that he prevailed upon his firm to buy one of the new cars so that it could be tried out on English roads. In order to be sure of getting exactly the car being offered the public in the United States, the car, bearing motor No. 530, was purchased at retail in New York and shipped to London.

Cadillac No. 530 proved to be a Mayflower in reverse, with Bennett playing the captain's role. It was a chill and hostile shore on which the little car landed when it reached London. The English and Europeans generally held manufactured goods from the United States in low regard. Limited importations of early American motorcars had further entrenched this European attitude. Some shipments of American bicycles were so far below English and European standards that entire lots had been sent directly to the scrapyards, rather than be offered for sale.

Europeans recognized themselves for what they were—the foremost workers with metals to be found anywhere in the world. Any machine from the United States would have to give spectacular performance in order to break through this hard shell of pride and respect for the labels reading, "Made In England," "France," "Belgium" and "Germany."

What the Europeans did not realize when they first saw the Cadillac was that it represented an entirely new approach to manufacturing complex machines. The ghost of Eli Whitney had finally crossed the Atlantic.

Bennett uncrated his Cadillac and was impressed with its performance from the first time he turned its crank and heard the purring smoothness of its Leland & Faulconer motor. He lost no time in introducing it to the British. The Midland Automobile Club staged its 1903 hill-climbing contest up Sunrise Hill soon after the Cadillac arrived. The result was a thrill that Bennett never forgot. His report on his participation in the event included:

> "Among the competitors was a dark horse ... a dinky little American car and a tall, spare, young man ... the performance of both was so much of a surprise to everyone that even the staid judges, who rarely allow anything like enthusiasm to creep into their official report, pronounced the feat of car and driver as 'Best Yet'."

The Cadillac had maintained an 8.09 miles per hour average on the hill described by some observers as the "worst in all England." Bennett moved quickly to follow up the initial conquest. In the fall of 1903, he entered No. 530 in the *One Thousand Mile Reliability Trial* sponsored by the Automobile Club of Great Britain and Ireland. The Cadillac was entered in the class of cars costing $1,000, or less. The cars were driven over a fixed course with each driver being accompanied by an official observer representing the judges.

Midway through the exhaustive trial, the Cadillac encountered a disaster that, except for Bennett's determination, would have taken the car out of the event. At the foot of River Hill, near Sevenoaks, a large steam-powered bus left its course and smashed into the car. The steering mechanism and one wheel were crushed, and the front axle was badly bent. Even Bennett's observer felt there was nothing he could have done to avert the crash. The observer, convinced the Cadillac was out of the contest, left for his home. But he did not reckon with Bennett's capacity to meet an emergency. After surveying the damage, the intrepid driver helped his mechanic to remove the mangled steering mechanism and front axle and get them repaired in a machine shop nearby.

Since the Cadillac was the only car of its type east of the Atlantic, there were no parts available anywhere in England. The wheel was broken beyond repair. Suddenly Bennett recalled that W. H. Wells, agent for Fiske tires in England for whom he had demonstrated the Cadillac, had commented that his Fiske tire display had a wheel which looked to be the same size as that on Bennett's car.

Bennett caught a train to London, got the wheel out of the Fiske display, took a train back to Sevenoaks, only to find on arriving, that, while the wheel was the same size, it had a much smaller hub. Undismayed Bennett went to a cottage nearby, built an open fire, heated iron pokers redhot and, by burning, increased the wheel's hub to accommodate the large Cadillac axle. By the time this was done, his mechanic had returned with the steering mechanism and front axle restored to working condition. The men installed the parts, found another observer and went on to complete the race.

At the end of the exhaustive trials, the Cadillac had a near-perfect score, being accorded 2,976 points of a possible 3,000. The car earned a perfect score for engine power and restarting on hills.

The fame of the Cadillac spread in England. Sales increased and Bennett was able to establish his own agency, dealing exclusively in Cadillacs, at 24-27 Orchard Street in London. Despite the successes of the Cadillac, the general belief that any machine made in the United States was inferior continued to be a limiting factor in sales.

In 1907, Bennett made his first trip to the Cadillac plant in Detroit. He met Henry Leland and heard firsthand the story of precision and the resulting magic of the complete interchangeability of parts. He was amazed with the ease and speed at which cars were assembled, without the need for grinding or final polishing of parts. He was familiar with the procedures of car assembly in England where a great deal of hand-work was still required. Perhaps, more than any other Englishmen of his time, Bennett was able to see the sweeping advantages of the American precision method of car manufacturing.

Before Bennett left Detroit he decided on a scheme to demonstrate and dramatize for European engineers and public, the advantage of precision in manufacturing of motorcars. The original idea came from Henry Leland himself. Once back in England, Bennett explained his plan to the officials of the Royal Automobile Club of England. They were interested, but all the remainder of 1907 was taken up in discussion of the plan and preparations for the grand demonstration.

In January of 1908, the Royal Automobile Club of England an-

Henry Leland, with his grandson. One of the nation's
great machinists, head of Leland & Faulconer Machine
Shop of Detroit when the directors of the unsuccessful
Henry Ford Company asked him to appraise the
defunct firm's equipment for purposes of liquidation.
Leland offered the directors an outstanding motor,
and the directors immediately formed the
Cadillac Motor Car Company.

nounced *"The Standardization Test"* open to all the automobile producers in the world. The Cadillac Motor Car Company of Detroit was the only firm to enter. The start of the test was set for Saturday, February 29th. The rules of the contest provided for six steps. First Step, club officials would have the opportunity to select three Cadillacs from a pool of new cars. In Step Two, the cars would be driven several times around the new racetrack at Brooklands in Surrey, about 20 miles from London. Step Three, the cars would be taken by Royal Club mechanics and completely disassembled. When the cars were completely disassembled, the Royal Club mechanics would (Step Four), have the opportunity to select any number of parts they wished. They would then exchange the used parts for new ones provided by Cadillac. Step Five, the Royal Club mechanics would scramble all parts of the three cars. Then would follow the crucial Step Six, under which the mechanics would reassemble the three cars. They could use only screwdrivers and spanners in the assembly work. After this had been done, the three cars would be taken back to the Brooklands track and driven 500 miles. The judges would then determine whether the performance of each was satisfactory.

On February 29th, the London area was hit by a record snow storm, but the test began on schedule. Three Cadillacs had been selected from a pool of fifteen horseless carriages. The cars had to operate in 2 feet of snow on the Brooklands track before judges motioned them into the garage where disassembly began at once. The Royal Club mechanics selected sixty-five parts and exchanged them for new ones. They scrambled the parts of all three cars. Then they began the long task of reassembly. The Cadillacs presented a strange appearance with wheels and even body parts of different colors since the three original cars had purposely been selected in three different colors.

When the work had been completed, the cars were taken back to the Brooklands track, several days later. By that time, the snow had been removed. The cars were driven 500 miles. The judges found that all three cars performed up to new car standards. As a result, the Cadillac Motor Company of Detroit received its first Dewar Trophy for the world's outstanding automotive achievement of the year. During the first decades of the motorcars, the Dewar Trophy was the most distinguished recognition for automotive achievement on either side of the Atlantic.

The Dewar Trophy took the form of a large, beautifully engraved silver cup. The cup was large enough to allow Wilfred Leland to place his small son, Wilfred Leland, Jr., in it and have a picture taken of the event. He sent a copy to Sir Thomas Dewar, originator of the award.

For Henry Leland, the Dewar Trophy came as a public and world-wide confirmation of the worth of precision and interchangeability, and of the superiority of the new American method of manufacturing. To mark the event, he published a special booklet entitled, "To The Men In The Shop." The publication described the standardization test conducted by the Royal Automobile Club of England. A copy was presented to each Cadillac workman. In it, he paid tribute to the men who produced the Cadillac.

"The honor belongs equally to every honest, sincere and conscientious member of this organization, no matter what his position, who has striven constantly and patiently to acquire and maintain in the work he is doing each day that fine accuracy which has made possible the absolute interchangeability of parts in Cadillac cars."

Unexpectedly, the Royal Club decided to retain one of the three Cadillacs after the standardization tests, and entered it in the July, 1908, International Touring Car 2,000 Mile Trial, held that year in England. Bennett drove the car. The trial included all types of road conditions and the last 150 miles included a straight-away race over the Brooklands track. The French car, Zedel, and others in the competition were capable of higher speeds. It was a race to see whether a dependable tortoise could outperform the hare.

Bennett and his multi-colored Cadillac easily won the competition over the first 1,850 miles, coming in hours ahead of its nearest competitor. The final run-down was clearly between Cadillac and the Zedel. The matter was still in contention as the final lap of the race began. With more than 1,998 tough miles behind them, there proved to be just a little more performance left in the Cadillac than in the Zedel. Bennett won by a small margin.

In 1913, Bennett recalled that just ten years before he had driven No. 530 to victory in the *Thousand Mile Reliability Trial*. He decided to locate his victory car, which he had lost track of long before.

The little car had been sold to a chemist in Slough who used it as a truck. When Bennett located the car again, it had been driven 50,000 miles. Yet, when Bennett raised the floor boards, he found the original Cadillac parts still there. Without special servicing, No. 530 made the run over the same course with Bennett himself driving on the final day. The Leland & Faulconer motor still moved the car along at 20 to 25 miles an hour on good roads.

Bennett did not allow No. 530 to get out of his possession again. He drove the car for half a century. Unbelievably, in 1953, he drove the first Cadillac to make the trip across the Atlantic fifty years earlier over the same course of the original 1,000-mile trial run. Still with its original motor, No. 530 averaged 21.2 miles an hour over the 1,094 miles of the course. Bennett reported that the roads were much better, but the traffic was so much worse that most of the advantage was lost.

Demand continued, both in the United States and Europe, for the small Cadillac after all other carmakers had discontinued similar models. Even the Curved Dash Oldsmobile had been discontinued more than a year earlier. At the end of its final day of production in 1908, there had been assembled and sold 16,126 of the little "one lungers," the record for horseless carriage production. The Leland & Faulconer motor remained to the end virtually unchanged since that day, long before, when Henry Leland had offered it as a gift to Ransom E. Olds.

The contribution of the single-cylinder Cadillac stands with that of any model ever made by any company. The little car proved that the Whitney-Brown-Leland precision technique was so superior that carmakers of the future would be forced to use the procedure.

More remarkable than the car was the man who created it, Henry Leland. For all practical purposes he controlled a monopoly, yet he worked almost as hard at sharing his advanced production secrets as he did developing them. He schooled men like Olds, Ford and Dodge, but he did vastly more. He not only taught others his new ideas, but also forced the early suppliers of vital motorcar parts to adopt the precision procedures.

On one occasion, Leland told the salesman of a supplier company, "You can't afford to sell this to us for so little . . . we buy the best parts we can find. We are not looking for cheapness."

The president of the leading supplier of roller bearings got the same blunt advice. His firm supplied components to almost every important automotive producer in the United States. Leland knew that forcing this supply organization to adopt precision methods would benefit his competitors, as well as himself, but he tackled the problem vigorously. The head of the firm recorded the incident.

"On his desk were some of our roller bearings, like culprits before a judge under Mr. Leland's brown hand with its broad thumb was a micrometer. He had measured the diameters of several specimen bearings. Then he had drawn lines and written down the variations from the agreed tolerance. I listened humbly as he went on talking."

"Your Mr. Steenstrup told me these bearings would be accurate, one like another, to one-thousandth of an inch. But look here. You must grind your bearings. Even though you make thousands, the first and the last should be precisely alike."

Henry Leland was lecturing Alfred P. Sloan, Jr., who, a few years earlier, had graduated from Massachusetts Institute of Technology as an engineer, and was then president of the Hyatt Roller Bearing Company in New Jersey.

Of this meeting with Leland, Sloan later said, "We discussed interchangeability of parts. A genuine conception of what mass production should mean really grew in me with that conversation."

Shortly after, Sloan, who also sold his roller bearings to Pierce-Arrow, Packard, Ford, Northern, Oldsmobile, Thomas, Stearns, Buick and numerous other cars, bought a Cadillac for his personal car. More important, his firm adopted the Whitney concept and began advocating its importance to all the car companies it served.

Alfred Sloan was but one of the many powerful personalities through whom Henry Leland communicated positively and decisively concerning the new motorcar industry.

By the close of 1903, the achievements of Ransom E. Olds and Henry M. Leland had all but assured that Michigan would become the seat of the motorcar industry in the United States, with Detroit becoming the Motor City. Because of the record-breaking production of the "Merry Oldsmobile" and the major production at the Cadillac plant, Michigan produced about half of the horseless carriages in the United States in 1903. Although far behind Michigan's record, the other leading states were Ohio, Wisconsin, Connecticut and New York.

Strong, additional action occurred in 1903 that would swing the motorcar pendulum to Michigan and Detroit. Designed by the young architects, Julius and Albert Kahn of Detroit, a new kind of factory especially suited to motorcar manufacturing was built by Henry B. Joy and his Packard Motor Car Company. Albert Kahn later built scores of such factories all over the world as a result of his first Detroit creation for Packard. Recognizing that a factory where motorcars were being assembled would have a ravenous appetite for materials and component parts, the Kahns designed a steel-reinforced concrete building that extended the entire block, north from

East Grand Boulevard in Detroit to Concord Avenue. The raw materials and component parts moved into the plant on Concord Avenue and new Packards were driven out the other end of the building on Grand Boulevard.

Spring and summer of 1903 also produced the first coast-to-coast horseless carriage trips. Two of the three tours were made with Michigan-produced motorcars. All three began in San Francisco and all ended in New York, then the foremost market.

The first trans-continental trip was driven by Dr. H. Nelson Jackson, a physician in Burlington, Vermont. He bought a used Winton and engaged a mechanic and driver, Sewall K. Crocker, and left San Francisco May 23rd. Sixty-four days later, on July 26th, Jackson and Crocker, drove up in front of the Waldorf Astoria Hotel in New York and touched off a celebration. The second was a solo trip, with driver Tom Fetch. He used the single-cylinder Packard, "Old Pacific." (The car is now at Ford's Greenfield Village Museum.) Fetch drove from San Francisco to New York in fifty-three days. He began on June 20th, and arrived in New York on August 12th. The third trip was made by L. L. Whitman and E. T. Hammond in a Curved Dash Oldsmobile. The two men left San Francisco July 6th, and reached New York on September 17th.

Not all of the lasting motorcar developments that year took place in Michigan. The Peerless Motor Car Company of Cleveland developed and used for the first time a new-type pressed steel frame. It was eventually adopted by most motorcar makers in the United States. In Detroit, Jonathon D. Maxwell, who joined Charles Brady King to build the Silent Northern, invented the siphon-cooling system which was manufactured by Benjamin and Frank Briscoe. Packard was granted a patent on the H slot-type gearshift which became universally used on automobiles produced in the United States. It still is the standard gearshift on motorcars that do not have automatic transmissions.

Of little importance in 1903, but with great future import, was the organization of the Buick Motor Car Company and the Ford Motor Company in Detroit. The major public attention to Henry Ford, up to this time, had been focused on his racing car, the "999." The car was driven to one new speed record after another by Barney Oldfield.

7

David Buick Goes to Flint

Early in the fall of 1904, a rising excitement gripped the citizens of Flint, Michigan. The town, with a population of 14,000, was the manufacturing center in the United States of horse-drawn vehicles—carriages, buggies, wagons and carts. Billy Durant, at forty-four, the carriage king, and one of Flint's best known, most admired and wealthiest men, seemed at last to be developing a case of horseless carriage fever. He had been exposed to the motorcar several times before, but had nothing but disdain for the self-propelled road vehicle.

On the first Sunday in September, Dr. Herbert H. Hills, who a month before had become the first man in Flint to own one of David Buick's new two-cylindered horseless carriages, had taken Durant for a ride. He was particularly impressed with the car's appearance, which was not a strong point of the first horseless carriages. Durant called the new Buick "very beautiful"; high praise from the man who had made some of the most attractive horse-drawn carriages ever built.

Almost every day during September and into early October, in sunshine and in rain, Billy Durant had climbed into the little Buick and driven out of town. Sometimes he had been gone two or three days. On occasion, his motorcar would come limping back into town. When that happened, he would take the vehicle directly to David

Buick and his assistant, Walter Marr, who would set everything else aside and repair the mechanical difficulty. Undaunted, Durant, on the following day, would drive out of town for another cross-country tour. He was studying every phase of the Buick's operation. One thing both impressed and puzzled him.

Durant was not mechanically-minded but he knew that everything depended upon the mechanical evaluation which he must make. The heart of the horseless carriage was its motor. All of the power plants he had seen in horseless carriages had been large, loud and weak. Was this two-cylindered motor of Dave Buick's the miracle that it appeared to be? The motor was small, powerful and remarkably quiet, removing the chief objections Durant had to earlier horseless carriages with which he was familiar.

Durant had ridden in three. In 1889, he had been persuaded to ride in the steam-powered motorcar so proudly owned by his cousin, W. C. Orrell, one of the first to be seen in Flint. The noise of that "contraption," as he called it, disturbed Durant so much that he told friends, "I was mighty provoked with anyone who would drive around annoying people that way."

Next, Durant rode in the first horseless carriage built in Flint. Judge Charles Wisner of Flint completed his car in 1900. Durant didn't ride in it until 1902. Wisner hoped Durant would take over the car and go into the horseless carriage business. Again, the carriage-maker was not convinced the motorcar had any real future. However, proving that he was aware of the implications of the new horseless carriage, later in the summer of 1902, Durant subjected himself to his first cross-country drive. The trip was made in a steam-powered Mobile from Lansing to Detroit. He traveled nearly 100 miles and the journey lasted all day. The carriage-maker was unimpressed.

But, as the days of October of 1904 slipped away, it was obvious to Billy Durant's friends that he was, for the first time, seriously interested in a horseless carriage. To the people of Flint, this meant that the horseless carriage was heading for a real showdown with the horse.

The citizens of Flint regarded Billy Durant as the most exciting man in town. And he was. He had rather few close friends, largely because he was away continually in connection with his carriage business. A small man, but with the proportions of an athlete, Durant did not overpower people, yet he often made a quick and lasting impression. Soft-spoken and gracious, his prominent nose and chin marked a face that spoke confidence. Both in his business and social relationships, he exhibited a keen interest in others, yet he was actually a self-contained individual, not infrequently almost lost in his own thoughts.

One of Durant's most remarkable qualities was his ability to remain calm even when dealing with critical matters. He was a brilliant conversationalist, yet he could be a good listener, too. Many an acquaintance spoke of him as, "the greatest salesman I ever met." He had a personal magnetism that caused his close associates often to refer to him, not as "the boss" (which he was at all times), but as "The Man." "The Man wants it done this way" or "The Man was pleased," they would say. This was the Durant that Flint knew in the years when he quickly rose to national leadership in the manufacturing of horse-drawn vehicles, and before he began his motorcar career.

There was no question that Durant was the foremost figure in the horse-drawn vehicle industry of the United States. By sharpness of intellect, rare business audacity, exceptional marketing skills and willingness and capacity to work eighteen and twenty hours a day for long periods, Durant had, in less than twenty years, marketed several times the number of horse-drawn vehicles sold by the Velie Works at Moline, Illinois, the Studebaker Brothers at South Bend, Indiana, the Fisher Family Carriage Works at Norwalk, Ohio, or any of the other builders of wagons, carts, buggies or carriages.

The Durant-Dort Carriage Company had been so successful that Durant, and his longtime associate, Josiah Dallas Dort, had, within fifteen years, become millionaires and many other Flint associates had been made wealthy. Billy Durant knew more about the mass-marketing of transportation vehicles than any man living. As he became seriously interested in the Buick horseless carriage, his Flint neighbors knew that exciting days were ahead.

David Dunbar Buick's car was not the only one being made in Flint. Another, the Flint Roadster (fire-engine red with brass trim and, in some ways, even more advanced than Buick's 1904 model), had been introduced two years before. Despite its attractive appearance, the Flint Roadster got off to a slow start in 1902, and did little better in 1903. In October of 1904, the Flint Automobile Company went out of business. The Association of Licensed Automobile Manufacturers, holders of the Selden patent, refused to extend a license because the firm was not in a position to invest $200,000 in its business of making motorcars.

In 1895, George Selden, inventor, of Rochester, New York (who never built a car himself), applied for and received a United States patent for a motorcar. His association used the patent, not only to collect royalties, but also to regulate the new business of carmaking. In an effort to weed out the weak firms, it established a minimum investment of $200,000 as one of the requirements to obtain a license to make motorcars. The Olds Motor Works and the Cadillac Motor Car Company jumped to high-volume production so quickly that they qualified for a license under the Selden patent.

Most of the events leading up to the Durant interest in Buick had taken place in Detroit. David Buick had an inquiring and inventive mind. Earlier, he had devised the process of fixing porcelain to an iron surface which he used to develop the first modern bathtub. He had established the Detroit firm, Buick and Sherwood, to manufacture the new bathtubs and other plumbing fixtures.

Soon after, Buick developed his own stationary gasoline motor for use on lake craft and for industrial and farm use, much as Pliny Olds, his son, Ransom, and Henry Leland had done earlier. Buick motorized some of the craft of the Detroit Yacht Club. So successful were his new motors that he was made a "Commodore" of the club.

By 1899, Buick was so sure that he could built a gasoline motor small enough, and with enough power, to propel a carriage that he organized a separate business to produce his motors. The title of the new firm left no doubt that the objective was to build a self-propelled vehicle. It was the Auto-Vim and Power Company, later changed to Buick Manufacturing Company. The firm was housed in a small plant on Holmes Avenue in Detroit. Buick's decision to build a horseless carriage came just before the Olds Motor Company announced its plan to build the first factory in Detroit to make self-propelled road vehicles, and well before there was any production of Oldsmobiles. Buick was acquainted with William Metzger, who had established Detroit's first motorcar agency the year before in connection with his bicycle business. Buick had undoubtedly seen, and probably ridden in a Winton.

Buick's serious work on a horseless carriage motor began in 1900. Although various tests were made in highly experimental vehicles, it was 1902 before anything was produced which could, even in approximate terms, be described as "the first Buick." It was the "Model-A," and only one was produced. The vehicle was powered by an L-head-type motor which, in basic design, was similar to the marine and farm stationary gasoline engines Buick continued to produce.

Two young engineers in Detroit were drawn into the exciting work by Dave Buick; exactly when and on what basis is not known. Certainly, Walter L. Marr, a young man with a will so strong that he and Buick frequently quarreled violently, was working at Auto-Vim, at least part-time, in 1899 and 1900. After one of their quarrels, Marr quit and went to the Olds Motor Works, just in time to assemble some of the first motorcars to be produced in Detroit.

Eugene C. Richard also worked with David Buick during 1902, and, possibly, in 1901. He was there when the first Buick horseless carriage was produced. He had received his training as a machinist in Philadelphia before moving to Detroit. Buick and Richard got along better personally than Buick and Marr. For this reason, Richard became the chief engineer during that period.

It was Buick's ability to draw around him outstanding young engineers that resulted in a lasting contribution to the American motorcar. Buick and his young associates were probably not aware that the valve-in-head principle had been used earlier; but they advanced the concept further than anyone else, effectively demonstrated its value and secured a patent.

"In an explosion engine, the combination of the cylinder-head, of induction and deduction valves, having their stems extending through said head . . ." is the description of the United States patent No. 7771095 that was issued to the Buick Manufacturing Company on May 23rd, 1903. The "valve-in-the-head" motor was soon adapted to use on a horseless carriage motor, and has been a feature of the Buick ever since. The added efficiency of the overhead valve principle was so great that, in time, the entire automotive industry of the world adopted the valves "having their stems extending through said head."

The first 1902 Buick, produced in a small plant on Holmes Avenue in Detroit, was similar, in many respects, to the Oldsmobile of 1901. The car had the standard L-head motor, the valve-in-head feature having not yet been perfected. Buick himself was largely responsible for the designing and building of the motor and most of the chassis and body parts.

In 1903, the work of the Buick-Richard-Marr team began to produce results. Soon after the year began, a new single-cylinder engine was put in the experimental car. Before the summer was over, they had on the drawing board an entirely new, two-cylinder-type engine, and in this the valves were designed into the head.

Despite the improvements and the performance of the new, experimental cars made in Detroit in 1903, there was no production of a

Buick for sale. Buick soon used up all the funds he could take out of his plumbing business. The firm was at the point of having to dissolve, even with a potentially promising motorcar, for lack of capital. Buick turned to two Detroit friends, the Briscoe Brothers, for financial help. The senior member of the sheet metal firm was the thirty-four-year-old Benjamin Briscoe. His brother, Frank, was twenty-eight. The young businessmen had done well in their sheet metal business. Their important product was a new garbage can made from metal.

Keenly interested in the new horseless carriage, the Briscoes advanced $2,000 worth of materials and components and invested $1,500 in cash in the Buick firm. They brought about a reorganization of the company, changing the name to the Buick Motor Company, with a capitalization of $100,000. Little additional money, beyond the initial $3,500, was invested in the business.

The Briscoe Brothers had no experience with a motorcar. Almost immediately they realized that even the funds which they could invest would not be enough to put the Buick car into production and on the market. Once again the Buick horseless carriage seemed ready to go the route of so many early cars and disappear before the public ever had an opportunity to see and appraise it. The Briscoes soon lost interest in going ahead with the Buick program and began seeking ways to get the $3,500 they had invested out of the enterprise.

The critical situation facing David Buick, and Benjamin and Frank Briscoe was more than a Buick problem. Although horseless carriages were already being sold in the United States (largely along the East Coast at a rate of 10,000 motorcars a year), there was hopeless confusion in the new business. New motorcars had been coming into the market at the bewildering rate of 40 to 60 a year since 1900. Many of the manufacturers went out of business the same year they announced their new models. This state of affairs made it difficult if not impossible to finance even a superior motorcar such as the Buick with its patented valve-in-head motor.

The fate of the more than 50 new horseless carriages, introduced in the preceding year, clearly indicates the odds for the Buick's chances of survival. Nearly one-third of these horseless carriages had gone out of business. A total of 37 would be out of business within three years. Only 7 would still be in production ten years later.

The names of the motorcars introduced in 1902 follow, the length of time each remained in production given after the name: Adrian, two; Apperson, twenty-three; Berg, five; Bramwell, two; Binney-

Burnham, one; Brazier, three; Bristol, two; Capital, one; Centaur, two; Champion, one; Church, one; Cleveland, two; Cloughley, two; Columbus, three; Covert Motorette, five; Crest, three; Davenport, one; Decker, two; Dyke, three; Fanning Electric, two; Fisher, three; Flint, three; Four-Wheel-Drive, six; Franklin, thirty-two; Fredonia, three; Garford Truck, one; Goethmobile, one; Holsman Autobuggy, nine; Jones-Corbin, six; Junz, one; Law's Car, one; Locomobile, twenty-eight; Long Distance, one; Meteor, two; Moore, two; Motor Truck, one; Northern, five; Pan-American, three; Pomeroy, one; Pope-Robinson, three; Rambler, eleven; Rapid Truck, eleven; Reber, two; Shain, two; Shelby, two; Standard, one; Storck, one; Stevens-Duryea, thirteen; Studebaker, sixty; Thomas, ten; Toledo, one; Twyford, six; Union, four; Upton, three; United Motor, one; White-Truck, sixty-six; Wick, one, and Wildman, one.

Well over 200 horseless carriages had been placed on the market in the United States between 1894, when Duryea demonstrated the practicability of the gasoline-powered, self-propelled road vehicle, to the end of 1902. Only five firms in the United States had produced as many as 100 cars in 1902. They were the Olds Motor Works, now moving to Lansing and producing the Oldsmobile; the Winton Motor Company of Cleveland, Ohio, making the Winton; the Thomas B. Jeffery Company of Kenosha, Wisconsin, making the Rambler; the Pope Manufacturing Company of Hartford, Connecticut, making the Columbia; and the Apperson Brothers Machine Shop of Kokomo, Indiana, making the Haynes-Apperson.

There was not a producer of motorcars based completely in Detroit in 1902. The Olds Motor Works had a plant in Detroit, but operated mainly in Lansing, Michigan. The Cadillac Motor Company had been organized late in the year, but had not begun producing other than pilot models. The same was true of Buick, Packard and Northern. The Ford Motor Company had not been organized.

Such was the picture early in 1903 when the future of Buick hung in the balance. Neither bankers nor stock brokers would consider investing in another horseless carriage, no matter how outstanding the features might be. The only hope seemed to be in finding a private investor, as had been the case with all the other successful motorcars of the time. It took capital, and lots of it, to produce motorcars in volume. There was no important money available to the Buick Motor Company, and it, too, was in the first stage of going out of business.

Unexpectedly, a major development occurred. Early in the sum mer, a chance circumstance changed things for Buick. Frank Briscoe visited relatives in Flint, Michigan. His cousin was the wife of Dwight T. Stone, a young Flint real estate dealer, and a member of one of Flint's pioneer families. Briscoe told Stone of David Buick's remarkable horseless carriage and the need to find additional capital to make it possible to produce and market the vehicle.

Stone thought there might be a solution to the Buick problem in the small city of Flint. He arranged for Briscoe to meet James H. Whiting, president of the Flint Wagon Works. Whiting, an older man (regarded by his associates as being highly conservative), did show interest and arranged to call a meeting of the Wagon Works directors to hear about Buick from young Briscoe before he returned to Detroit. Whiting was more interested in the stationary gasoline engines than in the motorcar because he thought the farm agents, who sold wagons and carts to midwest farmers, could find an additional business opportunity in selling engines for farm use.

The directors agreed with Whiting, but some of them thought the manufacture of the horseless carriage might also have a future. They remembered that the *Flint Journal* had earlier editorially observed that the "Horseless carriage was here to stay."

The directors arranged to go to Detroit to meet David Buick and see the work being done at the Buick Motor Company plant. The work of reaching an agreement lasted through August. On September 10th, 1903, Whiting took a cashier's check to Detroit for $10,000, binding the sale of the Buick Motor Company to the Flint Wagon Works.

The Briscoe Brothers turned over their controlling interest in the Buick Motor Company for the $3,500 they had invested. David Buick, on the other hand, accepted his compensation in 1,500 shares of stock.

The purchase was reported in the *Flint Journal* the next day, September 11th, which announced, in addition, that ground had been broken earlier in the day for the new plant at the west end of Kearsley Street. The building's first story was ready in a short time and, within the year, two more were added.

While community leaders hoped that the purchase of Buick Motor Company meant the making of a new motorcar, officials of the Wagon Works were unwilling to commit themselves to such a course at the time of purchase. The *Journal's* announcement, on the 11th, said only that the Flint firm would produce "stationary and

Winner of the New York Times trophy in the 1968
ceremonial rerunning of the New York to San Francisco
leg of the 1908 race, Warrent S. Weiant, Jr., of Newark,
Ohio, driving his Simplex, a car that cost $6,000 in 1909.
Mr. and Mrs. Weiant are seen with their Simplex at
Hebron, Nebraska, during the commemorative 1968 trip.

marine engines, automobile engines, transmissions, carburetors, spark plugs, etc."

When the *Journal's* reporter asked President Whiting specifically about the production of a Buick motorcar, "he smiled pleasantly and suggested that for the present the engines and accessories would be built by the new factory and that the broader opportunity was one for further consideration." On the following day the newspaper editorially pleaded the cause of producing a new car, observing:

> "Flint is the most natural center for the manufacture of autos in the whole country. It is the vehicle city of the United States and in order to maintain this name, by which it is known from ocean to ocean, there must be developed factories here for the manufacture of automobiles."

But, while the leaders of Flint astutely looked to the future, for the present, the city lived in the era of horses. In the same issue of the *Journal* announcing that the Buick Motor Company was moving from Detroit to Flint, a front page story reported that blacksmiths in convention in the city had voted $5,000 for a State College of Horseshoeing, demanding that the State of Michigan examiners raise the standards of the blacksmithing trade.

Early September produced several interesting signs of the times. The Whitman-Hammond transcontinental motorcar trip in their Curved Dash Oldsmobile was within one week of being complete. The Oldsmobile had already made its stop in Lansing and Detroit and was on its way to New York, "spinning across the country from San Francisco to Detroit," the *Detroit Free Press* reported. The day before the Flint-Buick deal was closed, Barney Oldfield's racer, the Ford "999," went out of control at Grosse Points track near Detroit, plowing through the fence and taking the life of a spectator. The same month, the *Detroit News-Tribune* published a full-page illustration of "The People's Automobile." The picture was of a crowded streetcar.

Three days later, the *Flint Journal* carried another news item, reporting that a solid train of forty-two carloads of carriages made by the Durant-Dort Carriage Company and the W. A. Paterson Company had pulled out of Flint to deliver the horse-drawn vehicles to distributors in the Midwest and Northwest. The special train carried huge posters proclaiming the carriages to be from Flint, the "vehicle capital of the U.S."

With Whiting himself as manager of the new motor works, there was, from the first, no question about the seriousness of the new enterprise. In reorganizing the Buick Company, capitalization was actually reduced from $100,000 to $75,000, but the entire amount was subscribed. The sum of $37,500 was set aside to get production of engines started.

Even before the new building was ready, Arthur C. Mason, steeped in the precision artistry of Henry M. Leland, was hired away from the Cadillac Motor Company which had already produced more than 1,000 motorcars since start of production nine months earlier. Mason was hired before the new Buick building was ready so that he might oversee the purchase and placement of the production machines in the new factory.

Pressure was exerted upon Whiting from the first, both within and without the organization, to plan for production of a horseless carriage in addition to making stationary gasoline engines. The pressure mounted after it became known that the Flint Automobile Company was going out of business, yielding to the ultimatum of the holders of the Selden patent.

About the time of the move to Flint, Buick and Marr settled their differences and Marr rejoined Buick, giving added thrust to the interest in producing a new motorcar. Since he and Buick had parted in anger, something more than a year before, Marr had introduced his own motorcar, the Marr Autocar. It was produced in Elgin, Illinois, in time for the 1903 Chicago and Detroit Automobile Shows. When it became apparent that the move to Flint could make Buick a going concern, Marr returned to the engineering staff, lured largely by a desire to work with the exciting new valve-in-head engines.

Whiting was reluctant early in 1904 to move into motorcar production. The demand for Buick stationary motors was beginning to develop. Also while he had heard the praises of the new two-cylinder, valve-in-head Buick engine, neither he nor anyone else had ridden in a car propelled by the new power plant. Aware of this, Marr and Buick kept pleading for an opportunity to build a pilot car with the powerful two-cylinder motor. They became more persistent after May 27th, when the first of the new two-cylinder motors was actually completed. On stationary trials, it was very successful. Buick and Marr knew they had the most powerful horseless carriage motor in existence, pound for pound.

Finally, about the first of June, Whiting relented and gave approval for the building of a complete Buick car with the understanding that it would have to prove that it was as good as the best, including the Curved Dash Oldsmobile and the New Cadillac. Buick and

Marr went to work and by the end of June had the pilot machine running around the Wagon Works property in Flint.

The time had come to decide what would constitute an acceptable test of performance for the management of the firm. This was really the first demonstration of a Buick motorcar. The earlier runs of the Buick "Model-A" had neither been witnessed by the public, nor reported in the press. Whiting himself decided upon the course over which the test run would be made. It would be a trip from Flint to Detroit and back. In order that as many people as possible could see the new Buick and that there be a wide range of road conditions, Whiting decreed that the cross-country run to Detroit should be made over an indirect route that permitted stops at five specified towns.

The cross-country drive was handled by Marr and Thomas Buick, son of the inventor. The first stop was at Davison, 10 miles directly east of Flint. The next was at Lapeer, another 10 miles further east. The third was at Oxford, 17 miles to the south of Lapeer on the way to Pontiac. The fourth was at Orion Lake between Oxford and Pontiac. The fifth stop was at Pontiac. From Pontiac, the drivers were free to choose their route into Detroit. The return trip was to be made over the same route. The circuitous route totaled 115 miles while the direct road from Flint to Detroit was only 65 miles.

Buick and Marr left from the Buick Motor Company plant in Flint on Saturday, July 9th. At all the stops on the way, they gave people a chance to see the new horseless carriage and advised them that they would be returning on a fast run to see in how short a time the Buick could make the trip. As a result of the stops, they did not reach Detroit until Monday.

The big day was Tuesday, the 12th. With Marr driving the entire distance, the men drove the 115 miles in two hundred and seventeen minutes. It was a record for open country driving that had not been equalled by another car.

"We took the hills handily without high-speed gear," reported Marr. At one point, near Pontiac, they became involved in a race with an electric car and ended up "showing the way" to the adversary. Buick and Marr roared into one small town going so fast that neither of them saw the sign limiting speed in the village to 6 miles an hour.

When they arrived in Flint, a photographer took pictures of the Buick and the passengers on the cross-country run, both in the downtown section and out at the Buick plant. The verdict on the test run was given in the next issue of the *Journal* which devoted half a column to the trip. The newspaper article reported: "Tom Buick and W. L. Marr of the Buick Motor Company who left for Detroit on Saturday to give the first automobile turned out by that concern a trial on the road, returned late yesterday afternoon. The test of the machine was eminently satisfactory, and in fact exceeded expectations."

The Buick was put into production. Orders accumulated before the first Buick was ready for delivery. The first delivered in Flint went to Dr. Herbert H. Hills. A total of 27 Buick horseless carriages were built and delivered in the remaining weeks of 1904. The chassis, the valve in-head motor and the transmissions were produced by the Buick Motor Company. The Flint Wagon Works built the first bodies but, before the year was out, body making had been turned over to the W. F. Stewart Company of Flint, another of the "Big Four" carriage builders in the city.

Dave Buick's car was, at last, in production.

At the moment of the Buick's first important success, when it would have been logical to expect Manager Whiting to be elated, he was deeply worried. He had made an important and painful discovery in the ten months since the Flint Wagon Works bought the Buick Motor Company. There were really few similarities between the horse-drawn vehicle business and the production of a horseless carriage. The requirement for invested capital was much greater for horseless carriage production. Whiting actually did not know how much greater, but far greater than the Flint Wagon Works could provide.

Nor could the two businesses be run together. The motorcar business was so exciting and demanding that it soaked up all available workmen and working capital and left nothing for anything else. It was impossible to give adequate attention to the Buick stationary engine business. Whiting's judgment that the Wagon Works dealer organization could sell these motors had proven correct. Just one dealer, Edward W. Cumings, in Michigan, had sold enough motors to keep the factory busy for some months, but, in the press of getting a motorcar produced, few of the engines were actually ever made and delivered. Whiting knew that he could not continue to manage the affairs of the Buick Motor Company and the Flint Wagon Works, too. Another deeply interested, younger man, Whiting thought, was needed to take over direction of Buick.

But, most frightening of all was the way the small Buick enterprise devoured financial resources. The $37,500 set aside in cash at the beginning was gone, and Wagon Works executives and other Flint community leaders owed each of the three Flint banks $25,000. This represented a large part of the capital of these financial institutions upon which Flint business and commerce depended for existence. Whiting knew that the stage was set for a crisis that could not be long delayed. They could not go ahead producing Buick horseless carriages for lack of investment funds; on the other hand, to allow the program to collapse could push the community into a business crisis.

Despite the engineering successes, the Buick was once more threatened with the same kind of disaster that it faced earlier when Buick-Sherwood, and later the Briscoe Brothers, found they could not invest the kind of money required. As Dave Buick and the Briscoe Brothers had been forced to decide earlier, the Flint Wagon Works had to find a buyer for the Buick Motor Company.

Meanwhile Dr. Hills and some twenty-six other owners of Buick horseless carriages were delighted with their new motorcars. The vehicles were operated in mud, sand and other arduous road conditions that had stopped other horseless carriages. The Buick handled them without difficulty.

8

"No Thanks, I'll Walk"

James Whiting didn't know it, of course, but in these early months of 1904 the future of Flint was virtually in his hands. Had he been an ordinary man, he would have conceded that there was no solution.

Whiting understood the difficult circumstances of the Flint Wagon Works in raising enough money to finance the Buick production. He had know it almost from the time he concluded the agreement with David Buick and the Briscoe brothers the fall before. Early in the winter that followed, he attended the 1904 Chicago convention of carriage manufacturers. In some respects it looked like a Flint meeting, for many of the men attending the convention were from Whiting's hometown. There he had an opportunity to talk, at length, about the Buick problem with Fred A. Aldrich of Flint. Aldrich was secretary-treasurer of the Durant-Dort Carriage Company. As such, he had an intimate knowledge of the business and was in close touch with the principals, Durant and Dort.

To sell Buick motorcars from ocean to ocean, as Flint carriages were being sold, there would have to be much more money invested than the Flint Wagon Works was able to invest, Whiting told Aldrich. In addition, the business would require the undivided attention of some capable businessman, and the Wagon Works did not employ such a man.

Aldrich asked if Whiting had thought of talking to William C. Durant. Whiting admitted that it had not occurred to him that Durant, with his wealth and prominence, might be interested. Aldrich said that he thought Durant might be interested in an entirely new venture. Durant, Aldrich reported, was in New York and would be there for some time. He suggested that Whiting also discuss the matter with Dallas Dort, the man in Flint who knew Durant better than anyone else.

When Whiting later talked to Dort, he, too, thought that Durant would be the ideal person to take over the direction of the Buick Motor Company. He gave Whiting the address in New York where Durant could be reached. Whiting delayed writing Durant until Dave Buick and Walt Marr began building the pilot car, in the hope, perhaps, that there would be something to demonstrate for Durant.

It was August before Durant returned to Flint. Whiting and Durant met and Whiting soon found that Durant was not greatly interested in horseless carriages. They were old friends, but had not visited in a long while. Whiting had known Durant's parents and had known Billy Durant since he was a schoolboy in Flint. They recalled many things, including Durant's early struggles to succeed.

After dropping out of the seventh grade in school, he had gone to work in the company store that had been established by his grandfather. He had sold cigars, patent medicines, matches, whiskey and, most important of all, bicycles; and had developed unusual skill in working with people, and as a salesman.

Even while working as a store clerk, he had begun to branch out. Selling insurance added to his sales experience. Setting up his own insurance business soon provided his first opportunity to travel to other towns—Pontiac, Detroit, Lansing, Jackson—seeking insurance business from important men and businesses in southern Michigan.

Important as were his business contacts in places like Jackson and Detroit, it was in the small town of Coldwater that opportunity struck with full force. There Durant met a man who had sometime before received a patent on a light, two-wheeled horse-drawn road cart with a novel type of suspension. The inventor contended that it was impossible to turn the car over, no matter how great its speed or how rough the road might be. He offered Durant a demonstration behind a spirited horse over rough ground. It was a wild affair. The

134

riders could have been thrown from an ordinary vehicle and injured or even have lost their lives. Durant got out of the cart, thanked the driver for the ride and meant it.

Durant was attracted to the cart because it was largely made of wood. It had few parts and was easy to assemble. In large quantities it could be made, Durant was sure, for no more than $10.00. Road carts were not common, largely because they were generally made by hand in blacksmith shops or small town machine shops. The Coldwater inventor had been disappointed that he had not been able to find anyone willing to build his patented road cart. After some bargaining, Durant bought the cart patent for $50.00 which he paid immediately, in cash. His days in the insurance business were over. The year was 1884.

With the patent in hand, Durant went back to Flint and talked to Flint's first wagon builder, William A. Paterson, who fifteen years before, in 1869, had converted his blacksmith shop into a factory and had begun making wagons for the lumbermen who worked the virgin forests up the Flint River to the north.

Paterson was interested in young Durant's proposal. Within days they reached an agreement under which the wagon builder consented to reorganize his factory and set up a new mass assembly procedure never before used in Flint's wagon or carriage plants. Paterson agreed to deliver 10,000 of the road carts at a cost of $8.00 each. His firm had not produced 10,000 vehicles since it began business.

Durant then went to the Flint hardware store and talked to Josiah Dallas Dort, the store's chief clerk, a young man of Durant's age. Dort gave up his job to become Durant's partner in marketing the road carts. They formed the Flint Road Cart Company and sold the carts for $12.00 each, to distributors of farm supplies.

The venture turned out well for both Paterson and The Flint Road Cart Company. Before the Paterson plant could complete manufacture of the 10,000 carts, Durant and Dort returned with a contract for another 10,0000, then another and still another. The Flint Road Cart Company eventually sold 100,000 carts in a single year.

Farm families used them for quick trips from farm to farm, or from farm to town. These were the trips that involved more than an individual on horseback could carry, and less than was needed for a buggy or a wagon. The cart could be used over muddy roads or other terrain too difficult for the carriage or wagon.

Using profits from the two-wheeled cart business, the young Flint businessmen organized the Durant-Dort Carriage Company. Employing the same principle of making a limited number of models, and standardizing the steps in production, the Durant-Dort Carriage Company lowered the cost of passenger horse-drawn vehicles and soon became the leader in the carriage trade. To provide better service and to hold down costs, Durant-Dort established plants in other locations to make component parts and to assemble complete vehicles in regional markets.

In diversity of production, number of plants and gross sales, the Durant-Dort Carriage Company reached a peak in 1895. A total of 75,000 vehicles was produced in fourteen plants in the United States and Canada. Gross sales were approximately five million dollars.

By the time Billy Durant was thirty-five years old, he had established a nation-wide organization for the manufacturing of road vehicles, initiated assembly-line production in his plants, set up a system of component suppliers, marketed his product to both farm and urban customers and constantly expanded sales and profits that defied even the depression of 1893.

When the discussion between Whiting and Durant got around to the problems of the Buick Motor Company, Durant admitted his unsatisfactory experiences with the several horseless carriages in which he had ridden. Later, commenting on the talks with Whiting, he stated, "I didn't have any more faith in the automobile then than Dort or Nash or any of the rest of us in the Durant-Dort Carriage Company.... I wasn't the least bit interested in managing an automobile concern."

When it became evident to Whiting that the major stumbling block was Durant's lack of confidence in the horseless carriage, he knew that the Buick motorcar would first have to sell itself to the carriage king. Meanwhile, the cross-country road test to Detroit and back had been made and the first Buicks were being produced for sale. Dr. Hills, in Flint, had bought one and Whiting proposed that Durant take a ride in it.

The car, like most horseless carriages of 1904, had no top, no windshield and no brakes. The engine used its planetary transmission for braking purposes. In an emergency, the reverse pedal, which enabled the car to back up, could be pushed to achieve immediate and effective braking. Late in 1904, Michigan passed a law requiring all motorcars to carry two independent brakes. Marr quickly designed brakes for the Buick, and had them installed on cars produced and sold earlier in the year.

Built in the Leland & Faulconer machine shop in
October, 1902, the first Cadillac, just as Test Driver
Al Brush was ready for the introductory public
demonstration. Wilfred Leland is the passenger.
Back of the left rear wheel are the engineers: Ernest
E. Sweet (large hat), Walter Phipps, Frank Johnson
(bareheaded) and others who, under Henry M. Leland's
direction, advanced Cadillac into the front ranks of
American motorcars.

The September 4th demonstration for Durant by Dr. Hills was a success. It convinced the carriage maker that he should investigate the Buick proposition further. He began his cross-country driving tests in September and continued them into October, subjecting, not only the Buick, but the motorcar, itself, to a searching study. He was sifting out new factors important to the car that were unimportant or did not exist in Durant-Dort horse-drawn vehicles. A motorcar agent, or dealer, he concluded, would have to be prepared to provide continual service to each customer who bought a motorcar. That meant that the agent would have to have a place of business conveniently located, and well-equipped to repair and service the vehicles.

Unquestionably, Durant took the opportunity to compare Dave Buick's horseless carriage with the other leading motorcars of 1904. Certainly he had the opportunity to compare the three leaders in Michigan. Oldsmobile was the nation's sales leader with a production of 5,000. Cadillac production was in excess of 2,000 cars. Both were selling their horseless carriages for less than $1,000. The Ford Motor Company, in its second year, ended 1904 by selling 1,695 machines. Totally, Durant found that motorcar sales in the United States were up sharply from the year before. When the reports were all in, sales had almost doubled from 11,235 self-propelled road vehicles in 1903 to 22,130 for 1904. Truck production was reported for the first time. Production and sales of trucks numbered 700 in 1904.

At frequent intervals, Durant met with Whiting and other members of the Flint Wagon Works to consider the problems of securing components, and of financing the production. By early October, Durant was tremendously impressed with the Buick motor. The real issue was in financing, producing and marketing a high volume of motorcars. He was aware that the Olds Motor Company was successfully meeting all these problems. The question was whether it could be done in Flint.

Sometime between the 10th and the 20th of October, William C. Durant decided that he would cast his lot with the motorcar and the Buick Motor Company. The biggest problem, he knew, would be to raise enough money to finance large-scale motorcar production. At the time of his decision to direct the fortunes of Buick, he did not know how the money could be obtained. He acted on faith that somehow the capital could be raised.

The Durant decision to take over the destiny of Buick introduced a fury of developments that rose in numbers and importance with

Proof that Cadillac's Leland & Faulconer single-cylinder
motor had power to climb hills! Thousands watched
as Al Brush drove the first Cadillac up the steps
of the Wayne County Building in Detroit.

each passing month. The agreement under which Durant took over direction of Buick was signed November 1st, 1904. Durant was elected a director, replacing Charles A. Cumings, general manager of the Flint Wagon Works. He would have been made president, but, at his request, he was not burdened with the work of such an office. Whiting resigned as president and was replaced by Charles M. Begole, a Flint Wagon Works executive, whose personal stock holdings of 1,000 shares in the Buick Motor Company was third in size, second only to Whiting with 1,505 shares and David D. Buick with 1,500.

Logically, Durant's first act as manager of Buick operations was to increase the capitalization from $75,000 to $300,000 by selling stock in the company. Durant handled the sale of the stock, his task being greatly simplified by the fact that the stockholders of a Flint utility company were paid $325,000 the same week that Buick's capitalization was increased. Durant persuaded the utility company stockholders to invest $275,000 of their stock payment in the Buick Motor Company.

Recognizing that there was not enough room for the Buick enterprise to grow on the west side of Flint, where the carriage factories were located, Durant bought the 220-acre Hamilton Farm on the north edge of Flint for $22,000. For the people of Flint, this was the tip-off as to how Durant regarded the future of the Buick.

Durant knew that he must move Buick quickly into a higher level of production in order to provide a basis for securing additional capital and further expansion. He had no intention of waiting until a factory could be built on the Hamilton Farm. While there was no available plant in Flint capable of housing a motorcar assembly operation, there was such a facility in Jackson. It was a large factory with a railroad siding, formerly used by the Durant-Dort Carriage Company to turn out wheels.

In December, 1904, the assembly facilities, as well as the general offices, for the Buick Motor Company were moved to Jackson. Soon 5 to 8 cars were being produced every week. The three-story Buick plant in Flint produced the Buick motors and transmissions. The bodies were also made in Flint, chiefly by the Stewart Carriage Company.

Money problems continued to require most of Durant's time. Setting up operations in Jackson, plus building a new factory on the Hamilton farm immediately put the company in a critical financial position. Only two months after having raised the capitalization to

$300,000, it was necessary to raise the figure to $500,000. Durant turned to friends, from Flint to New York, to raise the money.

With more than a car per day being produced in the new Jackson facility and a capitalization of $500,000, the holders of the Selden patent issued the Buick Motor Company a license and a membership in the Association of Licensed Automobile Manufacturers. Durant and Buick had secured what had been denied A. B. Hardy and his Flint Automobile Company fifteen months earlier, and Flint was respectably back in the motorcar business. The Selden group recognition eased Buick's financial position somewhat by making it easier to do business with important suppliers.

Jackson has long believed that the Buick got its start there and, to a degree, it is true. Although David Buick built experimental motors and a complete car in Detroit, and 27 Buicks were made in Flint late in 1904, the first important production of Buick motorcars took place in Jackson in 1905.

The "Model-C" was so named because the Detroit Buick had been called the "Model-A" and the 1904 Buicks, built in Flint were known as "Model-B." The "Model-C" was very much like the "Model-B." It was equipped with the same two-cylinder valve-in-head engine developed by Walter Marr and David Buick.

The "Model-C" engine was rated at 12 horsepower, though Marr claimed it could "develop 18 to 21 horsepower." Power was transferred to the rear wheels by means of a belt chain, adopted directly from the bicycle. The "Model-C" Buick's major advance was its brakes. Brakes were standard equipment on all cars for the first time. A foot-operated brake pedal controlled the brakes mounted on both rear wheels. The car could travel at top speeds of 30 to 35 miles an hour, and it sold for $1,000.

For an additional $100.00, the car was equipped with a buggy-like top. A front curtain contained a window of celluloid, the forerunner of modern plastics, and was available for an extra $20.00. It was the first windshield. For an additional investment of $75.00, the new Buick owner could purchase the powerful, new acetylene headlights, brass kerosene side lights and buggy mud guards. All told, the "Model-C" was an ingenious combination of the best features of the fine carriages and the new horseless carriage.

Even with all the demands of finances and of higher production of new Buicks, Durant found time to work on the marketing side of the new business. He appointed Charles Van Horne of Jackson as the first sales manager. He began appointing the first Buick dealers, with special attention to securing dealers who could provide a smart showroom coupled with a good service and repair department. The firm's first slogan, "When Better Buicks Are Built, Buick Will Build Them" was adopted. Later the slogan was changed to "When Better Cars Are Built Buick Will Build Them."

The first Buick communications to dealers and the public dealt with the fact that the new motorcars would be sold to customers who had formerly traveled in horse-drawn vehicles. Buick salesmen were trained to press the advantages of a horseless carriage over the horse and buggy. "Can you hitch up your horse that fast?" the salesman would ask, as he cranked a Buick for a new prospect. Driving along at 15-to-20 miles an hour, the question often was, "Can your hay-burner run this fast?"...."Does your old gray mare wait this calmly at a railroad crossing?"...."Can you back up a horse this easily?"

As 1905 progressed, the disadvantages of having major Buick operations in both Flint and Jackson, roughly 100 miles apart, became more apparent. Engines, transmissions, wheels, springs and bodies were being made in Flint and shipped by railroad to Jackson. By the summer of 1905, Durant realized consolidation in one city or the other had to be brought about. Although it is doubtful if he ever thought seriously of any place other than Flint as Buick's headquarters, it served his purpose to give the impression in both cities that the solution was a matter of financing. If Jackson could raise an additional $500,000 in cash so that the Buick Motor Company could be capitalized at $1,000,000, the city would become the home of the Buick.

Durant's offer to Jackson was little more than a means of getting the message across to the leaders of Flint that even more than the $500,000 already invested in Buick would be needed. During the spring and summer, a plan was developed by Durant and the leaders of Flint, under which the investment in the Buick Motor Company would be raised to $1,500,000 in order that the entire operation would remain in Flint. It was this plan that made it possible, eventually, for more than 500 acres in the Flint area to be covered by Buick factories.

The capitalization was raised to $1,500,000 on September 11th, 1905, exactly two years to the day after the Flint Wagon Works had completed the purchase of the Buick company. The banks, all four of the major carriage and wagon companies and hundreds of Flint organizations and individual investors bought the stock that advanced the capitalization, assuring Flint of being the permanent headquarters of Buick.

The next day an unusual dispatch appeared in the newspaper covering the Buick expansion indicating a great confidence in the future for the firm. The *Journal* reported:

"Yesterday afternoon Buick stockholders voted to increase the capital stock from $500,000, to $1,500,000, divided $900,000 common and $600,000 preferred shares. A large amount of the additional stock has already been taken by local interests, and the balance has takers in sight. The majority of the entire amount of stock is held in this City, and the controlling interest will remain here."

The directors of all four Flint banks personally pledged $90,000, in cash, for which they received $100,000 in Buick stock. So there could be no misunderstanding, the directors of the Genessee Bank included in their pledge agreement the following provision:

"This subscription is made with the understanding that the Buick Motor Company will discontinue its Jackson plant and locate its entire business at Flint, commencing construction work upon its new buildings as soon as plans can be prepared and weather will permit."

Again it was Durant who sold most of the new Buick stock. His friends always insisted that on one day, Tuesday, September 12th, Durant sold $500,000 of the additional million dollars' worth of Buick stock. It had to be the greatest personal tribute ever tendered to the soft-spoken, little man from Flint. Twice in the previous ten months he had been instrumental in selling stock in the untried Buick Motor Company for well over $250,000, most of it going to friends and neighbors in Flint, then a town of less than fifteen thousand people. Until September, 1905, there had been no such achievement demonstrated by any motorcar company or any city.

Following the reorganization and recapitalization, heads of all four of the big carriage firms were named to the board of Buick. The nine directors included the carriage makers, James H. Whiting, W. A. Paterson, J. Dallas Dort and William F. Stewart; banker, Arthur G. Bishop; superintendent of the Jackson plant, H. George Field; president, Charles M. Begole; treasurer, George L. Walker; and general manager and director, William C. Durant. Six of the nine were executives of the wagon and carriage firms in Flint that, during the year, would ship 100,000 horse-drawn vehicles to all parts of the United States.

In the reorganization, the final settlement with the Flint Wagon Works was made. The wagon and buggy firm received $200,000 in Buick stock in recognition of its $75,000 investment that brought the company to Flint two years earlier. The contributions of David Buick were similarly recognized and rewarded.

Work was intensified on the new Buick plant on the Hamilton farm. Durant had expanded it until it was a sprawling factory with 14 acres under its roof, by far the largest plant yet built in the young motorcar industry of the United States.

Production continued to rise at the assembly plant in Jackson. More new Buicks were turned out every month than had been produced during the corresponding month of the previous year. Production for 1905 climbed to 627 cars. Output was climbing rapidly as the new year opened. Durant had appointed so many excellent dealers that there was a backlog of orders, assuring that whatever could be produced would be sold.

By March, production at Jackson was up to 250 cars a week and climbing rapidly. By the end of 1906, the firm had produced and sold 2,295 cars. Buick had moved up among the leaders two years after Durant took over its management.

The year also concluded Jackson's contribution to Buick progress. Most of the year's production had been assembled and shipped from Jackson. Final assembly of Buicks was shifting to Flint before the year ended, and the Jackson plant, from which Buicks had been shipped by the trainload, was closed within a few months.

At the time of the agreement to concentrate all Buick operations in Flint, Durant took another important step. In the fall of 1905, Durant shared his future plans for Buick with Charles S. Mott and offered the Utica firm an inducement to relocate in Flint.

Mott, who had seen Michigan grab the leadership in the horseless carriage industry away from the eastern states, saw the advantages of being close to the rapidly expanding motorcar business in Flint, Lansing and Detroit. The Weston-Mott move to Flint took place so rapidly that its new building was being built nearby, on the Hamilton farm, at the same time that the big Buick assembly plant was being erected.

Weston-Mott was eventually bought by General Motors, and its head became an officer of that giant firm. Still living, Charles S. Mott has outlived Durant, Buick, Chrysler, Sloan and all the other founders of the motorcar. He had known them, and had helped in their hours of trial and triumph. He is the only man who has served General Motors as a director for fifty years. His name will always stand in the front ranks of the men who made the motorcar possible.

Weston-Mott was but the first of many motorcar component producers that Durant induced to move to Flint and to give Buick first call on their services. Shortly after, he enticed the former French racing star, Albert Champion, to Flint to set up his business, making sparkplugs for Buick. The former world-racing champion had emigrated to the United States and established his own company, marketing "Champion Sparkplugs." Durant persuaded him to sell his business and move to Flint.

When Champion arrived in Flint, the only place available was a corner of Buick's main office in the Buick plant on the Hamilton farm. The newborn sparkplug operation used the front office until a building could be erected for the new company. Champion gathered a small staff around him and began turning out approximately forty sparkplugs a day. Soon, Champion was turning out thousands of sparkplugs each week. Buick had provided all the funds and facilities to get Champion's new operation started. The enterprise could easily have become a department of Buick, but Durant wanted to provide Champion with greater incentive. He proposed that Champion establish a separate business, become its president and retain 25 percent of the stock.

The naming of the product of Champion's new company presented some difficulty. Champion sparkplugs had already been marketed. Finally, it was decided that Champion's initials, "A. C.," would be the name. This explains how, today, two major brands of sparkplugs, "Champion" and "AC," trace their origin to the same man—Albert C. Champion.

During the Durant era in Flint, from 1905 until 1910, the population of the city doubled. There were years, during the period, when more men were at work building new factories and homes than there were making Buicks. The north side of Flint took on the look of a boomtown reminiscent of the West, when railroad work camps and mining towns appeared overnight. So important did the night shift become, that hotels and boarding houses rented the same rooms "for the day or for the night."

Flint became the fastest growing industrial city in the United States. Its factory employment more than doubled in the months between early 1908 and the end of 1909. The work-week was seven 10-hour or longer days. The Flint payroll jumped to third in the state, exceeded only by Detroit and Lansing, the other cities most deeply involved in Michigan's takeover in the motorcar business.

Employment agents ranged as far as the East Coast looking for craftsmen and into the deep South seeking laborers. Plants paid rail road fares to Flint and furnished meals until employees received their first paychecks.

The town struggled to maintain community services as tent villages sprang up near the new plants. At one time, a thousand men were camping on the banks of the Flint River and in unused, wooded areas. From 1907, three thousand houses were built in three years. Seven square miles of outside territory were annexed by Flint in one twelve-month period, and the Hamilton farm industrial complex soon found itself in the city rather than on its edge. Four new schools were built on the north side of Flint in an effort to provide public schooling for children of the new population.

Flint would grow even more in the next decade but, by then, the stimulation would involve other factors. The record growth that began in 1905 stemmed directly from the economic explosion led by the town's little giant, Billy Durant. He was in the process of accomplishing again, in the age of horsepower, what he had done in the horse-drawn era.

The one man who deserves to share the spotlight with Durant was Walter L. Marr, a native of Lexington, Michigan. Marr became noted for his subtle humor, a Van Dyke beard and great motors. The motorcar advanced only as the motors advanced. Although overshadowed by the comet-like Durant, Marr was one of the five builders of the motors that made today's automobile possible. The other four were Frank Duryea, Ransom E. Olds, Henry Leland and Henry Ford. Great motor builders, such as Fred Zeder of Chrysler and Charles F. Kettering of General Motors came later, but, by that time, the worldwide prominence of the motorcar made in the United States had already been established.

Marr, like Durant, got his start in a sawmill town. In 1887, he began working for a firm that made motors for lake steamboats. A year later he had his first opportunity to build a small, one-cylinder internal combustion engine designed by the superintendent of the firm. An enterprising man, he opened, in 1896, his own, small bicycle factory in Detroit, where he used stationary gasoline engines for power. He had become acquainted with the stationary gasoline engines built by Olds, Leland and Buick. He built a motorwagon, powered with his own engine, a motor tricycle and at least one other motorwagon before he began working with David Buick and Eugene C. Richard at Buick's Auto-Vim Shop.

Marr built the two motors that moved Buick into greatness. Proving that ideas belong, not necessarily to the conceivers but, to those who embrace them, Marr became the first to see the real potential in the valve-in-head motor. Both his great engines for Buick had the overhead valves. The first was the two-cylinder, horizontal-style motor that became the power unit in Buick's famous "Model-F," the first Buick car that skyrocketed sales and attracted national attention.

Marr himself drove the "Model-F" horseless carriage in the hazardous hill climb at Eagle Rock, New Jersey. Like most of the hill climbs, it was an open event. The spectators gave a "Bronx cheer" when the spunky little Buick pulled up to the starting line, almost lost in the maze of big cars. The jeering turned to cheering when, at the firing of the starter's gun, Marr immediately moved so far out in front that the "Model-F" set a new record at 2 minutes and eighteen seconds. The previous record was 4 minutes. Reporters gathered around Marr at the finish, demanding to know how he could slash the record with such a small car. "It's the valve-in-the-head motor," Marr explained.

He took the "Model-F" directly from New Jersey to the 6,000-foot Mount Washington hill climb in New Hampshire. The Marr-Buick entry won there, also. Later, a Marr valve-in-head Buick set a new record for the climb up Pike's Peak, making the 58-mile round trip to the top of the 14,000-foot peak in 3 hours and twenty-two minutes, using but four and one-half gallons of gasoline. A year later, another Marr valve-in-head Buick became the first motorcar to cross the Andes, threading a 13,000-foot pass in which it had to wallow through heavy snow.

The public was quick to respond to the phenomenal power in the small motor. Many a steep hill from New York City to Flint was labeled "a Buick Hill." This was an important factor in doubling Buick sales in 1907, the year of national financial panic. Sales climbed to 5,000, from 2,300 the year before.

Marr's second motor was the four-cylinder engine of the "Model-10" Buick introduced in 1908. The basic motor had been developed by the Janney Motor Company of Jackson, another component supplier brought into existence by Durant. When Janney became a part of Buick, the experimental motor was turned over to Marr and his engineering assistant, E. A. DeWaters, who redesigned it, adding the valve-in-head feature.

The "Model-10" was an evidence of the Durant concept of success in the motorcar business. Departing from the one-model concept exemplified by the Curved Dash Oldsmobile, Durant believed Buick should have a line of cars, as soon as possible. It was natural that he should, since much of the success of the Durant-Dort Carriage Company had resulted from providing several types of buggies to fit varying budgets. It was the same concept that later led him to found General Motors.

In 1907, Buick introduced its first four-cylinder motorcar. In 1908, the firm offered two two-cylinder cars, one of which was the "Model F," and two four-cylinder cars, one of which was the new "Model-10." The "Model-10" was Buick's bid for the new car buyer with a low budget. The "Model-10" had a planetary transmission, as did Ford's "Model-T," and sold at a price range which began at $850, slightly less than the "Model-T," that year. The "Model-10" quickly became the hub of the Buick line and was the main reason that sales tripled in less than three years.

Walter Marr's career as Buick's chief engineer was cut short, in 1913, by ill health. He retired to Signal Mountain, Tennessee, in the Blue Ridge Mountains, but continued for another decade as a special engineering consultant. During those ten years, new Buick models were submitted to him at Signal Mountain for his reaction or approval.

Durant had the capacity to attract good men and, so long as things went well, he allowed them an unusual degree of freedom to carry out their work. He was able to give his attention to every phase of the rapidly expanding Buick business by working sixteen to twenty hours a day. Although he was never president, not even an officer of the firm, the big problems always found their way to "The Man." This was also true of engineering and performance problems, even though he had Marr and a strong corps of engineers to handle these matters.

Howard Crawford, a former Flint farm boy, was hired to handle parts inventory at the new Hamilton farm Buick factory even before it was opened. In his memoirs, he paints an eyewitness account that explains Durant's deep interest and direct involvement with Buick performance and engineering.

One afternoon in 1906, Durant, from Jackson, phoned to William Little, Buick's salty, Flint factory superintendent, reporting he had received many complaints on the Buick brakes. He wanted an improved braking system built as quickly as possible. Little called in Crawford and O'Brien, an expert mechanic. Little explained the call from Durant and then said, "O'Brien, I want you to make a set of brakes that will hold this car. Howard (Crawford) will take care of getting the stuff for you. You can put everything else aside and stay

Half a century of difference in producing motorcar
engines. *Top:* at the beginning, the Cadillac motor was
built on a stationary platform by two-man teams.
Bottom: fifty years later, the motors were being
mass-produced on a moving assembly line, with scores
of skilled men adding a particular feature to the engine.

right with it until you have the new brakes on the car for testing. Mr. Durant is always in a hurry."

O'Brien got the assignment in midafternoon. He and Crawford worked on through the evening and the night and completed the new brakes about noon the next day. O'Brien had developed a new feature involving the linkage that gave the new brakes greatly increased effectiveness.

Little called Durant and reported that the new brakes were ready for his check. Durant expressed pleasure and directed Little to pick him up at Flint's Dresden Hotel at seven the next morning. Little took Crawford and O'Brien with him and together they met Durant at the Dresden, then went to the new Hamilton farm Buick plant.

There was a level piece of farm meadow immediately back of the new plant, and Little suggested that they check the brakes there. With Crawford looking on, Little got into the driver's seat and Durant got into the back seat. Anxious to offer a decisive demonstration, Little built up speed and then jammed his foot down hard on the brake pedal. The brakes locked the wheels and Durant was thrown head first into the front seat and rolled out onto the ground. Front doors had not yet been developed.

Little was shocked. Durant picked himself up off the ground and, while dusting off his clothing, turned to Little. Speaking softly (as though nothing unusual had occurred), he said,

"Well, you certainly got some brakes, Bill."

"Get in, Mr. Durant and I'll drive you back to the plant," Little proposed.

"No thanks, I'll walk," Durant responded.

"Durant had the Buick completely in his hands," Crawford comments. "He was a small man and talked in a very soft voice. He could get the confidence of people. He was the best salesman I ever saw. He was an awfully nice chap."

One of the quickest ways in which to get Durant's personal attention was to raise a question about Buick's performance. He hired Buick's first outstanding sales manager by listening to such a complaint. Charles Van Horne, the first sales manager remained with Buick while the firm was located in Jackson. The second sales manager was Harry A. Shiland, a motorcar dealer in Worcester, Massachusetts, and was one of the first Buick agents Durant appointed after he took over the firm in 1904.

The mechanic in Shiland's repair shop called the first Buick they received the "worse lemon in America." Shiland did not entirely share the view, although on a 120-mile test drive the chain drive had broken and the transmission had locked. The carburetor had caused a lot of trouble, too. Shiland was impressed with the valve-in-head engine. He had his shop put on a heavier drive chain, service the transmission (which had been carelessly machined and improperly adjusted), and install a Kingston carburetor.

The next day, he took a drive in the hills west of Worcester and found, to his amazement, that his Buick was the most powerful and dependable horseless carriage he had ever driven. Soon he had issued a public challenge to any car owner to a race through the Green Mountains to the Canadian border. After a demonstration in the little Buick, there were no challengers. Shiland began selling Buicks faster than he could get delivery from Jackson, but he found, to his sorrow, that he had to overhaul the new cars before he could be sure of their performance.

Finally, he wrote the account of his experience directly to Durant. When he didn't get a response he traveled to Jackson to call on Durant.

"You aren't selling cars to mechanics," he told him. "Cars have to be foolproof for the average doctor or lawyer or businessman to want them."

Durant, at once, ordered a switch from the Hartford drive chain to a stronger one made by the Diamond Company. Despite the fact that Buick had a department set up to make its own carburetors, Durant ordered the use of the Kingston carburetor, as Shiland suggested. Durant then inquired how soon Shiland could arrange to leave his Worcester dealership and come to work for Buick.

That fall, Durant and Shiland both drove Buicks, the new "Model-F," in the 1906 Glidden Tour, the second of the annual fall tours conducted by the American Automobile Association, with Colonel Charles J. Glidden offering the trophy to the owner of the motorcar that gave the best performance within the regulations of the tour. Glidden, an associate of Alexander Graham Bell, offered the Glidden Trophy for tours conducted in various parts of the United States until 1912. The first Glidden Tour, held the year before, had been run from New York to Boston, to Bretton Woods, New Hampshire, and back to New York. Billy Pierce and his Pierce-Arrow, from Buffalo, had won the Glidden trophy.

The second tour was from Buffalo through Canada, to Bretton Woods and back to Buffalo, a distance of 1,200 miles. The two Buicks were but two of 48 cars that took part. Buick engineers had recently

151

begun using a new steel bushing around the two main bearings in the motor. On the first day out, one of the main steel bearings in the Buick driven by Shiland, froze and stopped the car instantly. He managed to get a bronze bushing and have it installed in time to catch up with the tour the following day. Shortly after rejoining the tour, the other steel bushing froze and Shiland was out of the Glidden Tour. The other Buick was disqualified later the same day when Durant stopped to help another Glidden Tour contestant. The tour rules did not permit offering assistance to contestants. Durant, who loved to win at whatever he was doing, was keenly disappointed at the poor showing made by Buick. As a result, he had the steel bushings removed, saving, not only hundreds of thousands of dollars, but preserving the Buick reputation. The great accomplishment of the Glidden and similar tours was to show up imperfections in early motorcars.

There was a time, soon after the new "Model-10" was introduced, when the people of Flint had an opportunity to see acres and acres of new Buicks standing in a field behind the big Hamilton farm plant—sidelined there because of a faulty part. A new distributor was used instead of the separate coil for each cylinder. The distributor worked well in tests, but, after the car was used for some time, oil from the flywheel caused a short circuit. Durant authorized an immediate return to the use of coils. Bill Little telephoned all the coil makers in the country but, before the coils arrived in sufficient numbers, there were acres and acres of Buicks ready for shipment, except for coils, parked in the open.

On another occasion, Shiland insisted that Durant meet him in Buffalo so that they could ride back to Detroit in a new Pope-Toledo car Shiland had borrowed. Shiland wanted to demonstrate the superiority of the sliding gear over the planetary transmission then used on Buicks. Durant quickly saw the advantage of the sliding gear. He was never too busy to study an improvement for Buick cars.

No early horseless carriage became successful without participation in hill climbs, races and demonstrations. Ransom E. Olds had already set the pace for picking up publicity. From the time he took over Buick, Durant was determined to collect his full dividend of publicity. Within months, after the Durant takeover, the Buick was setting records.

On Saturday, September 9th, 1905, Marr's valve-in-head Buick established a new world's 5-mile record for two-cylindered machines on the Readville Track in Boston. The Buick covered the distance in six minutes, nineteen and two-fifths seconds. The same day in Newark, New Jersey, another Buick established a new track record for 1 mile, traveling the distance in one minute and two seconds. A Pope-Hartford and a Wayne came in second and third. In other events the same day in Newark, Buick made a clean sweep, turning back the bids of the Knox, Reo and other cars.

Buick racing activities intensified until his drivers became some of the most outstanding in the country. Organized personally by Durant, the team was placed under the direction of William H. Pickens, in 1908. There were scores of drivers on Buick teams, but the three great champions were Robert R. (Wild Bob) Burman, Lewis Strang and Louis Chevrolet. Behind this group of regulars came a long list of noted drivers, such as Gaston Chevrolet, William Oldknow, J. R. Bradley, Peter de Paolo, George DeWitt, Charles Nyquist, Bill Farr and Phil Hines, all of whom, sooner or later, figured prominently in the "World Series" of racing at the Indianapolis "500." Strang, Gaston Chevrolet and Burman later lost their lives driving other cars.

Walter Marr, and other Buick engineers, built special Buicks for racing. The "Model-17," the "Buick-100," the Buick "Bearcat" and the "No. 60 Special Buick," also known as the Buick "Bug," were all racing cars. Most of the honors were won by regular stock cars with few, if any, modifications. Perhaps none of them won more honors than Marr's "Model-F."

National and international acclaim accounted for no small part of Buick's quick rise to leadership in sales. Buick racing drivers produced a steady flow of newspaper headlines in their victories and performances on the race tracks, hill and mountain climbs and in endurance contests.

In 1909, Durant set up an expense budget of $100,000 for the Buick racing team. He was so pleased at the end of the year that, at impressive ceremonies in Flint, a special purse of $10,000 was divided among Louis Chevrolet, Burman and Strang.

Bob Burman, who tested the first Buick built in Flint in June of 1904, drove a Buick "Bug" 105 miles an hour at the Indianapolis Speedway, July 1, 1910—the fastest time ever recorded, to that date, by a motorcar made in the United States. In 1912, a Buick "Bug" driven by Gaston Chevrolet and Bob Burman won the greatest race of them all, the Indianapolis "500." Practically every race track or steep hill in the United States had been used to set Buick records, and the Buick drivers won in all the big racing events throughout the world.

Between 1908, and 1911, the Buick Racing Team had captured more than five hundred trophies, more trophies than had been won by all other United States entries combined! The Buick trophy room was a tribute to Billy Durant, a man incapable of small thoughts.

In a Buick publication issued late in 1908, appeared a statement: "The Buick Motor Company has reached the point where we can, with pardonable pride, point to the largest production of automobiles in the world by any one concern."

Billy Durant had accomplished what no other man had then done, or would ever do. He had moved from horses to horsepower and had been the pacesetter in both. He had directed the production of more horse-drawn vehicles than any other man who had ever lived. Within four years, he had also scaled the same heights with the self-propelled vehicle.

The Durant achievement was greater than the Buick publication claim. Buick was not only the leading maker of motorcars in 1908, but also the producer of more than the next two firms combined. This achievement was fully reported later by an authority on the development of the motorcar in the United States, Alfred P. Sloan, Jr. Of the Durant achievement Sloan states:

"It may not be generally known that, at the turn of the century Mr. Durant—who started from scratch—was the leading wagon and carriage producer in the United States; that he entered and reorganized the failing Buick Motor Company in 1904 and by 1908 was the leading motorcar producer in the country. He built 8,487 Buicks in 1908, as compared with a production in that year of 6,181 Fords and 2,380 Cadillacs."

9

The Emergence of Henry Ford

As the century was about to turn, Fred J. Wagner, an advertising salesman for *Cycle Age,* called at the Detroit Electric Company's main office. Wagner, soon to become America's dean of race starters during the years when the motorcar advanced from an experiment to a necessity, had a few days before received a letter written in long-hand on blue-lined school tablet paper. The communication, written to the Chicago office of the magazine, was a one-sentence letter asking Wagner to stop and see the writer the next time he was in Detroit. It was signed, "H. Ford, Engineer, Detroit Electric Company."

Here is how Wagner described the visit:

"When I inquired for this H. Ford at the offices of the Detroit Electric, none there ever had heard of the man. As I was about to leave, however, the girl at the information had an inspiration. 'Say, perhaps he's the engineer—you know, the fireman—of the building,' she suggested. 'You might go around to the basement door at the rear of the plant and ask, anyway.'

I played her hunch.

Reaching the foot of the stairs, I found myself in a small dark chamber, in the opposite wall of which was a steel door. I tried the handle, but it was locked.

Next, I pounded on it with my fist and, when that brought no response, I lifted a foot and began kicking at the heavy portal. I knew there was someone inside, for I could hear a shovel scraping coal off the concrete floor.

But I had to lose the heel off my shoe before I succeeded in attracting attention.

When the door eventually opened, I was confronted by a tall gaunt fellow, his face covered with the grease and grime of the boiler room. He was just finishing banking his fires for the night.

'Are you H. Ford?' I asked.

'Why yes!' he said, his tone tinged with surprise, for I don't suppose he was in the habit of receiving visitors at his place of employment.

'My name is Wagner,' I told him. 'I'm with *Cycle Age.*'

'Well,' he declared, grinning and extending a blackened hand, but before I permitted him to say anything more, I gave him a piece of my mind.

'Hell of a way to welcome callers,' I told him. 'I've just kicked the heel off my shoe trying to get in here!'

'I'm sorry, Mr. Wagner,' he answered, 'but if you'll be seated in that chair over there, I'll fix it for you in a jiffy.'

Hobbling over to the designated seat, I made myself comfortable while H. Ford bent down on one knee and removed the shoe.

'Just a minute now,' he added, as he walked over to a bench, where with hammer and nails he repaired the damage.

'As good as new,' he informed me, laughingly, as he replaced the oxford on my foot.

'I have a letter from you, in which you asked me to call,' I explained.

'Yes, Mr. Wagner,' he replied.

Then he straightened his sparse frame, and plunged into a discussion of gasoline engines, convincing me that I was in the company of a nut or a genius. It was a most embarrassing situation for me. He bombarded me with questions that my better judgment told me were best left unanswered, and, finally, I was forced to tell him that, as an authority on the subject, I was America's best advertising solicitor.

'Well,' he shot back good-naturedly, 'what I really wanted to see you about was this. I'd like to subscribe to your magazine, but I haven't got the two dollars to give you right now, and I was wondering if you would take my order, and wait for the money until the first of the month, when I get paid off!'

Then and there the name 'H. Ford' was entered on the subscription lists of *Cycle Age,* and I made a most inglorious exit, saying to myself:

'I don't care whether that guy ever pays up or not, because it's worth two dollars just to get away from him!' "

This account of a first meeting with the thirty-seven-year-old Henry Ford reveals the man as he was while he was still unknown.

It constitutes a carefully-drawn portrait of a remarkable man before he was wrapped in half-truths that were often woven into complete myths.

Ford was a much more accomplished individual than Wagner knew at the time of their first meeting, and it is interesting that Ford preferred to reveal so little about himself and his plans. He had reached agreement in principle with a group of sponsors to develop a horseless carriage. The sponsors included some of the best known and wealthiest citizens of Detroit, including Mayor William C. Maybury. In a few days, on August 5th, 1899, the project would be formalized with the founding of the Detroit Automobile Company with "H. Ford" as the chief engineer. It would be the second horseless carriage company organized in Wayne County, Michigan, with offices in Detroit. The Olds Motor Works had been established three months and three days earlier, on May 8th, and its new factory on Jefferson Street in Detroit, first to be built in the United States, was underway.

This "H. Ford," at the turn of the century, was a friendly man. He was concerned about the heel Wagner had kicked from his shoe, and he moved immediately to repair the damage. He did a good job and was proud of his work. It was this quick concern for the welfare of others, rather than his mechanical wizardry, that contributed most to his success for which there is no parallel in American industry.

But, that was not all. Ford showed that he was aggressive and knew what he wanted. Otherwise, he would not have written Wagner at all. He was eager to learn, determined to educate himself. He sought *Cycle Age* for the information it would bring him about the self-propelled vehicles in which he already planned to have a career. Although he was scooping coal and dressed as a common laborer, the Henry Ford of 1900 exhibited a confidence that ruled out inferiority. He did not have the $2.00 for the subscription, but he felt no hesitancy in asking for credit until his next pay day. Finally, he accomplished his objective.

Because so much has been attributed to Henry Ford, it is useful at the outset to consider what he did and what he did not do. A bright future for the motorcar in the United States was already assured before the cars of Henry Ford became important. Ransom E. Olds had built, at least, 2 self-propelled vehicles before Ford thought seriously about building a motorcar, at all. The remarkable horseless carriages and their motors built by Duryea, Olds and Leland were well known to Ford before he designed his first car engine in 1903.

Durant's Buick factories in Flint had, at least, twenty acres under roof while the Ford Motor Company was operating in a small rented building on Mack Avenue in Detroit. Henry Ford was so late in his start that he missed much of the horseless carriage era.

The leadership of the State of Michigan and of Detroit in motorcar production was clearly established before the first Ford car had been sold. In the early months of 1903, before the Ford Motor Company was organized, the Olds Motor Works and the Cadillac Motor Car Company were the two leading producers of self-propelled vehicles in the United States. In May, 1903, before the Ford Motor Company existed, the Olds and Cadillac plants, between them, produced nearly 1,000 motorcars.

Nor did Ford come onto the market with the lowest priced car. His first car, the Model-A two-passenger runabout, sold for $850 which was about the price of the Cadillac and higher than the Curved Dash Oldsmobile, the leader in the market during the first years of Ford production. Some Ford models produced in the first four years were priced from $2,000 to $2,600. It was not until the Ford Model-N was introduced, after marketing medium and higher priced cars for nearly five years that the company made its first entry into the low-priced field.

Even when Ford turned to the production of an inexpensive motorcar, his firm was not alone in this field. Much of the time, during the spectacular and completely unprecedented rise of the Ford, from 1909 to 1924, good motorcars were available at prices as low, or even lower. One of those cars was Harry Ford's small motorcar, the Saxon. Another was the Hupp, of which Henry Ford later commented, "I recall looking at Bobby Hupp's roadster at the first show where it was exhibited and wondering whether we could ever build as good a small car for as little money."

Many of the mechanical advances that make today's cars so useful were not developed at Ford. The valve-in-the-head feature, the self-starter, the modern electrical system, the V-8 motor, the automatic transmission, the four-wheel brakes, the hydraulic systems that operate brakes and other vital features, the glass enclosed bodies, air conditioning and other features, so important to today's cars were developed by others.

While this is true, The Ford Motor Company in its period of greatest achievement from 1908 until 1924 did introduce many new engineering features that made the Model-T a superior car at the time. Most of these advanced Ford features, such as the planetary transmission and the flywheel magneto, have since been replaced by more recent advances. Two of these earlier Ford engineering achievements, however, have remained in universal use. The Ford Motor Company was the first to cast all of the cylinders in the engine block in a single operation, and Ford introduced the use of high-strength alloy steels, opening the way to the superior weight-to-power ratios employed in all cars today.

How, then, was it that the Ford car carried the American motorcar to new heights and precipitated a new kind of life in the United States and, gradually, throughout the world? There were scores of reasons, and most of them were to be found within the man himself.

The greatness of Henry Ford rests on his implementation of the motorcar. By 1907, Ford had developed two basic ideas about the motorcar that were to set him apart from everyone else. He persisted in them against the toughest kind of corporate opposition, even to eliminating from the firm the man who made possible the founding of the Ford Motor Company. Ford then went on to apply his ideas relentlessly until he had precipitated the most important of all changes in human transportation.

Ford's first objective was to build a light, utilitarian car that was so simple to operate and to maintain that any person capable of driving a horse could handle it. His second goal was to sell the car at a price most families could afford. Finally, he introduced another idea which had a great deal to do with carrying out his idea of replacing the "family horse" with a motorcar. He shared the earnings of his company directly with his employees so that they could afford to own and drive a motorcar. Because his firm was the leader in the motorcar industry, the concept of higher wages for men in the factory spread rapidly throughout the car industry and shortly after to most of the other important industries in the United States.

Because Henry Ford is the key figure in making the car universally available, he stands as the greatest figure of all in the long story of transportation.

Most of the reasons for Henry Ford's greatness were lodged within himself. The reasons were both general and specific. He grew up on a farm. He knew the same hard work and pinched finances that most farmers knew from time to time. Farmers constituted nearly 70 per cent of the American population when Ford was growing up. Ford didn't like the hard work of the farm and said so, reflecting exactly what most of his fellow Americans thought about the drudgery (and that is what it was) of farm life. Ford saw the motorcar, not as a vehicle, but as a means to give the rank-and-file of his countrymen, especially farmers and laboring people, the escape from the same kind of isolation and hardship he endured as a boy on a Michigan farm. Although he became wealthy within a period of five years, he remembered that he had been poor—never poverty-stricken, but poor—and always maintained a wide-eyed wonderment about it all. He was never ashamed or apologetic about his earlier circumstances.

Ford was not present for the first motorcar contest in the United States, the one sponsored by the *Chicago Times-Herald* in 1895, but it was not because he did not know of it or want to be present. When, fifteen years later, he met Henry H. Kohlsaat, the publisher who had been responsible for the event, he said, unabashed, as they were shaking hands, "I never wanted anything so badly in my life as to go to that race, but I couldn't get anyone to lend me the carfare to Chicago."

Ford quickly came to the position of wealth and influence that made it possible for him to meet and know the famous people of the country and the world. Many of them sought appointments and came to call on him at his second-floor office in the Ford plant at Highland Park. Ford enjoyed this opportunity, and always maintained the same friendly, quiet and direct manner that he exhibited when Fred Wagner went into the Detroit Electric Company to meet him. Ford probably never enjoyed any of his associations with the noted people of his time more than he did the friendship and confidence of Thomas Edison, Harvey Firestone and John Burroughs. The noted naturalist, who was older than Ford, in his later years was a distinguished figure with a flowing, white beard.

There were frequent newspaper reports of Ford's travels with Edison, Firestone or Burroughs. There were many stories of their experiences together, some of them humorous. These stories tended to tighten Ford's relationship with the American public. Most people of the country would have enjoyed, just as Ford did, meeting and knowing these famous persons. In a sense, Ford became the representative of the common people, something of the same relationship that Will Rogers achieved later. The general attitude developed over the land—"rich, but he's one of us. He understands our problems. If only there were more Henry Fords."

Here is an example of the stories that were legend for years, this one directly from Ford himself. Late in the summer of 1919, Henry Ford was coming down the steps of the Penobscot Building in Detroit. Herbert R. Lewis of General Motors was passing. Ford called to him, "Hey, Herb, have you got a minute. I want to tell you a funny thing that happened just the other day." Lewis, known for his humor and collection of funny stories, many of which Ford had enjoyed from time to time, responded, "Why sure, Henry, I've always got time for a good story."

Ford related, "I just got back yesterday from a little trip with Firestone and Burroughs. We drove south through Indiana to Louisville." They had taken the trip in a new Ford touring car, the motorcar owned by at least a third of those Americans having cars in that year.

"I drove into a little store to get some gas," Ford continued. "Firestone was sitting in the back and Burroughs was sitting in the front seat with me. I got out of the car as the man came out of the store. While he was filling the tank, I said to him, 'I'm Henry Ford. This is my car. Do you know who that man is sitting in the back seat? He's Harvey Firestone and the tires on this car are his tires'."

The countrystore owner looked over his shoulder, while holding the hose in the gas tank, with obvious disbelief registered on his face, and said in his best southern Hoosier drawl, "Yeh, now I suppose you are going to tell me that other old bird you have in the front seat is Santa Claus'."

Ford enjoyed this harmless joke and used it on many other occasions. The responses were not always printable, but he enjoyed the experiences, and so did the millions who heard the story, perhaps because it was about what they would have done if they had been in Henry Ford's place.

There were more specific reasons why Ford became an American hero quickly. The "Tin Lizzie," as Ford's "Model-T" was affectionately known from Maine to California, was everywhere providing families with entirely new opportunities. These people were enjoying life more than ever before, and they credited much of the opportunity to Henry Ford.

Another factor that solidified Ford's bond with the American public was that almost every year, from 1909 until 1925, the Ford Motor Company was able to reduce the price of the country's basic item of personal transportation, the Ford Touring Car. The price slid from $950, in 1909, down to a hard-to-believe $240, in 1925, for an even better car. While the prices of other cars went up and up, the price of Ford came down and down. No other carmaker was ever able to reduce prices regularly over this period when the inflation of World War I upped the cost of everything. Henry Ford not only got the credit personally, but also came to be recognized as a genius.

A lesser matter, but still a factor in lowering car prices (Ford again appearing to be the public's representative and protector) was Ford's battle to break the Selden patent. The holders of the patent on the motorcar first refused to recognize the small and under-financed Ford Motor Company. By the time the business had grown enough to qualify for a license under the Selden patent, Henry Ford had decided not to pay the patent fee. The Selden group took the matter to court, and Ford battled to break the patent. It took him seven years, but he won, and knocked out of existence the nearest approach to monopoly the motorcar industry ever knew in the United States.

The lowering of "Model-T" Ford prices was but the outward manifestation of the Henry Ford desire to be helpful. He had a special objective of his own that no other motorcar magnate ever possessed to such a degree. Ford knew that he was placed in a position of opportunity, greater than had ever come to any man in the area of transportation. He had the capacity to see it all in light of the welfare of the people he knew best. He wanted farm people to have a chance to own a car, so they could go to town, to church, to school or the hospital, as people in town did. Thinking of those even more closely linked with him, and even before the "Model-T" was on the production line, Ford was telling his associates, again and again, "I want to make a car our workers in the plant can afford to drive."

There were many other factors that made Henry Ford the best known, and one of the most favorably known, men in America, before World War I, but one overshadowed all others. This event shattered the old order as much as the Ford car had done.

Even with the reductions in the price of the "Model-T," money continued to pile up in the Ford Motor Company banks. Ford hit upon a new and bold scheme to move swiftly toward his goal of having a car his workmen could afford to own. On January 5th, 1914, when Ford plant workers were being paid an average of $2.30 a day, the Ford Motor Company announced that, immediately, it would pay every man, even the janitors, a minimum of $5.00 per day, and cut the working day down to a standard eight hours for everyone. A new concept of compensation for factory work had been introduced. Henry Ford got the credit, and well he might. The $5.00 minimum wage was his own idea, instituted over the objections of his financial advisors, who were certain that the policy would wreck the company. In a single week, Henry Ford became a world figure.

As Americans learned more of Ford's background, the more they admired him. He was born in the Ford farm home east of the village of Dearbornville. The farm was also located 2 miles east of the Rouge River on which he would, one day, build the mightiest motorcar producing complex of them all. From the Ford farm, on a clear day, it was possible to see the smoke of the river boats tied up at the Detroit docks.

Henry Ford was born July 30th, 1863, during the darkest hours of the Civil War and in the same month that the great Battles at Gettysburg and Vicksburg took place. His uncle was lost in the war. He was the eldest of the eight children of William and Mary Ford. As is often the case with an eldest son, he was very close to his mother, whose influence unquestionably shaped many of the great qualities which contributed to his later success. His mother was his first teacher. Henry did not enter the little red school of the Scotch Settlement District until after he was seven, not unusual for farm children facing Michigan winters. There was no car to take them to school and walking was the only means of getting to their classes. The Scotch Settlement School was a mile and a half north of the Ford farm.

As the twig is bent! By the time he entered school he could read, and wrote well enough to begin keeping a diary in his first year, something his mother undoubtedly encouraged. She instilled in him a keen interest in being orderly, keeping records and taking care of his toys and tools. He continued all his life to keep day-by-day reports of the things he did. His love of tools led him, in his later and wealthy years, to collect them on a vast scale. He specialized in collecting the objects which were so much a part of his life as a boy, a way of life largely obliterated in his lifetime. His Ford car was the primary catalyst in the change. The result of his collecting, and a tribute to his mother's influence, is the Ford Greenfield Museum, at Dearborn, Michigan, one of the great institutions of its kind in America. It is located near the site of the Ford farm, where Henry Ford spent his childhood.

His concern for others, his confidence in himself, the dependability of his word and, above all, his love for mechanical things appear to have been traits in which his mother played a large role. He was, in after years, Lincoln-like in his praise of her, saying in his autobiography, "Even when very young, I suspected that much might be done a better way. This is what took me to mechanics—although my mother always said I was a born mechanic. I had a kind of workshop with odds and ends for metal for tools before I had anything else. In those days we did not have the toys of today; what we had were home made. My toys were all tools—they still are. From the beginning I could never work up much interest in the labour of farming. I wanted to have something to do with machinery ... I have followed many a weary mile (walking) behind a plow and I know the drudgery of it."

Ford was good in mathematics and reading; poor in spelling. Judged by later achievements, his classmates may have been an above-average group. Some of them became good farmers, some of them became teachers. J. Dallas Dort, later to be a partner in the Durant-Dort Carriage Company, and who later created his own motorcar, the Dort, and a founder of General Motors, was one of Ford's classmates. Another was Alanson Brush, who assisted Ford with the technical matters at the Selden patent court hearings and who also developed his own motorcar, the Brush Runabout.

School afforded young Ford his first opportunity to exhibit leadership. Many examples have survived, indicating that he possessed the ability to develop plans and win the cooperation of his fellow students. Often there was mischief involved in his plans, and he spent time in the "sinners seat" in the front of the room in clear view of the teacher.

Tragedy struck the Ford family when Henry was thirteen. His mother died in March of 1875, following the stillbirth of her eighth child. He described the Ford home then as "a watch without a mainspring."

In July of the same year, he accompanied his father, by way of horse and buggy, on a trip to Detroit. Just after they left the Ford farmstead they met, coming down the road, a steam engine of the type used to provide power for sawing logs and running threshing machines. It was the first self-propelled road machine the youth had ever seen. The elder Ford stopped the horse to let the engine pass. Henry was so impressed that he jumped from the buggy, ran to the steam engine and began asking Fred Reden, the driver of the engine, a storm of questions. Later Reden let the boy shovel coal into the fire-box, operate the machine and assist with its service and repair. In this way, Ford became completely familiar with the design and functioning of the only self-propelled road vehicle to be seen on the farms of the Midwest in the years following the Civil War.

At the end of July, on his birthday, he received his first watch.

Using the clumsy tools at hand, he several times dismantled the watch completely, studied parts, and put it back together with satisfactory results. Within a year, he was repairing other watches. Later he worked for a Detroit jeweler as a watch repairman.

His watch repairing and work with the steam engine led directly to his getting the opportunity to repair other machines in the Dearborn community. His father was anxious to involve his son in work of the farm, expecting that he would take up farming. Henry would always prefer any work that involved use of machines, a fact that led to friction between them.

When Henry was nineteen, he decided to go to Detroit and work. He held several jobs and, for a time, attended a business school. He got a job with the Westinghouse Company, the firm that made many of the steam engines of the type Henry had learned to operate in his home community. He had become so expert at handling and servicing the big steamer engines that Westinghouse hired him as their southern Michigan troubleshooter. He checked out new machines and repaired older ones. The Eagle Iron Works of Detroit, distributors of the Otto gas engine, engaged young Ford to service some of their engines in the same area. He moved back to his farm home, and traveled from there as his services were needed. Ford could now repair almost any machine from a watch to a thresher.

Early in 1885, Henry Ford, at a party in Greenfield Township to the north of the Ford community, met eighteen old Clara Bryant, a girl whose family farmed in northern Greenfield Township. She was the eldest of ten children, capable, charming and vivacious. She, too, had a good rural school education. A year after meeting, the young couple made plans to marry as soon as they could manage, financially.

Henry's father, still seeking an opportunity to get his son into farming, offered a plan by which his son could be in a financial position to marry reasonably soon. A mile to the east, William Ford had an 80-acre tract of virgin timber, one of the few stands of virgin timber in this part of Michigan. There would be good money from the lumber, and, once the land was cleared, there would be a farm large enough to support a family. William offered to give Henry forty acres and allow him as much time as was needed to buy the remaining forty acres. Henry accepted the offer, although he probably did not intend to farm permanently. The offer had two aspects that appealed to him. It provided a chance for him and Clara Bryant to make definite plans to be married, and the timber could be removed with machinery. Henry modified a Westinghouse steam engine to pull stumps, a job that ordinarily required one or more teams of horses and several men. The same machine could furnish power for sawing up the lumber.

Henry Ford and Clara Bryant were married on her twenty-first birthday, April 11, 1888, in the Bryant farm home. The young couple moved into an old house on the Henry Ford farm where the removal of timber and stumps was well started. In the year that followed, Henry built his bride a new house, using the lumber sawed from timber on the farm. It was a comfortable, square, story-and-a-half frame house with an attached workshop for Henry.

The farm and the new home of Henry and Clara were located at the intersection of Ford Road and Southfield Road. A good deal of the farm today is taken up with the big cloverleaf at the intersection of Ford and Southfield Roads, both now grown to expressways. The village of Dearborn has grown to embrace the entire area. Directly across the intersection is the headquarters of the Ford Motor Company, whose property extends south along the west side of Southfield Road for several miles, with the proving grounds and the Henry Ford Museum and Greenfield Village at the southernmost point. Two miles to the southeast of the land where Henry and Clara farmed is the Ford Motor Company's River Rouge complex that each day receives thousands of tons of iron ore and sends out trainloads of new motorcars.

The marriage to Clara Bryant proved to be a major factor in Henry Ford's later achievement. They were a devoted couple, who enjoyed their home life as well as travel to the ends of the earth. Clara Bryant Ford was also her husband's business partner. She followed and understood the vast developments with which they were involved.

Clara Bryant Ford was the one person who could change Henry Ford's mind (once he had set a course) and leave no scars. Fifty-three years after their marriage, Ford left his office at 7 o'clock one evening, vowing to his closest associates, including his son, Edsel, that he would never give the union a closed shop at Ford Motor Company. The Ford plants had been strikebound for weeks. There had been bloodshed, and more was inevitable. He went home and talked with Clara, and two hours later called the union and agreed to the terms that would end the strike and avert further violence. Ford Motor Company executives were astounded when they heard the news of the break on the radio the next morning. Henry Ford's only explanation, given sometime later, was, "Never underestimate the power of a woman."

Charles L. Sorensen, who was more closely associated with Henry Ford over a longer period of time than anyone, has explained Clara Bryant Ford's role in Ford's life. He said, "From the earliest days on, I saw the Henry Fords often . . . Henry and Clara Ford were as closeknit and devoted a married couple as I have ever seen. She was ever loyal and ambitious for her husband . . . always cheerful and bright, and gave him the encouragement he needed. All her married life she was Henry Ford's balance wheel. When he listened to no one else, he listened to her. He relied on her judgment. She watched his health carefully, was always convinced that he worked too hard and occasionally was able to get him away for a rest."

Henry Ford tried farming the land as he cleared away the virgin timber. Surprisingly (for Ford kept records of everything), there was no report on just how well the crops turned out, but the foremost of his many biographers, Allan Nevins, concluded that the farming went well and added substantially to the income from the lumber being harvested. But Henry Ford didn't like farming any more this time than he had earlier on his father's place. In late 1891, when all the timber had been cut, Henry and Clara left the country and went to Detroit, but continued to own the farm. Henry became an engineer with the Edison Company. A year later, they bought a house at 58 Bagley Avenue in Detroit, the house in which their son, Edsel, was born November 6th, 1893.

Just before leaving his farm in 1891, Henry Ford became specific for the first time about building a horseless carriage. He had many times talked to Clara about his belief that a self-propelled road vehicle could be built which would not only replace the service of the horse, but which could be greatly superior. He had been convinced of this since the time when, as a boy, with his father, he met the steam engine coming down the road. He had, also, expressed the belief that he could one day build such a machine.

But when he brought the matter up in the fall before they moved to Detroit, his attitude had advanced another step. He said that he now knew how to do it, and, if he "had a piece of paper," he could explain it. Clara got him the paper and he sketched his thoughts about a horseless carriage. He told her, at the time, that he needed to know more about electricity. This may have been a major reason for him going to the Edison company as an engineer.

There is nothing in the fall of 1891 to indicate that Ford knew of work being done on a horseless carriage by anyone, either in Europe or the United States. The Duryea Brothers had not advanced beyond the thinking stage, and would not attempt a public demonstration of their internal combustion motorcar for two years. Ramson Olds had already built steam-powered motorcars and had completed the one that soon would be shipped to the Times Company in Bombay, India. Had Olds or Ford met before this time, certainly one or the other would have, at some time, mentioned it. Ford had not met Charles King or David Buick in Detroit. They would be his contemporaries, along with Olds, in building the first horseless carriages in the city. Elwood Haynes in Kokomo, Indiana, already was beginning to think seriously about a self-propelled vehicle, as was Alexander Winton in Cleveland, but neither had plans much more definite than those Ford sketched for his wife in the kitchen of their farm home. There is no indication that Ford was aware of the work going on in Europe. What he sketched for his wife, in the fall of 1891, represented his own thinking, exclusively. He was beginning to struggle with the same problem that concerned Olds, Duryea, Haynes, Winton and others at this time—how to adapt the large stationary engines with which they were all familiar, and develop a small engine with enough power to move a buggy without a horse.

By Christmas Eve of 1893, with six-weeks-old Edsel asleep in the next room and Clara rushing her preparations for Christmas dinner, Henry Ford came home and demanded that his wife stop everything. He needed her help in demonstrating the first, small internal combustion engine he had ever built. With Clara administering the gasoline a drop at a time, and with electricity from the electric light over the kitchen sink, where the historic experiment was performed, the first Ford engine worked. It was an extremely simple affair and can be seen in the Henry Ford Museum attached to the same kitchen sink. From studying it, it is certain that Ford had still not learned of anything being done in Europe, in Massachusetts or elsewhere. If so, he certainly would have incorporated some of the advancements already worked out in Europe, or by Frank Duryea, who by this time, had already driven his first horseless carriage down the streets of Springfield, Massachusetts, and was at work on his second vehicle that would be put in service within the month.

Two important events took place in 1896. In August, Ford was sent to a convention of the Edison companies held in the Oriental Hotel in Brooklyn. Here he met Charles P. Steinmetz, Samuel Insull and Thomas A. Edison. At a small dinner meeting, the evening of August 12th, Edison learned of Ford's work with a self-propelled vehicle. He asked Ford to be seated next to him so that, despite his hearing deficiency, he could still follow Ford's conversation. Edison showed great interest in Ford's work. The conversation (that may have been Edison's first penetrating discussion of the self-propelled road vehicle) lasted much of the evening. Ford reported that, earlier in the summer, he had road-tested, in Detroit, his first horseless carriage. Edison asked about the power unit. This was a touchy question by the father of modern electricity. Ford explained why he was not using Edison's power source or steam.

Edison seemed pleased. Apparently he had given the matter of motorcar propulsion some thought, and Ford's conclusions paralleled his own. At the close of the discussion, the foremost inventor of his time gave Henry Ford his complete blessing, saying, "Young man, (Ford was thirty-three) that's the thing; you have it. Keep at it. Electric cars must keep near to power stations. The storage battery is too heavy. Steam cars won't do, either, for they have to carry a boiler and fire. Your car is self-contained—it carries its own power plant—no fire, no boiler, no smoke, no steam. You have the thing. Keep at it."

The meeting with Edison gave Ford a new motivation that greatly intensified his interest in his work with the horseless buggy. To have the foremost inventor America had yet produced give him not only his blessing but a directive to continue was a powerful experience. It is not surprising that it constituted a turning point in Ford's career with self-propelled vehicles. He returned home, soon began his second car. Before long he was thinking of making cars a full-time occupation, rather than something which would be done on a part-time basis.

Nor was the meeting with Edison any flash-in-the-pan affair. Even during the remainder of the convention in Brooklyn, Edison and Ford continued to converse. Ford had bought his first camera to use on the trip, and he took a number of pictures of the "Wizard of Menlo Park" which are in the Ford Museum. The meeting ripened into a friendship that ultimately meant a great deal to both men and lasted until Edison died in 1931, having lived to see Henry Ford become perhaps the only living American to gain a worldwide fame that equalled his own. The department in the Henry Ford Museum at Greenfield Village devoted to Edison's work is the outgrowth of their dinner together that evening in Brooklyn.

With the exciting developments that came later, it is easier to put the triumph of Ford's first self-propelled vehicle into perspective. He drove his quadricycle (as he properly called the first Henry Ford built motorcar) for the first time on the streets of Detroit just two months and a week before he met Edison. The date was June 4th, 1896. The quadricycle revealed how far he had advanced from Christmas Eve, 1893, when he hooked up his first motor on the kitchen sink. The engine, well-machined and plainly showing Ford's artistry as a mechanic, was mounted in a neatly arranged compartment at the rear, which extended forward under the driver's seat. Otherwise, the vehicle was mostly bicycle. Although it regularly seated but one person, Clara (whatever may have been her emotions in the matter) managed to ride with her husband and keep young Edsel in her lap on a trip into the country outside Detroit. The car performed well.

Two features about the little car were significant. The engine and many of the other parts of the car were distinctly Henry Ford's own. By this time, he had seen and followed closely the development of the horseless carriage built by his friend, Charles King. King became the first to drive a self-propelled vehicle on the streets of Detroit. King drove his car in March of 1896, about ten weeks earlier than Ford's debut. This was the same King who had ridden as the official observer with a Benz car in the Chicago race on Thanksgiving Day, 1895.

Ford's quadricycle was an entirely different kind of vehicle from King's. Ford had his own ideas about building cars, from the very first constructed in the barn behind his home at 58 Bagley Avenue to the "Model-T." At the time he built his quadricycle, there were much more advanced cars and Ford knew it. But—he went right ahead and built his own car in his own way. It would always be so.

The quadricycle's three outstanding characteristics were the dependability of its motor, the simplicity of operation and the ease with which it could be repaired and maintained. He knew from his days on the farm that machines that didn't work were worthless. He would build the machines that would work, even though not the fanciest or prettiest.

The first little Ford-built car provided ample proof of these performance features. In the fall of 1896, at about the time Ford decided to build a second car, he sold the quadricycle to "Chappie" Annesley who used it for several months without trouble. Then, Annesley sold it to A. W. Hall, a bicycle dealer, who used it for two years as an errand car and conversation piece for his business, after which he sold it to a third owner. Although there were no mechanics in Detroit, other than Ford and King, who had experience in adjusting and repairing a self-propelled vehicle, not one of the three owners had to bring the machine back to the man who built it. Ford actually never rode in the car again until years later when he bought it for the Henry Ford Museum. At the time Hall sold the little car, he wrote Ford a letter that must have meant almost as much to him as the visit with Edison. Hall said:

'You will be surprised when I tell you that the little carriage is still doing its usual duty. I disposed of it this spring and the little rig was still in fair shape after all the banging around that it had and I guess you know that was considerable. I ran it almost two years ... about the only trouble I had was that one tire (failed) and the springs on the sparkers worked loose ... I put on a binding bolt (on them) and after that I never had any trouble ... I think if you have made the one (car) you told me about last summer a year ago it ought to be a corker. You know I have the Horseless Carriage fever and consequently if you are still in it I would like to have you call around to the store and see me ... I want to get into the business with some responsible concerne that is going into this line for it is the coming thing ... I trust I will see you (soon). I am always in of an evening so call around. Until then I remain
Yours sincerely,
A. H. HALL

The Hall letter contained the blueprint of the future of Henry Ford. He, too, had the job of getting with "some responsible concerne." The letter contained the seed of a great, nationwide dealer organization. Hundreds of dealers contacted Ford seeking a dealership after they experienced, as had Hall, the dependability of the Ford-built motor, the simplicity of operation and the ease of making repairs. A generation of Americans paid Henry Ford his greatest tribute when, in unison and millions-strong, they said, "With a piece of baling wire and a pair of pliers you can drive a Ford around the world."

The matter of finding the right concern took Ford years. Twice he brought about the organization of companies and twice they failed, but each time he kept on building more cars. Finally, in 1901, he built a racer that became the first self-propelled vehicle in the United States to travel a mile a minute. It was so powerful that Ford, a racing driver, would not attempt to run it, but the famed Barney Oldfield took over the Ford "999" and kept lowering the record until Ford's racer traveled a mile in only thirty-eight seconds.

Undismayed by his failures, Ford kept on doing things the way he wanted to do them. Although his wife never once mentioned it, this must have been the most trying time of her life. Henry Ford's father said what Clara probably often thought, when he remarked to a neighbor, "John and William (younger Ford sons) are alright, but Henry worries me. He doesn't seem to settle down, and I don't know what's going to become of him."

Once the Ford Motor Company was organized, Clara did not have to wonder again. He made his contribution, and his cars changed the way people lived in the United States and did it in ten tumultuous years, from 1906 until 1916. These were the years when, with the remarkable men he drew around him, he developed the "Model-T," broke the Selden monopoly on the motorcar and built a manufacturing empire such as the world had never seen. His industrial complex could produce the parts, and the world's first moving assembly line could assemble those parts into 10,000 cars a day. The cars sold at constantly lower prices so that, "our men who work in the plant can afford to own one."

None of the frictions and weird happenings that would surround Ford later in his old age and most famous years occurred during this "Golden Age" of Henry Ford. This was the period during which Ford's genius broke through the bonds of time and space which had always held man in a state of relative immobility.

Part Two

The
Ford-Durant
Era

10

"Dead or Dead Broke"

The "Horseless Carriage" era came to an end in 1906, the year the United States took over world leadership in the manufacturing of self-propelled road vehicles. The Oldsmobile, Cadillac and Buick plants set records that year and total motorcar production in this country increased by 25 per cent with the construction of 32,200 vehicles. France had been the previous world leader.

Despite the depression, motorcar production in the United States increased another 25 percent in 1907 but, for the first time, the horseless carriage models were not the pacesetters. The Olds Motor Works cut back its Curved Dash Oldsmobile production in 1907. Cadillac had begun producing larger and more powerful cars as early as 1905. Buick introduced its first four-cylinder motorcars in 1907. In 1906 and 1907, the first important production began at the Ford Motor Company in Detroit.

The "Horseless Carriage" era had lasted a decade, during the first half of which vehicles powered by steam engines or electric batteries were popular; but by the end of the second half, the internal combustion engine had moved ahead of steam and electricity. Electric cars were produced for town use in considerable numbers for another ten years, and the manufacture of steam cars continued to a degree even after World War I. But, by 1925, all production of electric and steam motorcars had ended in the United States. The horseless carriage power issue had been settled in favor of the gasoline engine.

When the horseless carriage decade began, motorcar production was heavily concentrated in southern New England with Hartford, Connecticut, apparently destined to become the nation's motor city. But, by the end of the decade, the star of the motorcar was fixed over a small tip of southeastern Michigan. The Flint-Lansing-Detroit triangle produced more than 50 percent of the nation's automobiles in 1906.

The first solid indication of the permanent pattern of the automobile industry in the United States had appeared. Some 300 makes of motorcars were being sold to the public as the horseless carriage era ended, but fewer than 25 were emerging from the pack in terms of craftsmanship, financial resources and marketing. The leading producers at the end of this first era were Oldsmobile and Reo in Lansing, Cadillac and Ford in Detroit and Buick in Flint, all located in southeastern Michigan.

The men who had brought the motorcar into being during these pioneering ten years were Frank and Charles Duryea, Massachusetts; Colonel Albert A. Pope, Connecticut; Alexander Winton, Ohio; Elwood G. Haynes, Indiana; Thomas B. Jeffery, Wisconsin; Ransom E. Olds, Henry Leland, Henry B. Joy and William C. Durant, Michigan. On the basis of what Henry Ford and his companies had accomplished by 1906, this automotive pioneer had broken through but had not yet attained a position of leadership. Yet he became the dominant figure of the motorcar business before World War I.

The unprecedented success of Henry Ford (which began in the summer of 1903), after ten years of work and the failure of his first two firms, came as a result of several favorable factors, many beyond Ford's control. Even failures contributed to Ford's achievement by providing the fortunate timing for launching his third company. His Detroit Automobile Company, organized in 1899, had engaged Ford's attention for nearly three years before it had gone out of business. The second firm, the Henry Ford Company, had existed during the last days of 1901 and the early months of 1902.

In the second half of 1903, the Ford struck the market at the most favorable time. The sales of motorcars in the United States had approximately doubled during the first twelve months that the new Ford car was on the market. Most of this demand had been developed by Oldsmobile and Cadillac, particularly by the Oldsmobile.

William C. Durant founded General Motors in 1908 and introduced all of the following cars of today in this order: Buick, Oldsmobile, Cadillac, Oakland-Pontiac and Chevrolet. He was the first to develop a firm producing a full line of cars. He planned today's General Motors Building, and selected the proposed famous "bow-tie" trademark for Chevrolet.

177

By the time the first Ford car was sold in July of 1903, the Olds Motor Works had produced and shipped nearly 3,000 Curved Dash Oldsmobiles that year, and would carry production for the entire year to more than 4,000 cars.

Henry Ford and his associates in the new Ford Motor Company were aware of the Oldsmobile achievements. They understood the importance of taking full advantage of everything that Ransom E. Olds had accomplished. And, not to be outdone by "Oldsmobile," the men at Ford named their first car the "Fordmobile."

It would be difficult to overestimate the degree to which the Oldsmobile had opened the way for the new Ford. The Olds Motor Works had invested $150,000 to reach car production and had quickly increased the investment to $300,000. The Flint Wagon Works had put up $75,000 to get the first Buick produced in Flint, but the Buick Motor Company had not achieved stable production until William C. Durant brought in investors who supplied $500,000. The Ford Motor Company got into production with a cash investment of $28,500!

Advantage was stacked on advantage to get the Ford Motor Company off to its start. Even though the demand for motorcars was strong, on the increase, none of the scores of other new car companies formed during this period was in a position to produce enough cars to take advantage of market conditions.

Fords were made and sold so quickly that, within the first year, it was possible to pay out dividends equal to 100 percent of the invested capital. Some shareholders who had signed notes for their stock actually paid off such notes with dividend money received from the company, investing nothing but their faith and their signature for the privilege of becoming rich.

The Ford legacy from Ransom E. Olds and Henry Leland was richly rewarding. Ford had studied the success of the Oldsmobile. He had spent hours in the Olds Motor Works factory in Detroit. Firsthand, he had seen the success achieved by making a single model of a lightweight and inexpensive motorcar. He had a keen understanding of the precision production procedures introduced into motorcar manufacture by Henry Leland at Leland & Faulconer and, later, at the Cadillac Motor Company.

An incident which occurred at the first Detroit Automobile and Outdoor Show held in February, 1902, revealed how fully aware Henry Ford was of the value of precision as practiced at Leland & Faulconer. Two Curved Dash Oldsmobiles were on display at the show. At intervals, their motors were allowed to run at idling speeds for long periods so the spectators could see the engines in action. It was Henry Ford who pointed out to an interested visitor that the Oldsmobile motors had been produced in different factories. The motor in one car had been produced at the Olds Motor Works, while the motor in the other had been produced by Leland & Faulconer. The Leland & Faulconer engine was so much more efficient, because of the high degree of precision built into the power unit, that it was necessary to brake it in order to get the two motors to idle at the same rate.

But, none of the great advantages Ford fell heir to detract from his own abilities or contributions; they serve, only, to underline the man's remarkable power of observation and ability to apply what he had learned. Henry Ford eventually got a third chance after his first two business opportunities ended in failure. For tenacity, at least, Ford should get full credit.

A shrewd judge of human relations, Ford knew that he must have some special means of attracting public attention. He turned to the development of a racing car. He was encouraged by William H. Murphy, who personally provided funds for materials and parts.

Alexander Winton had become the racing champion of the United States. He had built cars and driven them to victory in both this country and in Europe. He had lowered the mile speed record to one minute, fourteen and a half seconds.

Ford was greatly aided by Oliver E. Barthel, a young man of twenty-four, who had worked with Charles B. King to develop the first self-propelled road vehicle built in Detroit. They constructed a racing car with a big, two-cylinder horizontal motor. Rated at twenty-six horsepower, it was not as powerful as the machines built by Winton and other track aces, but it was, by far, the most powerful engine Ford had built for a motorcar of any kind. The motor had 7-inch pistons. Ford and Barthel tested the machine late in the summer and found that it could, under favorable conditions, reach a speed of about 70 miles an hour.

The first opportunity to meet Winton came October 10th, 1901, at the biggest racing event ever held in Detroit up to that time. The parade of steam, electric and gasoline cars (more than 100 vehicles) moved through the city on the way to the race track. The assault on the mile record was scheduled as a part of the 25-mile race, the finale of the afternoon's program. Because the earlier races took so long, the major event was shortened to 5 miles. There were three entries—Henry Ford, Alexander Winton and W. N. Murray. Tom Cooper, the cycle champion, rode two laps around the track with Ford, in advance of the race, offering suggestions.

Murray's car developed engine trouble as they lined up for the start and had to be withdrawn. Ford's mechanic, Ed Huff, who had begun working at Edison with him nine years before, rode with him during the race and leaned out on the curves to help keep the machine on its wheels. Both cars got off to a fast start, although Winton's ability as a racing driver gave him an advantage. He got the inside position and Ford lacked the power to pass on the outside. After 3 of the 5 miles had been run, Winton was a third of a mile ahead. The huge Detroit crowd, anxious to have the hometown man win, urged Ford on. He did gain on Winton but not enough to win. After the sixth lap the Winton began to overheat and lost speed. Accompanied by thunderous cheers, Ford passed Winton on the eighth lap and went on to win the race and the $1,000 prize.

The big race was historic in a number of respects. Clara Ford wrote of her husband's victory to her brother, Milton: "I wish you could have seen him. Also have heard the cheering when he passed Winton. The people went wild. One man threw his hat up and when it came down he stamped on it, he was so excited. Another man had to hit his wife on the head to keep her from going off the handle. She stood up in her seat and screamed, 'I'd bet fifty dollars on Ford if I had it.' "

Ford enjoyed the thrill, too, and the $1,000 prize was more than welcome. But the race ended his interest in driving racing cars. He realized Winton's great advantage as a driver and told reporters, "Put Winton in my car and it will beat anything in this country." He announced that he would not race in competition again. He never did. Several times he drove his racing cars against time, but he did not, again, engage in competitive racing.

The race was a great turning point. Even though it was the fall of 1901, a hundred cars had paraded the streets of Detroit, streets that had never felt the weight of even one car only five years before. At the racetrack, which had been developed to race horses, only a few of those animals were to be seen. As a preliminary attraction, two of the country's greatest cyclists, Tom Cooper and Barney Oldfield, had run a motor-tandem race against time, but the large crowd that had come to see motorcar racing was bored with the performance. Cooper was so shaken by the unfavorable reception that he retired from cycling competition.

The race pointed up the transition within the new realm of the motorcar. The initial race of the day was a 5-mile event for steam cars. R. H. White of Cleveland won with his best mile being clocked at 1:52. The second event featured electric cars with the best mile taking more than four minutes. Ford's time in the main event for the best gasoline-powered vehicle was 1:20.

After the racing victory, Tom Cooper met with Ford and together they planned to build a racing vehicle that could run 100 miles an hour. It was obvious that the long-sought goal of driving 60 miles an hour was close at hand. With Cooper providing financial support, Ford began designing the car. He planned and built two, identical machines, one for himself and one for Cooper. Eventually they became known as the "999" and the "Arrow."

Ford's triumph in building the racer and winning the big race against Winton quickly rekindled interest of the stockholders of Ford's Detroit Automobile Company. Founded nearly three years before, nothing had been produced for the market. The firm had not lost a great deal of money, but inactivity had amounted to a slow death. However, William H. Murphy and most of the other backers had witnessed the racing victory. Immediately, they proposed closing out the records of the old company and organizing a new firm to be known as the "Henry Ford Company." The new company name indicated their interest in continuing their association with the thirty-eight-year-old Ford.

The directors also showed their interest in other ways. The new firm was capitalized at $60,000 with $30,500 supplied in cash. Of the remaining $29,500 stock, $10,000 was given to Henry Ford so that he controlled a one-sixth interest in the firm. The stock was in addition to his salary as chief engineer. This was much more favorable for Ford than the arrangement with the first firm had been.

Organizing the new firm began almost as soon as the race was over. The second week in November, Ford went to New York to study the 88 cars exhibited at the city's second automobile show. The formation of the Henry Ford Company was announced in the Detroit newspapers on November 20th, just after Ford returned. Headquarters were established at 1343 Cass Avenue in Detroit.

Attending the New York Automobile Show had been a stimulating experience for Ford. He had become acquainted with C. H. Sieberling of Goodyear Tire and Rubber Company, Alfred P. Sloan and many others. Later a key figure in the motorcar industry, Sloan was then president of the Hyatt Roller Bearing Company of Harrison, New Jersey. The firm had a booth at the New York Show. Peter S. Steenstrup, Hyatt sales manager, had already met Ford on his calls in Detroit. He saw Ford walking past the Hyatt booth. Steenstrup called to him, "Come in. Where could you find a better place to rest? Sit down at the railing and see the show from a box-seat." Ford accepted and, in a short while, had his chair propped back with his feet on the front rail, a habit of his when he was at ease.

Despite the enthusiasm which accompanied the organizing of the Henry Ford Company in November, within sixty days it was clear to everyone, that nothing was going to come of the effort. Murphy and his associates wanted results too soon. Ford continued to work on the big racing cars which both encouraged yet distressed the stockholders. Most of them had been in the old Detroit Automobile Company and seen Ford exhaust the firm's working funds without producing a motorcar for the market. They began to believe, with some foreboding, that their chief engineer was a brilliant mechanic who would never buckle down and develop a car for public consumption.

February, 1901, became a period when, to the directors of the Henry Ford Company, the chief engineer *had* to show evidence of getting his car ready to produce for the spring market or face up to some changes. Nothing happened to impress the stockholders during that critical month. The showdown came in the first days of March. The job of handling the confrontation fell largely to Murphy. He used a two-pronged strategy. He talked with Ford but, fearing he might quit, kept the discussion general, mostly about the need to get on more rapidly. At the same time he talked bluntly to Barthel, the assistant to the chief engineer. He told Barthel that work on the big racer had to stop.

"He told me not to do it (work on the racer)," Barthel reported to Ford, "and that he would fire me if I did. If I valued my job, Murphy said I'd better not do any work on it."

Matters came to a head, quickly. On March 10th, an understanding was reached under which Henry Ford resigned as engineer, left the firm entirely, received $900 for his sixth interest in the firm and received the drawings for the big racers. The organization would have to find a new name to replace the "Henry Ford Company" before marketing a car.

The debacle logically should have ended the motorcar career of Henry Ford once and for all, and deserves examination as a means of understanding events that were to follow. Murphy and his associates were understandably impatient. They knew the opportunity was there. Roy Chapin, had, about a hundred days earlier, driven the horseless carriage Oldsmobile all the way from Detroit to New York. Ransom E. Olds had taken enough orders to make the Olds Motor Works successful overnight. It was even an open question whether Olds could produce enough cars to fill his orders in view of the fact that the new Oldsmobile factory had burned and the company was relocating in Lansing. Murphy, and the other directors, saw a fortune slipping away because their chief engineer simply would not settle down and build a car. They thought he could even use the Curved Dash Oldsmobile as a prototype, improving it enough to make the resulting car their own.

What the directors of the Henry Ford Company could not understand was that their chief engineer was having great difficulty designing a gasoline engine that was superior, or even as good, as the one already in use in the Oldsmobile. He faced the problem—the same one that Frank Duryea and Ransom E. Olds had faced—of reducing the big gasoline engine that he knew so well to a small motor that could fit into a car and still represent an improvement.

He could build a large motor such as he had developed for his racing car. He had used the two-cylinder opposed style of motor, similar to that developed by Frank Duryea, but he had not had time enough to reduce the motor to the size required. Later, he would use this type of motor in the first Ford cars to go into production. The simple fact was that Ford had started late and was not ready with a motor.

The cause for the failure certainly was not due to inattention. Ford had worked long and hard. Except for the motor, he had practically completed the design of the entire car at the time he left the Henry Ford Company. He had completed a strong chassis, an advanced type of power linkage and a good body.

This was the car Henry Leland found when he was called in, the following August, to make an inventory for liquidation purposes. He persuaded the directors to continue in business and to use the Leland & Faulconer motor. The production of the Cadillac horseless carriage began two months later. The bodies and external appearance of the Ford and Cadillac in 1902 were almost identical.

If the failure of his second company distressed Ford he failed to show it. He blamed Murphy and the other directors, stating they were more interested in making money than a good car. Later, he explained, "In March, 1902, I resigned, determined never again to put myself under orders." There was no suggestion at any time that he had made mistakes. The episode seemed to call forth in him a new confidence and determination to succeed. Most significant was the fact that he was able, in this difficult period, to retain the loyalties of the several young men who were working with him.

He moved his equipment to Barton Peck's small machine shop on Park Place, a rather dreary isolated area. The unheated building had been at one time a barn, no doubt. The rent was modest and Peck owned tools that would be useful in his work. Ford could be found at the shop in overalls most of the day and night. In the evenings, and on Sundays, he was joined by Oliver Barthel, Ed Huff, and a young newcomer, C. Harold Wills. Later, Barthel and Huff quit their jobs and devoted full time to working with Ford.

The weather was cold in March and April. Wills and others later explained how they worked into the nights, their hands and fingers numb with cold. To overcome the cold, Ford, Wills and the others would don boxing gloves and stage an exhibition until circulation had been restored. Work on the big racers progressed rapidly during the spring.

During most of 1902, Ford thought the quickest way to develop important income was to build racing cars capable of establishing new speed records. He may have even thought of racing cars as a means of getting working capital with which to build a car for the market. Whatever his plans, he did not completely neglect the work on an improved horseless carriage.

It took Ford, Barthel, Huff and Wills six months to build the "999." Toward the end they were joined by John Wandersee and Gus Degener. It was the biggest and heaviest racing car yet built on American soil. The wheel base was 9-feet, 9-inches and the distance between front and rear wheels was 5-feet, 2-inches. The motor had four upright 7-inch cylinders and developed at least 70 horsepower. The huge frame was of wood reinforced with steel. The wheels were 34 inches in diameter in front and 36 inches on the back and were fitted with pneumatic detachable Sieberling tires.

A novel feature of the racer stemmed from Ford's experience in racing. Instead of a steering wheel, there was a large tiller whose bar pointed straight ahead when the wheels were in a straight position. With such a device, the driver could operate the car by touch when the dust and smoke on the track obscured vision.

As the "999" began taking shape, Cooper and Ford discussed who would be the driver. Ford was already on record. He would not race again. Cooper had intended to do the driving, but as the size of the monster machine became more apparent, he became less sure he could handle the assignment.

As early as September 13th, a writer for the *Detroit Journal* saw the "999" and reported that it could develop 100 horsepower. Four days later Ford test-drove the machine. "The roar of those cylinders alone was enough to half kill a man," he reported, after he drove the racer a mile in 1:08 without pushing it. With only goggles to protect his eyes, Ford was the first to experience the sensations of the sheets of flame pouring from each of the four exhausts and of the intolerable noise from the roadway and the open crankshaft whirling at 1,500 revolutions a minute.

The next day the *Journal* reported, "But the oily appearance of the fence is nothing to the look of Chauffeur Henry Ford, after he had made a few dashes around the track yesterday, in his new speed machine which he and Tom Cooper built. Mr. Ford was a daub of oil from head to foot. His collar was yellow, his tie looked as though it had been cooked in lard, his shirt and clothes were splattered and smirched, while his face looked like a machinist's after 24 hours at his bench." The paper added, "It is a low, rakish-looking craft, and makes more noise than a freight train."

Detroit's big race of the year was scheduled for October 25th. Cooper proposed that they see if they could get Barney Oldfield, Cooper's former cycling antagonist, to drive the "999." They reached Oldfield by telegram in Salt Lake City. Oldfield replied that he had never driven a motorcar, but that he was willing to try it. Meanwhile Ed Huff took the "999" to a race in Ohio for its shakedown. The racer was shipped back by train the middle of October, arriving at about the same time Oldfield reached Detroit.

Oldfield arrived a few days early so that he could learn to drive a motorcar and learn something about piloting the "999" around a race track. Since the big race was to be run on the Grosse Pointe track, north of the city, Huff and Oldfield had the "999" towed by a team of horses through Detroit. Even at idling speeds, the big car was so loud that it would cause considerable disturbance. Oldfield was so excited at the prospect of driving the monster that, as soon as they arrived at the track, he said to Huff, "Let me try it now."

Huff, (who had driven the machine in Ohio) tutored Oldfield for several days at the Grosse Pointe track, and was able to report that Oldfield was soon getting more speed out of the "999" than he or Cooper had been able to command.

October 25th was a beautiful Indian summer day for the Manufacturers' Challenge Cup races. The grand finale was a 5-mile race for which there were five entries, two of the cars, Wintons—one being driven by Winton himself and the other by his sales manager, H. K. Shanks. There were 10,000 spectators in the stands for the maiden race of the "999."

Oldfield and Huff arrived at the track well ahead of race time to make last-minute preparations. They took several turns around the track, Huff riding along to check Oldfield out. When they first brought the car in, Ford was waiting for them. He was concerned about Oldfield's safety and, at one point, implored the speedster not to start. It was a moment of high drama. Ford's future was tied up in the "999"—this was the big race of the year! Winton had come to avenge himself for the loss the year before. Ford was asking Oldfield not to put the racer on the track and Oldfield understood what Ford was saying and why he was saying it. Nobody knew at this moment whether any man could tame the big racer in the heat of open track competition; Ford feared he had built a machine of murder. Still Oldfield went methodically about his preparations and, finally, turning to Ford, he said:

"Well, this chariot may kill me, but they'll say afterward that I was going like hell when it took me over the bank." Turning to Huff, Oldfield shrugged, "I may as well be dead as dead broke."

All five cars lined up at the starting line and got off without incident. Winton's superior ability as a racing driver gave him an early lead, but the others closed the gap, the lead changing hands several times. Before long, Oldfield, gaining confidence in the machine and in his ability to manage it, threw caution to the winds and began using a full throttle, even on the curves. By the middle of the race Oldfield had pulled ahead by a narrow margin, but Winton remained close. Other contestants fell behind. With but little more than a mile to go, the race was clearly between Oldfield and Winton.

Again, mechanical failure removed Winton from the contest. Even then, Oldfield, seeking to set a new record, ran the race out at full power, although he had won. The crowd broke down the board fence and rushed out onto the track. They lifted the exhausted Oldfield on their shoulders and carried him to the clubhouse. From that day on, and for years to come, the greatest commendation any racing driver in the world could receive was to have it said of him, "He beat Barney Oldfield at . . ."

Despite the failure of his second company, Henry Ford advanced rapidly during 1902. There were several reasons but the greatest was

Henry Ford conceived and checked every detail of the
development of the "Model-T" launched in 1908.
Introduced as a replacement for the "family horse,"
the model remained in production until 1927, and was
greatly responsible for making the United States the first
nation on wheels. Here are Henry and Edsel Ford
beside the first Ford-built vehicle (1896) and
10,000,000th "Model-T" made in 1924.

the assistance provided by his new associate, Childe Harold Wills.

Wills was only twenty-four when he began helping Ford build the "999." He started working evenings, even before the end of the Henry Ford Company. He became more important to Ford's work after the change to the Peck machine shop. The young engineer had a rare combination of talents. Trained by his Welsh father as a machinist, he had already completed a full apprenticeship with the Boyer Machine Company, forerunner of the Burroughs Adding Machine Company. Night school had provided formal training in engineering, chemistry and the then relatively new science of metallurgy.

As hard a worker as Ford, Wills arrived and worked at the Ford shop early in the morning, before going to his regular job. He even returned and worked during the evenings. He might not have been paid, but his work on the "999" earned him a strong foothold in a pacesetting career with the Ford motorcar.

Wills filled a major gap. Ford was never without an adequate motor again after he befriended the young draftsman and engineer. Without any formal training in drawings and blueprints, Ford had to visualize and actually build before he could correct mistakes and press on to improvement. Ford was a "cut and try" inventor. At no time in his life did he develop a set of blueprints. In fact, he read them with difficulty; some of his associates said he could not read them at all.

For the first time, Wills provided Ford with the advantages of an engineering department. The younger man had a unique ability to detect weaknesses in design and correct them on the drawing board. More than that, he could explain the problems to Ford. It was almost inevitable that there would be a great upswing in Ford's engineering work after he acquired the capabilities of Wills.

Ford had a larger role in the matter than may appear. He was quick to sense the vast abilities of Harold Wills when he was an unknown apprentice at the Boyer Company. And he had a remarkable capacity for presenting what he was doing as something so exciting and important that young men quickly developed a desire to join him. He did it again and again.

11

The Chosen Twelve

After Oldfield's triumph with the "999," Ford talked of building more racing cars, especially if Winton expected to build one that might take the Detroit race trophies back to Cleveland. He was even willing to drive racers against time, if need be, but his peak in the world of speed had been reached that afternoon when Oldfield drove Ford's "999" to easy victory. Ford had turned to racing as a means of getting attention from potential backers and from the public. His objectives had been achieved.

Even before the completion of the "999," Ford began talking of building a "family horse." This was a new concept, the first indication of what was to become Ford's unique contribution to the motorcar.

Almost everyone interested in making self-propelled vehicles had hoped to replace horses. Winton, with his powerful engines, focused on displacing horse-drawn vans and wagons in public transport, as well as producing motorcars for the wealthy. Olds and Leland concentrated upon replacing the horse in the carriage trade and in the professions.

It remained for Henry Ford to dare to set up the objective of *universally* replacing the family horse. There were tens of thousands of families able to own a team and carriage, but there were millions of families whose only form of transportation consisted of a family horse.

With his memory of the farm families he knew as a boy, and the laboring families he had come to know in Detroit, Henry Ford now had a roughhewn idea that would revolutionize living standards in the United States. Ford was thinking of a self-propelled vehicle that could be owned by most farm and town families and enable them to get from place to place quickly to enjoy a host of things they had never been able to before.

The horseless carriage, such as the Oldsmobile, was not powerful enough to replace the horse. The larger and more powerful motorcars, such as the Winton, were too expensive for ordinary people to own. In addition, they were unsuited to the dirt streets of most towns and the dirt roads in the country areas.

In Ford's mind a new kind of motorcar took shape. It would be nearly as powerful as the most expensive cars, only a little heavier than the horseless carriage, with wheels sturdy and high enough to move over muddy roads and streets. The car would be big enough so that the whole family could travel together, and it would be simple to operate, easy to repair and inexpensive to drive.

Produced in large numbers, Ford thought in 1902, he could market such a car for about $500, not much more than the cost of a good team of horses, a harness and a buggy. But, Ford's new idea was so far out and so far ahead of the times that most people dismissed him quickly as a crank who might even be a little mentally unbalanced. The idea of a grown man in his prime talking of a motorcar that most families in town and on the farm could own stamped him as a crackpot.

Fortunately, not everyone thought so. One who did not was Alexander Y. Malcomson, Detroit's foremost coal merchant. Born in Scotland, he had arrived in Detroit in 1885 at the age of twenty-one. In 1890, just before Ford went to the Edison Company, he established his coal business. Twelve years later, it had blossomed into an enterprise of many coal yards with two receiving stations directly on the Michigan Central's right-of-way. In addition to coal for home stoves, he also supplied coal for steamships, factories and even railroads in the Detroit area. He had established coal businesses in other towns, some as far away as Ohio, and had acquired his own coal fields in West Virginia.

Malcomson and Ford had been acquainted nearly ten years. One of

Ford's jobs at Edison was to visit Malcomson's headquarters, once or twice every month, and check the quality of the coal the firm was supplying to the Edison company. Even after Ford left the Edison Company, he continued to buy his coal for home use from Malcomson. The two men met from time to time at the Episcopal Church, too, where Malcomson was superintendent of the Sunday School in which Edsel was enrolled. The coal merchant was among those who had attended the race in the fall of 1901 in which Ford had driven his own racer to victory over Winton.

By early summer, after the termination of the Henry Ford Company, Ford began talking to Malcomson about the new type of motorcar he was developing, as a replacement for the family horse. Malcomson was already a motorcar user; he owned a Winton. Malcomson was interested in Ford's proposal and followed the work on the "999" with keen interest. By mid-summer, the two men agreed, in principle, to form a partnership under which Malcomson would provide the funds to complete the development of the new motorcar. As soon as there was a pilot car, they would use it to generate interest among other investor prospects, hoping to realize the money that would enable them to produce the new car for the market.

On August 16th, Malcomson took Ford to the office of his young attorney, John W. Anderson, at the firm of Rackham and Anderson and a partnership agreement was drawn up. In the law office, Ford first discussed the motor he was developing for the new car. It was a two-cylinder opposed type, the kind Ford had built for his racer in which he had defeated Winton the year before. The motor was more powerful than either the single-cylindered power unit in the Oldsmobile or the one that Henry Leland, within a matter of weeks, would present in the Cadillac horseless carriage.

The new Ford-Wills motor was the same type so successfully used by Duryea almost ten years earlier. Notwithstanding, the new Ford motor was the most powerful in Michigan until David Buick and Walter Marr began producing their motor of the same type, with the addition of the valve-in-head feature.

The Ford and Malcomson partnership required that Ford give a half interest in his designs, patents and tools to Malcomson. The coal magnate would provide funds to complete the design and the building of a pilot car. Ford would manage the engineering and manufacturing work and Malcomson would take charge of finance and marketing. At such time as the first car was complete and public interest aroused, the partners would form a new company in which they would, in like shares, hold a 51 percent interest with the remaining 49 percent going to the investing stockholders.

A report persists that, at the time of agreement on the partnership, Malcomson and Ford "sealed" it by shaving off their mustaches. Regardless of the validity of the incident, it is certain that both had worn mustaches for years and neither wore them again.

At the same time, a contract for employment was drawn for Harold Wills. He received $125 a month and began devoting his full time to working with Ford. The other men employed at Ford's Park Place shop were paid to work on the "999" from funds provided under the agreement with Tom Cooper.

In order to keep the venture separate from his numerous other business interests, Malcomson set up a partnership account at a separate bank in the name of James Couzens, his office manager at the coal company. A few days later, Ford met Couzens for the first time. By September, Ford was working with two of the six men who would carry the leading roles in the years of spectacular Ford achievement.

It was the iron will of Couzens (later to become mayor of Detroit and United States senator from Michigan) that would drive the Ford team to success. Born in Canada, the son of Joseph Couzens, a grocery store clerk, who later operated a small soap factory, Couzens early exhibited a restless ambition that all during his brilliant career left him little calm in which to enjoy life. When a hard-working teenager, he once berated his mother for having allowed him to be born in Canada, "I can never become King of England," he told his mother, "but if I had been born in the United States I could be President." He meant it.

Ford's first meeting with Couzens was cordial but nothing more. The Canadian, just thirty years old the day he met Ford, regarded handling the Malcomson-Ford special account as an extra chore, involving something in which he saw little futuer. He, grudgingly, paid the bills under the agreement.

In 1890, when he was 18, and when Henry Ford was still living on the farm, Couzens had gone to work on the Michigan Central as a freight car checker. In this way he had come to the attention of Malcomson who admired the thorough manner in which he checked out the Malcomson coal cars, regardless of the weather or the personal inconvenience. Malcomson hired him. A couple of years later, Couzens had advanced to the position of "Number Two" man in the big coal business.

With the triumph of the "999" the last week in October (coupled, as it was, with the victory over Winton a year before), Henry Ford became a famous name in Detroit. More than Olds and Winton, he was now the man most closely identified with the new motorcar in a city where interest in the horseless carriage was mushrooming. Even Couzens gradually became convinced that Ford and his machines were headed toward an important future. There were many inquiries about the new car that Ford expected to make, including some offers of down payment for an early delivery.

In the wake of the "999" victory, Malcomson thought the time was right to take the next step and organize the stock company. He thought the victory of Ford's racer would provide the proper environment for the sale of stock. In November, the partnership gave way to the Ford & Malcomson Company which provided for a capitalization of $150,000 divided into 150 shares of a thousand dollars each.

Malcomson put more cash into the business, and work on building the pilot car began seriously that month. Wills finished the drawings and by Thanksgiving the first of the new two-cylinder motors was completed. At the same time, work was being done on the frame, transmission, power linkage and wheel attachment. The B. F. Everett Carriage Shop in Detroit had the contract to build the body.

Assembly work was rushed in December and through the holiday period in an effort to have the pilot car ready to exhibit in the winter shows. Wills wrecked the first pilot car, after the first of the year, while driving on Mack Avenue, but Ford had become dissatisfied with the car and no effort was made to repair it. Instead, it was stored under a stairway at the Park Place shop to yield up its parts as they were needed. The second pilot car became the prototype of the first Ford, the "Model-A."

During November, Malcomson, with help from Couzens, launched the program to sell stock that would provide funds to produce the new Ford car. The victory of the "999" was not enough, and the stock solicitation was premature. Without a pilot car most people with investment money looked upon Ford as a racing car specialist, and were wary. The coal business was at its winter season peak, leaving Malcomson little time to give other matters his personal attention. Much of the work of solicitation fell to Couzens who spent day after day following up appointments with Detroit businessmen, appointments made for him by Malcomson. He was received with courtesy and generally aroused considerable interest, but sold no stock.

It was one of the most disheartening jobs the tough and unquench-
able Couzens ever undertook. There was to be a pleasant aftermath,
but that was some years in the future. After the success of the Ford,
Couzens could not appear at a public function in Detroit, without
one or more businessmen remarking, "Jim, you did your best to cut
me in. If I'd only had the sense to put in the money. I could have
done it, too. You only asked me to invest $2,500, or was it $1,000?"

Either amount would have been enough to have made the investor
a millionaire within ten years.

From the first, Ford and Malcomson had planned to contract with
outside firms for the important components of the new car. They
had seen the subcontracting for motors and other major components
save the Olds Motor Works after its fire early in 1901. With the difficulty of selling stock and raising working capital, it became obvious, by December that, if the car could be marketed in 1903,
there would have to be almost complete dependence upon subcon-
tractors—providing they could be found.

The most important thing was to find a firm willing and capable
of building the new motor. The outstanding machine shop in Detroit, besides Leland & Faulconer (already committed to the new
Cadillac), was operated by the Dodge brothers. They were building
transmissions for Oldsmobile and had just been offered a new contract for another year. The Great Northern, with John Maxwell who
had worked both with Haynes and Olds, was also bidding for the
future services of the Dodge Brothers Machine Shop which had recently moved into new quarters at the corner of Monroe and
Hastings.

Malcomson approached the hard-working, fun-loving John Dodge
on the matter. Dodge was thirty-eight years old, a few months
younger than Ford and a few months older than Malcomson. Discussions led to Ford and Wills turning over the blueprints for the
new, two-cylinder motor to the Dodge Brothers. John Dodge, well
acquainted with both the Oldsmobile and Cadillac motors, was immediately impressed.

Soon, for all concerned, the cards were on the table. The Dodges
wanted to get into the new motorcar business in a larger way. The
new Ford car offered them the role they wanted, but Ford & Malcomson were short of money.

Often, during critical discussions, Dodge was on the point of
pulling out and remaining with the Olds Motor Works. It could pay
its bills immediately and its work required almost no additional

John and Horace Dodge made Henry Ford and his car possible. Enticed by the prospect of a 10 percent ownership in the Ford Motor Company, the Dodge brothers gave up a dependable contract to make Oldsmobile transmissions and risked a long gamble with Henry Ford. The Dodges built, except for bodies and wheels, all Ford cars for the first three years and most of the first 500,000 Fords produced, including a third of a million "Model-Ts." In 1914, they introduced the Dodge car.

purchase of new machine tools. Each time that happened, Malcomson would make his proposal more attractive, and John Dodge would agree to go back and talk it over with his brother, Horace, who owned half the business. Finally, Malcomson played his trump—Ford & Malcomson would contract with the Dodge Brothers Machine Shop for all the important components for the new car, including the motor.

As February arrived, discussions were being held almost daily. By now there was a definite proposal. Ford & Malcomson would order 650 packages, or "rigs," as John Dodge called them, each consisting of radiator, motor, transmission, power linkage, axles and chassis, everything but the body and wheels. The Dodge shop would produce the complete rig for $250. From the time they reached an agreement, three months would be required to tool up for the big job and deliveries could then be made, hopefully, at the rate of ten, per day or at least fifty, per week.

The proposal amounted to the largest subcontract then developed in the motorcar business, but the risks were of equal proportion. If all went well, the job would bring the Dodge factory $162,500 in a period of three months with an attractive profit margin. Almost certainly, more contracts would follow. The risk for the Dodges was magnified by the fact that they would have to invest approximately $40,000 in new machines. (Actually, it proved to be $60,000.) If the deal were attempted and failed, it could wipe out the Dodges.

Finally, the matter came to a standstill. The Dodges had not turned the proposition down, but they were unwilling to approve the terms and begin work. No Malcomson & Ford stock was being sold, the chief obstacle being an inability to offer prospective investors a firm production program.

Malcomson got the Dodge talks going again by propounding an extraordinary idea to the Dodge brothers. Malcomson, undoubtedly, discussed this next move with his partner, and Ford must have agreed. Ford and Malcomson proposed setting aside 10 percent of the stock in their new firm for the Dodges who could pay for it with money received under their contract. This meant the Dodges could pay for their stock out of profits from the making of Ford components.

The Dodges were impressed with the new offer. Both John and Horace liked the idea of owning an interest in the Malcomson & Ford company. Nonetheless, they did not make their decision immediately.

By that time, the Dodges had learned about developments at the third New York Automobile Show, particularly the success scored there by Cadillac who had accepted 2,200 orders with down payments. This strongly indicated that the year 1903 would provide a new record in horseless carriage sales.

In mid-February, John Dodge and Alex Malcomson reached an agreement. Malcomson made some additional concessions. The Dodges were to be paid in advance for the first sixty rigs. For the next forty rigs, they would be paid as delivered. After that, they would settle accounts on the first and fifteenth of the month.

Even with Oldsmobile and Cadillac sales reaching record proportions, in the early months, Malcomson and Couzens still could not sell more than a fraction of the shares needed to provide adequate working capital. Orders started coming in when the "Model-A" pilot car was completed. That new development came close to solving the financial situation.

One day in May, Charles Bennett, young president and chief engineer of the Daisy Air Rifle Company of Plymouth, Michigan, came into Detroit to buy a Curved Dash Oldsmobile. Before going to see the Oldsmobile, he stopped to buy a suit. He was talking excitedly about buying his first motorcar, while the suit was being fitted.

Frank Malcomson, Alex's cousin, was just beyond the next fitting curtain. He called out to Bennett, "Pardon me. I couldn't help overhearing your conversation. Have you heard about the Ford car?" Bennett had not. He bought the suit and went to see Ford who gave him a ride in the new "Model-A" pilot car. As they traveled up and down Detroit's Gratiot Avenue, Bennett was so impressed that he agreed to wait for the new Ford. Asked about the price of his new car, Ford replied, "We're going to hold it down to somewhere near the Olds price."

Now it occurred to Malcomson that, if Daisy Air Rifle were to take a substantial part of the unsold stock, Malcomson & Ford's financial problems might be over. He and Couzens talked to Bennett and interested him in their plan by which his company would buy half the stock and Ford & Malcomson would hold the rest. Bennett brought in his partner, Ed Hough, and together they went to the Dodge factory. They decided that the new Ford motor was superior to either the single-cylinder Oldsmobile or Cadillac. Everything was proceeding well until lawyers for the Plymouth company pointed out that the firm's charter forbade such an investment in another company. Bennett was willing to look for a legal loophole, but

Hough ruled against that. Bennett agreed to buy 50 shares for $5,000 and gave his personal note. He paid it off a year later, after his dividends from the Ford Company had equalled the amount of his note.

The net result was that, although a shareholder had been gained, the critical financial crisis remained. Efforts to sell stock were intensified, but with all his business influence and enthusiasm, Malcomson could not find anyone, outside his personal connections in Detroit or elsewhere, willing to back Henry Ford's new car.

Malcomson and Ford were paying the price for Ford's two earlier failures. Only a year before, he had turned his back on a group of investors (some of Detroit's wealthiest citizens) who could have supplied the entire amount of money needed in a few minutes. Some of them had been involved in both of Ford's failures, and the word had been passed around among the men in Detroit with money to invest, so now Malcomson could only get support from those indebted to him in one degree or another.

Malcomson and Couzens managed to sell just enough stock to keep the Dodge agreement intact and the vital preliminary work on car production progressing. By spring, Malcomson decided that a new firm would have to be formed to absorb the functions and assets of both the original Ford-Malcomson partnership and the Ford & Malcomson Company.

On the evening of June 13th, the stockholders assembled at Malcomson's office in the McGraw Building at the intersection of Griswold Street and Lafayette Boulevard. There were only twelve of them, including Henry Ford, Alex Malcomson, and John and Horace Dodge. The other eight were James Couzens, John S. Gray, Albert Strelow, Vernon C. Fry, C. H. Bennett, Horace H. Rackham, John W. Anderson and Charles Woodall. Except for Bennett, the eight shareholders were either relatives or had close business ties with Malcomson.

They agreed to organize the Ford Motor Company. The name is evidence of the excitement the group felt about Ford's new engine—the most powerful horseless carriage engine yet made in Michigan. Malcomson suggested the name.

Deleting his name was an unusual move. It had been the Ford-Malcomson Partnership and the Ford & Malcomson Company. The coal tycoon was not a man to shrink from public acclaim. It is likely that he feared being prominently involved in the highly speculative horseless carriage business and the effect it might have on his already strained credit. It is not inconceivable that the principal reason for

Alex Malcomson, Detroit's leading coal merchant, organized the Ford Motor Company on a shoestring. He brought in all the investors (except Ford, who contributed only his genius), released from his coal business James Couzens to manage the Ford enterprise and got the Dodge brothers to make the first Ford cars. Malcomson differed with Ford over the future of the light, inexpensive car and gave Ford control of the company by selling the Malcomson stock to him for a nominal sum.

forming a new company was to give Malcomson a chance to remove his name from the project.

The shareholders agreed that the Ford Motor Company would be capitalized at $150,000, the same figure at which the Ford & Malcomson Company had been capitalized. There were so few shareholders that only $100,000 of the stock was issued. The remaining $50,000 was to be held as treasury stock.

The sale of 1,000 shares valued at $100 per share was authorized. The division of stock was John S. Gray, 102 shares; John F. Dodge, 50 shares; Horace E. Dodge, 50 shares; Albert Strelow, 50 shares; Vernon C. Fry, 50 shares; C. H. Bennett, 50 shares; Horace H. Rackham, 50 shares; John W. Anderson, 50 shares; Charles J. Woodall, 10 shares and James Couzens, 25 shares. Malcomson and Ford received 255 shares, each. Five days later they turned over to the new company all assets of the Ford-Malcomson Partnership and the Ford & Malcomson Company.

Other important decisions were made that Saturday evening. John S. Gray, the banker, largest cash investor and Malcomson's financial advisor, was named the first president of the Ford Motor Company. Henry Ford was elected vice-president and general manager. Though Malcomson was named treasurer, and Couzens was elected secretary, the books were immediately turned over to James Couzens to handle the work of both secretary and treasurer. Five directors were elected—Henry Ford, Alex Malcomson, John S. Gray, John Dodge and John W. Anderson.

The contributions of Ford and Malcomson were valued at $25,500 each and together they received 51 percent of the stock. The remaining ten shareholders paid in $28,000 in cash and supplied personal notes for $21,000. They received 49 percent of the stock. Except for Ford and the Dodges, none of the stockholders knew anything about a motorcar. Several of them had never owned a car or driven one.

The shareholders of the new Ford Motor Company had three immense assets—the capabilities of Henry Ford, the Dodge Brothers and a tremendous market potential.

They had, in Henry Ford, a rare man in the prime of his life, with an entirely new concept of what the motorcar could accomplish. Ford spelled out his ideas on making and marketing the car to Lawyer Anderson in an effort to convince him he should buy stock. Ford and Anderson had been to the Dodge factory to see the new motor being made. Ford drove Anderson home in the pilot car and explained, "The way to make automobiles is to make one automobile

The Hudson, one of the original cars of the American
Motors Corporation, was introduced in 1909. Produced
for half a century, the car was named for J. L. Hudson,
founder of the Hudson Stores of Detroit. In the front
seat of this 1910 Hudson are President Roy D. Chapin
(right) and Chief Engineer Howard E. Coffin.
Both were former associates of Ransom E. Olds.
They guided the destiny of Hudson for two decades.

like another automobile, to make them all alike, to make them come through the factory just alike; just as one pin is like another pin when it comes from the pin factory, or one match is like another match when it comes from the match factory."

"You need not fear about the market. The people will buy them all right. When you get to making the cars in quantity, you can make them cheaper, and when you make them cheaper you can get more people with enough money to buy them. The market will take care of itself."

The stockholders already had a contract with the Dodge brothers who were immediately capable of producing the car. Because of the daring and determined attitude of the Dodges, they were willing to invest more than all the other shareholders combined. It was the only firm in the city able to back the new car to such an extent.

Finally, the Ford Motor Company shareholders had the great, good fortune to be assembled at a moment when a large number of Americans, particularly doctors, lawyers and salesmen, were ready, able and even hungry to own a motorcar. They were the people most severely handicapped by the limitations of the horse as a means of conveyance.

Although the total invested for launching the Ford car was small, some of the shareholders found it difficult to fulfill their commitments in cash. Disregarding Ford, Malcomson and the two Dodge brothers, only one of the eight remaining shareholders, Banker Gray, paid cash in full. Anderson paid for his stock, in cash, two weeks later. Albert Strelow, the contractor, did not pay anything for a month. Charles J. Woodall, Malcomson's bookkeeper, and C. H. Bennett, the air rifle maker, supplied notes for the entire amount of their stock; Woodall for $1,000 and Bennett for $5,000 (two $2,500 notes to fall due on different dates). Vernon E. Fry, Malcomson's cousin and a variety store manager, paid in $3,000 and gave a note for $2,000. James Couzens paid $1,000 in cash and gave a note for $1,500. Horace H. Rackham paid in $3500 and gave a note for $1,500.

No one found it more difficult to find a way of making an important investment in the new company than Couzens. His total savings consisted of $400. Yet he had grown so sure of the success of the new car that he would, as he told a friend at the time, "Beg, borrow or steal every cent" he could to buy Ford Motor Company stock. Understanding his plight, Malcomson made it possible for him to do extra work at the coal company so he could earn another

Louis Chevrolet,
encouraged by William
C. Durant, began
designing his own car at
the peak of his racing
career. Earlier, Durant
had hired Chevrolet as
one of the big three
—Chevrolet, Bob Burman
and Lewis Strang—for
the Buick racing team.

$500. Also, through further assistance from Malcomson, Couzens was able to borrow $1,500 on signing a personal note at the German-American bank.

Couzens then had $2,400 to invest. He talked to his sister, Rosetta, a school teacher in Detroit, and asked her to invest with him. Her savings, at the time, consisted of a $200 bank account. She was so impressed with her brother's description of the new car that she considered investing the entire amount. But, after talking to her father, she decided to invest only half of her savings. While her stock purchase was a part of the $2,500 pledged by Couzens, her $100, later, was converted into a single share of Ford stock, the only such share ever sold. By 1915, the returns on her $100 investment in the Ford Motor Company gave her financial independence for the rest of her life.

John S. Gray, a former candy manufacturer in Detroit, was at the time president of the German-American bank. He was an uncle of Alex Malcomson. Before the June 13th meeting he bought $10,000 worth of stock in the Ford & Malcomson Company and paid for it in cash. It was this money that was used in March and April to meet the advance payments due the Dodge Brothers Machine Shop. The money from Gray kept the contract with the Dodges (and the car) alive.

On the evening of June 13th, Gray bought another $500 worth of stock for cash. One of the great ironies to be found anywhere in the early financial annals of the motorcar can be spotted in this purchase. A good customer of Gray's bank had called on him, shortly before the meeting at which the Ford Motor Company was organized. He was a Detroit physician, Dr. Frederick E. Zumstein. Gray explained the unusual opportunity and told Zumstein that he himself had already invested $10,000. That was good enough for Dr. Zumstein. He wrote a check to Gray for $500 worth of Ford stock, and told him, as he handed over the check, "Well, why not. Put me down for five shares." Then he added, "You know, we doctors are invariably simpletons in investments."

On June 13th, Gray reported that Dr. Zumstein had subscribed for five shares of stock and paid for them in cash, but could not attend the meeting. Surprisingly, and although they were meeting on the thirteenth day of the month, Henry Ford spoke up, calling attention to the fact that the doctor's investment would make thirteen shareholders which might be bad luck. However, he conceded that the new company was in no position to turn down any money. After

By 1911, Louis Chevrolet had developed a pilot car,
and the first of the millions of vehicles to bear his name
was produced in 1912. The first cars designed by
Chevrolet were large and powerful, reflecting
his racing background.

some discussion, Gray agreed to return Dr. Zumstein's check and invest an additional $500 himself. Zumstein, comfortably fixed financially, often recalled in reasonably good humor that, on the evening of June 13th, 1903, he was only the cashing of his check away from becoming a multimillionaire.

Albert Strelow was an unwilling investor all the way. He became more important for another reason. He was a major contractor in Detroit and he had built the Edison Electric Company building in which Henry Ford had worked for eight years. He had done construction work for Malcomson. Strelow owned a one-story building at the corner of Mack and Bellevue Avenues, formerly used as an icehouse.

Malcomson prevailed upon Strelow to build a second story on the structure so that it might be used as the first factory of the Ford Motor Company. Located on a siding of the Michigan Central Railroad, the building covered one-third of an acre and was 172 feet long and 72 feet wide. Strelow didn't like the idea of adding the second floor, for which he was paid $5,000, for fear it would make the building difficult to rent, "later."

Malcomson and Couzens tried repeatedly to get Strelow to buy at least as much stock as he was being paid for the remodeling of his building. He said, several times, that he would not buy Ford stock or back the new car, but he came to the organizational meeting. He left the meeting without investing, but a month later he bought $5,000 worth of stock and paid for it in cash.

Horace H. Rackham, the lawyer who drew up the Ford-Malcomson agreement with the Dodges in February, saw the opportunity and was anxious to buy stock. He talked to his wife about it who was quick to say, "But we haven't got $5,000."

"No, but we have 4 acres of land out on Van Ness Avenue worth more than that. We can borrow the money," her husband responded.

Mrs. Rackham left the final decision to her husband. He struggled with the problem and finally went to see the president of his bank, George Peck, who knew Henry Ford well. He had hired Ford at the Edison Company, and it was his son, Barton Peck, from whom Ford had rented shop space after the failure of the Henry Ford company. Peck advised Rackham against investing in a Ford Company. But Rackham went back to the bank and borrowed $3,500 with which, plus his $1,500 note, he was able to buy $5,000 worth of stock. Banker Peck told his wife the evening he made the loan to Rackham that he hated to see the Rackhams throwing their money away, but the security they gave was good and there was nothing he could do but loan them the money.

John W. Anderson, Rackham's partner, who had followed the developments closely, since the time he had drawn up the Ford-Malcomson partnership agreement nearly a year before, wanted to invest but had no financial resources. His father, a decorated Civil War doctor, was practicing in LaCrosse, Wisconsin, and was a man of means. Anderson wrote his father a 1,500-word letter, asking for a loan of $5,000.

The letter was written on June 4th, nine days before the organization meeting. In part, Anderson's letter stated the circumstances:

"...Mr. Ford of this city is recognized throughout the country as one of the best automobile mechanical experts in the U.S..... Years ago he constructed a racing machine which was a wonder, and since then has constructed others in which he has raced all over the country, East, and has won numerous contests on many tracks ... He then turned his entire attention to the designing and patenting of an entirely new machine. Mr. Malcomson, the coal man, backed him with money and the result is they have now perfected and are about to place on the market an automobile (gasoline) that is far and away ahead of anything that has yet come out. He has had applications (patent) taken out on every new point he has designed and has just received word that 17 of them have been allowed, everyone of which are incorporated in the machine ... So, they entered into a contract with the Dodge Bros. here to manufacture the automobile complete—less wheels and bodies—for $250 apiece, or $160,500.00 for the 650 machines which are to be delivered at the rate of 10 per day commencing July 1st, if possible, and all by Oct. 1st. I drew the contract, so know all about it. Now in order to comply with this contract ... Dodge Bros. had to decline all outside orders and devote the entire resources of their machine shop to the turning out of these automobiles. They were only paid $10,000 on account, and had to take all the risk themselves. They had to borrow $40,000, place orders for castings all over the country, pay their men ... (they have a large force) and do everything necessary to manufacture all the machines before they could hope to get a cent back. I go into this fully, so you may understand the faith that these experts and successful machinists have in the machine itself, in staking their whole business, practically, on the outcome ... In addition to this, contracts for the remaining parts of the automobile—the bodies, seat cushions, wheels and tires—were made so that they are supplied as wanted. The bodies and cushions, by the C. R. Wilson Carriage Co. at $52 apiece and $16 apiece respectively. The wheels by a Lansing, Mich., firm at $26 per set (4 wheels). The tires by the Hartford Rubber Co. at $46.00 per set (4 wheels) ... They found a man from whom Mr. M. rents a coal yard on the belt-

207

line R. R. with a spur track running into it. He agreed to erect a building, designed by Mr. Ford for their special use, for assembling purposes (which will cost between 3 & 4 thousand dollars) and rent it for three yrs. to Mr. F. and Mr. M. at $75 per month ... You will see there is absolutely no money, to speak of, tied up in a big factory ... The machines sell for $750 without a tonneau. With a tonneau, $850. This is the price of all medium priced machines and is standard. It is what the Cadillac and Great Northern sell for here ... On the season's output of 650 machines, it means a profit of $97,000 without a tonneau, and more in proportion to those sold with tonneau, and of course the latter is almost always bought, as it adds so much to the capacity of the vehicle."

The letter sparked the good doctor's interest. He appeared in Detroit almost as soon as he could secure train travel from Wisconsin. With his son he went to the Mack Avenue assembly plant and took a ride in the pilot car. Later he described the visit, "James Couzens was at the plant when we were there ... and he offered to drive us to town in his Ford car. On the way he attempted to drive through a small park, but the car stalled at a little hill. After frequent attempts to cross the little hill, Mr. Couzens was forced to detour around the block. That was my first auto ride."

Nevertheless, Anderson's father was sufficiently impressed to make the loan to his son. Needless to say, the doctor got his money back and he had assured his son a financial future of which few men dream.

The assembly of cars began in the Mack Avenue plant before the end of the first full week in July. All work was done on the first floor. The second floor had not yet been completed. Wills and his helpers did the design and engineering work behind an unpainted partition extending completely across the rear of the building. When the second floor was completed, Couzens' office was located in a small unpainted area at the front of the building. The car-painting operation required most of the upper floor. Henry Ford had no office.

The complete car, except for bodies and wheels, came over from the Dodge Machine Shop plant on Monroe Street. They were hauled on hayracks pulled by a team of horses, one at a time. There was little evidence of the famed Ford assembly line that developed later. The cars were assembled and, until the second floor was complete, were taken down the alley to a barn for painting.

August (Gus) Degener, a crack all-around mechanic, was in charge of the ten to twelve men who put together the first Fords. The men were paid $1.50 for a 10-hour day that began at 7 a.m. One of them was quick and cooperative, a young man named John Wandersee. He was a former Wisconsin farm boy who had trained to be a mechanic in Milwaukee and who was then beginning a storybook career with the Ford Motor Company that would span fifty years. Wandersee later explained how the work was handled in those first days on Mack Avenue.

"The motor, chassis and axles were all manufactured and assembled at Dodge Brothers. All we did was to put the wheels and the body on. The body came on a handtruck and they picked it out and put it on. The fellows could lift a car body easy enough. After the car was assembled, one fellow would take hold of the rear end and one the front end and lift the whole thing up.

"They were assembled on the spot and driven out. One or two men would do each assembly. There were ten to fifteen spots for assembling. The testing was done right on the blocks. You'd have to get the motor started and run it so it would be fit to run. Sometimes the valves would need grinding and we'd do it right there. The Dodges didn't do any testing."

Ford, whose starting salary had been set at $3,600 a year, was always at the Mack Avenue plant when the men arrived, and often long after they left. Couzens, whose initial salary had been set at $2,500 a year and Harold Wills, whose $125 a month from the old Ford & Malcomson Company was doubled at Ford's request, also worked twelve to sixteen hours a day, seven days a week. Everyone, generally, called Ford "Hank" or "Henry."

In that critical month of June, the 27th saw the Ford working capital reach a one-day peak of $19,500. The balance on the 26th was $14,500, but the following day Anderson paid for his stock in full. The check from his father in LaCrosse had arrived.

Couzens had written no checks since the company was formed two weeks before, and he had to begin paying bills. Check Number One was to Dodge Brothers for $10,000. The second check was to the Hartford Rubber Works in Hartford for $640, paying for 64 tires. By July 1st, the balance was down to $7,013.38, of which $5,000 was promptly sent to the Dodges.

That was the week car assembly began. Unlike Olds or Cadillac with a large backlog of orders before production, the Ford Motor Company started without a single order. Furthermore, after the first, full week of assembly, no orders had been received. On Thursday, July 9th, the day that the paint was dry on the Ford Motor Company's first cars, the bank balance was down to $595. Couzens had to write additional checks on Friday and the Ford Motor Company balance went down to $223.65, with the payroll for the men in the plant *due the next day.* The company had been in business one month. It had paid its way but its bank account was exhausted. The shareholders owed the firm more than $20,000, but the question was whether they would stay with the ship in the face of no sales and no bank account.

The reluctant Albert Strelow solved the problem. The next day, on July 11th, he paid in full for his $5,000 stock purchase and the company's bank balance increased to $5,223.65. Still the financial crisis extended into the next week. The following Wednesday, the big break came. C. A. Wardle, the company's first sales manager, telephoned from Chicago that Dr. E. Pfennig of that city had ordered and paid in full for a new Ford. He had bought the tonneau, at $850. Couzens was so excited that he misspelled the doctor's name in recording the event. Dr. Pfennig, who was weary of having to worry about his horse while on house calls, had placed the $850 in escrow to the Ford Motor Company to be paid out when he received the Fordmobile. On the day that the first order was recorded, the firm had but one dealer and he was located in Buffalo.

The Chicago doctor's order parted the curtain of financial adversity. Bills due on work done for firms in Indianapolis and Chicago were paid to the Ford Motor Company the next day. By the end of the week, even after the payroll of Saturday, July 18th, had been paid, the bank balance of the Ford Motor Company had risen to $6,486.44, never to be a problem again.

Twelve days later Henry Ford was forty years old.

12

This Is a Great Day

The demand for the new Ford car increased rapidly. It became available at a time when the market for motorcars was booming. The name, "Fordmobile," was quickly dropped and the car became known as the "Model-A." The little horseless carriage had a wheelbase of 6 feet and weighed only 1,250 pounds. Its two-cylinder motor was everything Ford and Wills had promised. The Ford was the most powerful motorcar produced in Michigan in 1903. The steering wheel was on the right. The car used the planetary transmission with three pedals on the floor. One controlled forward speeds, both on the same pedal to the left. Reverse was controlled by pushing the middle pedal and the pedal on the right was the brake. The general appearance of the car was similar to that of the Curved Dash Oldsmobile.

The judgment of Malcomson that 650 cars could be sold in the first year proved to be conservative. Malcomson's strategy of having the Dodges make the complete car, except for the bodies and wheels, worked magnificently. The Dodge Machine Shop held to its schedule and the Ford Motor Company was never without cars to sell.

With Oldsmobile and Cadillac having blazed the way, the new company found there was an intense interest throughout the country in motorcar dealerships. Couzens found he could investigate and appoint dealers via long distance telephone more rapidly than Sales Manager Wardle could by making personal calls. Accordingly at the November 13th, 1903, meeting of the board of directors, Alex Malcomson moved, and John Dodge seconded, a motion "that the President write to Mr. C. A. Wardle that his services can be dispensed with. That he write it in a courteous letter and pay his salary up to January 1, 1904." At the same meeting, the directors increased Couzens's salary from the original $2,500 to $3,000, as of December 1st.

The peak selling season for 1903 was over by the time the new Ford was available. Most of the cars sold in 1903 went to new dealers as demonstration cars. By the end of the year, Couzens had appointed dealers for the Ford in most cities of the United States. A dealer was appointed in Honolulu. Hawaii had become a U.S. territory only three years earlier. The first order for Ford cars from outside the United States was shipped that fall.

No dealer was appointed in Detroit. Anyone who bought the "Model-A" Ford in Detroit during 1903 transacted the sale at the Mack Avenue assembly plant. The following March, a spacious, company-owned salesroom, storage facility and repair shop were opened at 234 Jefferson Avenue with Charles A. Grant in charge.

John Wanamaker, the merchant genius in Philadelphia, was so intensely interested in Couzens's reports, and with the new car itself that, in 1904, he established Ford dealerships in both New York and Philadelphia. McCord and Company held the first dealership in Chicago. The Los Angeles Automobile Company was organized to sell Fords in all of Southern California.

By October 1st, Couzens was able to report that the business was doing well with a net profit of $36,957, about $8,000 more than the stockholders' original cash investment just three and one-half months earlier. By the end of September, 215 Ford cars had been assembled, and 195 had been sold, shipped and paid for. The average assembling cost was $36.75, per machine, and the advertising and sales expenses were $31.18, per car.

Early in November, the comapny placed a new order with the Dodge Brothers for car components to be delivered in 1904. It called for the Dodges to build the entire car, except for the wheels and bodies, as in the earlier order. Some improvements had been made and the directors agreed that the original price was a little low. In the new contract, the Dodges were paid $265, an increase of $15.00 per car, but the Ford company also provided the sparkplugs and coils.

On November 21st, the Ford Motor Company declared a 10 percent dividend. The firm had been in business four months and five days. Several of the stockholders used the money to pay off their notes for the purchase of stock. President John Gray received $1,050 of his $10,500 investment.

With so many of the shareholders, especially Malcomson, committed so heavily in their investment, dividends were paid as quickly as the directors considered it practical. A second factor in the early payment of dividends was the fact that several of the stockholders, who had offered notes to cover their shares, could be counted on to pay them off from dividend payments.

By November 21st, when the first dividend was authorized, Ford, Malcomson, Gray, Anderson, Strelow and Woodall had paid for their shares in full. The Dodges, Fry, Bennett, Rackham and Couzens, collectively, owed $20,000 to the company. After the November dividend, Fry, who owed $2,000 paid off $1,000 on his note and after the January dividend, he paid the remaining $1,000. The Dodges both paid for their $10,000 worth of stock the same day the January dividend money was received. Rackham, also, paid up more than half of his $1,500 note the day the January dividend was issued. He finished paying off the note after the big June dividend was received.

Although Bennett had signed notes for his entire $5,000 stock purchase, he collected his November and January dividends, totaling $1,500, without paying any amount on his notes. For months, early in 1904, Bennett was in the position of having received $1,500 in dividends on Ford stock upon which he had not paid any cash. Only after the large June dividend was declared, did he settle for his stock.

Couzens, who had borrowed most of his money on a bank note, used his dividend money in November, January and June to pay off the bank. On August 31st, 1904, he became the last shareholder to complete payment for Ford Motor Company stock. Henry Ford spoke for all of the shareholders, at that point, when he stated, "The business went along almost as by magic."

By the end of the first year, with only a few more than 1,000 cars produced and sold, the twelve Ford shareholders had received their original investment back in dividends and were launched on a golden flood of earnings.

By the end of March, 1904, all of the original 650 cars contracted for with the Dodges had been sold. Sales by March 31st totalled 658 cars. Exactly as Anderson had projected to his father when he asked to borrow money to buy Ford stock, the profits at the end of March stood at $98,851. The big sales season was just beginning and sales more than doubled in the next six months. By the end of September, 1,700 Fords had been sold. The high sales made it possible to meet the costs of expansion, out of profits, and it was at no time necessary for the company to borrow money at any bank or seek loans of any kind. All bills, including those from the Dodge Brothers, were paid in full, and on time.

Even with the company's success, Ford was looking ahead, thus demonstrating one of his most remarkable qualities. During the winter slowdown at the Mack Avenue plant, Ford hit upon an idea to promote sales, particularly of the new car, the "Model-B" which Wills had designed. The "Model-B" was to be put into production during the year. It was a heavier car with four cylinders.

On January 9th, a week before the opening of the fourth New York Automobile Show, Ford decided to have one more try at lowering the motorcar record for the mile. His plan was to use the "Arrow," sister to the "999." It had a four-cylindered motor, the forerunner of the one being placed in the new "Model-B." The men at the plant cleared the snow from a long stretch of Lake St. Clair's ice and scattered cinders the length of the clearing.

In bitter winter weather, Ford, Harold Wills and Ed Huff, accompanied by Mrs. Ford and ten-year-old Edsel (who wanted to watch the excitement), arrived at the lake. The Detroit newspapers had announced the event, and the Hotel Chesterfield at nearby New Baltimore had been handing out printed notices for several days announcing that: "the races will start at two o'clock and continue until Mr. Ford lowers the world's record."

Although Ford never admitted the fact, it was a foolhardy thing to do. The conditions were most unfavorable and Ford and Huff, who rode with him, easily could have lost their lives. Practice runs had been made for three days and the big event took place on the 12th. Ford, with Huff lying prone beside the motor to control the carburetor by hand, developed highest possible speed before entering the test mile. At that point Ford devoted his entire attention to the steering and it was Huff's responsibility to keep the big racer wide open. There were times when Ford could not keep the "Arrow" on the cindered path. The monstrous machine would ram into the snow banks on either side and was virtually thrown back onto the cinders. There were moments when it appeared the racer would turn over, but still the two daredevils thundered on to the finish line. The official timers of the automobile association reported the mile had

The "Baby Grand" Chevrolet of 1914 was the first to
carry the famous "bow-tie" trademark proposed by
Durant. This was the first Chevrolet to have a
valve-in-head engine, self starter and electric lights.

been run in thirty-nine and two-fifths seconds, knocking a full six seconds off the world record. Huff was paid a $50.00 bonus for risking his life. In his description of the race, Ford indicated that it had been a close call.

"The ice was seamed with fissures which I knew they were going to mean trouble the moment I got up speed. But there was nothing to do but go through with the trial, so I let the old 'Arrow' out. At every fissure the car leaped into the air. I never knew how it was coming down. When I wasn't in the air I was skidding, but somehow I stayed top side up on the course, making a record that went all over the world."

The "Model-A" established Ford in the motorcar market. It was the only car the Ford Motor Company had to sell in the spring and summer of 1904, the first full year the Ford was sold. To the "Model-A" fell the responsibility for breaking into an already very competitive market. There were more than two hundred different makes of motorcars sold in 1904, and some firms had several models. Seven cars, all gasoline-powered, were produced in Detroit. They were Oldsmobile (soon to be based in Lansing), Cadillac, Great Northern, Packard, Reliance, Mohawk and Ford. In 1903, the Reliance came on the market about the same time as the Ford, and the 1904 season was its last. The Mohawk was manufactured until 1909.

The Flint-built Buick arrived in 1904. Packard's "Model-L" was a four-cylinder, 20-horsepower, five-passenger car that sold for $3,000. The Great Northern also was a five-passenger car with a two-cylinder engine, and sold for $1,500. Oldsmobile, Cadillac, Ford and Great Northern produced two-passenger cars and all sold for the same base price of $750. The Buick had a two-cylinder motor, carried five passengers and sold for $1,250.

Colonel Albert Pope's Columbia factory at Hartford, Connecticut, produced the most complete line of motorcars in the United States in 1904, offering three gasoline models and two electric models. The Columbia gasoline touring car accommodated six passengers, sold for $5,000 and the Columbia electric runabout, a two-passenger vehicle, sold for $800. The two-passenger electric Studebaker runabout made in South Bend, Indiana, sold for $975. The Stevens-Duryea, complete with a heavy-duty top, carriage lamps and a padded dashboard, was made in Chicopee Falls, Massachusetts. It used a two-cylinder opposed motor developed by Frank Duryea, seated two passengers and sold for $1,300. Charles Duryea's firm in Reading, Pennsylvania, using his three-cylinder motor, sold its two-passenger phaeton for $1,350.

The air-cooled Franklin made in Syracuse, with a four-cylinder vertical engine mounted in front, carried two passengers and sold for $1,300. The Haynes-Apperson, made in Kokomo, Indiana, with a two-cylinder engine, seated two and sold for $1,550. Kenosha, Wisconsin's Rambler "Model-L" was a two-cylinder opposed engine and seated five persons. It had a top, curtains, four lamps, a horn and side baskets and sold for $1,350. The 1904 Winton in Cleveland had a two-cylinder horizontal motor, space for five persons and cost $2,500. The Peerless, made in Cleveland, had a four-cylinder 24-horsepower motor, also seated five ,and sold for $4,000.

There were 22,130 motorcars sold in the United States in 1904. The Olds Motor Works with its single model, the Curved Dash Oldsmobile, sold more than 5,000 cars. Cadillac was second with a production of 3,000 cars.

Success came at a high price on Mack Avenue. The problems and strife at the Ford Motor Company plant were on the same scale as the achievements. Only strong men with extraordinary abilities could have accomplished so much in so short a time. Disputes and sharp clashes of personalities and interests were as much a part of the success as the brilliant planning, shrewd judgment and plain hard work. Most of the men had grown up in isolation on farms, and under circumstances that provided for little schooling. They had labored alone or working with a man or two, in blacksmith shops, livery stables and small machine shops where physical strength was often the court of highest appeal. Suddenly they found it necessary to work as a part of a large team that constantly grew larger.

Jim Couzens and John Dodge were typical of the strong, domineering and often quick-tempered individuals who made the great success possible. Frequently, they did not get along well with each other. They had not met until the critical conference at which the vital agreement with the Dodges was hammered out. When John Dodge demanded cash in advance of delivery for motors and other components, Couzens jumped to his feet and thundered, "We'll not stand for that." In an instant Dodge was on his feet shouting back, "Who in the hell are you?" Malcomson had to step between the two men and order them to be seated. While the men were never friends, they developed a profound respect for each other and effectively pooled their great energies and abilities in the interest of the Ford motorcar for over a decade.

As important as his inventive and mechanical abilities were, it was Henry Ford's capacity to cool off the tempers of his high-strung associates, when things had reached the snapping point, that often counted most. He had a remarkable ability to avoid conflict even under great provocation. He was always able to keep in mind that solutions to problems had to be *thought* out rather than *fought* out. He was a flexible man, quick to sense tension when he entered a room. Under such circumstances, he was casual and always found the proper remark or joke to calm edgy workmen. Ford loved the practical joke. He would take time out from a busy day to wire a door knob for harmless electric shocks, and such a stunt often smoothed out difficult relationships. He nailed down many a man's hat and, at least once, nailed a pair of shoes to the floor while the owner was at work in rubber boots.

Ford got along with everyone, and one of the reasons he could do so was that Couzens met most of the human roadblocks first and plowed a wide furrow in which Ford could maneuver. Others would do it for Ford later, but none so well as the blunt, generally fair but often acid-tinged Couzens. His associates admitted that Jim Couzens smiled regularly but rarely more often than the ice went out in the lake. Couzens' capacity for business organization, his financial wizardry and an ability to direct the talents of Henry Ford constituted the very foundation of the Ford Motor Company's greatest achievements.

Almost from the very beginning the Ford Motor Company encountered a formidable problem. George B. Selden, an inventor and lawyer in Rochester, New York, took the first steps in 1879 to apply for a patent on a self-propelled vehicle powered by an internal combustion engine. After the success of the Duryea horseless carriage, Selden completed his application and received a patent in 1895.

By 1903, the patent had been accepted by nearly thirty producers of motorcars in the United States, including those firms that made Oldsmobile, Cadillac, the Great Northern and Packard in Detroit, Winton and Peerless in Cleveland, the Haynes-Apperson in Kokomo, the Stevens-Duryea in Chicopee, and the Pierce-Arrow in Buffalo. These firms, licensed under the Selden patent, had formed a group known as the Association of Licensed Automobile Manufacturers. In 1903, young Fred L. Smith, an officer of the Olds Motor Works, was president of the Selden group.

Ford, Malcomson and most of the other stockholders were aware of the Selden patent. Ford talked to Smith shortly after his company was formed about the possibility of securing a license to manufacture under the Selden patent. Smith was aware of Ford's first two business failures and did not take the matter seriously. He dismissed Ford's question by expressing doubt that a firm which was merely assembling cars could qualify for a license. He condescendingly suggested that when the Ford company was making its own cars and the firm had become a factor in the market, there would be no problem in securing a Selden license. Ford was upset at this but, characteristically, remained calm and even affable on the surface.

However, some of the stockholders thought the matter should be explored further. John W. Anderson, a lawyer and a Ford shareholder, arranged a luncheon conference with Smith at the Russell House. Ford officers, Gray, Ford and Couzens attended. The meeting was loaded with emotional dynamite. Smith was none too humble a young man, a son of one of Detroit's richest men and an officer in his father's company, the Olds Motor Works, the most successful firm in the business of making motorcars. Smith saw himself meeting with a former coal-yard clerk, a farmer from Dearborn (trying not too successfully to get into the motorcar business), a young lawyer who was a stockholder in a company that probably would not last out the year and the president of a small Detroit bank.

Although Smith showed deference to Gray, he firmly confirmed what he had earlier told Ford. This was too much for the explosive Couzens. He shouted in Smith's face, "Selden can take his patent and go to hell with it." When asked his views, Ford tilted his chair back against the wall and, with detachment, said coldly, "Couzens has answered you." Smith, by now beside himself, replied, "You men are foolish. The Selden crowd can put you out of business—and will."

President Gray immediately consulted Detroit's leading lawyer on patent matters, Ralzemond A. Parker. He was an ardent advocate of individual enterprise and free competition, and almost a fanatic on the question of getting justice for "the little fellow." Gray asked Parker to study the Selden patent and determine whether it could be overturned.

On September 18th, 1903, Gray called the directors together to hear Parker's report. The patent lawyer told the directors that the Selden patent could be broken. Ford and Couzens, supported by Gray and the other directors, decided to fight the Selden patent to the finish. The Ford Company had not then sold 200 cars, but decided to wager its life in a battle against the Selden patent which was already supported by most of the leaders in the new industry.

Ford and his associates were under no illusions, but they had unlimited confidence in Parker and they expected to win their case.

They were aware that a long period of time and a great deal of money (which the company did not possess) would be required to crack the patent. When the company's stand became known, the gauntlet was down. The Selden group had no alternative but to sue the small Ford Motor Company.

The suit was filed before the end of the year in a New York City court. The emotional, but realistic, Couzens commented, "It may take years to thresh the matter out in the courts . . . we have no apprehensions as to the result of this suit." Parker had a case that would bring him more fame than all the thousands of other cases he had already handled in his career. The job would take eight years. Meanwhile the economic fog of monopoly would hang over the motorcar industry in the United States.

Such problems, as well as the growth of the Ford Motor Company, had to be faced, constantly. Within months, after operations began in the Mack plant, it was evident that the company would have to seek larger quarters. On April 1st, 1904, eight and one-half months after the first car was assembled, the directors held a special meeting to approve buying land for a new factory on Piquette and Beaubien Avenues. There was easy access to several railroads in the new purchase. The land cost of the 3-acre site was $23,500. Within the next year a three-story brick building that fronted on Piquette Avenue was erected at a cost of $75,000. There was no foundry, or provision for much manufacturing of components. Like the Mack Avenue plant, it was essentially a factory to assemble cars along with space for engineering and the general offices. For the first time, Henry Ford had an office of his own.

The problems of worker cooperation, designing and building better cars and expansion were similar to those being experienced by all of the firms who were attempting to succeed in the motorcar business. From the first weeks of its existence, the Ford Motor Company encountered another problem that was particularly its own. It appeared to be strictly an internal affair, but it brought into focus an issue of such magnitude as to involve the future of the motorcar. It caused a cloud to gather over Henry Ford's vision of a car to replace the "family horse."

Within one hundred days after the first "Model-A" Fords were assembled, there appeared the first evidence of incompatability between Malcomson and Ford with respect to company policy. In view of his indispensability in arranging the financial support that made the company possible, it is not surprising that Malcomson might have

Charles W. Nash, hired by Durant, became president of Buick in 1910, served as president of General Motors from 1912 to 1916 when he acquired the Thomas B. Jeffery Company of Kenosha, Wisconsin. He established the Nash Motors Company, producer of more motorcars outside of Detroit than any other firm. The Nash-Hudson merger in 1954 formed the American Motors Corporation.

221

expected to have the final word in shaping policies. Malcomson had decreed that Couzens, his office manager at the coal company, should take over the same position at the Ford Motor Company. As a result, Couzens had assumed the responsibility of a general manager with special focus on finances and marketing. Ford did not object to the arrangement, as long as he had a free hand to run the engineering and production.

Then came the Malcomson thrust that struck a nerve. Malcomson was disappointed in the "Model-A." He wanted the new firm to get into the production of a larger and more powerful car, more like his Winton and the kinds of motorcars those who could easily afford cars would want to buy. This ran exactly counter to Ford's idea of developing a "family horse" that could sell for $500.

Ford avoided a showdown by effecting a compromise. He put Wills and his designers to work on two improved new cars fashioned from the "Model-A." These were the "Model-C" and the "Model-F." Both used an improvement of the original two-cylinder Ford engine. In 1905, the "Model-C" was a two-passenger runabout that sold for a hundred dollars more than the "Model-A," and the "Model-F" was the company's first touring car, a car large enough to seat five persons and rugged enough to travel across country. The "Model-F" sold for $1,000.

At the same time, Ford and Wills began engineering a heavier and more powerful car. It had the four-cylinder motor, a miniature of the "Arrow's" massive racing motor, and seated five passengers. The car also went into production for the selling season of 1905. It was given the name, "Model-B," and sold for $2,000. The car did not sell as well as the lighter, less expensive cars.

Armed with three new models, Ford dealers began establishing new sales records early in 1905. The new "Model-C" two-seater was especially popular. On the initiative of John Dodge, and without additional cost, the running gear was painted yellow and the car was fitted with new three-inch tires. The Dodge contract for the "Model-C" rigs, the package of motor, transmission, axles and chassis, was raised to 2,000—a record for one order. By March, they were being delivered to the new Piquette Avenue plant at the rate of 400 per month. By May, freight cars loaded with Ford cars were bearing large banners reading, "Loaded with Ford Automobiles." A giant sign across the new Piquette factory read, "The Home of the Celebrated Ford Automobile."

On June 16th, the company's second anniversary, the directors authorized a dividend of $100,000, approximately a 100 percent dividend. A month later, on July 26th, the directors authorized another 100 percent dividend. Obviously, much, if not all, of the second dividend could have been issued with the first, but Couzens thought the publicity of a second, walloping dividend in successive months would have a heartening effect upon the dealer organization and more effectively celebrate the firm's second anniversary.

Despite the rising tension between the chief owners, the spring and summer of 1905 was a period of great happiness for Henry and Clara Ford. In the earlier weeks of the year they had been living in the small house on Hendrie Avenue which they rented for $16.00 a month. Edsel was eleven years old, and he rode a bicycle to school where he was doing well. Henry's father, William, a very proud man, lived with them. The doubts he had harbored only two years before had evaporated; he knew what was going to "become of Henry."

Meanwhile, Henry was visiting his Dearborn farm more frequently. There he was experimenting with his motorcar engines. He began to see possibilities of replacing the "farm horse" as well as the "family horse." These initial experiments led him, fifteen years later, to the development of the first successful light farm tractor.

As the summer months of 1905 passed, the Ford and Malcomson crisis deepened. Ford decided to settle the matter. Ransom E. Olds had left the Olds Motor Works over the same issue. Ford and Wills were hard at work on two new models. They were planning to build (in 1906) the most improved, inexpensive light car of which they were capable, the "Model N." At the same time, they would build a heavier car with a six-cylinder motor, the "Model-K." The idea was to let the market decide the issue that was tearing the company management apart.

The question could have been settled amicably, but it would have taken time, and Malcomson was not willing to wait. He began to regret having sent his office manager, Couzens, to take his place at the motor company. Late in the summer, he attempted a solution. He ordered Couzens back to the coal company office so that Malcomson could take over the office management at the Ford Motor Company. Couzens refused to leave, and Ford resisted any move that would take Couzens away.

Malcomson's effort to remove Couzens brought the crisis quickly to a head and, in the end, greatly weakened his position. The issue became inmeshed with the struggle over making light or heavy cars.

Couzens, who had been relatively disinterested in the matter, began aggressively supporting Ford on the development of the new "Model-N" and emphasizing the inexpensive car.

The point of no return was reached at the directors meeting on September 9th, 1905. It was well known that Malcomson wished to have Couzens dismissed. Ford was known to oppose such a move. Directors Gray, Dodge and Anderson would have to make the decision. If one of them sided with Malcomson, the decision would be close enough to effect a deep rift that could handicap the company's operations. If two of them should side with Malcomson, Ford's position would then become something like the situation that took Ransom E. Olds out of the Olds Motor Works.

The moment of decision was purposely posed at a September board meeting. Aware that the issue was both the retention of Couzens as general manager and the question of specializing in either light or heavy cars, the motion was offered to the board to increase Couzens's salary from $4,000 to $8,000. Malcomson, for the first time, openly stated his reasons for wanting Couzens dismissed.

On the vote, all of the directors, other than Malcomson, backed Ford. Later, a check of the entire stockholder group revealed Malcomson had the support only of his close friend on the Board, Charles H. Bennett of Plymouth, and his cousin, Vernon Fry. Gray, both Dodges, Strelow, Rackham, Anderson, Woodall and Couzens supported the Ford views on policy.

Encouraged by such a strong vote of confidence, and convinced that Malcomson would take any steps (even to destroying the company, if need be), Ford and Couzens developed a hard-fisted plan. On November 22nd, 1905, Ford and Couzens organized a new company, the Ford Manufacturing Company, capitalized at $100,000. Ford was the major stockholder but equal blocks of stock were offered to each of the Ford Company shareholders, with the exception of Malcomson.

The objective of the new company was to make "Model-N" components exclusively for the Ford Motor Company, just as the Dodge Works was doing on other models. Directors of the new firm were Ford, Anderson, Couzens, John F. Dodge and Harold Wills. Ford was elected president, Dodge vice-president, Wills secretary and Couzens treasurer. The new company leased the factory at 773-775 Bellevue Avenue in Detroit, located about 4 miles from the Piquette Avenue Ford plant. The Ford Manufacturing Company began mak-

This 1912 Cadillac stands as the great divider in American motorcars. With the first electric self-starter, battery ignition and electric lights, it rendered obsolete the cars of the magneto and gaslight era and opened the way to today's cars.

ing rigs for the new "Model-N," leaving the manufacturing of parts for the new "Model-K" to the Dodge works.

On December 5th, 1905, the *Detroit Free Press* announced that Malcomson planned to organize a company to manufacture a new air-cooled engine for a motorcar to be named the "Aerocar." There were several other stockholders, but Malcomson held a majority interest. The announcement also mentioned that a new three-story plant on Mack Avenue was under construction and that 500 cars would be produced for sale within the coming year.

Stockholders of the Ford Motor Company reacted swiftly. A meeting of the board of directors was held the next day, December 6th, and a resolution was passed noting Malcomson's conflict of interest in motorcars and calling on him to resign as a director and treasurer of the Ford Motor Company within five days. Malcomson refused to resign, and promised he would seek redress in court against the Ford Motor Company. However, no suit was filed during the winter or spring.

The first four-cylinder model in the light car field, Ford's "Model-N," received an unprecedented reception. Trade journals declared the "Model-N" to be the "Number One" piece of motorcar news in 1906. After the pilot car had been shown at the early-year automobile shows, orders accompanied by checks flowed into the Piquette Avenue office. One order for 300 "Model-N" cars was received and accompanied by a $30,000 check. By May, the Ford Company began returning an average of $1,000 a day to dealers who had sent in orders with down payments, requesting delivery earlier than would be possible.

In sharp contrast, the new "Model-K" attracted few orders. Priced at $2,500 the car seated five passengers. Its six-cylinder motor was among the first in the price class to deliver top speeds of 50 miles an hour. Couzens tried many approaches to step up the sale of the big "Model-K." At one point, he insisted that dealers accept one "Model-K" with each ten "Model-N" cars ordered. Because the sales of the "Model-N" began so late in the year, and as a result of the buyer disinterest in the "Model-K," sales dropped for the year and the 1906 dividend was not authorized until October. Then, only $10,000 was distributed. There was little alarm, because the advance sale for 1906 and the following year exceeded anything experienced since the company started.

The failure of the big "Model-K" did produce one important result. It convinced Malcomson that his recommendation of a big car had been unsound and that, even if he won a court order to restore his rights at the Ford Motor Company, there could be no future there for him. In May, he suggested that Ford buy his shares. Couzens handled the difficult negotiations. The talks dragged on through June. On July 12th, Malcomson accepted Ford's offer of $175,000 for his 25½ percent interest in the Ford Motor Company. Ford's struggle for the right to make a car to replace the "family horse" had been won.

Ford was aware of the importance of the day. That evening, he asked the company's car tester and crack mechanic, Fred Rockelman, to drive him home. His mind was already focused on what was to come. As Rockelman stopped in front of the Ford home at 145 Harper Avenue, Ford said, "We're going to expand this company, and you will see it grow by leaps and bounds. The proper system, as I have it in mind, is to get the car to the people. Fred, *This Is a Great Day.*"

What Ford had always said since even before the company had been organized, he now began saying to anyone who would listen. He talked to Roy Chapin soon after he assumed command of the company. Chapin had been through such a management struggle when he had been the sales manager at the Olds Motor Works. He had left to join the Thomas Motor Company when the Olds Motor Works took the Curved Dash Oldsmobile out of production, instead of improving it, as Chapin and Olds had proposed.

Ford explained his plans to Chapin. He was going to create a four-cylinder motorcar, Ford said, that would have most of the advantages of any car then being made. Once it was perfected he was going to stay with the one, standard design. In this way he would drastically cut his production costs. Then he was going to reduce prices steadily until most of the families in the United States owned that car.

Chapin realized he was listening to a great leader in the new motorcar industry. Later, Chapin, who knew all of the early leaders, recalled the 1907 visit with Ford and commented, "He was the first man I ever heard enunciate that theory in our industry ... he practiced it and created a precedent which in fact is now being followed in all American businesses."

One morning soon after, Ford called to young Charles Sorensen, head of the pattern department at the Piquette Avenue plant. Together they went to the back of the third floor where assembly operations were not highly concentrated. Pointing to an area of some size, Ford told Sorensen, "Charlie, I'd like to have a room finished off right there in this space. Put up a wall with a door in it big enough to run a car in and out. Get a good lock for the door, and when you're ready we'll have Joe Galamb come up in here. We're going to start a completely new job." The "Model-T" was created in that room.

Couzens was thinking ahead, too. Within a month after Ford acquired control, he insisted that the company must find a new site and erect a factory large enough to assemble more cars than the company had then delivered in one year. Ford and John Dodge took over the search for the right site. In August, 1906, they agreed there was no satisfactory land in the city and that a move west to Highland Park would be desirable. They located, and soon acquired, a 60-acre racetrack property on the north side of Woodward Avenue. Within weeks, architects were busy planning what has been described as the "eighth wonder of the world," the Highland Park Ford plant.

It was early 1910 before actual production in the largest factory under a single roof in Michigan could begin. The Highland Park plant was so large that, when only one-fourth of it was constructed, it was possible to close down the Piquette and Bellevue plants completely. The Dodge Brothers also bought a new site in nearby Hamtramck where they built a great Dodge factory in order to be close to the new Ford plant.

Ford became president of the Ford Motor Company almost at the time he acquired Malcomson's stock. On July 6th, 1906, John S. Gray died, unexpectedly. He had been president during three turbulent and critical years. His contribution had been much more than that of the largest cash purchaser of stock at the time the company was formed. The high regard in which he was held gave the small company a standing that neither Malcomson or Ford could have provided during this period. He had been especially important in setting the company's course in the Selden patent fight. Although he had been pushed into involvement by his nephew, Gray had recognized Ford's qualities early and finally had backed him against Malcomson when the point of no return had been reached. Gray lived long enough to collect more than $50,000 in dividends on his original $10,500 investment. He had been delighted, but even at the time of his death, had not been sure that the motorcar was more than a fad.

In the reorganization of the board of directors, after Gray's death and Malcomson's departure from the company, Couzens was named to the position held by Malcomson on the board. A single share of

C. Harold Wills, first of the giants to join Henry Ford. This young Detroit machinist and engineer, directly out of night school, began working with Henry Ford on evenings and weekends, in 1902. He was the man who made possible the outstanding motors for the early Ford cars, including the famous "Model-T." He created his own car, the Wills-St. Clair, and completed his distinguished motorcar career with the Chrysler Corporation.

220

the Ford stock, held by John S. Gray's estate, was transferred to the principal Gray heir, David Gray, and he was elected president. The vote was unanimous. John F. Dodge was elected vice president and Couzens was named treasurer.

At the same time, plans were made to merge the Ford Manufacturing Company with the Ford Motor Company. The separate company had accomplished its original purpose, and had made a much greater contribution. Operations at the Bellevue plant marked the first time that the Ford Motor Company principals—Ford, Couzens, Wills, and others—had taken a direct interest in the manufacturing of motorcar components. What they learned set the stage for the revolution in manufacturing that was to come once operations were all concentrated in the new Highland Park Ford complex.

In the fourteen-month period between July 1st, 1906, and September 1st, 1907, six of the original twelve directors left the company. Malcomson invested his money in the Aerocar Company, which produced cars for three years. He continued in business and left a substantial estate, but only a small fraction of what it might have been had he elected to hold his stock in the Ford Motor Company. Charles J. Woodall sold his ten shares to Ford within two months after Malcomson's departure. He had invested $1,000, had collected $5,000 in dividends in three years, and would have become a multimillionaire had he held his $1,000 investment in the company.

The summer recession, in 1907, was mainly responsible for causing Vernon C. Fry and C. H. Bennett (the two men who had backed Malcomson against Ford) to sell their holdings. In 1906, at the peak of the Ford-Malcomson difficulties, Bennett had offered to sell his 50 shares to Percival Perry, Ford's British distributor, for $4,000. Ford personally urged Bennett to keep his stock, but interest had lessened in the motorcar venture for both Fry and Bennett when Malcomson had departed. With the decrease in business during the summer, they were easily discouraged and on September 1st, both sold their 50 shares the same day for $35,000, the same amount received by Malcomson.

Ford purchased all of Fry's shares. Couzens bought 35 shares from Bennett and Ford bought the remainder. There would be no further change in stock ownership for more than a decade. Ford then owned 58 percent of the company's stock. After September 1st, 1907, the distribution of shares was as follows: Henry Ford, 585; James Couzens, 109; Rosetta Couzens, 1; Gray Estate, 104; David Gray, 1;

James Couzens, Detroit
freight yard car checker
and coal business office
manager, was general
manager of the Ford
Motor Company from its
beginning in 1903 until
1916, during which time
the firm became the
world's largest and most
successful producer of
motorcars. Couzens's
contributions were on a
par with those of Ford
himself. He was later
mayor of Detroit and
senator from Michigan.

231

John F. Dodge, 50; Horace E. Dodge, 50; J. W. Anderson, 50; and Horace H. Rackham, 50.

The panic of 1907 cut into the company's cash position. For a few weeks, in the summer and early fall, it was necessary to delay some paydays and give suppliers notes instead of cash. The company continued making cars, and money was available to issue a 100 percent dividend on November 13th.

Of those who gave up their Ford stock early, the most pathetic case was that of Albert Strelow, the contractor who built some of Detroit's best-known buildings of that period. He thought he saw an opportunity to acquire much greater wealth in a Canadian gold mine and sold his 50 shares of stock for $25,000 to Couzens. He lost his entire fortune in the Canadian venture. Before long, he returned and took a job in the Ford plant at a time when he could have been among the city's wealthy, if only he had held his Ford stock.

The "Model-N" was the last of the Ford cars to retain much of the horseless carriage style. The model was actually a transition between the small horseless carriages and the full-sized cars to follow. It had a four-cylinder, 15-horsepower engine mounted in front, weighed only 1,050 pounds, could achieve a speed of 45 miles an hour and traveled as much as 200 miles on ten gallons of gasoline. It sold for $600, fifty dollars less than the lowest cost of the Curved Dash Olds-mobile. The "Model-N" had a personality of its own, perhaps as pronounced as that of the Curved Dash Olds. Nickel covered the radiator and the four lights. There were mudguards and short, snappy fenders.

The impact of the "Model-N" was so great that the company, de-spite some harsh inconvenience, was able to ride through the panic of 1907 and register, by far, its largest sales gain. Well into the 1907 sales season, Couzens halted all orders until further notice. There were several thousand unfilled orders for the little car. During 1907, the "Model-N" sales moved Ford into the position of an industry leader along with Buick, Cadillac and REO.

During this period, the company's new Hungarian engineering genius, Joseph Galamb, worked directly with Ford and a special staff developing the car that would replace the "family horse." It would become the most famous motorcar in the world, and would be known as the "Model-T." Although the new car was announced in 1908, it was 1909 before it could be bought.

Wealth had already been realized by Ford and the stockholders who stayed with him through the five years before the "Model-T."

They had received 100 percent on their investment by the company's first anniversary. Another 100 percent dividend, $100,000, was authorized on the second anniversary, June 16th, 1905. Still another 100 percent dividend was paid only five weeks later, July 24th, 1905. It was possible to pay only a 10 percent dividend in 1906. The 100 percent dividend was resumed in 1907.

In 1908, on sales of the "Model-N," Ford shareholders received a 100 percent dividend in April, May, June, July, October and November. The November dividend payment of $100,000 was authorized November 25th, the day before Thanksgiving, to be followed five days later by a financial blockbuster. On November 30th, 1908, the Ford Motor Company paid a 1,900 percent dividend totaling $1,900,000.

Lawyer Anderson, whose father had made a hurried trip from Wisconsin five years before to decide whether to lend his son the $5,000 to buy Ford stock, had earnings that November day of $95,000 —plus the $30,000 in dividends he had received earlier in the year.

All of this profit resulted from making Ford horseless carriages. The Ford motorcar that replaced the "family horse" was yet to come.

13

Durant Creates
General Motors

Two unrelated events occurred within the same month of 1908 that laid the foundation for today's motorcar industry in the United States. On September 28th, 1908, General Motors began operations. One month later, the first "Model-T" Ford car was produced.

The idea of bringing several motorcar companies into one super organization did not belong exclusively to William C. Durant. Anthony N. Brady of New York, one of the barons of American finance, had distinguished himself for his work in consolidating public utilities. Brady was working toward such a holding company in the automotive business as early as 1905. The possibilities had been pointed out to him by Herman F. Cuntz, an engineer for the Selden group. It was Cuntz's responsibility to visit the firms affiliated with the Association of Licensed Automobile Manufacturers. As a result, he knew of their operations, the capabilities of their staff and even the extent of their financial resources. Brady had put Cuntz to work, sounding out prominent firms in the Selden group about joining a larger organization capable of providing adequate financing, marketing assistance and other services. When Brady sensed that the financial crisis of 1907 was inevitable, he advised Cuntz to hold off until after the depression, hoping the good firms, then, could be bought for less.

The crisis developed, as Brady had predicted. However, the best motorcar firms, such as Buick, Ford, Cadillac and others that would be most useful in a combine, came through stronger than before. Cuntz was not able to advance the idea, and Brady lost his opportunity to play the part of kingmaker. He eventually had a minor place in General Motors.

Some combinations were formed only to fail in a short time, largely because they lacked a Durant. Benjamin Briscoe, owner of the infant Buick Company until he and his brother sold their interest to the Flint Wagon Works, organized the United States Motor Company. It brought together Colonel Albert Pope's Columbia car in Connecticut, along with several made in the Midwest, including the Maxwell. Pope invested a million dollars in an effort to make the United States Motor Company successful, but it failed in 1912. The fortune of the first important producer of both bicycles and motorcars in the United States was lost.

For Durant, building General Motors was simply an extension of his earlier career in horse-drawn vehicles. The Durant-Dort Carriage Company, with its coast-to-coast business and its component and assembly plants across the country, was the General Motors of the buggy industry. From the time Durant joined Buick, his moves pointed to the development of an organization which would provide the same service in motorcars. Bringing the Weston-Mott Company of Utica from New York to Flint, in 1905 was the first indication of his intention to establish a family of closely related businesses in the motorcar industry.

The Durant concept and that of Henry Ford were diametrically opposed. Ford was completely dedicated to the concept of building a single car capable of meeting a wide range of needs so that high volume could reduce production costs and, ultimately, the price of the car. Durant believed that the future would belong to the organization that produced a line of motorcars ranging from light, inexpensive vehicles to large, expensive automobiles.

When the Buick Motor Company came through the panic year of 1907 with a sharply rising sales volume and strong financial position, Durant moved quickly to organize General Motors. He approached J. P. Morgan & Company in New York for financial backing to weld a group of the leading car producers into a holding company. For a time, it appeared Durant would get Morgan's backing for a firm that would be called "International Motors."

The plan did not work out, and a few weeks later Durant crossed out the word, "International," and substituted "General." With a minimum of outside financial support, he filed the incorporating papers. General Motors came into existence as a New Jersey holding company in September of 1908, with an authorized capital of $12,500,000.

The first day on which the new firm could use its capital was September 28th. The following day, General Motors, in its first important transaction, bought from Durant 20,000 shares of Buick common and preferred stock. No money changed hands. General Motors exchanged its own stock for Buick stock, two thirds common and one-third preferred, made available by Durant.

Durant presented the benefits of joining General Motors so effectively that within ninety days the three foremost motorcar companies on Detroit's perimeter, Buick at Flint, Oakland at Pontiac and Oldsmobile at Lansing, came into General Motors. Buick was the largest producer of cars in the United States and Oldsmobile was the best known. Oakland was just getting started, but its new, four-cylinder "Model-K" (not to be confused with the Ford "Model-K," being marketed at the same time) was the country's hill-climbing champion that year, and was in the news. During this same period the young General Motors acquired the new W. F. Stewart Company body plant in return for $240,000 in General Motors stock. The plant, located within the Hamilton farm complex near the big Buick factory, was immediately leased to Buick.

At the end of the first three months, the new corporation was a going concern. On February 23rd, 1909, General Motors declared its first semi-annual dividend of $3.50 on its preferred stock. This dividend has been issued, despite two world wars and the great depression, every year to this time.

Durant knew that Detroit, home of nearly a dozen motorcars, now possessed the greatest capacity for the manufacturing of automobiles and car components, from screws to motors, of any city in the country. But Durant made it clear from the first, that at least some of the leading firms in Detroit must be acquired if General Motors were to become the greatest factor in motorcar production in the United States. He strongly desired to acquire all the leaders, Ford, Cadillac and Maxwell-Briscoe, and he quickly approached each of them.

"Ford bought by General Motors"—what a headline that would have been in Detroit and in the newspapers across the country! Such a possibility twice seemed close to becoming a reality, once as close as a single, confirming telephone call. The first near-miss occurred in

Detroit, in the fall of 1908, after the "Model-T" had been developed and announced to the public, but before production began. The second opportunity for the Ford Motor Company to come into General Motors occurred in New York City, a year later.

The first serious consideration of Ford becoming a part of General Motors took place in Durant's room at the Pontchartrain Hotel, at this time the unofficial headquarters of the motorcar industry in Detroit. During the last months of 1908 and throughout 1909, Durant frequently held conferences of this nature, once or twice a day.

The energetic Benjamin Briscoe, who by then headed the promising Maxwell-Briscoe Company that produced the Maxwell, had also met with Durant. Briscoe said, much later, that he helped arrange the meeting between Durant and Ford at the Pontchartrain Hotel and that Ransom E. Olds and he attended. According to Briscoe, a general agreement was worked out among Durant, Ford and Olds, under which both the Ford Motor Company and the REO Car Company would come into General Motors, and be paid the same price of $3,000,000. The purchase price makes the Briscoe report less than realistic. Ford earnings for the one year of 1908 approached the $3,000,000 figure with 100 percent dividends authorized almost every month. The meeting ended and the proposal collapsed, Briscoe said, when Ford demanded that the Ford Motor Company be paid in cash. Olds countered by stipulating that if Ford's terms were cash, REO would also have to be paid in the same manner. This was more cash, Durant is supposed to have said, than his new General Motors could raise.

In light of the facts, Herbert R. Lewis's account of this meeting between Durant and Ford is a more faithful report of what took place. Lewis, who knew both Durant and Ford well, was given the account by Durant a relatively short time after the meeting. As Durant explained it, those present with him were Ford and Couzens. The discussion went smoothly with Ford seemingly showing increasing interest as the talk progressed. The conference went on most of the day.

Agreement in principle had been reached, Durant thought, on a program that would bring the Ford Motor Company into General Motors. There was an apparent meeting of the minds on the price and the manner in which payment was to be made to the Ford Company. The conference ended with Ford seeming to express his general approval, although Durant recalled that Couzens had rather little to say, in the last stages of the discussion. They promised to

237

"sleep on it" and let Durant have a final answer within a few days. The next morning Couzens called to report that Mr. Ford had decided that "they would go it alone."

It was the first and only meeting of any length held between Durant and Ford. But, together they gave, within the next decade, a new and all but final shape to the motorcar industry in the United States.

Durant approached Maxwell-Briscoe and Cadillac at about the same time that he talked to Ford. Because of Maxwell-Briscoe's extreme capitalization problems and general financial weakness, nothing was to come of those negotiations. Durant had been able to acquire firms for General Motors through an exchange of stock with little or no cash investment by General Motors. Something entirely different took place in dealing with the Cadillac Motor Car Company. Perhaps this was a result of Durant having become aware that General Motors affiliation with either of the other Detroit leaders, Ford or Maxwell-Briscoe, was unlikely. Cadillac now represented the only opportunity to bring a Detroit leader into General Motors.

The negotiations with Cadillac extended over nearly a year and, until the last stages, were handled entirely by Arnold H. Goss of Flint, who had succeeded David Buick as secretary of the Buick Motor Car Company. He often served as Durant's personal representative. The first contact between Wilfred Leland and Goss was in the early fall of 1908. Cadillac had recovered from its tight-money situation experienced during the panic of 1907. The firm had introduced its new, four-cylinder "Model-30" early in 1908. The new car had sold well from the beginning and the company had produced and sold 4,500 cars, despite a late start.

On his first call at Cadillac, Goss explained the advantages of General Motors, said that they were interested in acquiring the Cadillac Motor Car Company and asked if Wilfred Leland thought the present owners would consider selling. Leland took the matter up with his father and the directors. The directors, who had been through the motorcar's first hectic decade, decided that they would give serious consideration to an offer of $3,500,000 cash. They designated Wilfred Leland as the Cadillac official to handle any negotiations that might result from their decision.

Shortly after, Goss called at Cadillac again and got Leland's report, after which Goss left to discuss the matter with Durant. The next day Goss returned with the news that General Motors would pay $3,000,000 in cash and an exchange of stock for the Cadillac Motor

Car Company. He then asked Leland to see if he could bring the stockholders down to the three million dollar figure, and offered Leland, personally, a commission if he could bring about a sale. Leland declined the offer of commission and again pointed out that if the sale were to be arranged it could only be on a strictly cash basis. Durant was not yet able or ready to pay cash.

Winter passed, during which Cadillac had been awarded the Dewar Trophy resulting from the standardization test conducted in England, and General Motors still had not captured a leading producer of motorcars in Detroit. In the spring of 1909, Goss came to see Leland again and another round of consultations and conferences followed. Cadillac was still for sale in a cash deal but the directors had advanced the price. With the widespread public acclaim following the awarding of the first Dewar Trophy to an American motorcar, and a continued upsurge in sales of the new "Model-30," the directors would not sell for less than $4,125,000. Goss asked for ten days in which to complete the sale, but there was no deal.

Early in the summer Goss made his third trip to Cadillac. By now the directors of Cadillac had raised the price tag to $300 a share for an even $4,500,000. Goss again took a ten-day option, but this time Durant came back with the cash and closed the deal. General Motors had moved into Detroit.

It was the largest cash property sale to take place in the motorcar industry of the United States up to that time. It proved immediately to be a bargain, something the shrewd Billy Durant had realized all the time. On August 31st, 1909, the Cadillac Motor Car Company reported a profit of $2,000,000. General Motors had nearly half its purchase price back, in cash, only thirty-three days after the purchase had been made! The buying of Cadillac served notice on everyone that General Motors was a new force with which to reckon in the motorcar business of the United States.

For those four Detroit entrepreneurs, William H. Murphy, Clarence A. Black, Lemuel B. Bowen and E. F. White, it marked the end of their illustrious careers in motorcars. Just ten years before they had founded the first self-propelled vehicle company ever organized in the Motor City involving only Detroit people. They had made possible both the Ford and the Cadillac.

The sale also made Henry M. Leland a wealthy man for the first time in his life. He had acquired enough shares in the Cadillac Motor Car Company to net him $402,000. Although there were no tax considerations involved, he immediately turned half of the money over to Wilfred Leland, who at his father's insistence had given up a promising medical career so that "they might work together."

The directors of Cadillac presented Wilfred Leland with a valuable watch on which was inscribed (obviously referring to Leland's refusal of the commission offered him by Durant):

> "In the old ordeal by fire, a man's body shriveled, while his soul remained unscathed. In the modern ordeal, the crucible of high finance blackens the soul, while the body remains un-injured. Happy the man who comes through both ordeals with body and soul unharmed.
>
> "May this watch be as true and faithful and loyal to you, as you have been to your associates, in this entire Cadillac transaction."

Soon after the acquisition of Cadillac, Durant decided to bid once more for the Ford Motor Company which he now had reason to believe was the leading producer of motorcars in the world. This time he would make an outright offer calculated to quickly sweep the Ford company into the growing General Motors family of cars.

The minutes of the General Motors directors' meeting, held in New York City, October 26th, 1909, show that the matter of purchasing Ford was discussed. In the end, Durant was authorized to offer nearly twice as much as General Motors had paid for Cadillac ninety days earlier. Durant was empowered to offer $8,000,000; two million paid immediately in cash and the balance spread over the next two years, "if arrangements can be made to finance."

Shortly after, Ford and Couzens were in New York. Durant called Ford at his hotel room, but Couzens answered and explained that Ford was not feeling well. Durant said that he would like to discuss once more the possibility of General Motors buying the Ford company. Couzens agreed to come to General Motors headquarters the next day to discuss the matter. In the conference, Durant made the offer of $8,000,000 with $2,000,000 immediately in cash and the balance in two years. Couzens took the proposition back to Ford who said that there was no use even discussing the offer, unless it provided for full and immediate payment in cash. Ford's reaction confirmed for Durant what he suspected; the Ford Motor Company had become the most powerful and richest firm in the motorcar business and was beyond the reach of General Motors. Durant never brought the matter up again.

From 1908 on, for the next quarter of a century, Henry Ford re-

240

peatedly received offers from others to buy his company, with the price to be paid in cash. Eventually, the price reached a billion dollars. He turned them all down, giving a wide assortment of reasons, perhaps none better or closer to the truth than, "What would I do for a job?" Ford, seriously, never considered selling the Ford Motor Company to General Motors.

Nor did Durant spend any time in mourning over his inability to bring Ford into the fold. On the same day that the General Motors directors authorized the purchase of the Ford Motor Company, Goss reported to Durant that the stockholders of the E. R. Thomas Company of Buffalo, maker of the famous "Thomas Flyer" had agreed upon a figure at which they would sell the firm to General Motors. The year before, the Thomas Flyer had won the first around-the-world New York-to-Paris race.

The success of that car is one of the dramatic developments in the record of the motorcar, sparkling evidence of the overwhelming power of an idea in the face of great odds. Contrary to the general banker reluctance to become involved in early motorcar financing, the banks in Buffalo, in an effort to make their city a hub of car production, had loaned the E. R. Thomas Company $2,500,000 to put the car into production, the largest such investment in the country at that time. The "Thomas Flyer" was placed on the market in 1902, and never got off the ground; nor did the situation greatly improve with time. Gradually, the firm's working capital was drained away until, in 1907, bankruptcy seemed to Thomas to be the only course open.

Thomas had actually begun notifying creditors, including the banks, that his company was without funds and would have to be liquidated, when he read a notice in a copy of the Paris newspaper *Le Matin*.

Le Matin announced that it was joining the *New York Times* in sponsoring the 1908 New York-to-Paris horseless carriage race. Thomas saw new possibilities for his "Flyer" in this race. He talked to some of his associates, especially Sidney H. Harris, who had designed the company's factory on Niagara Street in Buffalo and to S. H. Woodruff, the contractor who had built the plant. They agreed that the "Thomas Flyer" was a good horseless carriage, but that it was not well known. The Oldsmobile, Buick, Ford and other cars that were becoming highly successful had all been brought to public attention again and again by feats of speed or displays of power and endurance. Now, here was the opportunity to put the "Flyer" into the greatest test of endurance and speed ever undertaken by any automobile either in the United States or Europe. Woodruff pointed out that the New York-to-Buffalo race in 1901 had been the first important endurance contest in the United States. Since then, there had been runs against time from Cleveland to New York, Chapin's historic first motorcar trip from Detroit to New York, and several trips entirely across the United States from New York to San Francisco. But there had not been, they agreed, such an endurance race around the world by any motorcar. Woodruff was sure the investors, with millions at stake, would supply perhaps $50,000 in an effort to avert the impending financial disaster for Buffalo.

Harris went to the officials of the Buffalo banks and they agreed to loan the additional money to put the "Thomas Flyer" into the big race. The cost ultimately went up to $100,000 and the banks still underwrote the expenses.

Amid proper ceremonies, the "Great Race of 1908" began at New York on February 12th, with thirty-five-year-old George Schuster, the chief inspector and test driver at the Thomas plant, driving the "Thomas Flyer." Montague Roberts, one of the racing car greats of the century's early years, was engaged as the co-driver on the first hazardous leg of the trip across the American plains. Roberts turned the driving completely over to Schuster in Wyoming. George Miller of Buffalo went along as the chief mechanic allotted to each car on the round-the-world trip.

Roads through the western part of the United States had not yet been built. It was necessary to scout the trail which would be used and this job was the responsibility of each driver in the race. E. Lynn Mathewson aided Schuster as pathfinder through Wyoming, and Harold Brinker was the pathfinder from Ogden, Utah, to San Francisco, where the "Flyer" arrived a full ten days ahead of the three European entries, the "Zust," the De Dion" and the "Protos." Although Schuster didn't know it then, the other cars were never actually in the race after having taken ten days to cross the plains and mountains of the western United States.

Schuster and his "Flyer," accompanied by an adequate store of repair parts, were placed on a boat at San Francisco. A stop was made at Tokyo for a demonstration, and Schuster and his car went on to Vladivostok at the end of the Trans-Siberian Railroad, which had been completed just ten years before. They followed the course of the world's longest railroad into Moscow, then made a triumphant tour across Europe, with daily reports appearing in American and

European newspapers. Schuster drove the "Flyer" into Paris on July 30th. In the eighty-eight days that the car had actually been in use during the one hundred and seventy days since leaving New York, it had traveled 13,341 miles for an average of 151 miles per day. Schuster reported that his "Thomas Flyer" had to be driven in low gear on 8,000 miles of the trip.

On the sixtieth anniversary of the "Great Race of 1908," there was a ceremonial restaging of the New York-to-San Francisco leg of the big event. Sponsored by the American Automobile Association, the rerunning of the "great race" was open to any car made in 1914, or earlier. The original " Thomas Flyer" took part, the motorcar having been preserved in its original condition by William Harrah of Reno, the world's largest collector of early cars—with some fifteen hundred. The *New York Times* offered $1,000 for the car and driver giving the outstanding performance judged on the basis of a pre-arranged scoring system.

Stops were made at the twelve way-stations used in the original contest. The first highlight came at the Buffalo station. There the participants had the opportunity to meet and talk with ninety-five-year-old George Schuster, who had driven the "Flyer" to glory sixty years earlier. Also participating in the ceremonial race was Dr. Montague Roberts, son of the other driver who had driven the car through Wyoming in 1908. Dr. Montague drove his 1911 Abbott-Detroit automobile. The ceremonial trip began June 16th and ended at the Golden Gate, July 13th. At the race's end in San Francisco, the thirty-one drivers who completed the 3,300-mile trip were greeted by Alice Huyler Ramsey, the first woman to drive a motorcar across the United States. Living in New Jersey then, the twenty-one-year-old Alice and three other young women made their trip in a Maxwell. They left New York on June 9th, 1909, and arrived in San Francisco fifty-three days later.

The *New York Times 1968 Award* was presented in San Francisco to Warren S. Weiant, Jr., of Newark, Ohio, who had been accompanied by Mrs. Weiant on the entire trip. The Weiants drove their 1909 Simplex (whose original cost of $6000 did not provide for a windshield), from their home in Ohio to New York, across the continent and back to Ohio, a total distance of 6,700 miles.

"The Great Race of 1908" that took the "Flyer" from New York to Paris resulted in a high level of sales enabling the E. R. Thomas Company to pay off the banks and other creditors in thirty months. And it helped to make Thomas a man of wealth and distinction in the young motorcar industry. He financed the Thomas-Detroit car that became the Hudson, a motorcar that was produced in Detroit for half a century. But nothing came of the General Motors interest in acquiring the E. R. Thomas Company. Lasting fame eluded the Thomas, a name that might otherwise have stood along with the others on which Durant and General Motors conferred economic immortality —Buick, Oldsmobile, Cadillac, Oakland-Pontiac and Chevrolet.

In the two years after General Motors began doing business, Durant was in one continuous whirl of activity. In addition to his great personal abilities, he had the capacity to do at least two days work in one. A man who never weighed 150 pounds, he seemed able to draw on a bottomless well of energy. He would make appointments for midnight, one o'clock and even later in the morning. "I'll meet you at 1:30 a.m.," he once told a man who had waited long to see him. "You mean 1:30 p.m., don't you Mr. Durant?" "No, we'll get to this yet today. I mean 1:30 a.m.," Durant responded. But, he was always among the first to be at the office the next morning fresh and smiling.

Lee Dunlap, general manager of Oakland-Pontiac, described Durant during these first two years of General Motors.

"When Mr. Durant visited one of his plants it was like a visitation of a cyclone. He would lead his staff in, take off his coat, begin issuing orders, dictating letters and calling the ends of the continent on the telephone: talking in his easy way to New York, Chicago, San Francisco.... Only a phenomenal memory could keep his deals straight; he worked so fast that the records were always behind.

"On this visit of which I am thinking in 1910, I expected he would stay several days as we were to discuss the whole matter of plant expansion. But after a few hours, Mr. Durant said, 'Well, we're off to Flint.' In despair I led him on a quick inspection of the plant. Instantly, he agreed that we would have to build, and he asked me to bring the expansion plan with me to Flint the next day. There wasn't any plan, and none could be drawn on such short notice, but his will being law and our need great, something had to be done.

"So I called in a couple of our draftsmen to help me and that night we made a toy factory layout— existing buildings in one color, desired buildings in another. We drew a map of the whole property, showing streets and railway sidings, and then glued the existing buildings to it in their exact locations. Feeling like a small boy with a new toy, I took this lay-out to Flint and rather fearfully placed it before the chief ... He was pleased pink ... We placed those new buildings first here, then there, debating the

Charles E. Sorensen, starting in 1904, worked with Ford for forty years, longer than any of the Ford giants. He had an important role in building the world's first moving and fully mechanized assembly line, in the development of Ford's River Rouge complex and in the building operation of the Ford Willow Run bomber plant.

situation. When we agreed as to where they should go, he said. 'Glue them down and call W. E. Wood.'

"Mr. Wood came in after a few minutes and received an order for their construction ... Contractor Wood had men, materials and machines moving toward Pontiac within twenty-four hours, and we were installing machinery in part of the structures within three weeks."

In what must have been a record outburst of corporate expansion, Durant, in a period of approximately eighteen months, bagged these firms for General Motors: Buick Motor Company, Olds Motor Works, Oakland Motor Car Company, AC Spark Plug Company, Weston-Mott Company, Reliance Motor Truck Company, Rainier Motor Company, Michigan Motor Castings Company, Welch Motor Car Company, Welch-Detroit Company, Cadillac Motor Car Company, Jackson-Church-Wilcox Company, Michigan Auto Parts Company, Rapid Motor Vehicle Company, Cartercar Company, Ewing Automobile Company, Elmore Manufacturing Company, Dow Rim Company, Northway Motor & Manufacturing Company, National Motor Cab Company, Heany Lamp Company, Randolph Motor Car Company and McLaughlin Motor Car Company Ltd., which later became General Motors of Canada.

As well as acquiring these firms, there was the matter of giving them attention and leadership once they had joined the fold. The Olds Motor Company had slipped badly after the Smiths took over from Ransom E. Olds, phased out the light car and began making heavier machines. The fortunes of Oldsmobile had declined until at the time General Motors acquired the Olds Motor Works, Durant confessed to an aide that he had "just bought a million dollars worth of roadside signs." Although the larger Oldsmobile motor performed well, the larger cars were not selling.

Durant made one of his whirlwind trips to Lansing, met with the engineers and directed that a car body be sawed into quarters. Durant then moved the sides 6 inches further apart and lengthened the car by a foot. The Oldsmobile, with its new dimensions, was offered as a new model as soon as possible. Sales expanded rapidly and put the Olds Motor Works back into the black.

Durant always took immediate steps to retain the services of capable executives in the firms bought by General Motors. When the cash settlement was made with the Cadillac Motor Car Company, Durant withheld $100,000 of the Leland share. At the same time he called Wilfred Leland and asked that he and his father come to Detroit's Russell House to meet him. When they arrived, Durant explained that he was fully aware of the contribution the Lelands had made to Cadillac and that it was his desire that they continue to operate the business for General Motors.

Henry Leland explained to Durant that they had established certain standards and ideals in their development of Cadillac and that he and his son would be interested only in continuing to manage the firm if they were accorded the same free hand they had always had to maintain their standards and ideals. Durant slapped his knee and said, "That is exactly what I want. I want you to continue to run the Cadillac exactly as though it were still your own. You will receive no directions from anyone."

Durant was true to his word. The Lelands received no instructions. Durant's decision to retain the Leland management, unfettered, proved to be a tower of strength for General Motors in trying days just ahead.

14

The Model T:
There Was Only One

Late in the summer of 1908, the big door to the small engineering room Henry Ford had directed Charles Sorensen to build nearly two years before opened and the workmen got their first glimpse of the "Model-T." No one could know the impact this motorcar would have on the economic and social development of the United States and the world. However, Ford knew that a milestone had been reached in the life of his company and the business of making self-propelled road vehicles.

After the men had moved the pilot car out of the factory, George Holley, who had built the carburetor for the car, drove the "Model-T" for the first time in public. Ford asked Holley to take him for a ride. They were delayed when the new type of transmission stuck, but the engineers quickly corrected the difficulty.

Holley and Ford travelled the streets of Detroit for an hour or more. They drove up and down the quiet tree-shaded Woodward Avenue, Grand Boulevard, and Michigan Avenue. Ford was beside himself with excitement, but not to the point that he lost track of the agony and travail that had gone into the triumph. He told Holley to drive past the office of Alex Malcomson, the man who had made possible the founding of the Ford Motor Company, the man who had been driven from the company in a blast of carefully calculated corporate action. Malcomson had heaped words of ridicule on the Ford idea of developing a powerful, light and inexpensive car to replace the family horse. Holley reported that the drive had some of the elements of a triumphal parade of an athletic team along the streets of its home town after winning the game of the year.

Ford was impressed with the performance of the new car. Back at the plant he looked up Wills, Galamb, Wandersee, Couzens, Smith, Degener, Sorensen, and others who had carried with him the big load in the creation of the vehicle, and told them he was "tickled to death" with the way the car performed. He had a handshake, or a slap on the back, or that deepest of all Ford signs of fraternalism, a friendly kick in the pants, for each one. Finally, saluting them all, he grinned and told them, "Well, I guess we've got started." From the first day, Ford knew he had a winner.

The car was ready for production. The first few cars became availble in the early days of December as the motors and transmissions began coming in from the Dodge Works. Production did not begin on a big scale until February. It was destined to continue, without a major interruption, for almost twenty years.

No other motorcar has made such impact upon the country. The new creation hit with such force, even before the first car had been produced, that the "Model-T" became a separate contribution from the rest of the industry. The first promotion leaflet was issued in March to give dealers and the public an advance notice of what could be expected.

The New Castle, Pennsylvania, Ford dealer wrote immediately, "It is without doubt the greatest creation in automobiles ever placed before a people, and it means that this circular alone will flood your factory with orders." Other dealers were highly critical of the early announcement because so much of their time would be taken up with questions about the new car before it was available to customers. The Ford dealer in Rockford, Illinois, reported, "We have carefully hidden the sheets (leaflets) away and locked the drawer."

Pressure from agents and the public continued to build up. In September, when the pilot "Model-T" became available, Couzens was forced to invite the Ford dealers to Detroit and give them a forthright report. The company which would close out the 1908 year with a record production of 10,000 "Model-N" cars was prepared, Couzens told the dealers, to produce a record 25,000 "Model-Ts" in 1909.

It was a report calculated to get the heat off the Ford front office. Shortly after, contrary to the assurance given the dealers, Couzens told William C. Durant of General Motors that Ford production in 1909 would be stepped up to 15,000 cars. Interestingly, when the year was over, Ford had produced 17,700 cars. Buick was a close second with 16,500, Cadillac third with 7,500 and REO fourth with 6,600. Oldsmobile produced 1,750 and Oakland-Pontiac sales just cleared the 1,000 mark. On the basis of the 1909 returns, Buick was clearly in a position for the first and only time to contend with, or even overtake, the "Model-T" in 1910.

Instead, while Buick moved in 1910 to a new record for a non-Ford produced motorcar with 20,750, the "Model-T" increased its lead with a new single-year production record of 32,056. That, also, was the year that the United States first produced more automobiles than the rest of the world.

The following year, Buick faltered. The "Model-T" doubled its record volume to 70,000 cars while Buick ended the year producing 18,400; Cadillac, 10,000; and REO, 5,275.

The "Model-T" had broken away, but it was only the beginning. In 1912, Buick added to its production by 25 percent and set another, new record for a non-Ford produced car by making and marketing 26,800 automobiles. But, Ford gained by 100,000 for a total production of 170,000 "Model-Ts."

From that time on, and for a decade, there would be two sets of motorcar statistics; one for "Model-T" Ford production, and another for the remainder of the industry in the United States. "Model-T" volume climbed until, in 1923, Henry Ford's replacement for the family horse was sold to 1,817,891 customers. The nearest competitor that year was Chevrolet, with 454,000. In 1923, the American people bought as many "Model-T" Fords as all other national makes of motorcars combined. That one-year Ford production record for a single model stands to this day.

The "Model-T" remained so long without any important improvements that it was finally replaced by considerably superior motorcars. As a result, the public tends to remember this great motorcar in its old age as a funny little "tin lizzy" whose chief merit was that it was inexpensive and would perform ably on muddy roads. As a matter of fact, at the time of its introduction, and for fifteen years after, the "Model-T" was not only a light and inexpensive motorcar but also one of the most advanced in the world, at any weight or at any price.

Norval Hawkins, as
marketing genius behind
the "Model-T," became
the first man to sell more
than 25,000 motorcars in a
year. In 1916, he directed
the sale of three-quarters
of a million "Model-T"
cars. He suggested and
proved the worth of
establishing branch
assembly plants. The first
in the world was
established by Ford
in Kansas City.

251

The "Model-T" came on the market in a period when competition and contests for regular stock cars were being held in most cities and towns. No county, state fair or even big family reunion was held without featuring some type of automotive competition. The "Model-T" won hundreds of such competitions, but was the real champion on the long cross-country runs on dirt roads.

On June 1st, 1909, Mayor George B. McClellan in New York City fired a ceremonial gun to start six motorcars off on the 4,100-mile run to the Alaska-Yukon-Pacific Exposition in far-off Seattle. Two of the starters were the new "Model-T" Ford. Rules required that the cars should not travel on a railroad right-of-way, a considerable temptation in areas where well-defined roads did not exist. Repairs could only be made at two places enroute, Chicago and Cheyenne. Two scouting cars had been sent out in the spring to mark the route. The one moving east rammed into snow so deep in mountains of western Washington that the rest of the trip to New York had to be made by rail. The car going west made it to Idaho, where it broke down and terminated its scouting activities.

Both "Model-Ts" crossed the Mississippi River at St. Louis at the same time, some two hours ahead of the nearest competitor. The cars had to fight rain and mud and wet sands across Kansas, Colorado and eastern Wyoming. By that time, the two Fords were out of touch with each other and had no idea of where the other contestants were. The car driven by C. J. Smith reached the Snoqualmie Pass in the western Washington Mountains, where the scouting car had been stopped earlier, and found the snow still shoulder-deep. Smith was able to drive on top of the ice-capped snow for a while, but, finally, the car broke through and he had to assemble a crew to shovel out the pass.

They had worked only a short time when Henry Ford appeared. Ford had anticipated the situation, had approached the pass from the west and had directed the shoveling out of the snow on the long western rise to the summit. Ford, of course, had no definite way of knowing that one of his "Model-Ts" would be the first to reach the pass. Smith noted in his report, "When Mr. Ford saw us coming through, he was tickled to death to see we were the first."

Despite all of the road hazards (and having opened the Snoqualmie Pass for the others), Smith and his "Model-T" arrived at the Seattle Exposition on June 27th. He had driven through twelve states in twenty-two days, averaging just under 200 miles a day. Four years

This 1914 Jeffery truck applied power to all four wheels. The practice of selling the complete chassis without a body was common until World War I, permitting farmers and commercial owners to build their own truck bodies. The Graham Brothers of Evansville, Indiana, developed a national truck business, making bodies to place on Dodge engines and frames. Ford and Chevrolet did not make trucks until 1916.

earlier, the one-cylindered Oldsmobile had required forty-four days on the New York to Portland race.

The forty-five horsepower Shawmut arrived the following day. The second "Model-T" came in third, having lost one and a half days after turning the wrong direction at an important intersection in the mountains. The six-cylinder, 60-horsepower "Acme" arrived a week later; the only foreign car entry, the "Itala," was unable to travel beyond the second check point, Cheyenne.

In presenting the winner's cup to Smith and his "Model-T," mining-magnate Robert Guggenheim, one of the sponsors of the exposition, said, "Mr. Ford's theory that a lightweight car, highly powered for its weight, can go places where heavier cars cannot go, and can beat heavier cars costing five or six times as much on the steep hills or bad roads, has been proved."

That fall, the "Model-T" won the Munsey Reliability Run from Washington to Boston and back again to Washington. There were twenty competitors, including a Maryland, Renault, Chalmer-Detroit, REO, Columbia, Marmon, Maxwell and Hubmobile. The weather was bad and mud took nearly half the contestants out of the running. The Ford won with ease.

There is no mystery about the supremacy of Henry Ford's "Model-T." It was the first motorcar to offer so much for so little. It was the first car with the size and power to outperform a good team of horses and still come within the financial reach of most people. By the time the Ford Motor Company was established, in 1903, Ford was convinced that a proper balance of four factors—simple engineering, precision production, standardization of model and low price through high volume sale—could produce an entirely new kind of motorcar opportunity for everybody. The "Model-T" was that car.

The dramatic difference between Ford's accomplishment in his years of greatness and that of the other men who had similar opportunities is that this auto's career lasted so long and that it carried the almost solitary role of putting the nation on wheels. Five others —Olds, Durant, Jeffery, Leland and Pope (especially Durant and Olds)—also had the opportunity to lead the revolution.

It was Ford's emotional toughness that made the final difference. He maintained a stone-like steadfastness in seeking his goal. Within five years, some of his executives would have modified or scrapped the "Model-T," despite its unprecedented success. That had also happened at Oldsmobile, Buick, and numerous other plants, but Ford ruthlessly cut his objectors down. He prevented the change of even one major feature of the "Model-T" in the nearly twenty years the car was in production.

Ford himself was puzzled by the tendency of important competitors to move away from the production of light and inexpensive cars. "Within a few years," he commented, "Olds, Hupp, Buick and E. M. F. got out of my way, one by one, in something like that order. All of them went into larger cars after making a success of small ones. I recall looking at Bobby Hupp's roadster at the first show where it was exhibited and wondering whether we could ever build as good a small car for as little money."

The "Model-T" quickly changed the direction of the industry itself. Even in 1905, when only 25,000 motorcars were produced in the United States, the business had fragmented to such an extent that there were more than two hundred and fifty different makes of cars produced and sold. These were known as "assembled cars." They were largely made from the same standard components, and except for the name and some superficial features such as the hood or radiator shell, all were very much alike.

The "Model-T" was designed and engineered by one company. It offered numerous, superior features which were not to be found on the assembled cars. In 1908 and 1909, when the "Model-T" first arrived on the scene, the assembled car was in its heyday. More than four hundred different makes of cars were sold. As people turned to the "Model-T" with its exclusive and superior features, the number of assembled cars produced declined.

Couzens and his marketing men knew that they had a motorcar that would compete with any car made in the country regardless of its size, weight, and price. Advertisements told the public, "No car under $2,000 offers more, and no car over $2,000 offers more except in trimmings." There was much truth in the Ford proclamation. For the first time, a light and inexpensive car was available that could take a family anywhere that the largest and most expensive cars were able to go. It could do even more—it could travel muddy roads and through sand and across open streams where the heavy cars could not go. The "Model-T," in advertisements, was pictured moving across streams that had no bridges, climbing steep inclines (even climbing steps of public buildings) and perched on top of mountains no other car had yet climbed.

In the first two years, whenever a new "Model-T" stopped on a town street, a crowd would gather. The Ford dealer's first display of the car often attracted crowds like those that came to town to attend a fair or to see a circus.

What those people saw was a full-sized car with a wheel-base of 8 feet, 4 inches, standing 7 feet tall when the top was up, and with places for five passengers. It was called a touring car. The engine and body were carried high from the ground by unusually sturdy wheels. The steering wheel was moved to the left side and the seats were leather upholstered. When the car was introduced, the touring cars were painted red and the roadster was gray, but on June 1st, 1909, all "Model-Ts" were painted green with black trim and red striping. In 1912, black was made the standard color. Offering more than one color caused production delays and higher prices. Not again, until 1925, was a Ford car painted any color other than black.

The new car had an eye appeal all its own, but it was the mechanical improvements that set this car apart. The four-cylinder, 20-horsepower vertical-type motor was mounted in front. All four cylinders were cast at the same time. Earlier cylinders were cast one at a time and assembled into the motor. A new light vanadium steel, the first to appear in any American motorcar, was used in crankshafts, springs, axles and gears to make them both lighter and tougher.

Gone were the dry batteries and in their place was a magneto that provided electricity for the sparkplugs and lights. For the first time, the motor and transmission were completely enclosed. The car had two braking systems, one acting directly on the wheels and the other through the transmission. Front and rear springs were mounted above the axle and fastened to the ends of the axle in front, and to the ends of the axle housing in the rear. The gasoline tank was located under the driver's seat. The "Model-T" touring car weighed 1,200 pounds. In the first year, the touring car outsold the roadster four to one and in a short time was the most widely used car in the United States.

For the driver, perhaps the most appreciated new feature was the specially engineered planetary transmission. The "Model-T" planetary transmission, with its three pedals mounted on the floor, had some of the features of the modern automatic transmission. The two forward speeds were operated from a pedal on the left with an automatic shift from low into high at a given speed. The center pedal was reverse. The right pedal operated a braking system that functioned through the transmission while the emergency handbrake was completely independent and operated on wheel drums. The clutch and sliding gears of other cars were often difficult to use, especially in cold weather. The simple "Model-T" transmission offered many advantages.

On June 4th, 1908, the Ford factory became the first motorcar plant in the world to produce one hundred cars in a period of ten hours. Production of 70 to 80 cars a day had become customary during the spring. No record was planned for that June day, but the factory was pressing hard to complete its work on the "Model-N." By midafternoon the men became aware that a record was possible. When the whistle signaled the end of the day, 101 cars had been produced. During the late afternoon drive for a world production record, one car was assembled and tested in fourteen minutes.

By July and August, 100-car-days became commonplace on Piquette Avenue, but the limits of the plant had been reached. Ford's production men were already sure they could build 200 cars a day but that achievement would not take place until the move to Highland Park. While the activity in Highland Park was destined to attract the attention of the whole world, the foundation for the triumph was laid on Piquette Avenue where remarkable developments were directly related to the thunderous acceptance accorded the "Model-T."

Orders accumulated so rapidly that, by May of 1909, Couzens was compelled to announce that no more orders could be taken until further notice. Couzens had asked dealers to stop placing orders, briefly, when the "Model-N" was introduced, but that lasted less than three weeks. Nearly four months passed before orders were again accepted after the May announcement. Nothing like this had ever happened in the motorcar industry.

It was during this period that Ford and his men worked out another innovation opening the way to greater production and lowering costs. Norval Hawkins, Ford's marketing director, discovered that transportation costs could be sharply reduced when freight cars were used to ship maximum weights of components, such as motors, with the parts being assembled into cars near the point of sale.

In the summer of that year, work began on the building of the first Ford branch assembly plant in Kansas City. Albert Kahn designed a $30,000 assembly plant supplied by spurs from both the Frisco and Missouri Pacific railroads. Success came quickly to the Kansas City assembly plant and soon similar assembly facilities were being built in major cities from coast to coast. The first foreign assembly plant was built in Canada.

For instance, as soon as Henry Ford was convinced of the soundness of the "Model-T," he made a decision of the greatest importance to his company's objective of replacing the "family horse." He ordered that production of all other models be stopped and that all cars produced by the Ford Motor Company should be mounted on the same chassis. "Only one chassis from now on," he said, and with that order came the end of the four models then in production, including the six-cylinder "Model-K." For well over twenty years, the Ford Motor Company used only one chassis.

By 1908, Ford and Couzens had gathered together the cast of brilliant leaders who were to guide the destiny of the "Model-T" and the Ford Motor Company. Including Ford himself, there were only fourteen men who created the new and in many cases fantastic procedures that would soon make it possible to produce 10,000 cars in a twenty-four hour day.

They were Henry Ford, C. Harold Wills, James Couzens, John and Horace Dodge, Peter E. Martin, Charles Sorensen, Norval Hawkins, Joe Galamb, Fred Diehl and Walter Flanders. Later, three more were added to the group, William F. Knudsen, Clarence W. Avery and Edsel Ford. The fourteen men were never all together at the Ford Motor Company. However, for a period of three years, from 1911 until 1914, twelve of the fourteen worked together.

These twelve men deserve recognition as founders of the motorcar industry in this country. They were more important than many of the men who are widely regarded as motorcar pioneers because they produced cars bearing their names. The contributions of the Packards, Maxwells, Appersons, Stanleys, Hupps, Marmons and numerous others were modest compared to the achievements of any one of these giants who created the Ford Motor Company. The Ford group played the leading role in putting the people of the United States on wheels.

Of these men and their work Sorensen liked to quote a Danish poet, "To succeed is to realize what is possible." Henry Ford established the method that resulted in some of their unprecedented achievements when he told the men, "We must go ahead without the facts; we will learn as we go along."

Ten years were required to recruit this remarkable Ford team. The nature of their respective contributions is revealing. Twelve of the fourteen worked either with the creation or production of Ford cars. Only two, Couzens and Hawkins, were free of engineering or production responsibilities. After the first three years when he had responsibility for everything but engineering and production, Couzens was largely concerned with general management and finance. Hawkins was concerned with sales and marketing. First to join Ford was C. Harold Wills. He began working in 1902 on a part-time basis at the Henry Ford Company. Wills was mainly responsible for creating the great Ford motors. The Wills motors included the huge power plant in Ford's "999" racer, the 1903 "Model-A" that earned a place in the industry for the Ford Motor Company, and the "Model-N" with its first four-cylinder motor to be placed in a Ford car for general use. Wills had an important role in creating the "Model-T" motor, also.

Malcomson, who organized the Ford Motor Company, brought in James Couzens and John and Horace Dodge. Couzens in the role of management, and the Dodges' role in production were such, that had these men not joined, there would not have been a Ford Motor Company as it has existed through the years.

Peter E. Martin, universally known as "Ed," came to Ford Motor as a machine operator early in 1904. Friendly and popular with the workers, he quickly moved into production supervision. Ford Historian Owen Bombard says of him, "Martin was production superintendent at Highland Park for all those years from 1909 until assembly was moved to The Rouge in the 1920s. Production of the Model-T during its greatest years was Peter E. Martin's responsibility."

Charles E. Sorensen was hired in 1905. Ford had watched him as a pattern-maker in other Detroit firms. Son of a Danish immigrant, he worked with Henry Ford for forty years. He was the key figure in the creation of the moving, mechanized assembly line, considered to be the outstanding industrial advance of the century. One night, in his hotel room in Los Angeles, Sorensen conceived the idea of the great Ford Willow Run plant for making World War II bombers. Nineteen months later these complex giants of the air were moving out of the plant in half the time any similar plane had ever been produced before. Allan Nevins once remarked, "Charles E. Sorensen was a man who could have been head of a great country or played a decisive role in any of a hundred other callings and acquitted himself with distinction."

Walter Flanders was a member of the Ford staff only from 1906 until 1908. In that short time, he employed his genius in the use of machine tools and the placement of machines in the Ford factory to advance the company toward the magic of the moving, mechanized assembly line.

Norval Hawkins was head of his own Detroit accounting firm, with branches in several other cities, when Couzens retained him in 1907 to bring order to the records of the rapidly expanding Ford Motor Company. He took over the direction of Ford sales just as the "Model-T" entered the market. When he assumed the job, no sales manager in the motorcar business had marketed more than 15,000 cars within a year. Hawkins directed Ford sales for nine years and in the big year of 1916 achieved a record sale of 750,000.

Hawkins, who was accustomed to working on commission, saw the potential for the "Model-T." Couzens, who was noted for his miserly tendencies, offered Hawkins less salary than this new man thought was reasonable. But, instead of asking for a higher salary, Hawkins proposed that the Ford Motor Company pay him one dollar for each car sold. Both Couzens and Ford considered the arrangement fair. Before Hawkins resigned to become a special assistant to President Woodrow Wilson during World War I, that clause had made him a multimillionaire. The canny Hawkins had worked out the economic opportunities to be realized in establishment of branch assembly plants, a system since adopted generally throughout the industry.

Joe Galamb, who had received his engineering training in Europe, was hired by Wills in 1905 to work on plans and design. By the time the special office was established on the third floor of the Piquette Avenue plant to develop the "Model-T," Galamb was in charge of its engineering. The engine that literally became America's work horse was largely a creation of this engineer. And he had a key role in the last great engineering achievement under Henry Ford's direction, the building of the first successful V-8 engine for a low-priced car. It was introduced in 1932.

Fred Diehl joined the company in 1907 as a timekeeper. At the time, Couzens directed major purchases of materials himself. As he found it impossible to keep up with the constantly rising demands of purchasing, Diehl became an assistant and, soon after, was placed in complete charge. Diehl held the job for more than twenty years. He saw the job increase in scope and importance until he had the responsibility of seeing that the millions of items needed to complete 10,000 cars in a twenty-four hour period were ready and waiting. He bought billions in materials and components for the Ford Motor

Company and retired with the respect of his associates at Ford and throughout the industry.

In 1911, William S. Knudsen (later, president of General Motors), joined the Ford Motor Company. Knudsen had been employed, almost from the time he arrived in the United States from Denmark, by the John R. Keim Mills in Buffalo. The firm was purchased by the Ford Company in 1911. Knudsen developed most of the Ford branch assembly plants in the United States, as well as those in foreign countries. He joined General Motors in 1921.

Clarence W. Avery was the man who made the moving, fully-mechanized assembly line and completely synchronized manufacturing procedures practical. He joined The Ford Motor Company in 1912 as Sorensen's assistant. The idea of a moving assembly line had already taken root at Ford, but Avery translated the idea into reality in less than eighteen months. Within the period of a single year the time for the assembly of a Ford car was cut from 728 to 93 minutes.

Edsel Ford, along with Couzens, was the outstanding industrial management figure at the Ford Motor Company before World War II. A modest man, he was destined always to labor in the shadow of his illustrious father. However, drawing heavily on the genius of Sorensen, he cemented the great Ford empire together during the 1920s and 1930s, when he was often denied the cooperation of his aging father. Over Henry Ford's fierce opposition, Edsel marshaled the company's great power for the war effort in World War II, a task that so sapped his strength that he became a war casualty himself. The last Flying Fortress produced at the Willow Run plant was mounted on the grounds as a memorial to Edsel Ford.

15

The Golden Years

Between the evening of December 31st, 1909, and the morning of January 2nd, 1910, the Piquette Avenue Ford plant ceased to exist. Over the New Year holiday all the equipment at Piquette Avenue was transferred to the Highland Park plant, where the entire operation occupied only 25 percent of the main building. But, in the next five years, from Highland Park, would come, not only fantastic production of motorcars, but the ideas and practices which would revolutionize the industrial world.

"The Crystal Palace," so named because its walls and ceilings contained 50,000 square feet of glass, was designed by Albert Kahn and built, as the *Detroit Free Press* commented, "a way out in the country on Woodward Avenue." The main building was one-sixth of a mile long (865 feet), 75 feet wide and 4 stories high. It was the largest building in Michigan, and was constructed entirely of steel, concrete and glass.

The Highland Park factory was actually a complex with vast buildings spread over the entire 60 acres of what had been a racetrack. At one side of the main building was a one-story machine shop in which the motors and transmissions were turned out. The machine shop was 840 feet long and 140 feet wide. It was separated from the first floor of the main plant by another building that was 860 feet long and 57 feet wide. It was the first structure of its type in the world—a touch of the Kahn genius.

The building housed only a giant crane and its track. The crane was capable of picking up a railroad car of materials and delivering it to any door of the first story of the main plant or the machine shop on the other side. Cross-tracks enabled the crane to carry materials into the buildings. Functionally, the first floor of the main factory, the giant craneway and the vast machine shop were all one building.

The first floor of the main building was largely used for chassis construction. On the fourth floor, fenders, radiators, gas tanks, hoods and the upholstered appointments of the car's interiors were made. On the third floor, there were departments for wheels, bodies (including painting), lamps, floorboards, and other components. The second floor was devoted to assembly, the engineering department and the central office.

The Highland Park complex included many other buildings. The foundry (which had not existed at Piquette Avenue) was in a vast building, a square measuring 200 by 200 feet. The heat-treating plant, and numerous others, were also large. With all this vast array, it was possible to produce only a substantial part of the components that went into the motorcars leaving the Highland Park complex each working day. Soon the Firestone Tire and Rubber Company was delivering two million dollars' worth of tires a year to Highland Park. Firestone shipments were the largest of several from tire manufacturers. Lamp bulbs and other components arrived in carload lots.

Until 1914, the largest of all shipments received at the Highland Park factory was from the Dodge Brothers Works at Hamtramck. Those shipments constantly increased. When the two firms dissolved their relationship, the Dodge Works was supplying "Model-T" motors, transmissions and axles for 1,000 to 1,200 cars each working day. From 1909 until 1914, the Dodge Works (except for wheels and bodies), built more Ford cars than the total annual production of any other motorcar manufactured in the world.

As the "Model-T" led the Ford Motor Company to one unprecedented achievement after another in 1909 and 1910, Henry Ford was experiencing one of the most difficult periods of his life. The long-smoldering Selden patent suit burst into full flame. Four years, from 1904 through 1908, had been used by both sides to document their cases. In February of 1909, Attorney Ralzemond Parker advised Ford that the time was at hand when the trial would actually begin. The trial began on May 28th, in the New York District court before Judge Charles Merrill Hough, an acknowledged expert in marine law, but without special background in patent matters.

The trial lasted for two months. Ford was forced to devote practically his entire time appearing as a witness and assisting his lawyers in the conduct of the Ford Motor Company defense. Since the Selden group had filed patent violation charges against twenty other firms some years before, the Ford Company had emerged as the leader in the industry. This meant that the company, and Ford personally, bore the brunt of the attack. At times the courtroom proceedings took on the elements of an industry witch-hunt. The Selden lawyers attempted to make Ford's success appear as a social evil.

As tensions mounted, the trial became a great drama played through the press before the entire nation. Tempers flared, but Henry Ford kept his under careful control. His massive self-control mechanism was always at its best under heavy stress. Above all, he realized that the Selden trial could amount to a tremendous dividend for his company. He astutely assumed the role of a small David, being attacked by the giant determined to throw the blanket of monopoly over him and the entire motorcar industry of the United States. He used the trial as a pulpit to present his cause: that of a man and a company determined to bring to the working man, the farmers and the small professional man the rich benefits of the motorcar. He stressed that he was moving steadily toward this goal, despite the persecution of the Selden group who were determined to strangle his efforts by making him conform to their rules.

In an effort to break the tension, one of the lawyers said to Ford, "Mr. Ford, I came in from Oyster Bay by car. We didn't kill anyone, but everybody on the road hated us, and it was probably sheer luck that we didn't have a collision. I think you are creating a social problem with your car."

This touched a responsive chord in Ford and, in all seriousness, he responded, "No, my friend, you're mistaken. I'm not creating a social problem at all. I am going to democratize the automobile." He referred to the new Highland Park Plant that was within months of being completed, and added, "When I'm through everybody will be able to afford one, and about everybody will have one. The horse will have disappeared from our highways, the automobile will be taken for granted and there won't be any problem."

Ford made these observations in 1909, when as yet not 100,000 motorcars had been produced in a single year. There were then 25,000,000 horses handling the job of transportation and providing power on farms. As he looked out of the courtroom window, the ratio of horse-drawn vehicles to motorcars was, roughly, one to five. Recalling the incident years later, the lawyer who raised the point with Ford said, "And, by God, he was right."

On the afternoon of June 1st, Ford excused himself from court long enough to be present at the New York City Hall when Mayor George B. McClellan fired the shot that sent six motorcars off on the New York to Seattle run. Ford was disappointed that there were so few cars in the race and predicted that his 1,200-pound "Model-Ts" (lightest in the contest) would come in first and second. Two weeks later, he took time off to go to western Washington and help scoop the snow off the pass on the Continental Divide to allow his Ford and the other drivers through.

By July, the millions of words in the Selden trial had been spoken. Judge Hough had the records sent to his Rhode Island summer home. There he sifted the evidence for two months. On September 15th, he handed down his decision, in favor of the Selden patent group. Parker, in behalf of the Ford Motor Company, had argued that the engine George Selden had proposed for his car was based only on plans and was not the type of internal combustion engine that was used by the Ford Motor Company. In addition, Henry Ford had begun work before Selden received his patent in 1895 and, therefore, was not an infringer.

Judge Hough held that an internal combustion engine was an internal combustion engine no matter what frills might be built into it. The judge stated that even if Henry Ford had begun work before the issue of the patent, he had become an infringer as soon as he started producing motorcars after the date of issue; and would be for seventeen years more.

Judge Hough's decision set the stage for the first of the three greatest moments in the career of Henry Ford. They were all to occur in his five golden years, 1911 to 1916. These were the years, the last years, when the giants on the Ford team that made the "Model-T" possible—Couzens, Wills, Hawkins and the others— were with Henry Ford. Strangely, none of the three climactic achievements and the decisions associated with them contributed to the development or improvement of the car. Yet, these decisions smoothed the road to future success.

The Selden group was overjoyed. Many of the leaders had not

expected to win an unqualified victory, but they took quick advantage of the situation. The Association of Licensed Automobile Manufacturers filed new infringement suits against all of the motorcar firms that had encouraged or assisted Ford in his stand against the Selden group.

The suits soon brought about the desired response. Benjamin Briscoe, Ransom E. Olds and others who had stood with Ford in his fight, quickly surrendered and licensed their cars under the Selden patent. William Durant, who had no sympathy with the Selden group's objective and who had allowed the Oldsmobile permit to lapse after General Motors had acquired the Olds Motor Works, came to terms. He paid the Selden Association a million dollars in back dues and brought Buick, Oldsmobile, Cadillac, Oakland-Pontiac and the other motorcar producers in General Motors into the Selden fold. Ford was soon completely isolated from the other leaders in the motorcar industry.

A mounting anger developed among smaller companies attacked and pressured by the Selden Association, particularly the dealers representing Ford and other firms. The public, too, was aroused. The Selden patent group heaped fresh fuel on the rising flames by declaring that the dealers who sold and the people who bought non-licensed cars could be considered infringers. The Ford Motor Company countered by running advertisements stating it would pay for any damages assessed against a customer.

To a degree, the struggle had become a battle between the producers of the larger, heavier and expensive motorcars and the champion of the light, inexpensive car. Cadillac and Oldsmobile no longer made the light cars on which their early success had been founded. The Selden group attempted to stabilize the market at profitable levels by providing production ceilings.

The Velie Motor Company of Moline, Illinois, a former wagon manufacturing firm, which was reorganized to make cars, sued the Selden group for $500,000 damages, contending the action of the Selden association had deprived the firm of that much income. The Velie suit disclosed that the firm had been directed to pay $14,000 as an entrance fee to the association and to limit its 1910 production to 2,500 cars, and its 1911 output to 2,000 cars.

The Velie suit exposed the heart of the controversy. Ford was determined not to get shackled with industry planning or share the management of his company with outsiders. He had walked out on the Henry Ford Company over that issue and he had forced Alex K.

Malcomson out of the Ford Motor Company to earn the right to run his company with a free hand. For some years, the Ford Motor Company had been financially able to pay the fee levied under the Selden patent but, as the ability to pay increased, Ford's opposition mounted higher and higher.

Within hours of the Hough decision in favor of the Selden group, Ford promised that the case would be appealed. "We will fight to the finish," he proclaimed. "There will be no letup in the legal fight and I expect ultimately the Supreme Court of the United States will hold that the Selden basic patent is not valid."

The Ford Motor Company retained additional lawyers to work under the direction of Parker, and took the case to the Court of Appeals in New York. The process of legal preparations started over again. More than a year passed before the high court review began, in November, 1910.

There were signs of disruption of growth and car production after the Hough decision. In the period of uncertainties raised by the court decision, firms did not expand as they had earlier. Although "Model-T" production almost doubled during the first year of operation at the new Highland Park factory, the directors delayed a number of actions which would have increased production.

Three judges now conducted the review of the case. Among them was Walter Chadwick Noyes, a New Englander not only with legal training but also with business experience. He had been president of the New London Northern Railroad Company. President Theodore Roosevelt had appointed him to the New York bench where he presided over a number of important patent cases.

The judges worked rapidly, using the Yule holidays to put their decision in final form. Noyes read the decision January 9th, 1911, on the eve of the 11th annual New York Automobile Show. The Court of Appeals held that all internal combustion engines were *not* alike, and that the one included by Selden in his patent was of the Brayton type, while the engine used by the Ford Motor Company was completely different, being of the Otto type.

"We can see," said Noyes, "that had he (Selden) appreciated the superiority of the Otto engine and adopted that type for his combination, his patent would cover the modern automobile. He did not do so ... We cannot ... make another choice for him at the expense of these defendants, who neither legally nor morally owe him anything."

The first of the three great moments in the Ford career was over,

267

and the stage was set for the second and third. The fight against the Selden patent had begun the year the company was formed in 1903. For nearly eight years, until January, 1911, every act of the company had been conditioned to the possibility of losing the infringement suit brought against the company by the Selden group.

There had, however, been one enormous benefit from the great court fight. When the Selden controversy began, Ford and his company were unknown. When it ended Henry Ford was not only a national figure but had become an American hero at the same time. The trial and the front pages of the newspapers across the country provided Ford the opportunity to explain his objective of making it possible for most people in the United States to own an automobile. The Selden trial set Henry Ford apart from all other personalities and firms in the motorcar industry. His adversaries had conferred upon him and his company a benefit that might not have been achieved in any other way.

Ford was aware of this and, from the first moment of victory, made certain that he did nothing to detract from his priceless gains. He was about ready to leave for the New York Automobile Show when the news of his victory over the Selden group was flashed to Detroit. His reaction was one of remarkable restraint. He told a Detroit reporter, "Whatever I'd say now might sound like boasting. I think the decision speaks for itself." Nothing he said in public indicated how deeply he felt about the victory. That was revealed in the diary of his seventeen-year-old son, Edsel, who wrote in capital letters under the date of January 9th, 1911, "HEARD THE NEWS (WE) WON THE SELDEN SUIT."

Although the "Model-T" Ford had already established itself by 1911 as the most popular motorcar ever built, it was not until the restraints imposed by the long Selden court test were removed that the car began to fill its ultimate destiny of replacing the family horse. It is largely to Couzens's credit that the company's production capacity was expanded throughout the darkest months of the Selden fight. The hard-driving Couzens pressed Ford and the other directors to buy the site, draw the plans and build the greatest manufacturing facility in Michigan. It was Couzens who also had to find the money to build the new complex. He did, by raising the price of the "Model-T" in 1909, much to Henry Ford's regret.

The greatest Ford handicap imposed by the Selden litigation had been in marketing. Norval Hawkins had been all too aware of this. In commenting on the court victory, Hawkins said, "At last the

Ford Motor Company was placed in a position where it could market its product in the ordinary, customary and usual manner without the discouragements and intimidations of others. Prior to this time the company's contemplated program of expansion was, upon the advice and counsel of its patent attorneys, held in abeyance pending the ultimate outcome of the litigation."

But the Selden matter went much further than company management restraint, and Hawkins was the leading authority on that, too. He made a 1910 survey of the entire country. In his official report, he described "vast" areas, potentially rich in Ford sales, where there was no Ford representation at all. This had come about because Selden had licensed motorcar firms and had convinced those who would have become Ford dealers that they were taking too great a risk in being made party to infringement damages. Hawkins spent several weeks, in 1910, personally visiting more than fifty towns in the states where there were no Ford dealers. Great salesman that he was, he interested local businessmen in joining the Ford sales force, only to find when he returned to Detroit that every one of them had cancelled his contract.

It was true, as Hawkins suggested, that after the Selden verdict the company and its executives could conduct a more normal existence than had been known since the firm had been founded. Another sign indicating less tension was that Henry and Clara Ford took their son, Edsel, on a trip to Europe, something they could not have considered as long as the Selden matter remained unsettled. It was one of the happiest times Ford and his family ever had known. They went to Plymouth on the sleek ocean liner, George Washington, spent several weeks in Great Britain and France and returned from Cherbourg on the same ship.

Another evidence of the more confident mood was the purchase of the J. R. Keim Pressed Steel Mills of Buffalo. The company provided the pressed steel covers for the "Model-T" crankcase and transmission, contributing significantly to the car's light weight. Competitors, with less volume, used heavier cast iron for such purposes. Ford needed the entire Keim capacity and, on Sorensen's suggestion, bought the company's stock and moved the plant to Highland Park, using the former site in Buffalo for a Ford assembly plant.

The purchase of the Keim mill proved to be a major landmark in Ford development. The Ford Company acquired not only a vital supplier, but also three of its outstanding executives. One of those men was William H. Knudsen.

With the Highland Park plant coming into its own and the Selden suit shackles removed, "Model-T" production, already higher than that of any other automobile plant in the world, moved spectacularly upward. In 1911, Ford produced 70,000 cars, an increase of more than 100 percent over the 32,000 produced the year before. In 1912, "Model-T" production again increased 100 percent to a total of 170,000 cars. The total car production of General Motors, including Buick, Cadillac and Oakland-Pontiac, for the year, was less than 50,000. The Ford Motor Company produced almost half the motorcars made in the United States in 1912.

This sensational production enabled Henry Ford to make good his promise to use rising profits to reduce the price of the Ford car. The "Model-T" touring car, the backbone of the line, was priced at $850 when it was introduced in 1908, and raised to $950 in 1909, when the company was building and paying cash for the new Highland Park factory. Then, in 1910, the Ford Motor Company jolted the motorcar industry by becoming the first major producer to offer a significant cut in prices. The Model-T touring car price was reduced $170, to $780. In 1911, the price was slashed to $690 and, in 1912, was dropped again, to an even $600. The five-passenger, "Model-T" touring car was selling for $250 less than the two-cylindered, two-passenger "Model-A" produced nine years before, when the company started in business!

The second of Ford's exclusive contributions to the motorcar was at hand. The men of the Ford Motor Company were ready to work out and put into use the greatest advance in the production of manufactured products of the 20th Century. The introduction of *mass production,* not to be confused with quantity production, at Ford's Highland Park factory effected a more profound change and improvement in the lives of more people in less time than any other invention in recorded history.

The development of synchronized and mechanized production at Ford was the first advance in manufacturing since the concept of standardization of parts and specialized assembly announced and proven by Eli Whitney more than a century earlier. The new Ford procedure was built squarely on the Whitney discoveries, putting to full use the Whitney idea of building special machines to produce standardized parts to be assembled by semi-skilled workers. But the new Ford manufacturing procedure went much further.

The revolutionary moving assembly line was devised not only to speed the final building of the Ford car, but also to build the car's major components, including the radiator, the axle unit, the motor and the body. Further, the energy to move materials and components on both sub-assembly units and the final assembly line was provided not by men or animals but by electricity.

Many persons and many factors entered directly into the working out of this 20th Century miracle. Behind everything was the unprecedented success and acceptance of the Model-T. By 1912, Model-T production had moved above 75,000 cars a year while the production of all General Motors cars in that year was less than 50,000. Yet there was demand for an even much larger number of Model-T cars. Henry Ford encouraged his men to probe every possibility to increase production. He was ready to give quick approval to any expenditure for new equipment that held the promise of more production.

The idea of instituting a moving assembly line to take the place of the stationary assembly stations had been considered by Ford men for several years before 1913 when the new system of mass production was first put to use at the Highland Park plant. From the time the Model-N Ford, forerunner to the Model-T, reached full production in 1907, Ford production men, such as Sorensen, were under pressure to produce cars more quickly and less expensively.

In Sorensen's diary is a report of a first crude demonstration of a moving assembly procedure organized by Sorensen's men. It was held on a Sunday when the Piquette Avenue plant was closed. This was in the summer of 1908 after the Model-T had been announced but before production had begun and while Model-N cars were still being produced.

Among those present were Henry Ford, Harold Wills and Ed Martin, the three most important men to Ford production at that time and all of them in higher positions of authority than Sorensen whose responsibility included getting the constantly increasing number of components to the greater and greater number of assembly stations.

Putting a chassis on skids and pulling it past the points where components were located, Sorensen and his man actually went through the motions of assembling a Model-N Ford car. Wills and Martin were not impressed. Whatever Ford's inner thoughts on the matter may have been, he urged Sorensen to continue to experiment with the idea.

Such a radical idea naturally took hold slowly. Car production continued to be centered at the Piquette Avenue plant for two and one-half years longer, and this plant was too small and crowded to permit the full use of the new system. Fred Diehl was just beginning his pace-setting work in large scale procurement of materials and outside components upon which the new assembly procedures would depend. Hawkins's equally remarkable work in sales was also just beginning.

Production of Ford cars shifted to the new Highland Park plant in January, 1910. Although the Dodge Brothers continued to make Ford components, especially motors, more of the components were being made at the Ford plant. Another factor that hastened the coming of the moving assembly line was the installation of overhead conveyors to move components from storage areas to the first floor at the Highland Park plant where cars were assembled. Sorensen first installed an overhead conveyor to replace the parts carriers that moved radiators to the assembly floor. Time and cost savings were so great that conveyors were soon doing most of the transporting of big components.

The man who transformed the idea of mass production and its moving assembly line into reality did not come to the Ford Motor Company until the early weeks of 1912. He was Clarence W. Avery. Reared on a Michigan farm, he had graduated from the University of Michigan, become a teacher and was Edsel Ford's manual training instructor. The serious-minded Edsel developed a special fondness and respect for his manual training teacher. Avery was often a guest at the Ford home. During these visits Henry Ford interested him in quitting his teaching job to go to work for the Ford Motor Company.

Henry Ford introduced Avery to Sorensen who immediately recognized the 30-year-old Avery to be a man of unusual capacity. In Avery's first eight months, Sorensen sent him to work in each of the departments to give him a basic knowledge of each step in producing a Ford car. After the training period, Avery was made Sorensen's assistant and given the assignment of working out plans for a moving assembly line. Avery quickly grasped the importance of the program.

His first step was to make accurate time studies to determine exactly how many man-hours were required to build motors, radiators, axles and other components as well as the final assembly or building of the car. Next, he projected the savings in man-hours that could be expected when components were produced on a moving assembly.

The first breakthrough came in the spring of 1913. William C.

Klann, in charge of engine assembly, became interested in making the change-over to the revolutionary new method of putting together motors. The new procedure was soon adapted to the production of other major components, including the transmission. Major savings were effected, and the quality of the components was improved.

By summer, Avery was working toward an application of the moving assembly technique to the building of the complete car. He did a time study for almost a month on 250 men working at assembling stations and the 80 parts carriers who worked with them. Based on the production of more than 6,000 cars by this group of workmen, Avery found that it took an average of 12½ man-hours to assemble a car.

Starting with a moving assembly station actually pulled by Klann, Sorensen, Avery and the foreman in charge of final assembly, whose last name was Peterson, and with Henry Ford watching, the Ford men were able to cut the assembly time by one-half. A year later, when Avery had completed the development of the moving assembly, the time for building the Model -T car was reduced to one hour and thirty-three minutes.

Gradually, the moving assembly lines of the component plants were synchronized with the final assembly work so that the making of a car became one continuous operation. In time, iron ore moved from mines across the country into blast furnaces and into the Highland Park factory, becoming a part of a Model-T Ford, all in one continuous movement.

As was true of all the men, Ford regarded the development simply as a means of solving a company production problem. It was several years before he realized that his men had evolved the first important addition to the concept of mass production, since Eli Whitney first set down the fundamentals. It was a concept that within Ford's lifetime would spread to all American industry engaged in the production of large numbers of complex machines.

In 1913, even though the full moving assembly system was not in operation until close to the end of the year, a new record number of "Model-Ts" came off the line. For the first time, production exceeded 650 cars a day for a total of more than 200,000 motorcars for the year.

In 1914, the first full year for the moving assembly line, Ford production exceeded all previous records. For the three hundred working days that year, the company averaged just over 1,000 cars a day. The total for the year climbed to 308,000. Approximately three out of every five cars produced in the United States that year was a "Model-T."

High sales accounted for major cuts in the price each year. The new schedule announced on August 1st, 1913, lowered the price of the touring car to $550, three hundred dollars less than when the car was first introduced. In 1914, Henry Ford had the satisfaction of eclipsing the goal he had set for himself. He had promised to build a car for the entire family that could be sold for $500. On August 1st, the price of the "Model-T" touring car was reduced to $490. The price of the two-passenger roadster was cut to $440.

Henry Ford was elated, yet he had other emotions, too. Even with the deep slashes in cost, company profits were piling up in the banks more rapidly than ever before. The efficiency of the new moving assembly lines had reduced costs to an extent that even Ford had not thought possible. For the first time in the business of making motorcars, Ford had to worry about constantly rising profits. The stage was now in order for the third of Ford's great moments.

The year was 1914, the day January 4th. Unlike the secondary role held by Ford in the development of the moving assembly line, this line of action was to be his, alone. It was often his custom to meet with some of the key executives on Sunday morning in his Highland Park plant office. On this occasion, his production and employment chiefs were present, and the subject on the agenda concerned wages in the Ford plants for the coming year. Lee was in charge of employment for the company. Martin and Sorensen supervised most of the workers. The average daily wage of the workers was $2.30. The beginning wage paid in the plant was $2.00. Company profit-sharing had already been established. Before Christmas, employees who had worked for the company for three years generally received a bonus equal to 10 percent of their yearly wage.

The important facts bearing on the question of wages were known to everyone present. Although the price of the "Model-T" had been reduced by 40 percent since 1909, profits had taken a spectacular rise; $1,800,000 in 1909, $2,000,000 in 1910, $3,005,000 in 1911, $5,200,000 in 1912, and $11,200,000 in 1913. With the introduction of the moving assembly line, company earnings were rising well above these levels. In addition, the company had an inventory worth $7,000,000. This included a million lamps, 800,000 wheels, 800,000 tires, 90,000 tons of steel, the hide of 400,000 cattle for leather upholstery, 12,000,000 hickory billets for wheel spokes, and 2,000,000 square feet of glass for windshields.

As usual, Ford had thought the matter through and, undoubtedly, had talked it over with Mrs. Ford. From the beginning of the conference, he showed every indication of having made his decision on the matter under discussion. The question to be decided was the extent or degree.

Ford began by stating that the company had lowered costs of the cars for the benefit of customers, year after year, and that the time had come when he wanted to give a greater share of the profits to the men in the plants. He spoke of wanting Ford employees to be able to own and enjoy the benefits of the cars they were building. Lee and Martin said they favored regular raises for good workmen, but that they opposed any major, across-the-board increase in wages. The company was already one of the better places to work in the Detroit area.

Ford brushed aside the comments of Lee and Martin and went right on with his train of thought. He asked Sorensen to go to the blackboard and translate each million dollars taken out of profits into increases in average daily wages in the plants. The first projected rate was $3.00 a day, then $3.50, $3.75 and $4.00. Lee was sarcastic about the figures which seemed only to spur Ford on. Martin protested, too, but Ford asked how much profit would be required to support a daily wage of 4.25. Gradually the daily wage figure advanced to $4.50, then to $4.75. The conference lasted much of the day.

At this point Ford stepped to the blackboard, took the chalk from Sorensen and said, "Stop it, Charlie; it's all settled. Five dollars a minimum pay and at once."

As in the case of the moving assembly line, this decision to double the wages, from janitor to drill-press operator in the largest motorcar factory in the world, was merely the solution to a problem facing the Ford Motor Company. There was no thought about the effect such a drastic decision would have outside the Ford Company or outside of Michigan.

Ford had come to his office on that Sunday to meet with his associates in an effort to work out a problem that had concerned him for some months. Many explanations, friendly and unfriendly, were given for his decision, but those closest to Ford, agreed that he acted mainly, and perhaps impulsively, to help his workmen. The country was in the midst of the most severe recession since 1907, and this may have impressed upon him the need to use some of the wealth of his very successful company to improve the economic lot of the men in the plants. The increases applied to men in all branch assembly plants and branch sales offices across the country. The full increase applied to women only if they were head of the household. However, all women did get some increase over the average daily wage of $2.07.

The Sunday meeting was but the decisive one of several held on the matter about the same time. Wills, Couzens, Hawkins and others were consulted. On Monday, the 5th, there was a directors meeting which was a necessary formality. Ford, Couzens and Rackham were present and the $5.00 per day, minimum wage was unanimously approved. Early in the afternoon, Couzens and Ford met with reporters of the Detroit newspapers and announced the sensational wage increase. The news appeared in the evening editions.

There was sadness involved, too, further indicating that the move was made without much prior consideration. By 2 a.m. the morning of the 6th of January, men seeking jobs began to gather at the Highland Park Plant. By dawn police estimated there were ten thousand job seekers on Woodward Avenue. The company had to post a notice that there was no employment opportunity at that particular time.

Ford and Couzens immediately were in the limelight of the entire business world. Following on the heels of the Selden case publicity, the action on the $5.00 per day, made Ford as familiar a name as that of any living American. It had the effect of convincing laboring families across the country that Henry Ford was interested in them and believed in paying high wages. The relationship grew so strong that soon thousands of laboring families would not consider the purchase of any other make of car.

The management of other automotive firms in Detroit were generally bitter about the Ford action, especially because there had been no previous notice to them that the wage increase was coming. Alvin Macauley, president of Packard Motor Car Company, called Sorensen the Monday evening before the news appeared in the newspapers. He reported that they had heard of the $5.00 minimum wage decision during a meeting of their board, and that the directors were so shocked that the meeting was terminated. Macauley added, "What are you fellows trying to do? We all felt 'what's the use; we can't compete with an organization like The Ford Motor Company.' "

Two days later the editors of the *New York World* asked Thomas Edison for his opinion of the Ford move. Reflecting his understanding and friendship for Ford, as well as constituting a penetrating commentary on the times, Edison replied in a telegram, saying, "It is such a radical innovation that I cannot at present give an opinion as to its ultimate effect. Sometime ago Mr. Ford reduced the price of his wonderful touring car to the extent of fifty dollars. The user of the car received the entire benefit. Now he had practically reduced it another fifty dollars, but this time the men who make them get the benefit. Mr. Ford's machinery is special and highly efficient. This is what permits these results. This is open to all in nearly every line of business. Edison."

By 1915, the "immortality" of Henry Ford was secure. In a period of five amazing years, from 1909 when the "Model-T" went into production until 1914 when he adopted the $5.00 minimum wage, Henry Ford's career flashed like a comet across a dark sky, pointing the way to the future. During these golden years of his achievement, he carried on the fight, virtually alone, to break the Selden patent monopoly; he built, at Highland Park, one of the great industrial centers to be found anywhere in the world; he encouraged his men as they created the moving assembly line.

During these few years no controversies swirled about Ford or his company. Except for Walter Flanders and the Dodge brothers who left him to create their own motorcars, he had the confidence and loyalty of his fellow executives, his men in the plants, his thousands of dealers and of an admiring public across the nation.

His career would continue for more than three decades during which he developed a light tractor, built airplanes, owned a railroad and ships at sea and raised, on the banks of his beloved River Rouge, what is still one of the world's greatest industrial complexes. He fought for peace among nations as vigorously as he fought the Selden patent, but with less success. He spent much of his time and large sums of money creating a great museum at Greenfield Village, in Michigan, to let future generations know what our country was like in 1900, before the impact of the motorcar.

The "Model-T" stands as the memorial to his work and what he accomplished. The car introduced the advantages of the self-propelled road vehicle to more Americans than any other motorcar. This Ford car expanded the opportunities for millions of individuals to have better educations, better jobs, better health, better homes, better highways and, finally, the chance to escape human drudgery on the farm and in the factory.

In the short space of twenty years Ford and his company introduced into the lives of a majority of Americans the kind of living that only the wealthy were able to enjoy before 1900. The "Model-T" was the chief instrument of the greatest upgrading of opportunity in the lives of more people, in the shortest period of time, in all history.

16

The Night They Saved
General Motors

By the summer of 1910, General Motors was in trouble. Early in the fall difficulties had deepened until it appeared that bankruptcy and dissolution were only a matter of days away. For the first time, in a spectacular career in transportation that now spanned a full quarter of a century, William Crapo Durant was powerless. General Motors was out of money. Backers, such as Durant, could not provide more working capital and the banks would not advance more loans or even extend the loans already made.

Even worse, the Buick Motor Company, which had been the chief well of financial strength, was $8,000,000 in debt with loans overdue. The firm was reduced, literally, to shipping currency (paid the company by dealers) in suitcases directly from points like Boston to Flint so that the cash could be used for payrolls. If the money had been placed into regular banking channels, it would have been applied to pay overdue loans and Buick's operations would have collapsed because the men in the shops could not be paid.

General Motors had made good profits in the first two years. The first year, 1908, produced a gross sale of $29,000,000 and profits of $9,000,000. The second year was even better, with a gross sale of $39,000,000 and profits of $10,255,000. However, the seeds of trouble were to be seen in the second year report. An additional $10,000,000 income produced little additional profit. The crisis developed when it became necessary to invest in a much larger production for the spring selling season of 1911.

The problem was simple enough. Durant had not been able to get major investors to see the future possibilities in the motorcar. Even with the spectacular profits being turned in by Buick, Ford and Cadillac, the idea prevailed everywhere that the self-propelled road vehicle was a fad that would soon pass. The men who controlled the country's investment money would not believe that the horse was actually going to be replaced on the highways and streets of the United States.

Finally, Durant had yielded to the temptation to organize General Motors with little more at his disposal than the financial resources of his highly successful Buick Motor Company. Buick's net worth was the highest in the industry, being equal to the combined resources of Ford and Cadillac, but Buick's resources were not adequate to support the much larger financial responsibilities of General Motors. Matters brightened near the close of its first year when General Motors acquired the Cadillac Motor Company.

At this point, Durant's greatest weaknesses became apparent. Influenced, perhaps, by the fact that his own business career had begun when he acquired the patent for a new kind of two-wheeled horse cart, he chased patents the rest of his life, as boys chase butterflies. Instead of consolidating his gains around the great Buick and Cadillac potential, and their supplier companies, such as Weston-Mott and AC Sparkplug, Durant brought into General Motors a long list of firms that held patents on devices which he thought might provide important improvements for future General Motors cars.

Durant bought patents outright. He sent Herbert R. Lewis to Fargo, North Dakota, in the dead of winter to investigate a patent that Durant knew to be for sale. Lewis, himself well versed in patent matters, returned and reported that the patent could be bought for $10,000, but recommended against purchase. However, on learning that the patent could be secured for as little as $10,000, Durant bought it.

It was often impossible for Durant's close associates to understand his moves. It was one of these Durant decisions that played a major role in bringing General Motors to the brink of bankruptcy in the early fall of 1910. John Albert Heany of the Heany Lamp Company at York, Pennsylvania, claimed he was the inventor of the modern tungsten filament for the electric light. He had applied for the patent in 1908. Durant saw the possibility of revolutionizing the lighting system on a motorcar. He also knew once the patent was issued all companies making light bulbs, with the new filaments, would have to pay royalties to the holder of the Heany patent.

In January of 1910, Durant secured approval of the General Motors directors for the purchase of the Heany Lamp Company with its pending patent. The terms were unbelievable. General Motors turned over to Heany 8,290 shares of General Motors preferred stock and 74,775 shares of General Motors common stock, more stock than had been involved in the purchase of Buick and Cadillac combined. To make matters worse, the Heany Company was not a profitable company at the time. Its finances were in such poor condition, that by May, General Motors had to use scarce capital to keep the firm functioning.

The men in direct responsibility for operations in the important units of General Motors (such as Buick and Cadillac) grew deeply concerned. Henry M. Leland at Cadillac was planning a trip to Europe in the summer of 1910, to participate in the American Society of Mechanical Engineers study of European industry. Leland met with Durant and expressed his concern in having Cadillac profits heavily siphoned off into the General Motors expansion programs. Durant assured Leland that there were no grounds for alarm, and Leland went to Europe.

The crisis developed so quickly that Leland learned of it shortly after he got off the boat in England. At one point it was necessary to call an emergency meeting of the directors of the First National Bank and the Old National Bank of Detroit to approve a $500,000 loan to the Cadillac Motor Company, just hours before the money was needed to meet a payroll.

Durant first realized in July that there was trouble ahead. If his General Motors were to survive there would have to be more working capital both to meet the cost of producing additional cars to sell in 1911 and to meet present obligations. Knowing that banks were the only place where such help could be expected, but confident that he could secure the money, Durant went methodically about meeting the officers of banks from whom General Motors had already borrowed money, as well as to other banks, seeking fresh new loans. He talked to bank officials from Kansas City to Boston.

Durant took to some of these conferences men who were handling the finances at the most important car producing and supplier firms. At times he was accompanied by Wilfred Leland, who handled finances for the Cadillac Motor Company. Cadillac was one of the few firms affiliated with General Motors that was earning a high profit.

The conferences were often blunt. Durant learned, for the first time, that bankers were skeptical of becoming more deeply involved in the motorcar business. He also found they were disinterested in helping General Motors further, until Durant instituted better accounting, reports and projections.

The Leland reports on Cadillac operations received quick and favorable attention at the conferences. The bankers got a new understanding of the stability and profits which could come from a well-managed firm, engaged in producing a motorcar, largely of its own design. These conferences enabled bankers to compare the difference between the car assembled from parts as exemplified by dozens of other motorcars and the specially engineered cars like those made by Cadillac, Buick, REO or Ford.

For a time, some of the bank conferences appeared likely to provide a solution to the crisis. When Durant and Arnold Goss of Buick met with the officials of the big Chicago banking house, Continental and Commercial Savings and Trust Company, officials were willing to loan General Motors $7,500,000. On further investigation it was decided that General Motors needed a loan of $9,500,000. Then the Chicago bank showed some unwillingness to consider loaning even the lower amount, and a few days later withdrew entirely. Although Durant's round of bank conferences produced no new operating funds, there were results on both sides.

Early in September, the General Motors directors, at Durant's urging, began cutting back on expansion and reducing expenses. On September 7th, the directors authorized the sale of the Welch-Detroit Motor Company and the component supplier, the Michigan Auto Parts Company of Detroit. By the middle of the month, another car firm, the Marquette Automobile Company of Saginaw, Michigan, was up for sale in an effort to trim the sails. The first steps were taken to reduce payrolls, a process that, before the year was over, had cut the General Motors staff in half. Nevertheless, motorcar production continued to rise for a period and, despite the reduction in working force, General Motors' firms actually increased sales in the following year.

The confusion in operations increased as September passed. There

John and Horace Dodge, sons of a former Niles, Michigan, blacksmith, in the back seat of the first Dodge motorcar to come off the assembly line at the Hamtramck factory, previously devoted entirely to producing Ford cars exclusive of the wheels and bodies. Picture taken in front of John Dodge home, 75 East Boston Boulevard in Detroit.

was no established routine in the ordering of parts and materials by affiliates. There was nothing comparable to the magnificent purchasing work done at Ford by Fred Diehl, nor of the tight management controls maintained by Henry B. Joy at Packard.

General Motors directors soon discovered that it was not even possible to determine how much money was owed, or needed. Early in September, the amount required to bridge the crisis was estimated at $7,500,000, the basis of the first conference at the Chicago bank. Within the week, it became apparent that at least two additional million would be needed, and $9,500,000 became the figure for the next round of talks in Chicago. On September 19th, the General Motors Board was forced to acknowledge that there was no reliable record of the amount owed and a few days later it was thought that it would take at least $12,000,000 to muddle through. Since there was no money available anywhere, the idea was growing that complete insolvency was but days, perhaps only hours, away.

The extensive talks between General Motors men and the banks had made an impression on the financiers, too. No one ever recorded exactly who made the suggestion, but the banks decided that it would be unwise to permit General Motors to lapse into bankruptcy without a general conference of representatives from the several banks involved. The conference was held at the Chase National Bank in New York.

Durant headed the General Motors delegation and there was an executive present from each of the chief affiliated motorcar firms. Wilfred Leland arrived from Detroit to represent the Cadillac Motor Company, J. C. Van Cleaf, vice president of the National Park Bank, presided.

Durant reported that General Motors needed up to $15,000,000 in fresh loans to weather the crisis which had developed since early summer. Motorcar sales were good and General Motors could expect higher sales in 1911, and presumably a higher profit than the $10,000,000 earned in the previous year. The analysis of the situation at Buick was long and detailed. Representatives of Buick explained that while the firm owed $8,000,000, its sales were, along with the Ford Motor Company, the highest in the country. The conference continued on an increasingly sober tone. Bankers became pointedly critical of Durant's handling of the affairs of Buick with its high sales, low earnings and mounting debts. As other General Motors firms involved in the crisis reported, the bankers began saying openly

Wilfred Leland, son and
closest associate of
Henry M. Leland in the
development of Cadillac
and Lincoln, suggested
the V-8 motor, used first
in 1916 Cadillacs and since
adopted by practically
all American cars.

that they could not loan General Motors any more money. The conference (and General Motors) seemed headed toward collapse.

At about four in the afternoon, Van Cleaf noted that all during the day there had been little reference to the activities of the Cadillac Motor Company, noting that Cadillac had no debts and had not contributed to the problems of General Motors. At this point, he called on Wilfred Leland for a report and any statements he might wish to make.

Leland reported on the operations at Cadillac. He explained that the company had been in operation longer than any of the others, that it had always made a profit, constantly expanded its business, was in good financial condition and was looking forward to the best year in its history in 1911.

Leland's report took thirty to forty minutes and swept over the banker conferees like a fresh lake breeze. Bankers questioned Leland for another hour. They were impressed with the stability and profits a well-run motorcar company could produce over a period of several years. Some of them began to feel that a soundly operated General Motors might be worth saving. At 6 p.m. the conference was adjourned until 10 o'clock the next morning.

As Durant and his associates were leaving the conference, Van Cleaf took Leland aside and asked him to wait in an adjoining room, while some of the bankers met in executive session. A half hour later Van Cleaf told Leland, "Mr. Leland, up to the time of your testimony, we were convinced that nothing was possible except the complete dissolution of the General Motors Company. The operations you have explained to us have deeply interested us. We have appointed a committee of five bankers who will meet tonight in Parlor B of the Belmont Hotel at eight o'clock. We will appreciate it if you will arrange to meet with them and give them all the assistance you can. You have given us some hope."

At the Belmont meeting, the bankers asked Leland for his opinion on what should be done with respect to the General Motors crisis. Later, reporting on his role to Henry Leland and his associates at Cadillac, Wilfred said, "I told them that if they could only reorient their thinking in the direction of how General Motors could be saved, rather than why it should be dissolved, they would find many good portents of success. After all, Cadillac alone was earning almost two million a year and General Motors had made ten million. Surely fifteen million was not such a great sum to loan to a business earning at that rate."

The banker committee became more interested as the hours of the night passed. By midnight the conference turned entirely on what could be done to save General Motors. At 2:30 a.m., the bankers agreed to go to the conference when it would resume seven hours later, and recommend that the $15,000,000 loan be made to General Motors.

When Durant arrived for the resumption of the conference, he plainly showed the strain of a night of worry. Leland had not been authorized to report on the long, night conference and none of the bankers had talked with Durant. He said, later, that it was "the surprise of his life" when the banker committee recommended that the $15,000,000 loan be made to General Motors. Colonel Ralph Van Vechten, vice president of the Continental and Commercial Savings and Trust Company of Chicago, who had figured prominently in the proposed $9,500,000 loan during the summer, spoke in favor of it. Durant's talks with Van Vechten's bank during the summer had made their mark. The respected Chicago banker contended that he and his bank were convinced that the motorcar business could go on growing for years. He said that General Motors represented one means of bringing stability to the young industry and should be encouraged.

The bankers, at the conference, were asked to list the maximum amount they would be willing to recommend that their individual banks contribute to the proposed $15,000,000 loan. When the individual amounts were added up by Van Cleaf, they totaled $17,500,000. Van Cleaf turned to Leland and said, "Mr. Leland, I want to congratulate you, and I want to say that you have saved the General Motors Company."

The long night produced great changes on both sides of the conference table. For the first time, bankers realized that the young motorcar industry was moving toward stability and was making a major contribution to the American economy. This stability would evolve from a relatively few firms with good management that provided constantly improved cars and better service. The bankers, representing the major financial interests in the United States, acted to foster that growing stability.

Almost as soon as the conference at the Chase National Bank was over, the era of the assembled car, with its hundreds of small producing units, reached its high-water mark. For a brief period of time, a few months during the fall and winter of 1910-11, there were nearly three hundred different motorcars being made for sale in the United

States. With a highly similar product and almost no follow-through for customer service, these assembled cars would find it constantly more difficult to survive with their numbers thinning slowly until World War I. Then the disappearance became so rapid that, fifteen years later, the total number of firms had declined to fifty.

The action of the bankers that September night in 1910 was a major factor in pointing the face of the motorcar industry to the future. A shattered General Motors, with its potential for better cars, would have turned back the clock. General Motors and the Ford Motor Company became the chief architects of the better cars and service that led the new industry out of its wilderness into an economic contribution so broad that a new level of life evolved.

17

The Nash-Chrysler Team

Immediately after the banks made the decision to underwrite a $15,000,000 loan to General Motors, the heavy ice over the country's major reservoirs of financial credit began to break up. Several investment bankers were now willing to underwrite a loan extending over a period of years. Negotiations over the terms continued for six weeks and were completed November 11th, 1910.

A joint proposal by two investment companies was finally accepted. The firms of Lee, Higginson & Company of Boston and J. W. Seligman & Company of New York underwrote a loan for $15,000,000 in 6 percent notes that were to run for five years. The bankers were prepared to make a loan of $20,000,000 but, upon further investigation, it was agreed that $15,000,000 would solve the crisis.

Confirmation of public opinion on the future of the motorcar industry came when the notes became available for purchase. The bankers planned to offer them at public sale which would have been the first offer of its kind in the country. But with the well-known investment banking companies behind them, private investors (mostly the banks represented at the Chase Bank conference) took up the notes so quickly that there was no opportunity to make a public offering. There was, as yet, no offer of a motorcar stock on the New York Stock Exchange.

The financial terms for the $15,000,000 loan provided for repayment in five years as follows: 1911, $1,500,000; 1912, $1,500,000; 1913, $2,000,000; 1914, $2,000,000; and 1915, $8,000,000.

The schedule of payments clearly revealed the bankers' plan for getting repayment of their loan. The first two payments were low enough to be met from the almost certain profits of the Cadillac Motor Car Company, the one major asset of General Motors not deeply committed to financial problems. For two years after, the payments were still modest, probably low enough for Cadillac profits to cover them. At the end of four years or earlier, the bankers reasoned, the other units of General Motors would have recovered and should be able to meet the large final payment.

As is the usual practice, the investment bankers took out their designated fee for underwriting at the beginning. The fee amounted to $2,250,000, so that General Motors actually received $12,750,000 under the long-term loan. In addition, the underwriting companies received, at par value, $4,169,200 in General Motors Preferred and $2,000,000 in General Motors Common.

But there were more than financial terms to the agreement. The investment bankers demanded, and won the right, to run General Motors until the full amount of the loan was repaid. A five-man executive committee, to which the bankers would appoint three members, would handle day-to-day operations of General Motors as long as the loan remained unpaid. Durant would remain as vice president and chairman of the finance committee, and would be a member of the new board of directors. The bankers would have the final word on both policy and administration.

The terms of the General Motors-banker agreement have often been called excessive and unreasonable, but this was not a bank loan in the usual sense. General Motors was borrowing not money, but an extension of its life which was not available anywhere else at a lower cost; probably not at all. In total, the new lease on life cost General Motors approximately $8,400,000—$2,250,000 in fees and $6,169,000 in stock. For a firm whose previous year's profits exceeded $10,000,000, a cost of eight and one-half million for an opportunity to survive was not unreasonable, particularly in view of the fact that the bankers took 70 percent of their remuneration in stock.

In a quick transition, November, 1910, saw the resignation of eleven former directors of General Motors. These included President and Director William M. Eaton of Jackson, Michigan, who had served since the first days of the company's existence, and Director Wilfred C. Leland of Detroit. Durant was not on the former board of directors, but he was placed on the bankers' board which included five members from New York, four from Detroit and one each from Flint and Boston. The two most powerful members of the new board that took over, November 15th, were bankers, James J. Storrow of Boston and Albert Strauss of New York. Storrow represented Lee, Higginson & Company and Strauss, J. W. Seligman & Company. Both were on the five-man executive committee.

The bankers made a sincere effort to retain the interest and capabilities of Durant. They insisted that he accept a directorship as well as the chairmanship of the all-important committee on finances. The finance committee appointment was particularly sagacious since it paid tribute to the General Motors founder in an area where he had been most sharply criticized. Durant buried his pride and remained active for almost a year, at which time it suited his purposes to retain his stock interest but to separate himself from management.

Storrow was named president of General Motors on November 23rd and served a little more than two months, at which time a prominent businessman in Detroit, Thomas Neal, became president. After almost two years, the office went to Charles W. Nash of Flint who remained president for the ensuing years of banker control.

Storrow and Strauss soon made it clear that their trusteeship would be judicious, inasmuch as they were determined to see that General Motors would be successful, would pay off the loan and permit them to retire from all connection with the company. Storrow remained president only until a slate of Detroit men could be found to take over the top executive positions. Sixty days later, three Detroit men, all of them with successful experience in business, took over the top offices. Thomas Neal, manager of Acme Lead and Color Works, became president. James T. Shaw, with an accounting background, was named treasurer. Durant continued in the office of vice-president.

To accommodate the Detroit men, General Motors offices were opened in Detroit. The first offices were in a building across from the Pontchartrain Hotel on Woodward Avenue. In 1911, the headquarters were moved to the new Boyer Building at the southwest corner of Brush and Congress streets.

The bankers took immediate action, disposing of the worthless properties which had been acquired by Durant during the expansion of the first, hectic, two years. Some of the car companies were written off at one dollar and quickly forgotten. The Michigan firms of Rainier, Carter-car, Marquette and Welch were first consolidated and then abandoned. By 1912, there were only four producing firms left. They were Buick, Oldsmobile, Cadillac and Oakland-Pontiac.

Toughest of all the liquidation problems was that of the Heany Lamp Company, the bold venture taken by Durant that had brought on the crisis and banker control. General Electric had challenged the Heany patent but there had been no court ruling. Evidence brought into court was not favorable. In November of 1911, Durant took everyone off the spot by proposing that the Heany agreement be terminated, and that Heany be permitted to salvage what he might. The court eventually decided in favor of General Electric, and the Heany patent was worthless.

There was some forming of new companies, too. Using the Rapid Motor Vehicle Company of Pontiac and the Reliance Motor Truck Company of Owosso, Michigan, as a base, the General Motors Truck Company was organized. The same year, the General Motors Export Company was founded as a Michigan corporation.

During the first two years, the banker-management was unable to do a great deal to help the operating companies. There was no back-log of proven leaders to call into places where there was obviously trouble. When Neal became president, he moved against production problems in the affiliated companies by drawing upon the highly trained staff at Cadillac. When Neal appealed to Henry M. Leland to help iron out difficulties at Buick and Oakland-Pontiac, Leland responded quickly. He sent Joe Wilson, foundry expert from Leland & Faulconer days, to put Buick's foundry back on the track. Walter Phipps, formerly superintendent at Leland & Faulconer, was now in business for himself, but Leland arranged for Phipps to spend several weeks in Flint and Pontiac tuning up the production procedures at Buick and Oakland-Pontiac.

Fortunately, a number of the companies such as Weston-Mott, Cadillac and AC Sparkplug were under good management and continued to prosper. Just as the bankers were taking over, a costly management dispute developed at Buick Motor Company in Flint. The "Model-10," called the "Buick White Streak" (because it was painted "Buick gray") went into production late in 1907, even before Ford's "Model-T" was announced.

This was Buick's first light car with a four-cylinder motor, and it enjoyed a phenomenal sales success, greatest yet experienced at Flint. The "Model-10" accounted for half of Buick's record volume of pro-

The Cadillac Division of General Motors in Detroit
displays this memento as a tribute to Wilfred Leland.

TO
WILFRED CHESTER LELAND
IN RECOGNITION
OF HIS CONCEPTION OF THE HIGH SPEED
HIGH EFFICIENCY "V" TYPE ENGINE
AND ITS APPLICATION TO THE MOTOR CAR
FROM
CADILLAC OLD GUARD
PURSUANT TO THE RESOLUTION OF JANUARY 6TH 1910

duction in 1908, 1909 and 1910. Suddenly the "Model-10" was dropped from the 1911 Buick line. Buick sales dropped from 30,000 to 14,000 in the first crucial year of the banker take-over. It was something of a miracle that the management battle and the resulting decisions didn't crush the General Motors revival movement right at its outset. Such a disaster was averted largely because Cadillac sales and profits remained stable; even inched upward in 1911.

With Durant's personal leadership muffled in Flint, a bitter fight developed among Buick's directors over the future of the "Model-10." The small car had been a "Durant car" from its inception. The directors of Buick were made up of men who had generally devoted their careers to the building of fine carriages. They were largely responsible for adding to the language the term, "The Carriage Trade," a reference to the rich and powerful. There were exceptions. James H. Whiting, the man who started the whole Buick business in Flint, led the faction in favor of continuing to expand "Model-10" production. In the end, Whiting lacked the votes, and the only motorcar that was ever able to slug it out toe-to-toe with Ford's "Model-T" was abandoned.

Later, some of the Buick directors attempted to justify their dangerous and irresponsible action. They said they did not wish to compete with Ford in the low-priced field. It is true that they leaned toward such an action because, true to their carriage heritage, they wanted to be personally identified with a more expensive and pretentious motorcar. But the truth was that, without the Durant vision, they were unable to see the great future just ahead for the light and inexpensive car.

The decision was dangerous for the Buick Motor Company, and held the possibility of handicapping the entire industry. By suddenly removing the "Model-10" from the market, the primary burden of developing the light car and putting the nation on wheels fell upon Ford. As it turned out, Ford was equal to the responsibility, but the transition from horse to horsepower possibly would have been accomplished more quickly, had Buick continued the "Model-10."

It was but one of the hazards that developed as a result of Durant's loss of power. The bankers looked helplessly on as profits dropped to one-third what they had been the year before under Durant's management. The profits were hardly more than those earned at Cadillac, but enough to meet the first year payment on the loan.

Shortly after Storrow and the bankers took charge of General

Ralph De Palma at the wheel of the car in which he won
the 1915 Indianapolis "500," after 1910 cross-country
runs and hillclimbs declined and motorcar competition
shifted to the racetracks. Neither Oldfield, Chevrolet,
Rickenbacker nor anyone else equalled De Palma's
record of 2,557 victories in 2,889 major races
before he retired in 1934.

Motors, the presidency of Buick Motor Company had to be filled. Storrow consulted Durant. The General Motors founder said, without hesitancy, that the man best for the job was Charles Nash, production manager of Durant-Dort Carriage Company. Although without experience in motorcar production, Nash became president and general manager of Buick late in 1910.

As a boy, Nash had been bound out to a Michigan farmer. It was not an uncommon practice for parents with a large family to enter into an agreement by which a boy or girl would become a foster-child of another family. This meant that the youth worked for the new family in return for food and clothing. Often, it was a situation only a notch above slavery. In Nash's case, he had been fortunate enough to get some education while a boy. When he was able to handle a man's work, he went to Flint and got a job in the Whiting and Richardson Hardware Store. The store did a large business in farm machinery and Nash soon became important to the firm in the selling and servicing of farm implements.

Durant-Dort Carriage Company had only been in existence a short time when Durant observed that young Nash was a hard and careful worker. Durant hired him at $1.25 a day. Within a few days Nash came to Durant, saying, "Say, Mr. Durant, I've been pounding iron for Mr. McCruttin, the blacksmith, but I'm wasting time. You can get a little power hammer. Wouldn't cost more than $35.00, and it would do more pounding in a day than I can do in a month." This process continued until Nash had the Durant-Dort factory producing two or three times as many carriages in the same space and at a considerable savings in production cost, per vehicle. Because he was so valuable at Durant-Dort, he had not been invited to join the Buick operation. As production manager of Durant-Dort he had supervised the manufacturing of up to 150,000 vehicles a year. His talent for manufacturing was exactly what the strife-torn Buick Motor Company needed. He brought order to the Buick operation so quickly that within three years he was elected president of General Motors. Although four men had held that position, when Nash moved into the office November 20th, 1912, he was the first General Motors President who had had actual experience in a car factory.

Nash was able to give up his direct control of Buick, and assume the presidency of General Motors largely because of a man he had hired the year before. Like Nash, this man had an outstanding reputation in the building of vehicles, but he had never been inside a motorcar factory. Nash's new recruit was thirty-six-year-old Walter

Chrysler who came to Flint from the American Locomotive Company plant in Pittsburgh. The team of Nash and Chrysler was a major factor in making successful the years of banker-control at General Motors.

Chrysler, reared on the Kansas plains, had twenty years of experience in railroading when he joined Nash at Buick. His career had been devoted to railroad maintenance and, later, to the building of railroad engines. Six years before, while he was in charge of motive power for the Chicago Great Western Railway with his headquarters in Oelwein, Iowa, Chrysler had become intensely interested in the horseless carriage.

While attending a railroad convention in Chicago, Chrysler had committed his family's entire savings and a good deal more to buy a Locomobile. But, before he had attempted to drive it, he had dismantled it so completely that the motorcar had become nothing more than piles of parts and components on the floor of the horse barn behind the Chrysler home in Oelwein.

At the time he joined the Buick Motor Company, Chrysler was superintendent in the Pittsburgh factory where railroad engines were built. He had met President Storrow. The banker brought Nash and Chrysler together, first in Pittsburgh and, later, in Flint. It was a difficult decision for Chrysler, who gave up a $12,000 job in Pittsburgh and went to work for Buick at $6,000. He was determined to shift from building railroad engines to motorcars.

Chrysler brought a fresh viewpoint to Flint and, within a remarkably short time, became one of the wizards in motorcar production. In Herbert R. Lewis's memoirs there is an account of Chrysler's first week at Buick. Lewis had asked Chrysler what he first did when he shifted from building railroad engines to automobiles.

"I saved the Buick Motor Company my first year's salary the first week I was in Flint," said Chrysler. He went on to explain that, in 1911, there was no Buick testing ground as there is today. Buicks were checked out by test drivers who took the car (without its body) out for a run on the country roads near Flint. Even with a production of only two or three hundred cars a week, there was a constant stream of drivers coming and going with their test cars. Chrysler noted that neither the drivers nor the cars being checked were assigned numbers. How could accurate records be kept? He began a check that continued all week and, sure enough, each day one to four more Buicks were being taken out than were returned by the test drivers. Chrysler called the matter to the attention of Nash and immediately a system was created by which each car taken out was registered to make certain that it was returned.

The incident was typical of hundreds of new procedures Chrysler introduced at Buick. Most of them were directed toward cutting costs while doing the job as well and, on occasion, a great deal better. Chrysler's major contribution to the Buick Motor Company was to substitute metallurgy for cabinetmaking. Chrysler took the old carriage building practices out of Buick production procedures. Chrysler saw this opportunity, immediately, when he made his first visit to Buick late in 1911. He said later,

"What I saw astonished me . . . the opportunity to do things with metal in a factory where metallurgy was just beginning to be known. Of course, I was a machinist, and I was looking at workmen trained to handle wood. The bodies were being made of wood. In a big carpenter shop, long wide poplar boards were being bent and shaped in steam kilns. With wood they were admirably skillful, for most of them had been carriage builders, but wherever they were handling metal it seemed to me there was opportunity for a big improvement. I saw a hundred such opportunities, so that I was excitedly eager, saying to myself, 'What a job I could do here, if I were boss'."

When Nash became president of General Motors, Chrysler moved up to become president of Buick. Later, he was made a vice president of General Motors, and remained until 1920.

As Buick's boss, Chrysler led the company on to constantly higher production of better-built cars and to a restoration of profits. The former railroad mechanic had added a new, human dimension to the motorcar business.

18

Today's Cars
Come Into View

The motorcar, as we know it today, came into existence during World War I years, and just before. The year which proved to be the great divide between the super-horseless carriages and the modern car is 1912.

From the introduction of the Duryea, in Springfield, in 1896 and for ten years after, the builders of self-propelled road vehicles had been concerned largely with the problem of reducing the big, heavy stationary motors—steam, electric and internal combustion—to small size with enough power to drive a buggy or wagon. With the general introduction of more powerful motors, in 1907 and 1908, the five-passenger vehicles, large enough to transport an entire family (known as the "touring car") took over from the small runabout.

The touring car, with its hand-crank, carriage lamps or acetylene head lamps, right side steering, fabric tops for bad weather and absence of front doors, was good enough to replace an important part of the family horse-drawn transportation. But it was a far cry from the motorcars produced by the millions after World War I. The production figures are the evidence. In 1910, car production in the United States reached a new record and exceeded the output of self-propelled road vehicles of all other countries combined; but the total was still below 200,000. A decade later, car production in the United States was just under two million and in 1922 moved up to two and a quarter million cars.

In 1912, Cadillac Motor Company introduced the modern electrical system complete with self-starter on all its cars, wet battery, generator to keep the battery charged, battery-powered ignition in the cylinders and electric head lights. Within the year, Vincent Bendix invented the Bendix drive, which made the electric self-starter more effective. In 1912, the Hupp Motor Car Company in Detroit and the Oakland-Pontiac Car Company in Pontiac introduced all-steel bodies, although they were still open cars. The new steel bodies ruined one of vaudeville's best World War I jokes which purported that "the auto had a wooden frame, wooden wheels, wooden body —and wood'n run."

In 1914, the Cadillac Motor Company introduced the first high-speed V-8 motor. During this period, the steering wheel was moved to the left side, mudguards became fenders, and front and rear bumpers were introduced. Tilt-beam headlights were put into use in 1915, and hydraulic four-wheel brakes were perfected in 1918. In 1919, the Essex, a light six-cylinder car was built by Roy Chapin's Hudson Motor Company in Detroit. It was the sensation of the New York Automobile Show that year. The new Essex was a four-door, completely glass-enclosed car, known as a "sedan." Three years later, The Essex was selling one model of its sedan for less than $1,000. The days of the touring car were numbered.

The old order gave way, reluctantly, to the new. In 1919, the year Essex introduced the first inexpensive sedan, Studebaker discontinued making carriages and wagons to devote all the firm's energies to producing motorcars.

The public demand upon government for greater opportunities to use the motorcar began producing epic results during these first years of the World War when the United States was not yet directly involved. On August 1st, 1915, the gates of Yellowstone Park swung open to permit the first automobile to enter the park. Only one-way traffic was permitted on the hazardous road. The motorcar was beginning to smash age-old barriers and open up an entirely new opportunity for the American people. The excitement of the western mountain wilderness, until this time available only to explorers, mountaineers and wealthy sportsmen, was now open to families from every corner of the land as they became owners of that magic key—the motorcar.

300

Less than a year later, July 11th, 1916, the foundation was laid for the nation's modern transcontinental highway system. On that date, President Woodrow Wilson signed into law the first Federal Aid Road Act, under which federal funds could be used to meet up to half the cost of building new highways between towns.

To make the act constitutional, the infant law provided that the new highways could be built on "any public road over which the United States mails now are, or may hereafter be, transported." The real purpose was to provide the American public with the means of making more extensive use of their new motorcars. There were 1,500,000 cars sold in the United States in 1916, almost exactly half of them "Model-T" Fords. Some people suggested that the new federal law might more appropriately have been called, the "Ford Act."

One of the reasons for the accelerated development of the motorcar in this period was that scores of firms located all over the country were turning out cars. Although during these World War I years, Detroit and southeastern Michigan had become the hub of the industry, there were more than two hundred firms making cars in other states.

It was in this period that the Pontchartrain Hotel on Woodward Avenue became the functional headquarters for the industry. E. LeRoy Pelletier, advertising man who distinguished himself at Ford and other car factories, told William J. Chittenden, manager of the Pontchartrain, "Will, those are beautiful Persian rugs you've got on the floor. They should be taken up so the floor can be painted with a big red circle to enclose all those tables. In the middle of the circle you should have printed: 'This is the center of the world's automobile industry.' "

The men worked in their offices in the factories during the morning and went to the Pontchartrain Hotel at noon or in the evening to hold important conferences on new developments. Along with food and drink on the Pontchartrain tables, it was a common sight to see a new gear or some other experimental piece of equipment. On occasion, entire transmissions and other complex components were displayed on the tables in front of the Pontchartrain bar.

Supplier firms from out of town sent their representatives, as a matter of course, to learn what was new in the motorcar business. These meetings became a kind of a daily rehearsal for the New York Automobile Show where new cars and new features on cars were annually unveiled. Until the D. A. C. (Detroit Automobile Club) was opened, the Pontchartrain Hotel was the foremost communications center for this new breed of men responsible for establishing the greatest new business to emerge in this century.

The fact that many Detroit car builders and their numerous component suppliers were in close contact with one another largely accounted for the flood of major developments made after Detroit became the Motor City. The modern car body with four, rather than two, doors was one of them.

The Fisher Brothers had established their new body business in Detroit, indicating how the young industry was reaching out for trained men. The seven Fisher brothers were reared in Norwalk, Ohio. Their father, Lawrence, maintained a carriage and wagon business where the boys learned to be master craftsmen. Fred and Charles Fisher went to Detroit to work in the C. R. Wilson Body Company that started making the bodies for the Curved Dash Oldsmobile. When young Charles Fisher wanted to get married, he asked for a $5.00 a week raise. His request was turned down. Both he and his brother, Fred (who had become a department superintendent) quit. Hugh Chalmers, producer of the Chalmers car had recognized the Fishers' great ability and, rather than let them leave Detroit, Chalmers arranged a banking connection that enabled them to establish their own business, the Fisher Body Company. They were later joined by their brothers. In 1919, the company became a division of General Motors.

Walter Flanders, who had done so much to set up the manufacturing procedure at the Ford plants, left to produce his own car with two partners, Barney F. Everett and William C. Metzger, the man who operated the first motorcar agency in Detroit. Metzger, Cadillac's first sales manager, developed and began producing the E. M. F. motorcar. It later became the Studebaker. Flanders wanted to eliminate the horseless carriage feature of having an open front seat. He was sure that a four-door car body could be mass produced. He was also determined to have at least one to display at the New York Automobile Show, only weeks away. Flanders called on Charlie and Fred Fisher, swore them to secrecy, and told them about his idea for a new car body with four doors. The Fishers were constantly subjected to someone's new thinking about car bodies, but they admitted that Flanders had a novel idea. They had never seen such a body, and were not sure it was possible to build one that could stand the punishment a car body had to endure. Moreover, they were unable to undertake such an experiment since their factory already had more work than could easily be handled.

302

But the Fishers underestimated the flamboyant Flanders and, by the time of the New York show, they had produced a four-door body for his new E. M. F. car. The body was an immediate success and Flanders sent one large order after another to the Fisher Body Company. The Fishers had quoted him a price before the high volume of orders developed. With volume production, their costs were lowered and they decided that the cost to E. M. F. should be lowered, correspondingly. Charles Fisher went to visit Flanders. Malcolm W. Bingay of the Detroit *Free Press,* who knew the Fishers and Flanders personally, reported the conversation:

"My brother, Fred, and I have been thinking this thing over. We want to talk over with you the matter of a price adjustment."

"Here I am," shouted Flanders, "just getting my head above water and you fellows start gouging me! Holding me up! I won't stand for it."

When Flanders had finished his energetic lecture and Fisher could get back into the conversation, the body-maker said, "It is not our purpose to raise the price. What I am trying to tell you is that we think we are charging too much. We are making a big profit on this type of job and we want to lower the figure."

Flanders was a hard man to leave speechless but, for a time, he simply could not reply. Finally he said, "I don't get you. Are you fellows crazy?"

"Not at all," the soft spoken Fisher said. "We believe in a fair profit for our work. Father always did business that way. We intend to do the same."

The incident became a household story throughout the motorcar industry. Having the good fortune to build their business in a time when the appetite of the booming Detroit motorcar industry for bodies was almost endless, the Fisher Body Company never had to develop an expansive sales department.

The experience of Charles Fisher and Walter Briggs reveals the great opportunity the motorcar business afforded young men in Detroit from the early days of this century. When Charles Fisher married Sarah Kramer from his hometown of Norwalk, they lived in a modest apartment in a modest section of Detroit. Across the hall lived another young couple, Mr. and Mrs. Walter Briggs.

Briggs had started out as a switchman on the Michigan Central Railroad in Detroit and was yard foreman at a Detroit cement company when he met Barney Everett whose name later provided the "E" for the E. M. F. motorcar. Everett had a wagon and carriage painting shop when Briggs went to work for him as a trimmer. Everett left, Briggs took over the business and went on to build, along with the Fisher Body Company, one of the great car-body businesses in the world. Although business competitors, the Fisher and Briggs families continued their close ties. They built large homes side by side in Detroit. When Walter Briggs bought the Detroit Tigers baseball team "so he could get a seat whenever he wanted one for the games," the two families had their boxes, side by side. The first-born of the families, Charles T. Fisher, Jr. and Elizabeth Briggs, married, and later Susan Briggs and Everall Fisher also married.

In this greatest upsurge in motorcar performance, one firm stood out over the several hundred others making cars. The firm was the Cadillac Motor Car Company. It was strange, in a way, that these major developments should have come from Cadillac, which was not among the expensive motorcars of the period. With the exception of Packard, all the luxury cars of the World War I period were made in the East. They were the Winton and White, made in Cleveland; the Pierce-Arrow, in Buffalo; the Frankin, in Syracuse; and the Locomobile, in Bridgeport.

The major contribution to motorcar development came from Cadillac in the medium price range. The medium-priced leaders were almost entirely produced in Michigan. The Cadillac's competitors were the REO in Lansing, the Buick in Flint, the Oakland-Pontiac in Pontiac, the Hudson, Hupmobile, Chalmers in Detroit and the Willys-Overland just south of Detroit in Toledo. Ford's "Model-T" was the only important low-priced car.

The Cadillac advantage was its leadership. The firm was, despite the banker take-over of General Motors, still firmly in the hands of the Lelands. The earlier triumphs at Cadillac had been directed by motordom's patriarch, Henry M. Leland. Approaching seventy years of age, but a man of undiminished vigor, Leland had the help of a group of expert engineers headed by Ernest E. Sweet and Frank Johnson. Most of them had been with him since the days of Leland & Faulconer. Of equal consequence, he had the assistance of his son, Wilfred, in the prime of his life and possessed of a brilliance in the fields of motorcar improvement, finance and marketing that supported his father's unmatched ability to fashion miracles in metal. As 1912 opened, Henry and Wilfred Leland and Sweet, were ready to lead the motorcar into its maturity.

By far, the most important self-propelled vehicle improvement in the World War I period was its electrification. Ignition system, self-starting, and greatly improved lighting for night driving were the forerunners of later refinements such as heating and air-conditioning of car interiors. No one, not even the Lelands, foresaw these possibilities. Yet the era of the effective use of electricity in the operation of the motorcar was conceived and launched within a period of two years, and reached a climax in 1912.

In the early days of 1911, Byron T. Carter's death touched off a series of events that led to this important advance in the motorcar. Carter had developed the Cartercar and founded the Cartercar Company of Pontiac, acquired by General Motors in 1909.

On Christmas Day, 1910, Carter was driving through the Belle Isle Park in Detroit, when he came upon a woman driver who had stalled her motor. Carter stopped and offered to crank her car. The woman neglected to retard the spark, controlled by a small lever on the steering column. As Carter cranked, the motor backfired, as was often the case when the spark was not retarded, and before automatic spark regulating mechanisms were developed. Carter's arm and jaw were broken by the hand-crank thrown completely out of control by the backfiring motor. Even his face was deeply lacerated.

As fate would have it, the next car to pass brought the Cadillac engineers, Ernest Sweet and Bill Foltz, to the scene. The men were driving through the park with their wives on that pleasant, winter day. Sweet and Foltz cranked the woman's stalled car and rushed Carter to the hospital. Although Carter's injuries did not seem serious, complications resulting from his injuries and exposure developed and he died of pneumonia.

When Sweet reported the accident to Henry Leland, the head of Cadillac was very much upset. He blurted out, "I'm sorry I ever built an automobile. I won't have Cadillacs hurting people that way." The incident continued to depress him, and a few days later he met with Sweet and other Cadillac engineers.

Present, along with Sweet and Leland, were D. T. Randall, Lyle Snell, Fred Hawes, Frank Johnson, Herman Schwarze, R. T. Wingo and Herman Zannoth. These men constituted the foremost engineering group in the motorcar industry. Leland gave them a massive assignment. "The Cadillac car," he told them, "will kill no more men if we can help it. Lay all the other projects aside. We are going to develop a foolproof device for starting Cadillac motors."

This incident introduced the modern era of automotive research. No longer could the lone experimenter, responding to his own ideas and toiling day and night as Frank Duryea, Ransom Olds, Henry Ford and so many others had done, hope to work out the complicated improvements in highly complex motorcars. The era had begun when the research department combined the abilities of a number of men whose fulltime job it was to improve the firm's product.

The need for developing an effective self-starter for a motorcar had been recognized from the first. Hand-cranking was hazardous, even with the low-powered, single-cylinder cars, such as the Curved Dash Oldsmobile. When the larger, four-cylinder motors were introduced and, as the number of cars in use increased, the injury from hand-cranking reached such proportions that it became a factor that was limiting the usefulness of the self-propelled road vehicle. Women rarely attempted to crank the four-cylinder cars because it was hazardous, and because they lacked the strength to turn over the motors, as well.

There were many self-starters in use. Most of them used compressed air, springs or acetylene for power. The Winton, Packard and other luxury cars in the United States and Europe generally had some means of mechanical starting, but the trouble with all starting devices was that they were not dependable and they generally required constant checking and servicing.

Within days of the time Carter died, the 1911 New York Automobile Show opened and its leading, new exhibit was a display of self-starters. Thomas Edison had taken out a patent for an electric self-starter but had not developed it. The Cadillac engineers worked methodically. First, they assembled information on all earlier efforts to develop a self-starter. From this investigation they decided what general aproach offered the best opportunity to build an effective self-starter. They were benfitted by another experience that was fresh in their minds.

Months before, Sweet and several of his group had worked out an electrical power system for the Wilfred Leland's country estate on Lake Angelus in Oakland County, Michigan. Using a four-cylinder Cadillac motor for power, the engineers had installed a generator and connected it to dozens of storage batteries. The system supplied electric current for an extensive lighting system, including lights for nearly a mile of driveways on the estate. The system also provided power for a pressure water-system that, in addition to serving the several buildings, supplied enough water to irrigate the lawn and gardens.

The experience of the engineers with the Leland country lighting

The moving assembly line, developed at the Ford Motor Company and first used with full effect in 1914, quickly spread to all other firms producing large numbers of motorcars. Here is the Chevrolet assembly line at Flint, in 1916. The mechanized moving assembling line is regarded as the foremost industrial development in the first half of this century.

plant was an important factor in developing a self-starter for the Cadillac car. They decided that a starter, using electricity from a system that was a miniature duplicate of the Leland estate power plant, would be the most effective way to proceed. It would operate from a small electric motor powered by a storage battery which, in turn, would be charged by a small generator that would operate all the time the car-engine ran. One of the engineers, Frank Johnson, cut teeth in the flywheel, so that the starter's power could be applied to the motor at that point.

In a remarkably short time, Sweet was able to report to Henry Leland that they had demonstrated a practical means of mechanically starting a car. All that remained to be worked out was the production of the starting equipment. It would not take long to develop the generating system or the storage battery, but the building of a new electric motor small enough and with enough power to start the car dependably (especially in cold weather) would take some time.

Earl C. Howard, assistant sales manager at Cadillac had previously worked for National Cash Register in Dayton. Late in January, Wilfred Leland talked to him about the need to design a small electric motor for the self-starter being developed. Howard recalled that a young electrical engineer by the name of Kettering had solved just such a problem for the National Cash Register Company when that firm needed a tiny electric motor to replace the hand-crank on the cash register. Howard thought Kettering's experience might be useful and save a lot of time for Cadillac. Leland was impressed with Howard's suggestion. He picked up the telephone and called Kettering in Dayton, inviting him to visit Cadillac the following day.

When Kettering arrived, Leland explained that his engineers had perfected the first foolproof self-starter for a motorcar. They were at a point where they had to design a small electric motor powerful and rugged enough to turn over a car motor and do it long enough for the engine to start.

Kettering was delighted with the assignment. Sweet went to Dayton to work with him. When Kettering returned, he brought with him a small electric motor that functioned perfectly. The only adjustment needed was the filing of one side so that it could fit in the space available.

Then came the historic day. On February 27th, 1911, less than two months after Carter's death, and with the Lelands and all the Cadillac engineers looking on in the Cadillac engineering room,

The vacation trips of these four famous Americans,
Henry Ford (below), Thomas Edison (left), Harvey
Firestone and John Burroughs (right) made news,
frequently, for years after World War I. Each had a keen
interest in nature and out-of-doors. Personal ties were close.
Edison had encouraged Ford, when they had first met in
1896, to continue his experiments with a gasoline-powered
horseless carriage. Firestone established his tire business
to serve the infant motorcar industry, and Ford became
his best customer.

Henry Leland pressed an electric switch and the big Cadillac motor turned over and started in a fraction of the time hand-cranking would have taken. The modern self-starter for the motorcar was a reality.

Henry Leland shook hands with Sweet, Johnson and Kettering and with each of the engineers, congratulating them on their achievement. He expressed the hope that they might now solve the manufacturing problems in time so that every Cadillac turned out in 1912 could be equipped with a self-starter.

Within hours after the starter had been successfully demonstrated, Henry Leland, his men and Kettering made another major decision. It resulted in another improvement in the motorcar, almost as significant as the starter. Since the 1912 Cadillac was to have an electric self-starter with a storage battery and generator, why not use the electricity for ignition and headlights?

The acetylenc lighting system was almost as cumbersome to the car owner as the hand-crank. An acetylene tank had to be attached to the car's running board. The tank had to be refilled from time to time. When darkness came, the driver had to light the headlights by using matches. When windy conditions prevailed, it often required a handful of matches and much wasted time to get the acetylene lights ready for driving.

The "Model-T" Ford used electric lights that were supplied electric power from a specialized type of generator known as a magneto. There was no storage battery involved. As a result, there was no power for lights when the motor was not running. In addition, the lights were too dim for safety when driving at low speeds. The only time the magneto-fed electric lights were adequate, was after the car had attaind speeds of 25 miles an hour. Road conditions being what they were in that period, night driving was nearly always at slower speeds.

Sweet and Kettering worked together all summer to perfect the new system, and they were able, in a short time, to demonstrate the effectiveness of electric lights for the 1912 Cadillac. The lights were powerful, they provided light when the motor was not running, they could be turned on instantly regardless of wind or rain, merely by turning a switch. The new lights did not have to be recharged at a garage from time to time as was the case with acetylene lights.

With the self-starter and electric lights, both available at finger's touch, the self-propelled road vehicle ceased to be a competitor of horse-drawn transportation and moved ahead toward a destiny com-

pletely its own. No other means of transportation provided any reasonable comparison. The self-starter and electric lights greatly
extended the potential use of the motorcar. So long as it was necessary to crank the engine by hand and endure the hazards of either
acetylene or magneto-powered lights, women could make only
limited use of the motorcar. With the addition of these two features,
introduced by Cadillac, women could drive, as well as men. Also a
large number of men, especially in urban areas, who had continued
to depend upon public transport, could turn to the motorcar as their
primary transportation.

The inventions were complete, but the matter of getting them on
the 1912 Cadillac cars was beset by problems so great, that only the
capacity of men like the Lelands, Sweet and Kettering could have
solved them. It was the first of March, but seven months later
Cadillac dealers were viewing the first motorcar complete with a
modern electric self-starter and electric head lamps.

Cadillac Motor Company had neither the floor space, the time
nor the trained men to undertake the manufacture of the non-motor
components for the new self-starter and the electric lighting system.
There was no regular supplier to turn to in this eleventh hour situation. Battery companies had no stock batteries small enough and
powerful enough to be installed under the hood of a motorcar to
run the self-starter. No small generator existed that was rugged and
efficient enough to be installed on the Cadillac motor.

When introduction of the new inventions on the 1912 Cadillac
began to seem hopeless, Kettering offered to assume the responsibility for manufacturing the non-motor components for the self-
starter and the electric headlights. To his everlasting credit, the
young Ohio engineer did not hesitate, although at the moment he
controlled no facilities by which the components could be produced
in so short a time for the 12,000 Cadillac cars.

Kettering went back to Dayton, gathered his associates together
and told them what he had agreed to do. Most of them were still
holding their jobs at the National Cash Register Company and
working with his Dayton Electric Laboratory Company after business hours and on weekends. Kettering was the small laboratory's
only principal fulltime employee. He had resigned his job at National Cash Register Company only two years before and set up the
new laboratory. He had taken that step after he had agreed to
develop a new electric ignition system for Cadillac Motor Car Company. The laboratory was located in an old horse-barn at the edge of

Dayton. Undaunted, Kettering and his associates used their personal credit to rent more building space, buy equipment and hire men to manufacture the components for the new Cadillacs.

Henry and Wilfred Leland were aware of what a slender thread it was on which they depended. And in entrusting this formidable problem to Kettering and his new organization, they showed great faith. But, also, they had almost no other choice. If Kettering did not come through, the self-starter and the electric lights would have to appear on Cadillac at some later time.

An indication of the procurement problems was first realized when Kettering tried to get batteries. He wrote to a leading battery firm, Electric Storage Battery Company, to place an order for 10,000 batteries, listing the specifications. The battery firm had not heard of Kettering or his firm. It had never received an order from anybody for 10,000 batteries and the battery to the specifications listed did not exist.

Electric Storage Battery Company sent one of its executives, O. Lee Harrison, to Dayton to see Kettering. He introduced himself by saying, "I don't want to sell you any batteries, I just want to look at a fellow who thinks he wants to buy 10,000 batteries." Before the talk was over, Harrison had been won over to Kettering's point of view. He went home and, after considerable difficulty, convinced his company that it could and should make the special battery to Kettering's specifications.

The Lelands had no less of a roadblock to hurdle in getting approval from the banker-bosses of General Motors to take the great gamble in introducing a self-starter no one had ever seen and a new kind of lighting system. If the new features failed, or were only fairly successful, the Cadillac Motor Car Company could be crippled, or even ruined. Cadillac was the firm that chiefly was meeting the annual payments to the banks to keep General Motors alive. That the bankers urged the Lelands not to take such a step is understandable, but the Lelands were determined to push on and take the great leap ahead.

To break the deadlock, Storrow and his General Motors executive committee agreed to appoint a special group made up of outside engineers from the electrical industry to review what Cadillac was planning to do. The committee's recommendation would be final. One engineer was assigned to the investigating committee from Westinghouse, one from General Electric and one from the Haltske Company. The committee listed ten features on which their recommendation would be based.

The visiting engineers met with Cadillac officials for two days. They found that seven of the ten features they had elected to study proved satisfactory. Leland called Kettering in Dayton and, on the second day, he arrived from Ohio and joined the investigation. The visiting engineers were unanimous in their judgment. The self-starter and the new lighting system worked well.

There were other anxious moments, too. In April, Kettering broke his ankle when his test car went out of control and toppled into a ditch. Two days later, a fire occurred in the Cadillac plant. The pilot car for the 1912 models, the only car in existence with a complete installation of the new self-starter and electric headlights, had been so badly damaged that the Cadillac engineers could not get it back into operation. Kettering called his doctor, got crutches and took the night train to Detroit. The next day he and Herman Schwarze, the master electrician at Cadillac, restored the self-starter and cleared the way for resuming work on the new model.

Through all the ordeal of creating and producing the self-starter and electric lights in so short a time, it was Henry Leland who sustained the spirits of everyone. There came the day in summer when the decision had to be made as to whether the new Cadillac with its self-starter would be equipped with a hand-crank. When Leland proposed that the hand-crank be removed entirely, his associates were shocked. They urged that the hand-crank be installed as usual.

"Why not take it off," said Leland. "Haven't you any faith in your starter?" Leland reported that he had removed the hand-crank from the pilot car two months before and hidden it. No one had missed it.

In August, Cadillac announced the revolutionary development. Six weeks later, cars fully equipped were coming off Cadillac assembly lines. Cadillac was the only car to have the new self-starter in 1912, but the following year a number of other car companies adopted the self-starter and, two year later, a car in the medium and upper price ranges either adopted the electric self-starter or went out of business.

Worldwide recognition of the Cadillac Motor Car Company's contribution came quickly. In London, Frederick Bennett, who was in charge of Cadillac sales in Europe, developed an unusual demonstration for the new electric self-starter. Bennett built a small roadster only 4 feet long and powered it with the new Cadillac self-starter motor and its battery.

After it had been exhibited in all the countries of western Europe, the Bennett children drove the small car in the London park adjoining the royal palace. Queen Alexandra was so impressed with the car that she insisted on buying it for her grandson, Prince Olaf of Norway. After the Prince had outgrown the vehicle, Bennett bought it back. Later, he presented the small car to Wilfred Leland, Jr., as a present on his fifth birthday.

The Royal Automobile Club of Great Britain had made exhaustive tests of the new Cadillac features. These tests resulted in the second Dewar Trophy being awarded the Cadillac Motor Car Company for its invention of the electric self-starter and new lighting system. It is the only time that the Dewar Trophy was awarded twice to the same firm.

In November, 1936, twenty-five years after Cadillac engineers had developed the electric self-starter, two hundred and fifty leaders of the motorcar industry in the United States and Europe attended a dinner at the Waldorf Astoria in New York. Henry M. Leland was no longer living, but as had happened so many times before, he was represented by his son, Wilfred. Charles F. Kettering was present. In the center of the banquet room stage was a 1912 Cadillac mounted on a velvet-covered pedestal. On a smaller side pedestal, with its own spotlight, was mounted the complete electric self-starter. A plaque read: "This simple mechanism became the cornerstone of the modern motorcar industry."

New developments often lead to others. After the introduction of the electric headlights, there had been complaints that the lights were too bright for approaching vehicles. Cities began to pass ordinances, requiring that electric car lights be covered. When approaching these towns, drivers would stop their cars and tie handkerchiefs over their lights. In 1915, Cadillac introduced the tilt beam that permitted "dimming" the lights. The same year the Cadillac steering wheel was shifted to the left side of the car.

One of the most important results of the work on the Cadillac ignition system, self-starter and lighting system was the emergence and development of the young engineer, Charles F. Kettering. The Cadillac achievement launched Kettering on a long and unprecedented career in automotive research. In 1920, General Motors acquired the Dayton Electrical Laboratory Company, converted it into a General Motors research facility and named Kettering the first head of General Motors' research department. His contributions ranged from superior car paints to new motors and new gasolines.

In 1914, two years after the introduction of the self-starter, Henry and Wilfred Leland and their Cadillac engineers brought another sweeping advance to the motorcar technology of this country. The invention constituted the most important improvement in the motorcar's internal combustion engine since Henry Leland introduced precision machining for the engine of the Curved Dash Oldsmobile and increased engine power by 100 percent.

Henry Leland's sensitive engineering sense told him that the shorter the crankshaft in the motor, the more efficient, quiet and vibrationless the engine would be. He deplored the introduction of six-cylinder motors with their longer crankshafts which became popular after 1910. Sweet and the Cadillac engineers developed six-cylinder motors and, finally, had one that did not please Henry Leland, but which he regarded as superior to any then in use. The new six-cylinder engine was scheduled for the 1915 Cadillac. It was never put into production.

Wilfred Leland was aware of the limitations of the six-cylinder motors and his father's reasons for opposing them. Yet, he recognized that more powerful engines, with less noise and vibration, were needed for the larger and heavier closed cars in which the American public was showing increasing interest. In the summer of 1913, on a pullman trip from New York, Leland pondered the matter hour after hour. During the night an idea occurred to him that still fascinated him the next morning. When he arrived at the Cadillac plant, he went directly to his father's office and explained,

"The idea came to me that we were having good success with our four-cylinder motors; we would surely have equally good results with blocks of lighter four-cylinders and pistons. Why not make up those smaller blocks of lighter four-cylinders and pistons and put two of the blocks together at an angle and avoid that troublesome long crankshaft?"

The V-8 motor for American motorcars was the result.

Henry Leland was immediately impressed with Wilfred's proposal for placing more cylinders on the same length of crankshaft. He conferred with Ernest Sweet and the Cadillac engineers who also liked this proposal for a new kind of engine. The Lelands placed such a high value on the new motor, that they were determined to develop it secretly and time the announcement so that Cadillac could be sure of having it exclusively for at least one year.

Extensive engineering space was rented on the 22nd floor of the Dime Building that had just been built across from the Detroit City Hall. Not only were there offices for the engineers, but Henry Leland also outfitted a special office for himself so that he could give

315

constant attention to the development of the new engine. The engineering load was so great that new engineers had to be hired. One of them was an Englishman, D. McCall White. He went directly to the Dime Building headquarters so that he would not be known at the Cadillac plant.

As parts for the new motor were designed, they were turned over to a new company, the Ideal Manufacturing Company, organized for the sole purpose of producing the new motor. This company had its own plant at the intersection of Pelham and Drydock Streets in Detroit. Robert Pike, a young Cadillac engineer, was placed in charge of parts procurement. Henry Leland arranged for Pike to take designs of various new parts to six firms in New England capable of doing high precision work. As a result, no one manufacturer knew in what kind of motor his parts were to be used. Pike travelled to and from these New England firms during the spring and summer of 1914 to make certain that the individual parts were made accurately and on schedule.

As had been the case so many times before in motorcar development in the United States, when work on the new engine was well along, Henry Leland learned that a few V-8 motors had already been made in Europe, but with little success. This was disturbing. Perhaps there was some fault in such a motor that had escaped the attention of Cadillac engineers.

After an intensive search, Cadillac's purchasing department located one of the motors in New York. It had been built by the French automobile company, De Dion-Bouton. The motor was shipped to the Dime Building in Detroit where Cadillac engineers anxiously analyzed the French V-8 engine.

The French engine had been built largely by hand craftsmen. No wonder, Henry Leland observed, that they had not heard of the motor or that it had not become a success. It was so poorly made that it was not even a good test of a V-type engine. The new Cadillac V-8 being developed had so many superior features that the French motor was quickly discarded.

A difference in European standards of machining was involved in the only major crisis which developed while the Cadillac V-8 engine was being produced. The pilot engine worked well, but it had a constant loud knock at operating speeds. The vibration and noise were too great to be tolerated in cars. The Cadillac engineers could not find the reason for the unacceptable noise in the new engine.

Finally it reached a point where something had to be done

quickly. Sweet called a conference of all the key engineers who had worked on the new engine. The purpose of the meeting was to check over every engineering detail with Henry Leland to see if he could help them find the cause of the knocking and eliminate the noise.

Leland began at the start of the project and inquired about each step of the work. He discussed the work directly with each man who had been in charge of the design of particular parts. D. McCall White had designed the new connecting rods. Leland examined them with care and then inquired about the machining tolerances. White replied that he had "insisted on nine-thousandths of an inch" which the European engineer considered the highest practical degree of precision.

"That's too much" said Leland. "There is your problem." The old man turned to Charles Martens who had tested Leland engines since the days of Leland & Faulconer. "I'll leave it to you, Charlie, to determine how much the clearance should be reduced." Martens took the motor back to the laboratory and began a series of exhaustive experiments to reduce the machined tolerances. Finally, he was down to 2½ thousands of an inch and the motor noise was still high. Then he cut to two thousandths and it was reduced. When he reduced the tolerance to 1½ thousandths, the noise was gone.

The engineers had done more than build a V-8 engine. They had developed a number of other important new features for the motor. The crankshaft bearings were made larger and the number reduced to three. There was a new lubricating system. A multiple-disc clutch replaced the older cone-type clutch. Perhaps most important, the transmission was mounted right on the engine so that the motor and transmission became a single component in assembling a car. The new V-8 was so well designed that it weighed fifty pounds less than the four-cylinder Cadillac motor it replaced.

By July, the parts for the new engine were being received in the special plant of the Ideal Manufacturing Company on Pelham Street. George Clement, one of Cadillac's top machinists and tool men, was in charge of the new company's operations. He was at the plant all summer. Men at the Cadillac plant thought he had left the company. Even his wife did not know that he was in charge of the secret plant.

The new Cadillac V-8 motor was announced in August. Henry Leland was so sure of the success of the new V-8 motor that the four-cylindered engines were discontinued when production of the 1915 Cadillac began. The Smithsonian Institution recognized the V-8 engine as a major advance in motorcar development and displays one of the first Cadillac engines in Washington, D.C. The V-8 engine has been used in every Cadillac production-year since. Cadillac has used the V-8 engine longer than any other motorcar.

Although, other firms have, through the years, produced straight eights and V-type engines up to the V-16, V-24 and even the V-32, gradually all automotive engineers have come to accept Henry Leland's original judgment on the value of a short crankshaft. The motor was considered too expensive for a low-priced motorcar until Henry Ford created a V-8 engine for use in a 1932 Ford. Since then the V-8 has become the most widely used type of engine in the motorcar.

By 1916, the V-8 engine had become such a success that Ernest Sweet and the other veterans on the Cadillac engineering staff gave a dinner for Wilfred Leland, in appreciation of the inventor of the V-8 motor. Leland was honored with a platinum plaque on which was embossed a solid gold replica of the first Cadillac V-8 motor. The plaque's inscription read: "To Wilfred Leland, in recognition of his conception of the high speed, high efficiency V-type engine, and its application to the motorcar." Today the plaque is to be seen in the entrance to the Cadillac Division of General Motors in Detroit.

Although this upsurge of inventiveness and unprecedented improvement of the motorcar was brought to fruition by Henry Leland and Cadillac during World War I years, the major features of today's cars were almost complete. Since then, there have been refinements which at times were so important that they seemed like new inventions. But, there have been only three developments since that time that have gone beyond refinement. They are high compression rubber-mounted motors, new transmissions and air conditioning. These features were added in the decades of the 20s and the 30s, although major use did not come until after World War II, between 1950 and the present.

19

Chevrolet Takes Over GM

Louis Chevrolet contributed the name and the spirit that launched the Chevrolet motorcar on its career. William C. Durant provided the money, the first factories, the marketing, eventually the car and threw in the famed "bowtie" trademark for good measure.

Although Chevrolet left Durant and his namesake early in the game, he lived to see his name, year after year, placed on more motorcars than any other. The colorful Frenchman with the big mustache lived until 1941. In the last ten years of his life, his name was welded and stamped onto a million more cars than carried the name of any other man. The runner-up was Henry Ford.

Louis Chevrolet was a big man in just about every respect. He was especially big in courage. He was large physically. When he sat behind the wheel of the Buick Bug, or other racing cars, he seemed to dwarf the vehicle. His opinions and his emotions matched his size. He spent almost his entire career in transportation; his life, literally, a bridge from oxen to airplanes. He designed and built his own bicycles, racing cars, motorcars and, finally, airplane engines.

He was born in Switzerland on Christmas Day, 1878, the son of a Swiss watchmaker. Louis learned about machinery, design and repair work from his father. By the time he was ten, the Chevrolet family had moved across the border into the French province of Burgundy where his younger brothers, Gaston and Arthur, were born. The family was poor. As a result, the Chevrolet boys got little formal education and Louis began working, while a boy, to help support the family.

His first job was as a guide for a blind wine merchant. While still in his teens, he invented and built a wine pump that made the Chevrolet name well-known in the Burgundy wine industry. The bicycle soon captured his interest, and he designed, built and raced his own. The 17th century French governor in Canada, Louis Frontenac (for whom it is believed Chevrolet was named), was his lifelong hero. Chevrolet named his bicycle, the "Frontenac," and much later he gave the same name to the Stutz-backed sports and racing car. In 1920, with Louis, Arthur and Gaston working as a Chevrolet team, Gaston drove a Frontenac racer to victory in the Indianapolis "500." He lost his life, however, a few months later when the Frontenac went out of control during a race at the Los Angeles race track.

Louis became acquainted with self-propelled vehicles when he went to work in the French factories producing the Mors, Darracq, Hotchkiss and de Dion Bouton automobiles. He became an expert technician. He came to Montreal in 1900, and worked as a chauffeur, which at that time was a profession that required being able to repair, and even rebuild a car, as well as drive it.

By 1902, he was working in Brooklyn in the American factory of the de Dion Bouton car. On May 20th, 1905, he took advantage of the opportunity to drive a 90-horsepower Fiat racer at the Hippodrome in Morris Park, New York, where he competed against many of the most famous racing drivers of that period. He was twenty-seven years old. This burly, pleasant, powerfully-built man with wavy brown hair and a sweeping mustache won his first big race and immediately captured the hearts of racing fans as a rough-and-ready driver who would take chances without calculating the odds.

The victory won him an opportunity to drive the huge 110-horsepower Fiat in the second Vanderbilt Cup Race on Long Island. He was leading the field late in the race when a front wheel collapsed. The juggernaut crashed but Chevrolet walked away with scarcely a scratch. Arthur was critically injured in racing accidents, and Gaston lost his life in a racer, but Louis, who took many more, and often impossible, risks, escaped without serious injury. He set records on most of the big tracks in the United States and became a member of the elite group of drivers when, in 1905, he defeated Barney Oldfield three times in one season.

William C. Durant hired both Louis and Arthur Chevrolet, in 1907, as members of the Buick racing team. Within the next three years, the Buick accumulated twice as many honors in racing, hill climbing and endurance competition as any other car before or after. Durant also hired Arthur Chevrolet as his chauffeur, preferring him over Louis, "because Arthur took less chances." In 1909, Louis Chevrolet and Bob Burman, another racing immortal of the period, assisted in the design of the Buick "Bugs." E. A. DeWaters, assistant to Buick's chief engineer, Walter Marr, was in charge. E. C. Richards, who together with Marr and Buick had a major part in developing Buick's overhead valves, also helped develop the "Bug."

It was while the Buick "Bugs" were being developed and built that Louis Chevrolet began to think seriously about building a motorcar for the market. Racing experience had taught him a good deal about what made a car dependable. Since dependability was the major problem with cars at this time, Chevrolet believed he could develop a better car. Durant encouraged Chevrolet in his car-engineering efforts, but gave the matter limited attention until after the bankers took over the operation of General Motors.

The banker take-over from the highly successful Durant management had the effect of breaking the old Durant team into two factions. Both the new Nash management at Buick and the banker-management at General Motors were aware of this and tried to prevent the fragmentation, but it was impossible. The senseless and absurd fight that developed at Buick over the continuation of Buick's Model-10 and the outstanding achievement of the Durant management pushed the issue beyond the point of no return. This was the car that had moved Buick into leadership, making it the second most popular car in the country.

In a more mature business, the ouster of Durant from management and the cancelling of his "Model-10," would not have affected the future very much. But the motorcar business was in a highly volatile state with a large and expanding public demand creating the opportunity. It was just such a situation as this that resulted in the creation of REO when Ransom Olds was shoved out of the Olds Motor Company; the same condition that created Cadillac when Henry Ford suddenly terminated his relationship with the Henry Ford Company.

There was a lull that lasted from the fall of 1910 until midsummer

1911, during which time lines were being redrawn. At the end of July, the opening volley was fired and a second motorcar era in the life of William Crapo Durant was underway. It lasted for nine, decisive years and produced many, new wonders. Not the least of them was bringing into existence the Chevrolet, the most prolifically produced and sold car in the seventy-five years of this nation's self-propelled road vehicle history.

The Mason Motor Company was organized in Flint on July 31st. As its name suggests, the company's objective was to make motors rather than cars. On October 30th, the Little Motor Company was formed with an imposing group of incorporators. They included William H. Little, Charles M. Begole and William S. Ballenger all of Flint and all Durant men. Little had been Durant's general superintendent at Buick's "largest motorcar factory in the world" on the Hamilton Farm at the north side of Flint. Begole and Ballenger were Flint Wagon Works officials who had pooled their interest with David Buick and James Whiting to launch Buick on its way to success.

Three days later, the Chevrolet Motor Company was organized with an equally competent group of incorporators. They were Louis Chevrolet, the same William H. Little and Edwin R. Campbell, Durant's son-in-law who, until the banker regime, had been a director of General Motors.

Durant began building his new motorcar business on his General Motors formula from the very beginning. The Little was a light, four-cylinder car, intended to move into the void created by Buick's decision to drop the "Model-10." The car Louis Chevrolet had developed was a powerful, six-cylinder vehicle that could compete with Buick, Oldsmobile and Cadillac. The Mason Motor Company made the motors for both cars.

There was little evidence of revenge in Durant's new moves. There was more indication of a hedge against Buick disintegration. Buick's production in 1911 dropped to 13,889 as compared with 30,525 the year before when the "Model-10" was being produced.

Durant literally moved back into motorcar production with buildings and workmen turned loose by Buick in its retrenchment. The original building, erected on the west side of Flint to make Buick motors after the new factory became available, had been abandoned. Durant bought it and the Flint Wagon Works facilities nearby for the Little Car Company.

With the Buick work force cut back for the first time since the

Buick Motor Car Company began production, it was an easy matter for Bill Little to hire experienced and capable workers. The Little roadster, selling for $650, and with the same features as the former "Model-10" Buick, got into production in the fall of 1911, in time to produce and sell 3,500 cars in 1912.

The new Chevrolet went into production in Detroit on West Grand Boulevard in a rented factory that had been used for making lamps. The most important developmental work had been worked out by a small group of men directed by Louis Chevrolet, in a loft above a small shop on Grand River Avenue in Detroit. The prototype was completed late in 1911, and production began after the first of the year. Durant was so determined to get the Chevrolet into production, he asked Bill Little to leave the Little Motor Company in Flint and move to Detroit. Durant wanted to get Chevrolet into a high level of production so there would be cars to market during the spring sales period.

The car was exactly the kind of vehicle that would be expected of the big man, who had become famous in America for setting racing records with some of the most powerful self-propelled motor vehicles ever built. The first Chevrolet was a heavy, six-cylinder touring car capable of carrying five passengers with ease. It was a luxurious car which sold at the factory gate for $2,150. Three thousand of them were sold the first year, which was a tribute both to Chevrolet's fame and Durant's marketing ability. Louis Chevrolet was delighted with the car.

Although the first Chevrolets were produced largely with credit from firms supplying the parts and materials, Durant let it be widely known that he had high objectives for the Chevrolet car. Perhaps more to impress investors than anything else, Durant bought a factory site on Woodward Avenue in Highland Park, directly across from the Ford Motor Company. He erected a large billboard, declaring that a "large completely modern factory" would be built on the site by the Chevrolet Motor Company. It is possible that Durant had such intentions but, as matters worked out, Chevrolet did not build a factory in Highland Park.

By the early months of 1913, important things had happened on the nation's motorcar scene. Durant was able to see, to a greater degree than his associates or adversaries, that the potential for the motorcar had greatly increased. By that time, Walter Chrysler was in charge of Buick, and Durant was greatly impressed with the former railroad man. Nash had moved on to the presidency of

General Motors. Earnings were rising well above the level required to repay the bankers. At Cadillac, Henry Leland and his engineers had developed a successful self-starter and an electric lighting system.

But Durant's mind probed more deeply. He realized that General Motors stock was undervalued. In 1911, not Durant, but that organization's management received permission to list General Motors stock on the New York Stock Exchange. It was the first motorcar stock to be listed. Durant began, as early as 1913, to increase his holdings in General Motors. He began quietly to buy stock. The public was not alerted and the price remained low.

Furthermore, Durant had concluded that, with the surprising upturn in General Motors' financial health, the banker group would find ways to remain in control even after the $15,000,000 loan had been repaid. Durant knew he could never return to power in General Motors unless he could find a way to control a majority of the common stock. Although the showdown did not come for almost three years, subsequent events confirmed that the bankers had no intention of giving up their control once the loan was repaid.

Just when Billy Durant saw the opportunity to capture outright control of General Motors is uncertain. Judging from his actions it must have been early in 1913. Naturally, he kept his own counsel in the matter. The idea was so fantastic that it would have seemed ridiculous even if he had been willing to discuss it.

The plan that took shape in Durant's mind was threefold. He would use his General Motors stock as security to develop either the Little or the Chevrolet into a "name car" like Buick or Ford, with nationwide distribution. As the business and profits of the firm expanded, Durant would increase the capitalization. Finally, as the time approached for the bank loan to be paid, Durant would trade Chevrolet stock for General Motors common stock. He would accomplish his plan quickly by offering favorable terms to the holders of General Motors Stock. He planned to continue such trading of Chevrolet for General Motors stock until the stock holding of his friends, himself and Chevrolet equaled more than 50 percent of the total General Motors common stock outstanding. When this point had been reached, Durant would regain control of General Motors.

Durant had reached an important conclusion: he needed one car to execute his plan and that meant he could close out his operations in Detroit and draw on far more engineering and production resources in Flint.

Durant launched his plan in August of 1913, just before the 1914 cars were put into production. Without taking the sign down across from the Ford Motor Company in Highland Park, Durant closed down the Detroit operations of Chevrolet. He moved them to Flint, combining the manufacture of the Little and the Chevrolet. He placed in charge his longtime friend, A. B. C. Hardy, who had been president of Durant-Dort Carriage Company fifteen years earlier.

Next came the decision on which of the motorcars Durant should use to carry out his daring plan to regain control of General Motors. The decision went to the Little with its low price, but it would carry the Chevrolet name, in order to take full advantage of the great racing name. Durant knew he would need every possible advantage.

Durant tried to get Louis Chevrolet to stay with the company. He suggested that Chevrolet develop a better, small, six-cylinder engine for the Little car. To Chevrolet, who had won success and fame by achieving big and impossible things, the idea of starting all over to build a small engine was unthinkable. He left in a rage, and sold his generous allowance of Chevrolet stock to Durant for a modest sum.

Chevrolet went back to the speedways as a builder of powerful racing cars. His racer, the "Frontenac," won the Indianapolis "500" in 1920.

By the late 1920s, Chevrolet had turned his attention to aircraft engines. He joined forces with a Ford dealer, Glenn L. Martin from Baltimore. Martin attempted to work with Chevrolet in somewhat the same way Durant had done when Chevrolet began his work on a motorcar. They planned to establish a firm to manufacture Chevrolet motors for airplanes. Chevrolet designed four- and six-cylinder aviation motors that were adaptations of his racing car engines. He designed a ten-cylinder radial aircraft engine in 1932 and applied for a patent which was granted.

The Great Depression ended the hope of founding a Chevrolet company to produce aircraft motors. Martin kept the motors and, after the depression, with but minor refinement, used the Chevrolair-333 motor as the Martin 4-333. The six-cylinder version of the Chevrolet motor was produced as the Martin 6-500.

Louis Chevrolet had designed power units for every modern vehicle of transportation that followed the use of horses and preceded the use of rockets.

Durant moved rapidly in 1914. His Chevrolet Motor Company introduced two new models, the "Baby Grand," last of the big cars, and the "Royal Mail Roadster," first of the Little motorcars with the

Chevrolet name. Remembering the success with overhead valves at Buick, Durant introduced the valve-in-head engines in the Chevrolet that year. The 1914 models were also the first to use the now famous Chevrolet "bowtie" trademark. On a trip through France in 1908, Durant had seen the bowtie design on the wallpaper of his Paris hotel room. He was so impressed with its possibilities, he arranged to get a small section of the wallpaper. The design appeared as the Chevrolet trademark six years later.

There was great expansion in Chevrolet assembly and marketing in 1914. The demand for motorcars was so great that every Chevrolet that could be turned out was sold. In June, the Chevrolet Motor Company acquired the Maxwell Motor Company's factory at Tarrytown, New York. Regional sales headquarters, some of them with assembly plants, were soon opened in Oakland, St. Louis and Kansas City, Atlanta, and in Canada. In order to get assembly facilities established quickly, and at little cost, Durant worked out an area franchise arrangement. Under the plan, management was provided by Chevrolet with the plants and operational funds being supplied by the local franchise.

By 1915, Durant was again ready to do battle with the "Model-T" Ford. His Chevrolet Motor Company, that year, introduced the Chevrolet "490," named because Chevrolet's touring car sold at the factory for $490. In addition to being made in Flint, the "490" was also assembled in franchise plants across the country. For Durant, the Chevrolet "490" was a precise reenactment of his earlier development of the Buick "Model-10." It had a four-cylinder, valve-in-head motor, it was a full-sized car and it sold in the same price range as Ford's "Model-T."

For the first time, Chrevolet moved into a head-on competitive clash with Ford. The "490" touring car was just $50.00 higher than the "Model-T" Ford that year and it provided, as standard equipment (while the Ford did not), the new electric self-starter and electric light system developed earlier at Cadillac. The Durant philosophy of attacking Ford had been set. Chevrolet would concentrate on marketing a car for only slightly more, while offering features not to be found on the Ford. The Chevrolet-Ford war, to become one of the classics in competitive marketing in the American economy, had been declared.

Although the new "490" was just being introduced in 1915, Chevrolet production and sales recorded a significant jump upward. Production more than doubled from the output of 5,000 cars in 1914 to 13,500 cars in 1915. This was followed by a thumping fourfold increase in 1916 when Chevrolet production soared to 63,000. Chevrolet sales nearly doubled in 1917, climbing to a production of 111,500 cars. Only Ford, Buick and Willys-Overland marketed more cars that year.

With the adoption of the low-priced car and the high volume of sales that followed, the Chevrolet Motor Comapny began making money. From 1915, the firm's profits were in excess of a million dollars a year. In 1917, more than a quarter of a million dollars was added to profits when Durant sold the factory site in Highland Park to the Ford Motor Company. He then leased an eight-story building at 224 West 57th Street in New York City for company headquarters.

Besides building Chevrolet Motor Company up from nothing to one of the leading car producers in the United States in a period of just more than three years, Durant had carried out a task of equal magnitude in acquiring either ownership or control of General Motors common stock. During 1913 and 1914, he forged strong ties with powerful financial interests willing to invest in either General Motors or the Chevrolet Company, or both.

None was more important than the relationship he developed with John J. Raskob, an executive with the du Pont Company of Wilmington, Delware. Raskob interested Pierre S. du Pont, president of the company, in investing in General Motors and Chevrolet. This led to major investment in General Motors and Chevrolet by the du Pont Company until, in 1918, du Pont owned 26.4 percent of all General Motors common stock outstanding. In 1917, there was a single purchase of 25 million dollars of General Motors and Chevrolet stock by the du Pont Company.

In 1915, Durant announced that Chevrolet Motor Company common stock would be traded for General Motors common stock at the rate of five shares of Chevrolet for one of General Motors. The result must have surprised even Durant. Hundreds of General Motors shareholders took advantage of the offer. Most of them had bought their Buick and General Motors stocks from Durant in the first place. Both companies had prospered and these people were ready to stand with Billy Durant in whatever he wanted to do.

A. M. Bentley of Owosso, Michigan, traveled all the way to Chevrolet's headquarters in New York City to turn over a small suitcase full of General Motors stock. The certificates came in such numbers that they were stored at the Chevrolet offices in bushel baskets. In September, of 1915, the Chevrolet Motor Company of

Michigan was absorbed by the Chevrolet Motor Company of Delaware and the capitalization was raised to $20,000,000.

Time was running out, but Durant was ready. With his twin efforts succeeding—building a strong Chevrolet Motor Company and acquiring more and more bushel baskets of General Motors stock—by the spring of 1915 Durant was ready to state his intentions openly. The end of banker management would come with the final payment on the loan scheduled for the end of the year. Durant confided to trusted friends that he would, then, resume control of General Motors.

While Nash and his backers didn't believe Durant or anyone could assume personal control of General Motors, they did recognize that Durant would again become an important figure in company operations. This was revealed in June when Bankers Storrow and Strauss retired from the General Motors board of directors. Storrow's position as chairman of the important financial committee was filled by Louis G. Kaufman, president of the Chatham and Phoenix National Bank of New York. Kaufman was a close friend of Durant. Repeatedly, his bank had loaned the Chevrolet Motor Company large sums of money that made it possible for the firm to advance so rapidly.

Durant chose the September meeting (on the 16th, the seventh anniversary of the company) to make the frontal assault. It was planned to be an especially important meeting. It was expected that President Nash would announce that General Motors profits justified advancing the date of final payment of the 1910 bank loan from December 31st to October 11th. It was also expected that the first General Motors common stock dividend would be declared.

On September 13th, Wilfred Leland of Cadillac stopped at Durant's New York office in the Chevrolet Motor Company headquarters. Durant confidently predicted that he would regain control of General Motors at the annual meeting when new directors would be elected. He took Leland to a large walk-in type safe at the back of the building. Durant opened the door, turned on the light and showed Leland a huge stack of General Motors stock certificates which, he said, represented controlling interest in the company.

Durant and three of his associates personally stayed up through the night, at Chevrolet's headquarters, counting the General Motors stock certificates. To make absolutely certain there could be no mistake, they removed one certificate at a time and passed it from hand

One of the two hundred and fifty Dodge cars used by the
U. S. Army in the Mexican border bandit incident,
directed by Brigadier-General John J. Pershing in 1916.
First motorcars used in combat by the U. S. Army, put in
action as communications and command cars, replacing
horses. They were also employed in the final cavalry
charge in which the bandit leaders were killed. Here is a
field unit on the border during the campaign.

to hand so there was a four-way check of the results as they tallied the total.

At the director's meeting, Durant asked for an opportunity to speak. In his quiet and gracious manner, he announced that his $20,000,000 Chevrolet Motor Company owned a controlling interest in the $100,000,000 General Motors Company. The stunned officials and directors, unable to believe such a thing was possible, sat in silence during much of the remainer of the meeting. On Nash's motion and Durant's second, the directors authorized General Motors' first dividend on common stock. It amounted to $50.00 per share, a total outpouring to shareholders of $8,000,000. It was the largest cash dividend, per share, declared on a stock listed on the New York Stock Exchange up to that time. A large part of the cash flowed into the treasury of the Chevrolet Motor Company.

The reaction to the Durant announcement came later in the day when it became necessary to recommend the new directors to be elected in November at the annual meeting of General Motors shareholders. The situation quickly developed into a battle between the Durant faction and the directors in sympathy with Nash. Knowing of their interest in General Motors activities, Banker Kaufman had invited the du Pont Company officials, Pierre S. du Pont, president, and John J. Raskob, treasurer, to attend the meeting as observers. It was the first time that du Pont and Durant had met.

After the harsh talk had continued for an hour or more, Kaufman found a way to break the deadlock—in Durant's favor. Kaufman asked du Pont to leave the room so that he might explain the plan. When they returned, Kaufman proposed that du Pont name three members of the new directorate, with Durant naming seven members and the Nash banker management directors naming seven. The plan was accepted and du Pont agreed to serve as a General Motors director himself, and named two others.

Before the September meeting of the directors closed, Durant offered to bring the Chevrolet Motor Company into General Motors. The directors were so certain that Durant's Chevrolet company did not own controlling interest, they turned the offer down.

At the November 16th meeting of General Motors shareholders, Charles W. Nash was reelected president, and the compromise directorate worked out two months earlier was also seated. Pierre du Pont was elected chairman of the General Motors board, a position he held for nearly two decades. While the election gave Durant a majority of ten to seven on the board of directors, the directors challenged the alleged Durant-Chevrolet control of General Motors and pledged a court fight to determine the facts.

The threat was never carried out. It would have been a waste of energy if it had been A year later, on October 13th, 1916, the General Motors Corporation of Delaware was formed to take over the assets of the General Motors Company and the actual ownership of shares was determined. Of the 825,589 shares of General Motors common stock outstanding, exactly 450,000 shares were owned by the Chevrolet Motor Company. Billy Durant had not been bluffing.

20

"He Could Coax a Bird
Right Down Out of a Tree"

When Durant returned to power in General Motors in 1915, there was no resumption of the furious expansion he had directed earlier. General Motors was a highly profitable business. Durant had access to strong men, such as Nash, Kaufman, Raskob and Pierre du Pont in addition to the men operating the subsidiaries, the Lelands at Cadillac and Chrysler at Buick.

Except for the Chevrolet Motor Company, there was no major effort toward additional company acquisition. Even Chevrolet did not join General Motors for nearly two years. Durant's efforts, in 1916, were devoted to protecting and preserving the management team, securing control of more suppliers of vital components and improving the General Motors corporate structure.

He immediately approached Nash and asked him to remain as president. The relations were cordial. Nash agreed to stay, but it must have been evident to them both that Nash's days at General Motors were numbered.

Within a few days after Durant resumed control he made a trip to Detroit to meet the Lelands at Cadillac. He expressed his continuing gratitude to Wilfred Leland for working out the formula in the bankers meeting at the Chase bank in New York, five years earlier, which had led to the $15,000,000 loan that had pulled General Motors through. Durant told Leland that as long as he lived he would never forget the constant, "I will not lend another dollar" refrain of the first day of the Chase conference.

Durant explained how closely he had followed General Motors developments during the five years of banker control. He thanked the Lelands for having sent their outstanding machinists to Buick and Oakland plants to iron out production difficulties. He noted that the banker-management had forced the Lelands to accept a 50 percent cut in their own salaries. Durant further noted that the salary cut had not even partially been restored, although the Cadillac Motor Car Company had made a profit every year and had introduced both the new electric starter and V-8 engine.

"How much did you lose through reduction in salary made by the Finance Committee?" Durant asked Henry Leland.

"In excess of $500,000," Leland replied.

Durant realized what the Lelands had contributed and that there were few men, if any, who could have directed the Cadillac Motor Car Company to its unusual achievements. He restored the Leland incomes. He assured them that General Motors would "reimburse" them for the income which had been withheld and added, "You are entitled to another block of stock to reward you for all you have done."

In the same manner, Durant moved to make certain that Walter Chrysler's unusual ability remained available to the Buick Motor Car Company and to General Motors. He, too, had been mistreated. In his determination to get into motorcar production he had accepted the same 50 percent cut imposed upon the Lelands.

It is understandable that management felt it necessary to reduce salaries of its executives when it took over late in 1910. It is another question as to whether the move was justified in the case of Henry and Wilfred Leland since their company was providing the profits to meet the repayments to the bank. Things were extremely difficult when Chrysler went to Buick in 1911, just after the "Model-10" had been removed from the line, and Buick had lost nearly 60 percent of its business. Buick was fortunate that Chrysler wanted to change from railroading to motorcars badly enough to accept the $6,000 salary.

By 1912, management and Nash (as General Motors president), placed themselves in a dangerous position by failing to raise the salaries of men like the Lelands and Chrysler who were apprehending the General Motors return to financial stability. The Lelands asked for no restoration of income and received none, but their personal need was not as great as Chrysler's.

Chrysler worked for three years at the $6,000-a-year pittance, boiling inside at the sacrifices this required of his family. He worked through 1912, 1913 and 1914 at the low wage. Finally, early in 1915, he forced a showdown. Later in his autobiography, issued while Nash, Durant and many of the other principals were still living, Chrysler told exactly what he did on that day early in 1915 when his anger reached the exploding point:

"Executives out there in Flint sat in swivel chairs between a roll-top desk and a big flat-topped table.

.....I walked into Nash's office and rested my knuckles on his table. 'Charley, I want $25,000 a year.'

'Walter!' It was pretty nearly a scream, the way he uttered my name.

'Now, Charley, we've gotten along fine. We are making good. Here in Buick, we've got the one company that has been making money.'

'Walter—'

'Just a minute until I have finished. I've waited a long time before saying this. When I came here I was getting $12,000; I took this job for $6,000, and you haven't given me a raise. I want $25,000 a year, or I'm going to leave you.'

'Walter, this is something I'll have to talk about with Mr. Storrow.'

I walked out smoking one of my own panatelas.

In a couple of days I learned that Storrow had arrived in town. Nash and Storrow were in conference. Then word was brought that they would like to see me down in Charley's office.

'What's this all about, Walter?'

'Not much to it. You know how I came here. You know I was getting $12,000, and now I'm getting $6,000; after three years of the hardest—. I want $25,000 a year. By—.'

'Don't get excited, Walter.' Mr. Storrow did everything but pat me like a pet horse. 'Don't get excited; you're going to get your $25,000.'

'Yes? Well, thank you; and by the way: Next year I want $50,000.' I was forty years old. When I got home, I really started to enjoy that raise."

Since Chrysler, as a result of this confrontation with Nash and Storrow, was, in effect, under obligation to stay on at Buick as general manager, Durant visited the other General Motors executives first. It was early in 1916, when it was known that Nash was going to leave, that Durant went to see Chrysler who may have thought he was being neglected.

Chrysler and Durant were not acquainted at the time when it

Even the Medics used Dodges to get around quickly and dependably. This one was assigned to a surgeon, as indicated on the left rear door.

became known that Nash, with the backing of eastern banker friends, was going to produce a car of his own. There were reports that Chrysler might join Nash in the new venture. Actually, at the time Durant went to see Chrysler, Nash and Chrysler had made an offer to buy the Packard Motor Car Company in Detroit. Durant undoubtedly knew of the Nash-Chrysler discussions with Packard. He was noted for his uncanny faculty for gathering information relating to the production of motorcars anywhere in the country.

Durant took the initiative in his talk with Chrysler from the outset, with, "Mr. Chrysler I'd like to hire you as president of The Buick Motor Company." Making it clear that he was well aware of what was going on, Durant told Chrysler that he wanted him to forget, for the present, going into a production of his own car and to stay with Buick. Chrysler admitted that, if plans in which he was interested materialized, he planned to leave Buick. Durant asked Chrysler how long it would be until his plans were definite and Chrysler told him it would be in about thirty days. Durant left, after inviting Chrysler to call him at his home in Flint when his plans were settled.

Thirty days later the Packard deal fell through. Chrysler called Durant, reported his plans had not developed and he would like to meet Durant and discuss matters. Durant proposed to meet Chrysler at the Buick Plant at 7 o'clock the next morning. It was their second private conversation. Chrysler's account of the meeting is a splendid commentary on Durant as well as what happened. Of that spring day in 1916 he reported:

"I cannot hope to find words to express the charm of the man. He has the most winning personality of anyone I've ever known. *He could coax a bird right down out of a tree,* I think ... Seven o'clock found Billy Durant right on my doorstep. I dropped into my swivel chair between my roll-top desk and my wide table; Durant seated himself on the opposite side of the table. I was going to ask him for a raise.

'I'll pay you $500,000 a year to stay on here as president of Buick.' He just sprang it on me that way; he did not bat an eye. I couldn't think for a few seconds.

'Mr. Durant, the salary you offer is, of course, far and away beyond anything I had expected, but—'

'Now, Walter (we were getting well acquainted fast) you just put aside, for the time being, all your plans of getting into business for yourself. I don't blame you for ambition, but I ask you to give me just three years of yourself."

336

American trucks first became important as military
transport during World War I. General Pershing is seen
with a Jeffery military vehicle. The Nash Motors
Company, which took over Jeffery, became the country's
largest truck builder during the war, producing 11,000
trucks under one U. S. Army contract.

Durant knew what a man of Chrysler's experience and capability could do for Buick. Only months before Nash and Storrow—knowing they were getting a bargain, but not really knowing what Chrysler was worth nor appreciating his ability—were paying $6,000 a year to their man in charge at Buick. Durant, however, was willing to pay that same man $500,000. Chrysler chose to draw $10,000 a month and take the remainder, $380,000, in General Motors stock.

Time confirmed that Durant was accurate in his appraisal. Durant later raised Chrysler's salary to $600,000 a year. Four years later, when Chrysler left General Motors, his next job was directing the faltering fortunes of the Willys-Overland motorcar empire for which he received $1,000,000 a year. Until he established the Chrysler Corporation, Walter Chrysler earned such annual amounts. Only when he headed his own firm, did he accept a smaller salary.

Nash advised the board of directors on April 18th of his desire to leave the presidency of General Motors on June 1st. At the time it appeared that the closing of the purchase of the Packard Motor Company was only days away. By the time the Packard proposal had been turned down, Storrow and Nash had found that the Thomas B. Jeffery Company of Kenosha, where the Rambler motorcar had been made since 1902, was for sale.

Providing another dramatic example of the importance of one man's leadership in the motorcar business, Nash went to Wisconsin and used the old Jeffery facilities to create the Nash car. Eighteen months later, Nash's new firm became the largest builder of trucks in the world. In 1918, the Nash Motor Company turned out 11,494 trucks under a United States Army contract. Later, the Nash became one of the country's most prized motorcars.

Another example of the personal leadership in motorcars was unfolding during the same year at Detroit where Roy D. Chapin, who worked with Ransom E. Olds on the Curved Dash Oldsmobile, was leading the Hudson Motor Car Company to a position of prominence. In 1954, the Nash and Hudson firms were merged into the American Motors Corporation. Nash's protege, George Mason, was the first president. The man who followed Mason as head of American Motors was Roy D. Chapin, Jr., son of the man most responsible for making the Hudson, one of America's great motorcars for nearly half a century.

William C. Durant became president of the General Motors Company for the first time when Nash left on June 1st, 1916. Soon after, President Durant and Chairman of the Board Pierre du Pont ushered in a new era for General Motors by making a fundamental change in its corporate structure.

On October 13th, the General Motors Corporation of Delaware was created and quickly absorbed the assets of the General Motors Company of New Jersey. General Motors changed from a holding firm to an operating company. With the coming of the corporation, the capitalization of General Motors was increased from $60 million to $100 million.

On the date of its inception, the General Motors Corporation owned the entire capital stock of Buick Motor Company of Flint, Olds Motor Works of Lansing, Cadillac Motor Car Company of Detroit, Oakland (Pontiac) Motor Car Company of Pontiac, General Motors Export Company of Michigan, General Motors Truck Company of Pontiac, Jackson-Church-Wilcox Company of Jackson, Northway Motor & Manufacturing Company of Detroit and the Weston-Mott Company of Flint. The corporation owned 62.5 percent of the capital stock of AC Sparkplug Company of Flint and 49.85 percent of the McLaughlin Motor Car Co. Ltd. (General Motors of Canada) of Oshawa, Ontario.

For charter purposes, the annual production capacity of the new corporation was listed as 165,000 motorcars and 6,000 trucks, divided among the former member companies as follows: Buick, 100,000 cars; Oakland, 30,000 cars; Cadillac, 20,000 cars; Oldsmobile, 15,000 cars; General Motors Truck Company, 6,000 trucks.

In the transition year of 1916 the net profits were $28,812,287.96, net working capital was $43,664,671.40 and dividends were paid totaling $11,779,122.99. Under the corporation, the former operating companies became divisions of the General Motors Corporation with each manager becoming a member of the corporation's board of directors and a vice president of the corporation. The new division general managers and General Motors vice presidents were Walter P. Chrysler, Buick; Wilfred C. Leland, Cadillac; F. W. Warner, Oakland-Pontiac; Edward Verlinden, Oldsmobile; Charles S. Mott, Weston-Mott; W. L. Day, General Motors Truck (GMC); G. H. Hannum, Jackson-Church-Wilcox; A. L. Cash, Northway.

The change in corporate structure opened the way for a further expansion which centered largely around developing the facilities of the operating divisions rather than acquiring new companies. The Chevrolet Motor Company was brought into the fold in 1918, resolving the awkward situation where Chevrolet held control over General Motors.

Much of the new money for this expansion was provided by the du Pont Company. Under an agreement developed by Durant and Raskob, du Pont executives moved into General Motors and took over the financial responsibilities. Raskob himself became chairman of the finance committee in November, 1917. In the next two years, the du Pont Company increased its stock holdings until on December 31st, 1919, du Pont owned 28.7 percent of General Motors. At this point, the directors of the du Pont Company, becoming fearful of too deep an involvement, declared formally that there would be no further buying of General Motors stock.

Durant's expectations in forming the new corporation were soon confirmed. The General Motors Corporation, in a remarkably few years, became the largest corporate enterprise in the world. Its annual industrial output advanced until it was greater than that of all but the largest nations. These accomplishments rest on the achievements of the earlier General Motors Company whose life extended over a period of eight crucial years.

During that period, the General Motors Company brought about the first merger of motorcar companies. The company secured its major financing from privately owned banking companies and was the first motorcar manufacturer whose securities were traded on the New York Stock Exchange. Through crisis and prosperity, the first General Motors—as has the second—maintained prompt, semi-annual payments on preferred stock. When this company came into existence, the car itself was still on trial. Horseless carriages were widely in use. When it was reorganized, the car was already a vital part of American life and its permanence was recognized alike by farmers, city dwellers, bankers and government officials.

The new round of Durant expansion was primarily focused on companies that could contribute components to General Motors cars and trucks. There were a few exceptions.

Durant attempted to put General Motors into the farm tractor business. He acquired several companies making farm equipment and merged them into Samson Tractor Division with headquarters at Janesville, Wisconsin. The venture turned out badly, although great engineering opportunity and the market potential were both present. But no Henry Leland or Walter Chrysler was on the scene to carry the program to success. As a result, General Motors wrote off its losses and left the Ford Motor Company the only motorcar firm to find a permanent place in the farm equipment industry.

During this period Durant discovered an important future industry in an inventor's attic workshop in Detroit. In a matter of minutes he sized up the situation and said, "Next to the automobile, this is the greatest thing that could be put on the market." He had just discovered that an electrically-powered home refrigerator was a possibility. Looking over the inventor's loft, Durant commented to the friend who took him there, "This man's got an idea. ... I'll organize a company with one hundred thousand dollars new capital and give you people a quarter interest." He moved the inventor to a little brick building at the Cadillac factory. The result was the Frigidaire home refrigerator, the machine that a few years later introduced the blessings of electric refrigeration to millions of homes in the United States.

From 1917 to 1920, a number of manufacturing divisions were set up to provide axles, gears, crankshafts and other parts for motorcars. Two acquisitions were of special importance. One was the purchase of a group of Dayton companies that had been spawned from the genius of Charles F. Kettering. In the process, Kettering became an official of General Motors and director of the corporation's research effort.

The other was the purchase of the Hyatt Roller Bearing Company of Harrison, New Jersey. Hyatt was the leading producer of vital roller bearings for the motorcar. During 1916 and 1917, Durant acquired several important component manufacturers, including the Harrison Radiator Company of Lockport, New York, and merged them into the United Motor Company. He secured, as president of this largest motorcar component firm, Alfred P. Sloan, Jr., who had built the Hyatt roller bearing organization from a dirt-floor factory in an old barn to a multimillion dollar manufacturing concern. The United Motor Corporation was taken into General Motors in 1918. Sloan became head of the United Motors Division of General Motors.

Durant's greatest accomplishment during his second term as head of General Motors was his recruiting of Sloan and Kettering. They, more than anyone else, became responsible for the development of General Motors and what it now contributes to America's industrial strength.

21

John and Horace Dodge

The American tradition of rising from poor origins to positions of contribution, influence and wealth finds one of its best examples in the careers of John and Horace Dodge. Duryea, Olds, Leland, Durant and Ford all grew up in rural homes where pennies had to be watched closely, but John and Horace Dodge went to school barefooted, for lack of shoes, in Michigan's cold weather.

Untimely death cut short the Dodges' careers in 1920. Beginning at a time when no automotive industry existed in Detroit, the red-headed Dodge brothers began by producing complex parts, such as the transmissions for the first Curved Dash Oldsmobile. They made possible the success of Henry Ford. They created the Dodge motor-car. They died with combined personal fortunes in excess of one-hundred-million dollars. Today, the estates of John and Horace Dodge, despite depressions, high taxes and world wars, are each still valued at approximately fifty million dollars.

The world has known little about these remarkable men and their contributions to the modern motorcar. There are several reasons. They did not seek publicity, as did Olds and Ford. During more than half their motorcar careers, when they developed the largest motor factory in the world, they made no car of their own. Instead the Dodges poured their vast production of motors, transmissions, axles, radiators, running gears and other parts into the assembly plants of the Ford Motor Company. Their motorcars appeared under the Ford name.

However, the Dodge brothers, their vast achievements hidden under a contract with Ford, were often known by the Detroit citizenry for their gala parties. These stories have continued to be conversation pieces in Detroit for half a century. Perhaps none of the stories has been told so often as the various accounts of the party held in March, 1914, at Detroit's fashionable Book-Cadillac Hotel at which the Dodge brothers announced the introduction of the Dodge motorcar. John Dodge provided an impromptu finale that evening to end all finales. It consisted of his mounting the long white banquet tables, marching up and down with gusto and darkening the great hall by smashing the electric bulbs in the chandeliers with a cane.

At the time of their deaths, the Dodges were attending the 1920 New York Automobile Show. John died unexpectedly at the Ritz Carlton Hotel with no member of his family present except Horace, who was also ill and who lived only a few months. Many of their contemporaries believed high living contributed to their deaths.

The real tragedy has been that the accounts of the Dodge brothers' escapades failed to include the important details, too. For, if at times they were self-indulgent, this never interfered with their integrity and efficiency in business, nor with their close family ties and devotion to their families and friends.

John and Horace Dodge were sons of a blacksmith at Niles, Michigan, a small rural town in the southwestern part of the state. John was born in October of 1864. Horace was born three and one-half years later. The Dodge blacksmith shop was near the railroad station in the center of Niles, but the family lived in a small house at the north edge of town. Family ties were close but, with growing children, it was difficult to make a blacksmith's wage provide even the necessities.

John Dodge once explained to a newspaper reporter of the *Niles Star* some of the circumstances under which he and his brother grew up.

"We were born on North Fifth Street in a little wooden cottage close to where your (water) standpipe is now located. In those days we were the most destitute kids in town. Poor Mother, how she used to worry about her boys.

"I am three years older than my brother and, naturally, Mother always confided her trouble to me. When cold weather came, H. F. and myself were obliged to go barefoot and wear ragged clothes. We didn't grumble but tried to make Mother think it was all right.

"I drove a cow three miles twice a day for 50 cents a week and was mighty glad when pay day came. Later I carried sacks of bran with Tom Davis out of freight cars for 50 cents a day and when we left Niles I was earning $1.25 a day in the old Krick factory."

The most important training for John, and even his younger brother, Horace, did not come in tending cows or carrying livestock feed out of railroad cars. From the time they were small boys, they worked with their father at the Dodge Blacksmith Shop. Soon after John was graduated from high school, the Dodge family moved to Port Huron on the St. Clair River northeast of Detroit, where the elder Dodge operated a small machine shop. The St. Clair River, along with Lake St. Clair and the Detroit River, connects Lake Huron with Lake Erie. The Dodge Machine Shop's major business was maintaining and rebuilding marine engines, both of the steam and internal combustion types. This is where the Dodge brothers received their first training in internal combustion engines.

But, there wasn't much work in Port Huron for two young men who were capable mechanics and able to earn a man's wages. In 1886, when he was twenty-two, John went to Detroit and Horace soon followed. They worked in Detroit machine shops for six years, during which they became expert machinists. John's first job was as a mechanic in the Murphy Boiler Factory. After six months, he was made a foreman. Horace got a job at Leland & Faulconer and became one of the finest metal craftsmen in Detroit.

In 1894, John and Horace went across the Detroit River to Windsor, Canada, to work at the Dominion Typograph Company. John received a starting salary of $6.25 a day, a salary which indicated that he already had a reputation as a top machinist in the Detroit-Windsor area. He soon became superintendent of the small plant.

The two brothers were in Windsor for nearly seven years. These were the years when they put down the foundations for their unique role in the development of the motorcar. They had always been devoted to each other, even when they were small boys in Michigan. In Canada, they began an unusual business association and personal companionship that continued unbroken and unmarred until the death of John.

Soon after they went to Windsor, the two brothers undertook

their first engineeirng work. They developed a Dodge bicycle that rolled entirely on ball bearings. It attracted the attention of Fred S. Evans, a Detroit manufacturer. In 1897, with Evans' backing, the Dodges organized the Evans & Dodge Bicycle Company. They leased the Dominion Typograph Company plant and launched their career as manufacturers.

After two years of a successful operation, the Dodge brothers sold their business to a Canadian bicycle manufacturer. They returned to Detroit, with $7,500 cash and $10,000 in machinery. In 1901, they rented space in the Boydell Building on Beaubien Street between Fort Street and Lafayette Boulevard. There they established the Dodge Brothers Machine Shop.

Their first few months in Detroit, the young businessmen worked seven days a week and into the night, to get their new business established. Soon they were employing twelve men.

During the day, John and Horace worked side-by-side at the benches with their workmen. Almost, from the first, there was a divided responsibility. John went about the city looking for new jobs, while Horace remained in the shop to supervise the work. After their men left in the evenings, the Dodges often worked until after midnight. They labored at designing and engineering tasks and planning future work. John prepared the bills and handled the customer relationships. Horace translated their plans into action in the shop.

A few months after the Dodges had been in business, their big break came. In March, the new factory of the Olds Motor Works, first motorcar plant to be built in Detroit, burned. In the summer, after orders for the Curved Dash Oldsmobile came more rapidly than the crippled Olds Motor Works could produce the cars, Ransom E. Olds went to the Dodge Brothers Machine Shop for assistance. Olds drove to the Dodge shop in his own car. He wanted to see for himself whether these small businessmen could be depended upon to handle the production of an important part for his Oldsmobile. The Dodge brothers knew they could do the work and soon convinced Ransom Olds. They were given an order to produce the transmissions for the Curved Dash Oldsmobile. The Dodge work was so satisfactory that during the fall of 1901, all of 1902 and early 1903, the Olds Motor Works relied entirely on the Dodge Brothers Machine Shop to make the Oldsmobile transmissions. The Dodges made three thousand of the complicated components.

The business and number of workmen they required increased.

345

In 1902, the Dodges moved to larger quarters at 240 Monroe Street. They leased a large building and installed new machine tools. The Dodge brothers were operating on Monroe Street when Alex Malcomson of the Ford & Malcomson Company, predecessor of the Ford Motor Company, approached them to make parts for the new Ford car which was soon to be launched.

The relationship that followed was the only one of its kind ever to exist in the motorcar business. Except for the almost standard items of wheels, tires and bodies, the Dodges continued to make the Ford cars for several years. This agreement continued while the Ford Motor Company shrugged off its earlier heavy models and won complete dominance in the low-priced field.

The Dodges did more than supply components. They participated in the decisions on design and often built additional benefits into the Ford car at their own expense. When the Ford "Model-C" was introduced in 1905, the Dodge brothers surprised everyone at the Ford Motor Company by painting the wheels a distinctive yellow and added new larger three-inch tires—all for the same price. The new features helped make the "Model-C" highly successful.

When Dodge parts did not function well, Henry Ford or his engineers would step in. As an example—the decision on securing a carburetor for the first Ford engine was left to the Dodges. They equipped the car with a Kingston carburetor considered to be the best available in Detroit at the time. Ford did not regard the carburetor as satisfactory. He learned of a young man in Bradford, Pennsylvania, who had developed a superior carburetor, and was manufacturing a small, single-cylinder horseless carriage named the Holley "Motorette." Ford brought Holley to Detroit, and built him a small plant where he made superior carburetors for the Ford car.

Even when the "Model-T" Ford was developed, the Dodges continued to build practically the entire Ford car. The Ford Motor Company continued to be a firm largely engaged in assembly and marketing. The Dodge Brothers Company had enlarged its plant, year after year, at 240 Monroe Avenue. By 1910, the Dodge brothers had the most modern car factory in the United States. Its nearest rival was the big Buick factory on the north edge of Flint.

John Dodge was a director and vice president of The Ford Motor Company. When it became necessary to acquire a location for a new and larger factory for the Ford Motor Company to replace the one on Piquette Avenue, John Dodge and Henry Ford conducted the search. They were together the day they found the location on

Woodward Avenue in Highland Park, where the mighty Ford plant was opened January 2nd, 1910. In order to be near the new Ford factory, the Dodge brothers also developed a new factory in nearby Hamtramck. The new Dodge Works, on a sixty-acre tract, was completed and put into use in 1910. The Ford Motor Company was the firm's only customer. Each working day, the Dodge Works built one hundred motors and other major components for the "Model-T" Ford.

From the time Ford opened its new Highland Park plant, the unusual relationship between Ford and Dodge was doomed. With the opening of the Highland Park factory, the Ford Motor Company, for the first time, had the plant space, the financial resources and the staff to take over production responsibility from the Dodge brothers. Henry Ford and John Dodge knew that they had reached the culmination of their working relationship. It had made them both leaders in the motorcar industry, as well as wealthy and famous.

Ford was willing to lease the new Dodge Works at Hamtramck and integrate its factory space and workmen into the great Ford enterprise. Such an arrangement was agreed upon, in principle, in 1912, while the Dodge brothers continued to provide a vast flow of major components, including the motor for Ford cars. The lease terms were not to become effective until 1914. The proposal gave John Dodge time to think the matter out. The one thing which he insisted upon, all his life, was time to make decisions. To associates he repeated his axiom again and again, "If you have to decide quickly, don't do it."

From the Dodge point of view there were both advantages and disadvantages to the leasing arrangement. The major advantage was that it would immediately protect the thousands of men working at the Dodge Brothers Works in Hamtramck. Moreover, the lease plan would protect the Dodge investment in the big manufacturing complex.

The disadvantages centered upon the Dodge brothers themselves. They were men in their forties, approaching their most active and productive years. They had worked hard since they were small boys in Niles. The Dodges and their wives thought deeply about what new business they should enter. Everyone recognized that John and Horace Dodge would never retire to a life of pure leisure.

It was not that John and Horace Dodge lacked interests outside their business. John had served with zest and distinction on both the Detroit Board of Water Commissioners and the Detroit Street Railway Commission. He had his farm at nearby Rochester where he spent a great deal of time, especially when there were big decisions to be made. He had a special interest in politics and, by 1912, was regarded as a powerful political figure of the Republican Party in Detroit. A man free of financial problems would logically move into public life. There was talk of John Dodge running for United States Senator from Michigan.

Horace Dodge had his own interests, centered largely on his family, boats and music. Horace built yachts for his own use on the Detroit and St. Clair Rivers and the Great Lakes. Perhaps his favorite was the "Delphine," named for his daughter. When Horace went to the National Republican Convention in Chicago, as a Michigan delegate, he made the trip from Detroit on the "Delphine," going through Lake Huron, the Straits of Mackinac and south across Lake Michigan to Chicago.

The yacht, the "Lotus," which Horace owned with John, won numerous challenges and was regarded as the fastest racing yacht on the central Great Lakes. The Delphine II was being built at the time of Horace's death.

Both brothers possessed unusual musical ability. Horace was a close friend of the great Victor Herbert. He was so fond of the pipe organ that he learned to play, though he rarely performed, except for his own and his family's enjoyment. He had built, in his Detroit home, one of the finest pipe organs in the United States. Conductors often invited him to appear in public for benefits. Horace, joined by John, was the principal benefactor of the Detroit Symphony Orchestra. In appreciation, at the wedding of Horace Dodge's daughter, Delphine, the Detroit Symphony Orchestra, unannounced, appeared to play the wedding march.

As the months of decision passed on the impending lease of the Dodge Works to the Ford Motor Company, another question of much greater magnitude confronted John and Horace Dodge. They knew how to build a better car than the "Model-T." Should they, therefore, give up their Dodge factory and retire from the business or should they tear up the proffered lease from the Ford Motor Company? Should they become a competitor of the motorcar they had helped to make the most important in the world? Should they risk their wealth in an effort to make the first formidable entry into the Ford empire? Literally, dozens of cars had attempted to challenge the "Model-T" and had failed.

The Dodge brothers had special reasons for wanting to build a better car. They had repeatedly offered to make improvements on the "Model-T," only to be brusquely turned down by Henry Ford. Many times, since that car had gone into production five years before, John Dodge had proposed improvements, some of which would have reduced the cost of making the Ford car; and still he had been turned down. Ford had become a czar where the "Model-T" was concerned. In 1912, he had issued a personal order that every "Model-T" Ford, regardless of the body style, would be painted black. "Let 'em have any color they want so long as it's black," he joked as the order on color went out.

The Dodge brothers had come to regard the "Model-T" as something of a tragedy. Here was the opportunity to use their abilities to give the public a greatly improved motorcar at little, if any, increase in price. But Henry Ford refused to discuss the matter. His closest associates, Wills, Couzens, Hawkins and others, had attempted to reason with him. The memoirs of Herbert R. Lewis, who had known all those involved, records that a group of Ford's close associates built a pilot car to show Ford what an improved "Model-T" could be like. Ford, literally, destroyed the new car without even starting the motor.

Ford dealers and even the public, to a limited degree, were aware of the problem. There was talk, as early as 1912, that the Dodge brothers would cancel out on Ford to make their own car. Prominent Ford dealers called on John and Horace Dodge to ask them if it were true that they expected to build a Dodge car. They promised, that if one were put on the market, they would sell the car.

Dealers talked to Ford about improving the "Model-T." At times Ford listened with some interest, and minor changes were sometimes made. Front doors were added and the steering wheel was moved from the right to the left side, after most other cars had added such features. But on important improvements, such as the standard gear shift or a new lighting system to replace the magneto lights, Ford was adamant, often abusive. He always pointed to the rising sales of the car "as she is," and his objective to further reduce the price.

In the summer of 1913, the Dodge Works at Hamtramck was, on some days, turning out 1,000 Ford motors in a 24-hour period. John Dodge began spending a lot of time at his farm at Rochester. Horace visited him there to consider what their course would be. The second week in August, the brothers made a trip to Niles to visit old friends, pay their respects at their mother's grave and discuss the possibility of creating a new village park for Niles.

While on this visit, John Dodge gave the interview to a *Niles Star* reporter, explaining the conditions in the village and in the Dodge family when he and Horace were growing up and working in his father's blacksmith shop. In light of the decision as to whether they would remain active in the motorcar business, some of John's other comments to the reporter that day are of interest. In connection with the $100,000 he and Horace provided to buy a park site in Niles, John remarked,

"This amount sounds big but really it is nothing to us now. H. E. and myself are worth $50,000,000 and we have made most of it in the last ten years. We want to do something for Niles right away and I have suggested a donation of $100,000. We will double the amount if your citizens will advance a judicial manner in which it can be spent."

The trip to Niles gave John and Horace additional time in which to discuss what they would do about the Ford lease offer. A week after they returned, the decision came. On August 18th, 1913, John Dodge wrote James Couzens, resigning as vice president and director of the Ford Motor Company. He exercised the option to terminate the leasing plan worked out earlier, after a period of one year.

There was no suggestion of bitterness or recrimination. The Dodges agreed to deliver all of the components to Ford that would have flowed from Hamtramck had the permanent lease been allowed to go into effect. There simply would not be any further negotiating for the making of Ford parts after that year was up. John Dodge said to Couzens, "We expect to fulfill strictly all of the conditions imposed on us by the lease for the ensuing year...."

The Ford Motor Company had one year in which to secure the components that Dodge had supplied. Ten years had passed since the first Ford was assembled at the little Mack Avenue plant. The Dodge Works was mainly engaged in producing Ford motors during the last year. When the year was over, the Dodge brothers had produced 500,000 motors for the Ford Motor Company. That was more engines for motorcars than had been produced by any other firm in any country.

After nearly a year had passed from the time John Dodge retired as an officer of the Ford Motor Company, the announcement was made to the nation that there would soon be a Dodge car. On July 17th, 1914, the new firm, Dodge Brothers, Inc., was chartered in

Herbert Hoover used this 1917 Hudson during his term
in Europe after World War I as United States Food
Administrator, a service that made him a world figure.

Michigan. John Dodge promised that the new car would be coming off the Hamtramck assembly line in about one hundred days.

Automobile Topics reported, "... news that Dodge Brothers were to bring out a new car swept like wildfire throughout the industry. It was like the announcement of a new gold strike—another Comstock Lode or a second Klondike—that the famous Dodge engine builders were to have a car of their own."

The Dodges themselves were surprised by the reception given their announcement. By the time the first car was produced on November 14th, 1914, approximately 22,000 individuals and firms had applied for dealerships. Most of them, at the time, were selling other cars. Before that point, when a new firm began producing a motorcar, it had to seek salesmen. Consequently, the Dodge brothers could reverse the process and select the best dealers.

John Dodge was so impressed that he made a special effort to cultivate his Dodge dealers and let them know how important they were. He once sent a check to a New York City Dodge dealer for $15,000, the amount of commission the dealer had lost because Dodge Brothers, Inc., had failed to deliver the number of cars the dealer had ordered.

There was a touch of snow in the air at Hamtramck on November 14th, 1914, when the first Dodge car came off the assembly line. A crowd had gathered at the big plant to see the historic moment. John and Horace Dodge got into the back seat of the touring car. The driver placed his foot on the self-starter floor button, "Old Betsy" came to life and the career of the Dodge car had begun. At the idling speed, the car had a sound all of its own. The Dodge "chugged." Comedians soon quipped, "A Ford rattles, a Packard purrs, and a Dodge chugs."

The new Dodge was the kind of motorcar that the Dodges had hoped the "Model-T" Ford would become. The new car had greatly increased power. The 20-horsepower engine of the "Model-T," a sensation when it was introduced in 1908, was a modest power unit by 1914.

The new Dodge car had a 35-horsepower engine, and a 110-inch wheelbase, and weighed 2,200 pounds. Next among the improvements was the sliding gear transmission. Ford's associates had been pleading with him for three years to replace the planetary transmission that required so much service, with the improved standard sliding gearshift.

The third major departure was in the car's suspension system.

Instead of the two big cross springs that supported the "Model-T" body, the Dodge car had independent suspension for each wheel, as all of the medium and higher priced cars did. The body of the five-passenger Dodge touring car contained no wood. It was an all-steel single unit. It provided greater strength and less noise from vibration.

The new Dodge car included what the "Model-T" did not offer in appointments. There was a speedometer, windshield and the new demountable rims, which made it possible to carry a fully inflated spare tire. The new car had, as standard equipment, the entire electrical system introduced by Cadillac two years earlier. The Dodge included the self-starter and electric lights powered by a wet battery and generator. The "Model-T" continued to use the magneto until after World War I. The new car cost only about $100 more than the Ford.

Asked at the time how he thought the competition with the "Model-T" would succeed, John Dodge observed, "Just think of all those Ford owners who will someday want an automobile." As events later proved, Henry Ford would have done well to have pondered Dodge's statement.

The Dodge brothers, who found the "Model-T" underpowered and always needing to be repaired, were determined that their car would be dependable, even under difficult conditions. John Dodge personally rolled tires off the roof of a four-story building at the Hamtramck factory, observed their bounce and studied them for injury. Fred Lamborn, who retired as a department manager at the Dodge Works, was a young worker in the plant when the car was being developed. He reported that in these exhaustive tire tests, John Dodge came to the conclusion that U. S. Chain Tread tire stood up best. That was the tire with which the first Dodge cars were equipped.

Horace Dodge supervised the building of a high plank test track just outside the Hamtramck factory. His new cars could be checked out right on the factory grounds, rather than giving them road tests in the area as was the common practice. A "hill," fashioned from planks, severely tested Dodge engines going up and Dodge brakes coming down. The testing track, with its long, steep incline, became the forerunner of the modern motorcar proving grounds.

John Dodge carried testing to the greatest extremes. Lamborn was present on one occasion when John Dodge had two new cars, both unreleased models, driven into a reinforced brick wall at twenty miles an hour. "I've never heard such a crash," said Lamborn. When he asked Dodge why he insisted on such an expensive test, Dodge said "I might as well, because someone else is going to do it when these cars get out on the road."

The advent of the Dodge motorcar resulted in adding a word to the language. Customers responded quickly to the greater power and more rugged construction. Within months letters began arriving at Hamtramck reporting, again and again, that the car could be depended upon. Gradually Dodge men coined a new word to summarize these customer reports. They said it was the "dependability" that the Dodge owners liked most in their new car. Dealers began using the new word. In time it was placed on billboards across the nation. The word was adopted by others, became a standard reference and began appearing in dictionaries in the 1930s.

By 1915, the racing, hill climbing and across-the-nation endurance feats had ceased to attract public attention as they had a few years earlier. The new Dodge car received attention from the public, but in an entirely different manner. Late in 1915, the U. S. Army bought its first Dodges. The army repainted them olive and sent them to the troubled border area between Mexico and the United States. Pancho Villa and other Mexican bandits were terrorizing both Mexican and American people along the border.

In the early weeks of 1916, Villa and his men made several forays across the border into New Mexico. On one of these savage raids, Villa and his men attacked the town of Columbus, New Mexico, fifty miles west of El Paso. Several American civilians and soldiers lost their lives. The country's best known military personality, Brigadier General John J. Pershing, led a force of 12,000 soldiers to protect American lives and property and remove the threat of violence.

In April, Pershing led his men across the southwestern desert into the border region. For the first time motorcars, three Dodge touring cars, were used in a U. S. Army cavalry operation. They were driven against an armed enemy in exactly the same manner as horses, camels, elephants and other beasts of burden had been since time immemorial. There were no roads and the cars were driven over the open desert terrain, along with horses. The army officers were impressed with the cars, and Pershing ordered six more Dodges sent to his desert expedition.

The writer for the influential *Century Magazine* (traveling with the expedition) wrote, "Over the desert stretch, and by nature of the desert dust they themselves camouflaged, three automobiles swayed and lurched and banged in low gear, belching steam from their radiators, grinding their way through the sand."

Pershing's campaign progressed well. The American side of the border was cleared of Mexican bandits, and the leaders of the raiders retreated deep into Mexican territory. Their headquarters was on the big San Miguel de Rubis ranch, near the town of Chihauhua, 200 miles south of El Paso. The bandits were operating from a ranch building so well protected that a surprise attack appeared to be the only quick way to rout them. During the retreat southward, several thrusts by crack units of the horse cavalry had failed to capture the bandits.

By the middle of May, the American force had moved to within a few miles of the rebel headquarters. At this point Pershing introduced an entirely new tactic. At dawn on May 14th, fifteen heavily armed men climbed into three Dodge touring cars and carried out the first motorized charge, under combat conditions, in the history of the United States Army.

The approach to the bandit headquarters was across open country. During the last mile, the officer in charge ordered the army drivers to charge at the highest speed possible over the sandy ground. The three Dodges, driven in tight formation, approached the fortified ranch house at forty miles an hour. The Americans were within a few hundred yards before the bandit guards became aware they were under attack. The bandits were so completely surprised that they ran out of the doors and jumped half clad from windows in an effort to escape. Colonel Julio Cardenas, leader of the rebels, and two of his aides were killed. The other bandits were captured or dispersed and the rebellion was soon over. The Americans had suffered no casualties.

Pershing's young lieutenant in command of the daring attack at dawn stated in his report, "We couldn't have done it with horses. The motorcar is the modern war horse." The lieutenant was George S. Patton, Jr., who later became one of America's greatest generals. He, too, made lightning thrusts against the enemy, with motorized cavalry, during World War II.

Pershing immediately ordered two hundred and fifty more Dodge cars. He was so impressed with the ruggedness and performance of the cars that his entire staff used them. In less than a year, the United States entered World War I, and General Pershing was given command of the American Expeditionary Force in Europe. In France, one of the drivers of Pershing's Dodge car was Lieutenant Edward

Rickenbacker, the famed racing car driver who became America's first hero in the air.

The Dodge brothers had justified their decision to produce a new car at their Hamtramck factory rather than lease to the Ford Motor Company and retire. They had produced a more powerful car, capable of providing a wider range of service than Ford's "Model-T."

As might be expected, relations between Henry Ford and the Dodge brothers changed as soon as it became certain that there would be a Dodge car to compete with the Ford. Judging by his actions, Ford must have thought that the Dodge factory at Hamtramck would always, in some manner, remain available to the Ford Motor Company.

Soon after, he learned that this was not to be the case, and shrewdly judging that the demand for the "Model-T" would continue to rise for years to come, Ford began planning a colossal new production facility. Making the land purchases personally, Ford acquired a thousand acres of farm land along the River Rouge at Dearborn. A part of the tract was within sight of the farm he had purchased from his father. The house Ford had built for his young wife, soon after his marriage, still stood on the farm.

The loss of Dodge production came at a critical time at Ford and greatly complicated the planning situation. Except for Flanders and John Dodge, Ford was surrounded by his original team—Wills, Couzens, Hawkins, Sorensen, Diehl, Knudsen, and his son, Edsel— all at the very peak of their motorcar careers. In Ford, they had an aggressive leader who could commit tens of millions of dollars to any plan that met his approval. Stimulated into action by the unexpected loss of the Dodge production, the men at Ford arrived at what proved to be a brilliant projection of increased motorcar use in the next decade and the part the "Model-T" would have in the expansion. To support the projection, the plans for a new massive Ford factory at Dearborn was announced by Ford and Couzens in June, 1915.

At the time the decision was made, the Ford Motor Company was producing "Model-T" cars at the rate of 1,000 each working day for a total of about 300,000 annually. Buick in Flint and Willys-Overland in Toledo ranked next but were producing only 150 cars a day or a total of about 50,000 a year. At a time when total U. S. motorcar production was 500,000 cars a year, the men at Ford concluded that, within ten years, the American people would, if the opportunity

Food shortages, especially in Britain, accelerated
Henry Ford's development of a lightweight tractor
to replace the horse on the farm. Here is Harvey S.
Firestone, in 1916, using one of the first Ford tractors
at Columbiana, Ohio. With him are his two sons,
Leonard K. Firestone (left), now president of the
Firestone Tire & Rubber Company of California and
Raymond C. Firestone, now Chairman of the Board
and chief executive officer of the Firestone Tire
and Rubber Company.

could be made available, buy up to 2,000,000 "Model-T" cars annually. They made plans to produce them.

The Highland Park plant, without the production of the Dodge brothers factory at Hamtramck, could be expanded to produce 750,000 cars a year. The new factory on the River Rouge, Ford men reasoned, should be large enough to produce 1,250,000 cars. No such manufacturing plans had ever taken form in the mind of man before. To those who had less understanding of the motorcar potential, the Ford decision to build the huge River Rouge plant appeared to be madness, the act of men drunk with their own success, and a move which could destroy the Ford company.

As the plans for the great River Rouge complex took shape, the costs of development were taken from earnings of the Ford Motor Company. As a result, large dividend payments were no longer paid. This infuriated the Dodge brothers who still retained a ten percent ownership of the Ford Motor Company. They looked upon the Ford move as but a means of using dividend money, logically due them, to build new plant facilities so that Ford cars could compete more effectively with Dodge cars. The Dodge brothers had been paid more than a million dollars a year in Ford dividends, beginning with 1912. To have this income cut off at a time when they were launching a new car was inconvenient, even embarrassing. As early as January, 1916, rumors circulated about Dodge court action which was planned against the Ford Motor Company.

The historic court battle between the motorcar giants began November 2nd, 1916, and there was high drama in the selection of that date. The suit could have been filed November 1st, and, in fact, it was reported at one time that it would be filed October 31st. The Dodge brothers waited for personal reasons. On the evening of November 1st, they and their wives attended the wedding of Edsel Ford and Eleanor Lowthian Clay, niece of J. L. Hudson, Detroit's foremost merchant and principal in the Hudson Motor Car Company. The wedding took place in the Hudson mansion on Boston Boulevard East. Mr. and Mrs. Thomas Edison were among the guests. Henry Ford, too, showed that he could separate business and personal relations as he visited pleasantly that evening with John and Horace Dodge.

Dodge lawyers filed their case against Ford the following afternoon in the Michigan Circuit Court. The suit demanded, among other things, that the Ford Motor Company distribute as dividends 75 percent of $39,000,000 of the company's cash surplus. The suit also asked an immediate injunction to halt the building of the River Rouge plant until the dividends were paid. The court granted a temporary injunction, preventing further work on the new Ford factory, until the question of dividend distribution was settled.

The long trial that resulted was familiar ground to Henry Ford. It was basically a reenactment of the classic court battle against the Selden patent. In both court actions, the fundamental issue was the same—company management. The Selden group had sought to dictate to the Ford Motor Company how many cars it could produce and what standards of production it should maintain. The suit by the Dodge brothers sought to dictate to the Ford Motor Company how it should use its profits.

The testimony brought out much about the Ford-Dodge relations that had not before been public. A great deal of vital information of public interest about the motorcar industry was placed on record by men talking under oath. Between them, the principals, at the time of the trial, maintained half the productive capacity of the entire motorcar industry in the United States.

Ford, the Dodges, Harold Wills, and James Couzens, who had resigned from Ford by the time of the court case, and many other company principals of both firms appeared in the witness chair. Ford and the Dodges maintained a high level of courtesy in all their references to one another. There was a great deal said to the benefit of both companies. Ford, with his experience in previous court battles and his great capacity to remain calm and reasoning, even when placed on the defensive, was a highly effective witness. As in the Selden case six years before, Ford found the opportunity to spell out for the public his determination to make it possible for everybody to own a motorcar.

Ford had often said that he regarded the profits of The Ford Motor Company as "awful." The Dodge lawyer, Elliott G. Stevenson, had this exchange with Ford on the witness stand:

STEVENSON: "Now I ask you again, do you still think that those profits were 'awful profits?'"

FORD: "Well, I guess I do, yes."

STEVENSON: "And for that reason you were not satisfied to continue to make such awful profits?"

FORD: "We don't seem to be able to keep the profits down."

STEVENSON: "Are you trying to keep them down? What is the Ford Motor Company organized for except profits, will you tell me, Mr. Ford?

FORD: "Organized to do as much good as we can, everywhere, for everybody concerned .... to make money and to use it, give employment, and send out the car where the people can use it .... If you give all that, the money will fall into your hands; you can't get out of it."

In another exchange between Stevenson and his famous witness, the public learned for the first time the decisive role the Dodge brothers had played in the success of the Ford Motor Company.

STEVENSON: "Dodge brothers spent $60,000 to $75,000 (John Dodge in earlier testimony supplied these figures) to re-equip their plant and to do the work—to retool. They jeopardized everything they had."
FORD: "I don't know about that."
STEVENSON: "Well, you didn't have any risk, did you?"

Ford replied that he had taken a similar risk in turning over to the Dodge brothers the drawings for his cars to be manufactured.

STEVENSON: "You haven't forgotten that they produced the cars that brought the money to make you a success. There isn't any doubt of it, is there?"
FORD: "No."

A year later, on October 31st, 1917, the State Circuit Court handed down a verdict that was favorable to the Dodges, and greatly limited the role of Ford management in both how to declare profits and how profits might be used. The Ford Motor Company immediately appealed the verdict. The United States was then engaged in World War I. The Ford and Dodge companies quickly assumed major roles in the production of weapons, and the court fight was continued.

The verdict of the higher court did not come until after the war was over. On February 7th, 1919, the higher court held that the Ford Motor Company management and its directors had no monopoly over the motorcar business. As a consequence, the directors were free to manage the affairs of the company as they saw fit, including the building of a factory of any size on the banks of the River Rouge. The court did, however, rule that when profits of the company were great, the owners were entitled to an annual return of 10 percent. Under that formula the court ordered the Ford Motor Company to pay its shareholders $19,300,000 of which the Dodges brothers received $1,900,000 and Henry Ford personally received $11,100,000.

22

Legion of Honor

The role of the United States carmakers in the last days of World War I was a major factor in altering the balance of power throughout the world. It was not only the weapons the industry produced. It was the spirit of cooperation with their government and between themselves and, above all, the speed with which they converted to war work, that encouraged the Allied Powers and shocked their enemies.

The war in Europe had been in progress two and one-half years when the United States entered on April 6th, 1917. There had been little buying of weapons in the United States although the munitions manufacturers, such as the du Pont Company, had supplied a high volume of explosives to the European belligerents almost from the outbreak late in the summer of 1914. There had been almost no direct involvement of the motorcar manufacturers prior to the time the United States entered the war.

Still there was a deep awareness and uneasiness about the war. Henry Ford, whose sense of social concern was always unusually keen, had brooded over the war developments. He was an advocate of peace all his life. In August, 1915, he made a public statement to the effect that he would gladly give up all he owned if he could make any contribution to restoring peace. In December, 1916, he chartered a "peace ship" and headed a list of distinguished Americans who went to Europe hoping to interest the warring powers in a plan of continuous negotiation.

The United States had entered the war in early April. Before the end of June, the first American soldiers were in France. Motor transport from U. S. car factories arrived even before the first troops. While the conflict was the first war in which motorized equipment was important, it was essentially a war fought with horses.

The experience of the Studebaker Corporation at South Bend revealed this dual nature. On the day the United States declared war, Albert R. Erskine, president of Studebaker, sent a telegram to President Wilson: "Studebaker factories ... are at the disposal of the Government. Any orders given us will receive preference and cleared right away."

Studebaker had been one of the country's major builders of horse-drawn equipment. Just before the war, the company had closed out the last of its wagon and carriage business. With the expeditionary force and our Allies waging war with horses, Studebaker returned to the making of harness, heavy wagons, water carts and horse-drawn ambulances. Within one month after the United States entered the war, Studebaker had made a fifty percent conversion to war work. Within a year, Studebaker's entire factory was given over to the production of war materials.

In contrast to Packard, Ford, Hudson, Studebaker, Nash and most other carmakers, General Motors was slow to enter war work. William C. Durant, deeply engaged in consolidating his gains after resuming control at General Motors, at first opposed taking on government war contracts. His attitude cost General Motors the services of Henry and Wilfred Leland who were determined to place their great talents at the disposal of the government, immediately.

Before long, Durant began changing his mind about accepting war contracts, but his hesitancy resulted in a relatively limited contribution by General Motors to the war effort. Cadillac produced 2,350 staff cars for the army which were regular V-8 Cadillac cars painted army olive. Cadillac also made more than one thousand artillery tractor engines, using a heavy Cadillac V-8 motor as a power unit. The Jackson-Church-Wilcox Division produced trench mortar shells, reaching a production of 20,000 rounds, per day, by the time the war ended.

Through its English and French branches, the Ford Motor Company supplied at least 7,500 vehicles for war use before the U. S. entry into the war. The French government bought 4,000 "Model-T" Fords for use on the Western Front. The English Ford plant sold thousands of Fords for military use. In both England and France, Fords were made with special bodies as ambulances. The first war contract to Ford from the United States government was for 2,000 chassis to be equipped as Ford ambulances. Harvard and Yale students raised a fund and gave seventeen Ford ambulances to the Red Cross for war use. Early in the war the Ford Motor Company also made 820,000 steel helmets.

The War emergency stimulated the production of the Ford tractor, the "Fordson," which was the first successful light tractor for use in either England or the United States. Food shortages in England made the use of tractors urgent and the Ford Motor Company produced 7,000 tractors for the British and a similar number for national use by July of 1918. Production was at the rate of 130 tractors a day during the last months of the war.

The Ford Motor Company was engaged by the government to build a submarine chaser. It was a 200-ton craft, two hundred feet long with a 21-foot beam. It was named the "Eagle." An 18-acre plant was erected on the River Rouge to make the boat. The factory employed 8,000 men at the peak of effort. With William S. Knudsen in charge, the plant's first building was erected in February, 1918, the first keel was laid May 7th and the first Eagle boat launched July 10th. Fifty-two were produced (in eighteen months) before the project was closed out after the war. If the war had continued the Eagle boat could have become a decisive weapon. In the late stages of the conflict, Germany's control of the sea was almost solely enforced by the use of the submarine.

The Ford Motor Company developed for the U. S. Army a small, two-man tank and a larger, three-man tank. Only the smaller tank reached production, but had the war continued the new tanks could have been a factor in ending brutal trench warfare. Had not the war been brought to an end in the fall of 1918, the American motorcar plants would have provided an entirely new family of weapons for use in 1919.

The entry of the United States into the war dramatically unleashed the power of the newly developed American mechanized system of manufacturing. The war became a test between the Whitney system of standardization, combined with the fully mechanized and moving assembly line, and the European production system that depended upon handwork. Two war production programs handled by the new motorcar procedures in Detroit proved so decisive that they contributed directly to ending the war and were instrumental in an Allied victory.

The airplane, which was not considered as an important offensive weapon at the beginning of the war, had advanced to the position of being decisive by the time the United States entered the conflict. More powerful planes, in great quantity, were considered to be the Allies most urgent need when America was drawn into the fight.

J. G. Vincent, Parkard's chief engineer, had seen this need developing long before the United States got into the war. For three years he had been developing a 12-cylinder engine. Soon after war came, Alvan Macauley, who had become Packard's president upon the retirement of Henry B. Joy, offered to the government the designs for the only immediately useful airplane motor. Packard also offered to begin production of 100 of the motors, without a contract, so that airplane engines could be available quickly. Macauley urged that the government contract with additional firms who would be given the right to produce the motor without reference to the Packard name.

The Packard offer resulted in the calling together by our government of representatives of the hard-pressed British and French air forces, along with American participants, including Vincent of Packard. On June 4th, Great Britain, France and the United States agreed to place in the hands of the American motorcar industry the responsibility for building a new airplane motor capable of winning supremacy in the air for the Allies.

The conference had worked out some refinements for the Packard motor, originally designed as a racing car engine and rigorously tested on the race tracks. The new motor was named "Liberty." Colonel Edward A. Deeds, who with Charles F. Kettering had founded the Dayton Electrical Laboratory Company, was given the responsibility of producing the Liberty airplane engine. E. J. Hall, of the Scott-Hall Motor Car Company, an engineer who had worked with the Russians on aircraft design before U. S. entry into the war, was made chief engineer of the Liberty program.

Remarkable developments followed quickly. Packard began work on the 100 motors it had offered to make without a contract. On July 4th, exactly one month after the program had been approved, Hall turned the propeller to start the first Liberty engine at the Packard plant.

Meanwhile, on June 18th, Henry and Wilfred Leland resigned

from Cadillac, the organization they had created. At a farewell dinner, Henry Leland stated, "The Cadillac has been dearer to me than any other one thing in the world except my home, but there has arisen now a claim on my loyalty that is nearer and dearer still. I do not believe the people of this country realize the monumental nature of their task. The time is coming though when this realization will be forced upon us. The world's greatest need at this moment is America; and America's paramount need now is to provide means for mastery of the air."

Without waiting for a government contract to produce Liberty motors, Leland and his son, Wilfred, organized a new company. Henry Leland who with his own hands had made rifles for the Union army during the Civil War, and who supported and voted for the reelection of Abraham Lincoln in 1864, named the new company, the Lincoln Motor Company. Along with friends, the Lelands invested their own fortune in erecting a new plant on a 50-acre piece of prairie, on Warren Avenue, where 6,500 Liberty motors were eventually produced. Packard produced 6,000, Ford, 5,000, Buick and Cadillac, 2,000 and Nordyke & Marmon, 3,000.

Nor was the Liberty airplane engine the only work done by motorcar men on aircraft. Charles F. Kettering and his engineers at Dayton developed a pilotless airplane for the government. The project was producing operational airplanes by the end of the war. With a view to saving men, Kettering was asked to develop a small plane capable of carrying an effective bomb-load behind enemy lines and of dropping the bombs at a predetermined point. In the period before effective anti-aircraft guns existed, the little, pilotless weapon could have been of decisive character had the war continued.

An even more urgent matter developed, related directly to winning the war on the ground. The French 75 and 155 cannons were the backbone of the Allied ground attack. The war had lasted so long and the destruction of these guns had been so great that an acute shortage of these artillery pieces had developed.

The English and French could mold the huge cannon barrels and build the running gear for almost any number, but they could not produce the vital firing mechanisms. These had always been made by hand craftsmen. It was beyond capacity of all available men in Allied countries skilled in this work to make enough of the complicated and delicate recoil firing components to keep Allied armies supplied with the French 75s.

The need became so desperate that the famed French general,

Marshal Joseph Joffre, headed a delegation that visited Washington to lay the matter personally before Secretary of War, Newton D. Baker. Baker consulted a number of American firms, including some in the motorcar industry, without finding an organization willing to tackle the assignment. It had been suggested to Baker that if anybody could carry out such a undertaking it would be the Dodge brothers. Baker called John Dodge to Washington to meet with Marshal Joffre and himself.

Dodge said immediately that if the French could provide an accurate set of blueprints and if the government would leave the matter entirely in the hands of Dodge management, they could produce the delicate recoil mechanisms in almost any quantity desired. Joffre did not believe the firming mechanisms could be mass produced. Dodge was short of patience and tempers flared. Dodge shouted at Baker, "Do you want these things· or don't you?" "But this is not a mass-production task," Baker insisted. "The hell it isn't," Dodge retorted. "Look here, Mr. Dodge," Baker lashed back. "I am not accustomed to being spoken to in that kind of language." "The war would be a hell of a lot better off if you were," yelled Dodge. "Do you want us to do this job or don't you?"

Dodge's proposal was approved. Without waiting for a contract, John telephoned Horace in Detroit and reported they would build the firming mechanisms for the French cannon. He also added that he would be in Detroit the next day with the blueprints and directed that preparations for erecting the factory begin at once. The Dodges had an 18-acre tract of open land on Elliott Street. Earlier, they had planned the kind of building that would be required to make the French mechanism.

On Monday, two days later, the water and sewer lines were staked out on the location. On Tuesday, the Detroit Terminal Railway was building a spur line onto the property. Carloads of building materials were already enroute to the plant site. Within a week, what had been an unplowed field, was thick with steam shovels, cement mixers, cranes, switch engines and workmen.

One month later, eleven acres of concrete floor had been poured. Despite an unusually cold winter, the factory took shape. Eighteen hundred men had worked to erect the big plant at a cost of $10,000,000.

While the factory was being built, Dodge engineers and machinists were working just as furiously on preparations for mass-producing the cannon components. They designed, and built 129 special machines to produce the parts. By late February, the machines were being moved into the factory.

On March 1st, 1918, Horace Dodge gave the signal. The big factory came to life and began turning out the firing mechanisms. Only four winter months had passed since Baker and Marshal Joffre had given the job to John Dodge.

French military engineers took the cannon recoil units off the Dodge assembly line, put them into actual French 75 and 155 cannons. They worked flawlessly. The firing mechanisms were rushed to Europe by the fastest ships available. Some of the big guns were ready with Allied armies awaiting the firing components from Detroit that would make them operational.

After the war, the French Government awarded the Legion of Honor to John Dodge and his eight thousand workmen who had forged a vital link in the chain of Allied victory.

The contribution of the young American motorcar industry had altered the military map of the world. Its outpouring of weapons moved the United States up to the rank of a foremost world power and laid the foundation for the country to become, a generation later, the most powerful nation on earth. In the short period of eighteen months, the carmakers who had no previous experience in armaments were turning out quantities of weapons for use on the land, on the sea and in the air. Wiped out, too, was the old concept of a permanent industry for the making of weapons. Even as the war was being fought, the carmakers were making plans for resuming, at the earliest possible time, the producing of motorcars and other products of peace.

Part Three

The
Sloan Era

23

Parting of the Ways
in Detroit

World War I and its economic aftermath swept over the motorcar industry of the United States like a violent storm. Before it was over the weaker carmakers had been swept away and even the strongest had been sorely tested. The exception was the Ford Motor Company, whose "Model-T" provided a bridge over the chaos on which the motorcar moved to its present greatness. What was left after the war was the foundation of today's industry which is, by any measure, the most important-non-government enterprise in the world.

The war stress lasted a decade. The war had begun in Europe late in 1914 and, by 1915, shortages of materials began to develop. In 1917 and 1918, all of the major motorcar plants were filling war contracts, and by the end of the war, car production had come to a halt in most factories. Material shortages limited production of cars in 1919. The fall of that year and spring of 1920 brought recovery. But, just as this restoration was getting underway, the country's economic underpinning collapsed in a sharp postwar depression. It was particularly disastrous for the motorcar business just attempting to get its breath from the wartime shutdown.

The adjustments in the war period were made acute by another factor. Many of the strong men who had provided the stability that brought the motorcar through its horseless carriage years came to the end of their careers during those difficult years.

Frank Duryea, who had produced the first successful motorcar, retired just as the European war began. In 1915, he sold his interest in the Stevens-Duryea and retired, a rich man, to his modest but comfortable home in Madison, Connecticut. Free from the stresses of the business, he outlived them all, maintaining close contacts with his old friends. He died in 1967 at the age of ninety-eight. His brother, Charles, who interested him in working on a self-propelled road vehicle, had died in 1939.

Charles King, who in 1896 had demonstrated the first motorcar built in Detroit, and who later designed the Silent Northern, turned his attention to aircraft engines in 1916 and did not return to motorcars after the war.

The remarkable Stanley twins, Frances and Freelan, 1897 builders of the first Stanley Steamers, best-known of American steam-propelled motorcars, sold their Stanley Motor Company in 1917 and retired. Their 1906 steamer had set a mile-speed world record, travelling 127.66 miles an hour. The Stanley Steamer continued on the market until 1924, long after most steam cars had been discontinued.

Elwood Haynes also retired during the war years. With the help of the Apperson brothers in Kokomo, he had introduced his first Haynes motorcar in 1894. The last Haynes car was made in 1925. The Apperson brothers, who produced their own cars, including the Apperson "Jack Rabbit," completed their motorcar careers at the same time. The older brother, Elmer, who had worked most closely with Haynes, died while attending a race in Los Angeles, on the very track where Gaston Chevrolet lost his life. The Apperson motorcar was discontinued in 1925.

Alexander Winton, who had built the first powerful motorcar in the United States, turned his attention to heavy diesel motors during the war years and did not return to work with motorcars. The Winton was made until 1925. Winton organized a special company, the Winton Engine Company, and became one of the nation's foremost builders of diesel engines for marine, rail and industrial use. His company was acquired by General Motors in 1930 and became a part of the Electromotive Division of General Motors. With Charles F. Kettering's help, this division revolutionized railroad engines by developing the modern diesel locomotive.

The war shattered the Ford Motor Company team. With Henry Ford, these men had been responsible for producing one out of every two cars made in the United States from 1894 until the April day in 1917 when this country entered World War I. They became the architects of the first nationwide use of motor transport.

James Couzens was the first to go, and before the war aftermath was over Norval Hawkins, C. Harold Wills, John R. Lee, and William S. Knudsen were gone. Flanders, of course, had left earlier to build his own car. Couzens left to go into public service, becoming mayor of Detroit, and later, United States Senator from Michigan. Wills moved on to another distinguished career with the Chrysler Corporation. Hawkins and Knudsen went to General Motors where they contributed to the building of that organization.

The war years brought an almost complete changing of the guard in motorcar racing. Death or retirement had thinned the ranks of the great early drivers. Eddie Rickenbacker, one of the great ones on America's racetracks before the war, returned from Europe a national hero after having brought down twenty-six German planes. Rickenbacker came to Detroit where he was welcomed home at a gala dinner organized by Herbert R. Lewis in behalf of a legion of Detroit friends. Later, Rickenbacker, with Barney Everett and others as financial backers, designed and produced the Rickenbacker, a medium-priced car that was marketed from 1922 until 1927.

The importance of the role that car racing had in shaping the future of the motorcar and the early builders is pointed up by Henry Ford's reunion with Barney Oldfield. By this time, Ford was known to be one of America's wealthy men. Oldfield was operating a tavern in California. Ford paid Oldfield the honor of going to see him at his place of business, a gracious concession in view of Ford's lifelong aversion to alcoholic beverages of any kind. The old friends discussed the great experiences they had weathered together with the "999" Ford racer. "Yes, Barney," said Ford, "they were great days. I helped to make you and you helped to make me."

"Yes, Henry," Oldfield answered, with a smile. "But I did much the best job of it."

One of the most decisive events was the sudden and unexpected deaths of John and Horace Dodge. The brothers had attended the 1920 New York Automobile Show. Ten days later, John was dead and Horace was incapacitated. Both had been removed at a very critical period in the postwar adjustment.

Two women who had taken no direct part in the business suddenly had the responsibility of running the vast Dodge enterprise. Despite the trouble that had developed between the Dodge brothers and Ford, the Dodge widows went to see Henry Ford. Although there is no record of the conversation that took place, the ladies, soon after, placed their confidence in Frederick J. Haynes. Haynes was superintendent of the great Hamtramck factory. He had, years earlier, been chosen for the job by John Dodge. Haynes had become president of Dodge. At a time when many feared the Dodge business would distintegrate, and during a period when hundreds of car firms did go out of business, Haynes greatly increased Dodge production and sales.

One of Haynes's first moves was to reach a contractual agreement with the Graham Brothers Truck Company of Evansville. The Graham brothers, Joseph, Robert and Ray, had developed a small, pickup farm truck. At first they built it for their own use on the Graham farms in southern Indiana. In the beginning, the Grahams used a "Model-T" Ford running gear and motor. When the more powerful Dodge engine became available, they contracted for Dodge components. The Grahams made the truck bodies in their plant and mounted them on a modified Dodge chassis and motor. By 1921, the Graham Truck Company had become a good customer of Dodge. Haynes proposed that the nationwide Dodge dealer organization take over the marketing of Graham Brothers trucks. The trucks quickly became leaders, nationally, preferred for vehicles of their weight and for their price. Graham Brothers established a plant to make bodies in Detroit in addition to those produced in Evansville. In 1925, Dodge bought the Graham Brothers Truck Company and the three Grahams became executives of Dodge. Joseph became a Dodge vice-president. Robert became sales manager. Ray was placed in charge of manufacturing for Dodge. Later, the Graham brothers left Dodge to produce the Graham-Paige motorcar, one of the impressive cars in the upper-medium price range during the late 1920s.

In 1925, the widows of John and Horace Dodge sold the Dodge Brothers Motor Car Company to the New York banking syndicate of Dillon, Read and Company for $146,000,000. It was the largest cash deal made to that time in the motorcar business. Haynes continued as president.

The postwar depression, which suddenly developed late in the summer of 1920, was accompanied by a sharp drop in the raw materials needed to build cars. The carmakers who had been struggling to maintain inventories of components during the war years were expecting a record sale of cars in 1921. They were acquiring large inventories. Suddenly, car sales declined sharply, causing high losses

374

in inventories on hand due to the sharp drop in the general price level.

Scores of the assembled-type of cars were forced out of business. Others, such as Willys-Overland, Chalmers and Maxwell, managed to survive but lacked the vitality to regain their former positions of leadership. The misfortune of Hugh Chalmers was repeated, over and over again. Chalmers closed out his business after his firm lost a million dollars in the 1921 slump, ending his illustrious motorcar career. He had helped establish the Hudson, produced the Chalmers-Detroit (later, the Chalmers), backed his friend, Harry Ford, in the Saxon, served on the War Industries Board, headed a special firm that made anti-aircraft guns and had engineered the forming of Chalmers-Maxwell to bring together his high-priced car with the inexpensive Maxwell.

The financial storm also swept away an important number of promising new cars developed during the war years in anticipation of greater car use in the 1920s. C. Harold Wills's beautiful motorcar, the Wills St. Clair, had reached production in 1921 but was swept away by the economic adversity. Another member of the former Ford team, Norval Hawkins, backed an engineer at Cadillac in the development of a small car to compete with the "Model-T" Ford. Hawkins planned to call his creation the "Americar." He was ready to introduce it when the depression came. By the time the financial storm had passed, Hawkins had given up the idea.

Herbert R. Lewis tells of going into the lobby of the Ben Franklin Hotel, in Philadelphia, one evening in the spring of 1920. He had hardly put down his suitcase when an old friend rushed up to shake his hand. It was Dave Buick, who asked Lewis to follow him to one of the large conference rooms off the hotel lobby. Buick unlocked the room, switched on the lights and there stood one of the most beautiful cars Lewis had ever seen. Buick hastened to explain that he had designed the new car and that he was to exhibit the car the next day to a group of prospective financial backers. Lewis asked him what he had named the new car. Buick said, "Just call it Dave Buick's best."

Among those who developed a new postwar car was Henry M. Leland, with his son, Wilfred. Leland had available the factory in which he had produced the Liberty airplane motor. Although he was now seventy-five years old, he and others had devised new ideas and techniques during the war. The Armistice had hardly been signed when the man who had developed the Cadillac had decided

375

to create one final motorcar that would embody the best that he had evolved in his long career. His friends pleaded with him to name the new car the "Leland." When completed, it was the finest motorcar ever built, he said, and it should be named for the man he regarded as the greatest of all Americans—Abraham Lincoln. There was one concession to his associates, the motors of all first-year Lincolns were stamped "Leland-made Motor."

The Lelands had planned on the Lincoln being available for the big spring sales period in 1920, but suppliers were unable to deliver the components until late summer. The new car was announced just as the economic depression began and within a year the resources of the Leland company were exhausted. Although the arrangements were so unsatisfactory to the Lelands that they resigned, the Ford Motor Company, in an unprecedented move, acquired the new car and, in so doing, entered the luxury-car market. The Lincoln Division soon became one of the important operations of the Ford company. In 1939, Ford expanded into the medium-price-range by adding the Mercury to the Lincoln Division.

A few of the men who had been important in the horseless carriage era continued through the World War I upheaval and added to their careers through the 1920s and after. As a result of their work, several outstanding motorcars were developed during that period, with Ford dominating the low priced field, and others making contributions in the medium and upper range of the price scale.

Ransom E. Olds, whose 1901 horseless carriage Oldsmobile became the foundation stone of the industry, continued to be the driving force after the war, as his Lansing company marketed a series of fine REO motorcars. Charles D. Hastings brought the Hupp Motor Corporation through the war years and produced a highly successful car in the upper-medium price class. The Hupmobile remained on the market until motorcar production was stopped at the beginning of World War II.

Three independent firms made especially important conrtibutions after World War I, and each was directed by a man who had begun working with horseless carriages. The cars of these companies were the Hudson, the Nash and the Studebaker. Roy D. Chapin, who had begun working with Olds in 1901, was behind the Hudson. Charles W. Nash, who saw the birth of the Buick in Flint, provided, perhaps, the most dramatic example of one man's leadership in the business of making motorcars.

In the period between the two world wars, his Nash Motor Company in Racine, Wisconsin, became the outstanding carmaker outside of Detroit. After World War II, Hudson and Nash were combined into American Motors Corporation. Under the leadership of Albert R. Erskine, Studebaker became one of America's great cars and the South Bend carmaker became the second largest outside of Detroit. Studebaker's headquarters were located only blocks from Notre Dame University. The national gridiron fame of Notre Dame's Knute Rockne led to the introduction of the Rockne motorcar whose existence was cut short largely because the football hero lost his life in an airplane crash, just as the new car was being introduced.

Of all the remarkable motorcars that flourished in the United States between the world wars, none can entirely match the position attained by the Packard. Led by two outstanding leaders trained by the founder, Henry B. Joy, Packard quickly emerged as the foremost luxury car on the American market. Alvan Macaulay, chief executive, and Colonel J. G. Vincent, in charge of engineering, became one of the most successful leadership teams in the industry.

The foremost carmaker outside of Michigan in the early days, Willys-Overland of Toledo, continued to make cars in large numbers during the 1920s. From 1916, when Willys produced 141,000 cars, until 1921, the firm produced more motorcars than any other manufacturer, with the exception of Ford. Although Willys-Overland dropped back during the 1920s, this firm became important to the final development of today's motorcar industry. It provided a chapter in the career of Walter P. Chrysler. Chrysler left Buick and General Motors in 1920, just as the economic clouds were gathering, and went into a retirement that proved to be of short duration. In 1921, he took over the direction of Willys-Overland.

By the time the Dodge court case against the Ford Motor Company had ended, Henry Ford had decided that he would take no more chances with disappointed stockholders. He announced that he wished to buy all of the company's stock held by anyone outside the Ford family. The idea was not new, for the Dodge brothers had suggested that Ford buy them out before the court fight began. The Dodges, at first, offered to sell their 10 percent ownership of the Ford Motor Company for $15,000,000. Ford turned them down. The Dodges renewed the offer to sell at a later date, but this time they asked $25,000,000.

There were seven shareholders in addition to the Ford family, six of them from the original group of twelve. Of the six who had been present that hot June evening in 1903 when the Ford Motor Company had been organized, five were still living. Banker John S. Gray, was dead, but his estate still held his 105 Ford shares. The other five were John and Horace Dodge, the two Detroit lawyers, Horace H. Rackham and John W. Anderson, who had drafted the incorporating papers and James Couzens, the former general manager.

The seventh was Rosetta Couzens, the school teacher sister of James who had invested half her savings, $100. Her money had been added to the amount James Couzens invested, hence her name was not listed with the original stockholders.

After an investigation in which Daniel C. Roper, the U. S. Commissioner of the Internal Revenue Service, took part, it was decided that, for purposes of settlement, the Ford Motor Company, in 1919, was worth something over a quarter of a billion dollars. Therefore, for her one-thousandth part that had originally cost her $100, Mrs. Rosetta Couzens Hauss was entitled to $262,036.67. With the dividends she had received over the sixteen years her total income from her $100 investment was brought up to $355,000.

Mrs. Hauss, Rackham and Anderson were the only stockholders remaining who had strictly an investor's interest. To Ford, the Dodges and Couzens, motorcars had been their business, but Hauss and the two lawyers had, at personal risk and sacrifice, invested what they could. Anderson had borrowed the entire amount of his $5,000 purchase from his father. Rackham had had to mortagage the only property he and his wife owned so that he could buy $5,000 worth of Ford stock. None of them ever considered selling the stock until Henry Ford asked for the opportunity to buy it.

All three were profoundly aware of their good fortune. Mrs. Hauss and the Rackhams, despite their wealth, had changed their mode of living very little. The Rackhams who were worth millions within ten years after their purchase of Ford stock, took little notice of their wealth. He continued his law practice, took the street car to work and enjoyed the same friends as though the Ford Motor Company did not exist. They built a modest house—they probably would have built it under former circumstances. They left their millions in a trust to be used for the public good—projects such as the Rackham School of Graduate Studies at the University of Michigan, and the Rackham Memorial Park on Woodward Avenue in Detroit, affording welcome open space to the Detroit Public Library, Wayne State University and several hospitals in the immediate area.

The John Andersons had reacted differently. From the time their

Ford dividends became an important source of income, they became world travellers. They continued to travel extensively the rest of their lives, never entirely losing that American tourist thrill of a visit to far-off places. They collected antiques of rare value and gave many of them to the museum at the University of Michigan. In Italy, they bought a rare tablet inscribed during the reign of Trajan, the Roman emperor whose rule ended in 117 A.D. From Greece, the university received an original parchment of an oration Demosthenes had delivered in the third century B.C. From Egypt, came a rare collection of papyri, a legal document during the rule of Emperor Claudius I at the time of Christ.

An interesting result of Ford investment had occurred on June 16th, 1913, when Anderson and his wife were in Switzerland. It had been the tenth anniversary of the founding of the Ford Motor Company, but the anniversary had escaped their attention. A telegram was delivered to their hotel from Anderson's law partner, Clarence E. Wilcox. It was Wilcox's habit to send Anderson a telegram when Ford dividends were declared, merely reporting the percentage. Most dividends were 100 to 300 percent, meaning that Anderson had received $5,000 to $15,000.

Anderson had already received his 1913 dividends of 300 percent, on January 2nd and April 1st. Then he read the Swiss cable whose simple message was, "five thousand." Anderson immediately dispatched a cable to Wilcox, "Your cable probably mistake. Say it over again, Anderson." Wilcox who must have enjoyed the exchange of messages sent a second telegram, repeating, "five thousand." The Ford Motor Company had declared a tenth anniversary dividend of $10,000,000. The Andersons' share was $250,000.

The Andersons joined friends and went to Geneva's Kurtsall where they drank toasts to Mr. and Mrs. Ford. They drank to the health of Mr. and Mrs. Couzens. They toasted all Ford stockholders, including themselves.

Interestingly, Anderson never owned a Ford car.

The purchase of all stock was handled by the Ford lawyers excepting the shares owned by Couzens. Ford met with his former general manager, personally. Couzens secured a somewhat better deal than the others. Ford paid the former freight car checker $29,308,857.50. The Dodge brothers each received $12,500,000. Both Rackham and Anderson received $12,500,000. In addition, all of them had received millions in dividends.

All five of the original Ford shareholders who had previously sold their stock were still living. None of them sold because he was in dire need of money and all of them sold after the company had, in dividends, returned to them in a relatively short period of time at least three times their original investment. Alex Malcomson, who had been almost entirely responsible for the founding of the company, had been required to sell his interest to Henry Ford for $175,000. Had he been selling his shares at the agreed upon rate with the others in 1919, he would have received $64,000,000. The friends of Malcomson, C. H. Bennett, Vernon C. Fry and Albert Strelow, had let their stock go for $35,000, each. They would have been paid $12,500,000 each, if they had held out.

Malcomson was still in business and prosperous, though a man of modest means compared with the wealth that would have been his had he and Ford been able to continue working together. Bennett was still in the air rifle business in neighboring Plymouth just as on the spring day in 1903 when he had gone to Detroit intending to buy a Curved Dash Oldsmobile. Except for Strelow, the others were in comfortable cirmustances. Strelow had been poverty-ridden ever since he took his $35,000 from Ford stock and lost it in a Canadian gold mine venture.

The estate of John S. Gray was paid $26,250,000. Gray had made an investment of $10,000 which would have entitled his estate to $25,000,000. But, the Gray estate received the $1,250,000 that would have gone to Gray's friend, Doctor Zumstein, if Ford had not refused to accept Zumstein's check; because it might be "bad luck" to have thirteen stockholders, Gray had agreed to put in the extra $500 himself.

When the last share of stock had been purchased, a grand total of $105,000,000 had been paid to shareholders who had originally invested $33,100 in Ford stock. It meant the end of holding formal board meetings or issuing stockholder reports. Henry, Clara and Edsel Ford owned the Ford Motor Company, and would be the owners for the rest of their lives.

24

Sloan's Finest Hour

The General Motors career of William C. Durant came to an end on November 30th, 1920, with his resignation as president of the corporation. He had created and had been the central figure in the early development of General Motors. The former carriage and wagon maker had acquired a network of factories making components and assembling cars that extended from California to New England with production concentrated in the Flint-Detroit-Lansing area of southeastern Michigan.

Although General Motors had two other cars, the Scripps-Booth and the Sheridan at the time, and would introduce the La Salle later, Billy Durant had already brought together all of the cars that remain "General Motors" today. Buick and Chevrolet were created by the sheer power of his own personality. Oldsmobile and Oakland (later to become Pontiac) were rescued by Durant as they teetered on the edge of oblivion. At a time when General Motors cash resources were almost nonexistent, Durant produced the money to complete a cash-on-the-barrel purchase of Henry Leland's Cadillac, which, along with Ford in 1910, was the most successful motorcar in Detroit.

Durant was the first to bring about a merger—the blending of the manufacturing power of several companies into a single producing organization capable of catering to the full range of buyers. Of the scores of other such mergers attempted before and after 1920, Durant's was the only one with the potential to succeed.

Nowhere in the motorcar business did the postwar depression of 1920-21 strike more swiftly and work such profound changes as it did at General Motors. The effect was to expose weaknesses, force immediate solutions and, in the end, bring into being the powerful organization as it exists today.

Economic collapse did not cause Durant's downfall at General Motors. It only forced an immediate solution of a crisis which had been building up almost from the time Durant resumed control in 1916. The first evidence that Durant management was inadequate came when he failed to appreciate the importance of joining the war effort, and the resulting loss of the irreplaceable talents of the Lelands at Cadillac. Further confirmation came when his management was unable to retain for General Motors the services of Walter Chrysler.

Buick and Cadillac were the only dependable, profit-earning divisions of General Motors. Chrysler and the Lelands had built these divisions and were highly successful in operating them. In letting these men get away, Durant not only lost their efforts for General Motors but also soon gained direct competitors in the form of Lincoln and Chrysler cars.

Both of the automotive giants—Ford and General Motors—had grown beyond the capacity of one man to direct them. No such organizations had existed before. The limits of one man's management of, and the unique leadership required for, a vast consumer business were largely unknown. Both Durant and Ford sensed the problem and attempted to overcome it by working longer and harder, themselves. It was fortunate for the future of the motorcar in this country that the failure of the Durant management at General Motors occurred so early. The tight hold of the "Model-T" on the market and the high company earnings enabled Henry Ford to continue. With the same shortcomings, Ford's personal management by decree continued for more than two decades, while his great organization, inch-by-inch, retreated from its earlier position of leadership. With but one exception, the low-cost V-8 motor, the major new developments in motorcars between the two world wars were not introduced at Ford.

The events which led to the departure of Durant resulted from communication failure that stemmed directly from his own over-work. His break with Chrysler illustrated the growing problem. There had been increasing tension between the two men, but the incident that caused Chrysler to resign dramatized the nature of the growing crisis.

Chrysler had worked hard and long to complete an agreement with the A. O. Smith Company of Milwaukee to produce the frames for the 1921 Buicks. Smith was then (and still is) one of the country's foremost producers of motorcar frames. Not only was Chrysler glad to get the frames which he considered superior in quality, but also the proposed contract would save Buick a minimum of $1,500,000. Chrysler had talked to Durant about the new Buick arrangement with A. O. Smith and understood that he had the General Motors president's approval. Chrysler had been the "No. 1" man at Buick for eight years of unbroken profits and was being paid $600,000 a year to do the job.

Then, at the time the Smith agreement was ready to be signed, Durant announced at a civic meeting in Flint that General Motors would build a multimillion dollar factory there to make frames for next year's Buicks. Chrysler confronted Durant at New York head-quarters, resigned and walked out so angry that he slammed the door hard enough for Sloan to hear the noise in his office some distance away. Sloan said of the incident later, "I remember the day. He banged the door on the way out, and out of that bang came, eventually, the Chrysler Corporation."

Sloan very nearly banged the door, himself, shortly after. He was president of the United Motors Corporation, a General Motors-type of organization established by Durant, in 1916, and made up from vital component producing firms, such as Harrison Radiator, Hyatt Roller Bearing, Dayton Electrical Laboratory Company, Remy Electric, Klaxon Horn, and others. In 1918, Durant brought United Motor into General Motors. Sloan did not even change offices and continued to manage the component operation as a division. It was at this time that Herbert R. Lewis came into General Motors. Lewis had worked with Sloan as chief sales officer at Harrison Radiator.

Early in 1919, Sloan walked into Durant's office and found himself a part of a conference between Durant and J. Amory Haskell, a du Pont executive who was assisting General Motors in financial matters. The transfer of the General Motors headquarters from New York to Detroit and the location of the new building that would be erected was under discussion. Durant and Haskell had already

383

agreed that the building would be in the central business district in the vicinity of the Grand Circus Park.

Sloan, who knew the city well, broke into the conversation: "Mr. Durant, I don't feel that General Motors needs to have its offices downtown in Detroit. We're not brokers. We're not bankers. Primarily, our purpose is to keep in touch with the various plants."

"Where would you put it?" questioned Durant.

"Out on the Boulevard. We can shorten the journeys of all who have to run back and forth to Flint and Pontiac. Cadillac would be close by. Much of our office personnel will be saved an hour or more a day. Why pay downtown prices for land or downtown taxes?"

Durant liked Sloan's idea of locating on Grand Boulevard in what was then the western part of Detroit. He proposed that they go to the site which they did, shortly after. On that winter day, the two men walked along West Grand Boulevard between Cass Avenue and Second Boulevard. Exactly what was going through Durant's mind was never known but, at a given point, he stopped and said to Sloan: "Buy up to here." Later, he asked Sloan to buy the entire block, which Sloan did. That walk along Grand Boulevard eventually resulted in the transformation of a residential area into a commercial center, second only to Detroit's main riverfront business district.

Sloan knew that block well because the Detroit headquarters of his old Hyatt Roller Bearing Company was located there in a brick building. The Hyatt building was moved a block south so quickly that there was no interruption in its use. In all, forty-eight buildings were wrecked or moved while Detroit's architect, Albert Kahn, drew the plans. Ground was broken on June 2nd, 1919, and on November 18th, 1920, exactly ten days before Durant left General Motors, Herbert R. Lewis and his Harrison Radiator staff became the first to conduct business in the new structure. (Still the headquarters, it is known as "the General Motors Building.") The intention was to call it the "Durant Building." Four large "Ds" (still there), were cut into the granite at each corner immediately below the roof as a tribute to Billy Durant, in whose mind the building first took shape.

The building, for all its magnificence, disturbed Sloan from the first. So few people took part in its planning, and Durant had so little time to devote to it. Reeling under an overwhelming work load, Durant did not have enough time to give adequate direction to even the largest General Motors programs. There are numerous instances in which he would call important executives, including Sloan, to his office in New York, Flint or Detroit and then would not be able to see the individual for a day or two. At times, the visitor went home, in disgust, without seeing Durant at all.

After Chrysler had left, and just before the depression in the fall of 1920, Sloan took a month's vacation to consider what he would do. He had attractive offers for employment outside the motorcar industry. He and his wife went to England and ordered a Rolls Royce car preparatory to making an extended tour of European countries. While in London, Sloan decided to leave General Motors. He returned at once to New York intending to submit his resignation to Durant. When he arrived at New York headquarters, he learned that Durant had left for an extended vacation. Sloan sensed a crisis and decided to wait and see what would happen.

Matters worsened quickly. By October, General Motors production was all but halted. The inventory of cars and materials had risen from $137,000,000 to $209,000,000. This was $59,000,000 above the safe limit established earlier in the year. Car sales had been declining since summer and would fall even more, but the General Motors inventory reports failed to provide current information.

At Ford, where the reporting procedures were better and the problem much less complex (since the company made but one car), action had been taken in September on two vital fronts. Production of new cars had been more nearly adjusted to the downward swing of sales so that the inventory was less of a burden. Even in the face of losses, the Ford Motor Company had, on September 21st reduced "Model-T" prices by $135 on the touring car, and $180 on the sedan. Ford explained its action in this way: "We must, of course, take a temporary loss because of the stock of materials on hand, bought at inflated prices . . . we take it willingly in order to bring about a going state of business throughout the country."

Bad as was the situation at General Motors, until noon on the 11th of November, the life of the corporation was not threatened. On that day, Durant invited General Motors Board Chairman Pierre du Pont and John Raskob, Chairman of Finance, to lunch. Over the luncheon table Durant revealed that he had, since the break in stock prices in the summer, been personally buying General Motors stock on a grand scale with borrowed money in an effort to sustain its value on the open market. Durant had gambled that General Motors stock would not drop drastically.

To his chagrin, the value of General Motors stock had dropped from a high of nearly $50.00 a share, early in the summer down to

385

about $15.00 in November. Durant disclosed that he did not know how much he owed, but that matters were approaching the point where he could not meet his personal obligations. The banks deeply involved in the corporation's financing, Durant disclosed, were demanding that he resign as president of General Motors. Bankers feared, that should the public learn of Durant's bankruptcy, the news might bring about the collapse of the corporation.

Chairman du Pont and Raskob were astounded and shocked. They returned to Wilmington where they could talk with other du Pont executives and decide upon a course of action. Their discussions touched on the tremendous rise in importance of the motorcar and its industry in the United States economy in the decade between 1910 and 1920.

It had been just ten years before that Boston and New York bankers had made the first important financial deal in the motorcar industry when they had agreed to loan General Motors $15,000,000. General Motors stock had been first offered for public sale only nine years before. Now it was agreed that failure, which could be triggered by the bankruptcy of General Motors' president, might break several banks and big brokerage houses and, perhaps, push the entire nation's economy deeper in depression. The entire country was dotted with cities where real panic could develop were General Motors to collapse.

The du Pont executives came to two important decisions before Pierre du Pont and Raskob returned to New York late Monday. Durant insolvency must be corrected before it became a matter of public knowledge; to prevent a Durant bankruptcy, du Pont would invest up to $10,000,000 in cash and extend trade credit for millions more, if that should be necessary.

Raskob and du Pont attempted to meet with Durant early Tuesday, the 16th, but Durant was so busy with business callers and long distance phone conferences that it was 4 p.m. before they met. The du Pont men asked for a listing of Durant's obligations. Durant had some longhand notes on amounts he had borrowed from banks but he had no report on how much he might owe the several stock brokerage houses involved. While the conference was going on, the brokers (Jones & Reed) reported to Durant that $150,000 was needed to support his account with that firm.

Wednesday was given over to securing from the numerous stock brokers involved a completely current report on Durant's liabilities. Raskob and du Pont began working out a plan under which a special company would be organized to take over Durant's stock holdings with a view to settling all his obligations, in cash. The du Pont Company would provide the new company with $7- to $10,000,000.

On Thursday morning, conferences began on the Durant crisis that lasted almost continuously for two days. Thursday afternoon, Durant reported that representatives of Morgan and Company had requested a conference with him which he would hold late in the day. The House of Morgan had earlier made a substantial purchase of General Motors stock, but only as an investment. Before the November 11th luncheon conference, Dwight Morrow of Morgan & Company had come to du Pont to inquire about Durant's personal finances. Du Pont had told Morrow that he knew nothing of the General Motors president's personal finances and advised Morrow to go directly to Durant and ask him. The Morgan conference, late on the 18th, was the result of this du Pont suggestion.

After the Durant-Morgan conference, Morrow contacted du Pont at his hotel reporting that, in the Morgan view, Durant's finances were in a most critical condition. An all-night conference ensued in which Durant, Morrow, du Pont and Raskob took part. By 5:30 a.m., a plan had been agreed upon by which Durant's stock holdings would be taken over, his obligations paid, and under which he would still have stocks worth nearly $3,000,000 figured at the low current prices. In addition to the du Pont money going into the new company, it was the judgment of both the Morgan and du Pont executives that there would have to be an immediate loan of $20,000,000 which could only come from banks on such short notice.

The conference adjourned at 5:30 a.m. and was resumed three hours later. By 5:00 that afternoon, November 19th, 1920, Morgan & Company had secured the $20,000,000 loan from New York banks and had volunteered to keep its staff at work through the weekend in order to check out every item of Durant indebtedness and bring together every share of General Motors stock involved. The job was completed by Tuesday morning. In shares of General Motors stock Durant had more than a $60,000,000 interest.

Under the final terms of the arrangement, the du Pont Company received 60 percent of the General Motors stock held by Durant and he retained 40 percent. Morgan & Company received nothing. From the time they had entered the conferences, Morgan partners had made it plain they would accept no remuneration for their services. The Durant resignation as president of General Motors followed eight days later, allowing enough time for the transfer of the office to other hands.

The curious crisis in which General Motors was not directly involved at all was over. It was never entirely clear why Durant permitted himself to get so deeply involved in a one-man effort to support the price of General Motors stock. Sloan, who witnessed the entire episode as a minor participant, always thought that it was Durant's great pride in General Motors and his great confidence in the future that caused him to act as he did. No one was benefited. The du Pont Company ended up investing more heavily and owning more General Motors stock than its directors wished to own. The New York bankers showed no interest in taking over General Motors. Although Durant was accorded generous treatment under the circumstances, he came out with but a small part of the wealth he had enjoyed, debt-free, a few months earlier.

The directors of General Motors elected Pierre du Pont president, a responsibility he reluctantly agreed to take on an interim basis until the corporation's affairs could be put in order and a successor trained. At the age of fifty, and in good health, he had retired as president of the du Pont Company only the year before, insisting on turning du Pont management over to men ten to fifteen years younger than himself. In du Pont, General Motors had a chief executive in the prime of his life and experienced in every phase of management of a large business. Even in his short term of two and one-half years, General Motors took great strides. From the first, du Pont made Alfred Sloan his chief aide, and it quickly became apparent that he was grooming the former roller bearing manufacturer to become head of General Motors. Sloan had been a director of the corporation since 1918.

In the thirty months of du Pont's presidency, many notable things were accomplished. Fortunately, the depression was not of long duration; the worst was over in less than a year. The first step was to bring the inventory problem under control. Chevrolet, alone, had 150,000 cars unsold. The expensive venture into the farm machinery field was promptly closed out. The Samson Tractor plant at Janesville, Wisconsin, was closed and the facility turned over to Chevrolet as an assembly plant, which is still used today. The Heany Lamp Company matter was finally and completely closed out.

There were special problems. With du Pont officials taking over many of the highest jobs in General Motors and the du Pont Company holding the largest block of stock, rumors spread that General

Motors factories in Michigan and the midwest would be closed and relocated near du Pont locations in the east. To put these reports to rest, Pierre du Pont spent much of his time visiting General Motors plants around the country and talking with city officials to convince them that there would be no relocation. As evidence of the corporation's continued interest in Flint, General Motors financed the building of a new hotel which was given the name "Durant" in honor of the town's "Little Billy."

Some far-reaching procedures were introduced. A much more closely-knit system of communications was instituted. Each week, the number of cars in dealers' hands, cars completed at the factory but not delivered, the schedule of production in each plant and the number of cars on order by areas were reported.

Under du Pont leadership, General Motors became the first firm to use the machinery of the Federal Reserve system for a quick transfer of money from one part of the country to another. In October of 1920, the corporation had found it necessary to borrow $80,000,000 to meet payrolls and supplier bills. Later, it was discovered that a number of the divisions actually had more funds on hand than they needed for operation. Under the new system of fund transfer, each General Motors bank account throughout the United States was assigned a maximum balance. When that balance was exceeded, the Federal Reserve System was used to transfer the surplus to a central General Motors account. The Federal Reserve transfers were made by telegram and accomplished in a matter of minutes. Mailing of checks was ended. Later, other firms with many facilities across the country adopted the same procedure.

The same dictatorial type of management as practiced by Durant was being exercised even in a more rigid form at the Ford Motor Company. The great men developed at Ford during its early years were being driven away, and this proved to be a stroke of good fortune for General Motors. Norval Hawkins, who had built the first motorcar sales organization capable of distributing three-quarters of a million cars a year, came to General Motors.

In an even more disgraceful display of management brutality, the Ford Motor Company fired William S. Knudsen, who had built most of the Ford assembly plants in the United States and Europe. He also had managed the daring Eagle boat building program at Ford during the war. Henry Ford disliked Knudsen's personal habits and the Dane's independent thinking. He was determined to rid himself of Knudsen but, characteristically, lacked the courage to tell

Knudsen himself. He directed Ernest Kanzler to do the job. When Kanzler protested, saying that Knudsen was capable, Ford said, "I see that you don't want this job. I'll give it to Sorensen. He'd love to fire Knudsen."

Knudsen became general manager of a factory in Detroit making parts for cars and stoves. Sloan met him there and was immediately impressed with the man. Although he did not, yet, have a specific job in mind, Sloan offered the Dane a position on the executive staff. Knudsen accepted before the matter of salary even had been mentioned.

"How much shall we pay you, Mr. Knudsen?" asked Sloan.

In his last year at Ford, Knudsen had been paid $50,000, but to Sloan he replied, "Anything you like. I am not here to set a figure. I seek an opportunity."

Sloan welcomed executives from Ford who were familiar with the "Model-T," its production and its marketing. He had recently made a decision that General Motors would enter the low-priced field and challenge the "Model-T." Few cars had suffered more in the 1920-21 depression than Chevrolet and few cars had suffered less than the "Model-T." In 1921, Chevrolet production dropped to 64,375 cars from 125,767 the year before. The Chevrolet Division lost nearly $9,000,000. But Ford production actually advanced in 1921, outselling Chevrolet about thirteen to one. President du Pont hired a firm of engineering consultants to conduct an analysis of the low-priced field and make recommendations. The consultants concluded that, with the Ford Company selling half the cars in the low-priced field, the cost of capturing an important part of that market would be too high. General Motors resources could be better used, they said, in the middle- and upper-price ranges. They recommended that Chevrolet be dropped from the General Motors line.

When the report came to Sloan's attention, he denounced it in the strongest terms. With better engineering and better service, Sloan contended, Chevrolet could effectively compete with Ford. Du Pont was at first difficult to persuade, but Sloan pressed his views so strongly that du Pont finally said, "Forget the report. We will go ahead and see what we can do."

Pierre du Pont was a business executive of remarkable ability. He had already become the builder of the modern du Pont organization. Even during his short tenure as chief executive of General Motors, he provided Sloan, Haskell, Kettering, Raskob, Hawkins, Knudsen and other younger executives the opportunity to develop an entirely new kind of thinking about the technique of General Motors business. With Sloan as the ramrod, new concepts or objectives were developed, most of them surfacing in 1922-23. Much of this new thinking eventually was adopted by the entire motorcar industry in the United States. These were the new objectives:

> Research and marketing would become the critical areas. General Motors cars must be improved. Buick and Cadillac were already advanced cars, but major improvements would be made in Oldsmobile, Oakland-Pontiac and Chevrolet. Kettering and his new engineering department would work on the tough problems, such as new kinds of fuel, new kinds of paint, new comfort devices and basic improvements in motors, power linkage and bodies. The work of Kettering's department would be available to all General Motors Divisions.
>
> With research providing a constant flow of improvements, General Motors would initiate the practice each year of presenting new models of all cars. (The annual model concept was aimed squarely at the "Model-T" Ford which had been on the market since 1908 without a basic change.)
>
> General Motors must develop a strong car in the low-priced field. (Durant had this as one of his major objectives from the time he founded the firm, but Ford had made the low-priced car so important that no longer was it possible to be an industry leader without a low-cost car capable of selling at high volume. During the war, Durant had bought two small car firms, the Sheridan at Muncie, Indiana, and the Scripps-Booth in Detroit. They would be discontinued and efforts in the low-priced field would be concentrated on Chevrolet.)
>
> In the future, General Motors cars would not compete directly with one another. Cadillac would be the luxury car. Buick would sell in the upper price range, Oldsmobile would be priced just below Buick and Oakland-Pontiac below Oldsmobile. Chevrolet would be the only car in the low-price range.
>
> A new system of management, that made each division largely a self-contained unit, headed by a general manager with complete responsibility for production, marketing, purchasing, engineering and finances, would be created. The corporation's function would be one of service to the division through departments of engineering, general purchasing, sales assistance and institutional advertising.

The new system of management, simple enough to explain, was difficult to put into practice. Hardships developed and the new plan did not work well until men had been especially trained in its use. The corporation's experience with the "copper-cooled" motor provided an example of the early difficulties.

When Kettering became director of research for General Motors in 1919, he had already done a considerable amount of work on the development of an air-cooled motor. Several cars had already used an air-cooled engine, including the Franklin made in Syracuse, one of the better-known, higher-priced cars. Elimination of the car's water system could solve many problems for the owner and might even offer the possibility of reducing the cost.

On December 7th, 1920, one week after du Pont became president of General Motors, he made a trip to Dayton to meet with Kettering. He was accompanied by Sloan, Raskob, Haskell, K. W. Zimmerschied, and C. D. Hartman, Jr. Zimmerschied was head of Chevrolet, having taken over directly from Durant. Hartman was secretary of Raskob's finance committee. The most important thing the General Motors executives had to discuss with Kettering that day was the work on the new, air-cooled motor. The officials were impressed. It was decided that, as soon as the engine had been tested to the satisfaction of Kettering and his research engineers, a four-cylinder motor would be developed for Chevrolet. Everyone agreed that the new, air-cooled motor could become the decisive element in the forthcoming challenge to the "Model-T."

In 1921, the Executive Committee continued to be impressed with the air-cooled motor and decided that the General Motors new engine would henceforth be called the "copper-cooled" motor to distinguish it from this type of motor in other cars. The committee also decided there should be a six-cylinder "copper-cooled" motor for Oakland-Pontiac and Oldsmobile.

There were dates set for placing the "copper-cooled" car in production early in 1922, but Zimmerschied wanted to wait for a year. Du Pont was so convinced that this new motor would be useful he moved Zimmerschied out of the division and made him an assistant to the president in order to place Knudsen, in charge of Chevrolet. Knudsen had studied the "copper-cooled" motor and thought it had production possibilities.

Under Knudsen's direction a few "copper-cooled" Chevrolets were produced in time for the 1923 New York Automobile Show. The car proved to be the sensation of the show. There were plans for making 50,000 of these Chevrolets a month by the fall of 1923. As things developed, not one was sold. Only 759 "copper-cooled" Chevrolets were produced. Production men refused to let 239 of them leave the plant. Of the remaining 520, only 100 ever went to customers. There was so much operational trouble with the new cars that in June they

The General Motors Building, built by Durant, as it
appears in Detroit today. It was the largest office building
in the world when it was opened in 1920. This, along
with Ford's River Rouge production complex,
ushered in the modern era of the motorcar.

were all recalled, and the "copper-cooled" program was cancelled.

Kettering was convinced that the division engineers ruined the air-cooled motor when they adapted it for assembly-line production. He called it the bitterest experience of his entire career in research and wrote a letter of resignation, asking to be relieved as soon as his successor could be found. Sloan convinced him that he should reconsider, and in a few weeks Kettering and his men were busy with new research projects.

Kettering probably was right in his contention that the idea was sound and that if everyone had been willing to work with it a little longer a major development in the motorcar would have resulted. This was strongly indicated when years later Chevrolet introduced its "Corvair" with an air-cooled motor.

The motorcar year of 1923 was notable in several respects. With both the Highland Park and new River Rouge Ford plants working at capacity, and the "Model-T" touring car selling for $295, Henry Ford reached the zenith of his motorcar career. Ford passenger car and truck production reached 2,019,000. It was the first time that any firm had produced 2,000,000 self-propelled vehicles. The Ford increase over its previous year production (also a new record) was the largest ever recorded by the Ford Motor Company. The Ford production increase in 1923 was 712,421 over its 1922 output. Chevrolet's production for the year was 454,968, second-best in the industry. When the big year was over, almost half of all the motorcars bought in the United States were "Model-T's." The American public, before or since, never paid such a tribute to a motorcar.

Chevrolet's 1923 production of nearly half a million cars and trucks was double the production ever attained by any General Motors car before. The previous record for production in a single year was Chevrolet's output of 223,840 cars in 1922. The highest production ever achieved to that time by any other General Motors car was recorded by Buick in 1923, a total of 200,759. Harry H. Bassett was then president of Buick, having taken over from Chrysler.

The spectacular showing of Chevrolet in 1923 established Knudsen as one of the leaders in the industry. The Dane wasn't impressed. Soon after the end of the big year, he was asked to address a large gathering of very happy Chevrolet dealers. Knudsen's English always came in such a heavy Danish accent that it was often difficult to understand him. He was reluctant to speak before large gatherings. On this occasion, his address consisted of but five words, but it brought the dealers to their feet clapping and shouting. Holding up

Pierre S. du Pont, former president of the Du Pont Company, came out of retirement when the 1920-21 depression threatened the life of General Motors. Although he remained in that office for only thirty months, turning the presidency over to his choice, Alfred P. Sloan, Jr., he served as chairman of the Board of Directors from 1916 until 1929. He guided General Motors through years of struggle to the position of the largest private enterprise in the world.

two fingers, Knudsen said, "I vant von for von," driving home the point that he would not be happy until Chevrolet had, at least, caught up with Ford. Ford's treatment of the Danish immigrant was providing additional thrust for General Motors.

Close examination of the 1923 sales reports for all carmakers revealed an entirely new trend. An industry increase of 1,400,000 cars over the year before had been recorded. Nearly 900,000 of that gain was accounted for by two firms, Ford and Chevrolet; most of it by Ford. The remainder of the industry showed a gain of only 500,000, which meant that many firms registered losses in production. Producers of the assembled car and the producers of cars in the higher-price brackets were losing ground in the greatest car-buying boom the country had ever experienced. The American public was showing an increasing interest in the lighter, inexpensive cars which could be driven for shorter periods of time and traded in on a new model. The annual model policy introduced by General Motors was catching on. Those who could not afford a new car could now buy a second-hand car at half or less the cost of a new one. It resulted in a greatly expanded use of the motorcar.

On June 4th, 1924, the Highland Park plant produced the 10,000,000th Ford car. No other carmaker in the world had yet produced 2,000,000 cars. Yet, in the same year, came first indications that the era of the "Model-T" was coming to a close. In 1924, for the first time since the "Model-T" had been announced a decade and a half earlier, the Ford Motor Company was able to produce more cars than could be sold. Sales of the "Model-T" dropped about 70,000 cars below the high water mark set in 1923. For the first time, Henry Ford was powerless to apply the magic that enabled the "Model-T" to continue setting new sales records long after its prime. With the Ford touring car selling for only $295 it was no longer possible to announce a new sweeping price reduction.

In 1925, Ford dealers were forced to sell the same "Model-T" in competition with a new model of the Chevrolet which introduced an imposing list of new features, such as a one-piece windshield equipped with automatic wipers (they had been operated by hand before), an improved clutch system, an entirely new rear axle and new, larger brakes. The maker of the "Model-T" offered one small concession. For the first time, since 1912, the car was available in some color other than black. "Model-T" sales dropped 100,000 in 1925.

Under the Sloan-Kettering-Knudsen plan of a new model every

Charles F. Kettering
became director of
research for General
Motors in 1920. He stood
as symbol of the rapid
advancement of the
motorcar industry from
1912, when he built the
vital non-motor parts
for the first electric
self-starter, until World
War II, when the concept
of the modern internal
combustion motorcar
was complete.

397

year, Chevrolet presented a new car again in 1926. There was a heavier body from the Fisher plant that added greatly to the appeal of the closed cars. Easy-to-clean, disc wheels replaced the wooden spoke wheels. Unchanged, the "Model-T" sales in 1926 dropped a quarter of a million cars below the previous year's output. Still, the Ford production of cars for the year stood at 1,368,383. Chevrolet set a new record and moved its production above the half million mark for the first time, but the "Model-T" still sold two and a half times as many cars.

The end came for the "Model-T" in 1927. It was a pitiful situation. Henry Ford blamed the decline on the Ford dealers, saying they had grown rich and lazy. He castigated General Motors for its "new model every year" policy. "It does not please us," Ford said, "to have a buyer's car wear out or become obsolete. We want the man who buys one of our products never to have to buy another. We never make an improvement that renders any previous model obsolete." He might just as well have ordered the waves of the ocean to cease their roll.

The "Model-T" had become so much a part of Henry Ford that his personal grief at its decline hindered him from taking any kind of action. Greatly complicating the situation was the fact that it all happened so quickly; the crisis had developed in about eighteen months. In April of 1925, there had been signs of decline, but nothing to indicate that the end of the car's usefulness was so near. By the fall of 1926, it was obvious to Ford's associates and to Ford dealers that the end was close at hand. The nation became involved. There were rumors that Ford would replace the "Model-T," in his own good time, with a new "super" car. "Just you wait till you see what Old Henry has up his sleeve," was a common remark from New York to California.

For the public, it was unthinkable that "Old Henry" did not have something up his sleeve. But he did not. To be sure, he thought fondly of the possibility of introducing a new car that would continue Ford supremacy. As had been done twenty years before when the "Model-T" had been developed, there was another engineering room set aside in which to develop the new "X Ford Engine." No motor was ever forthcoming.

The dictatorial management that had become more ruthless with the passing of the years had long since driven away the men who could have provided a triumphant transition from the "Model-T." Gone were James Couzens, Harold Wills, John and Horace Dodge,

Edward V. Rickenbacker, the Eddie Rickenbacker famous as a hero on America's racetracks, as well as air ace in World War I, designed the Rickenbacker car that was marketed from 1922 to 1927. He was, for years, the chief executive officer of the Indianapolis Speedway, sponsor of the annual Indy "500."

Norval Hawkins and William S. Knudsen, who had pleaded for the opportunity to improve the "Model-T." Left with Ford were only the "yes" men—like Sorensen, Galamb and Harry Bennett.

One man was left in the organization who could tell the aging Ford the truth. It was Edsel Ford's painful responsibility to carry the burden of convincing his father that the time had come to halt production of the "Model-T." The relation between the two men was never again one of complete trust, the rift widening as the years passed.

It was 1926 when Ford pushed past the point of no return. Massive opportunity still existed for the Ford Motor Company as late as the summer of that year. By this time, Ford had become something of a recluse, like a sulking child offended that his friends would not play the game his way. Without leadership, executives of the Ford Motor Company were loath to act; some of the advisors even pointing out to him that the "Model-T" should not be discontinued. There actually existed, they said, an annual need for at least half a million cars of this type—roughly double the production at the time of any car, other than Chevrolet. The closing down of the "Model-T" left a great void for farmers in the Midwest, Mountain States and the Deep South and the army of country doctors and others who provided services for farms, ranches and rural homes.

It was true that the people living in the eastern cities were through buying the "Model-T" Ford, unless it could be improved. They were no longer driving on dirt and mud roads as most of the people still were, west and south of the Great Lakes. These eastern families had higher incomes and they could afford the new Chevrolet, or a more expensive car. Yet, everywhere the "Model-T" still had its substantial number of worshipers. Upon learning that the car was to be discontinued, thousands of families who were able to afford it bought *two* "Model-T" cars for use in the future. A woman in New Jersey bought seven. One well-to-do man in Arizona bought ten, so that he "would never have to learn to drive another car." He never did.

The year passed without action to meet the problem. In the early weeks of 1927, "Model-T" production was reduced but, by May, the yards surrounding the branch assembly plants, the grounds of the Highland Park factory and at the River Rouge were filled with unsold Ford cars.

On May 26th, 1927, the announcement came that the "Model-T" would be discontinued. That morning, the 15,000,000th "Model-T" motor was produced, at the Ford factory on the River Rouge. The

Walter Chrysler became, in the eight years before he resigned in 1920 as head of Buick and vice-president of General Motors, one of the production wizards of the motorcar industry. He combined this genius with the production capacity of Maxwell, Chalmers and Dodge to forge the Chrysler Corporation into the third giant of the industry.

401

eight men who had been with Henry Ford the longest, personally stamped the historic serial number on the block. Four of them—John F. Wandersee, August Degener, Frank Kulik and Fred L. Rockelman—had been in the Mack Avenue plant that early July day in 1903, when the Dodge brothers sent over the first Ford motor and the assembly of the first Ford car was completed. The other four —P. E. Martin, C. B. Hartner, Charles E. Sorensen and Charles Meida—had joined Ford in the first three years.

That afternoon, the 15,000,000th motor was assembled into a "Model-T" touring car. Henry and Edsel Ford walked beside the car as it was made on the moving assembly line. In a very real sense, the "Model-T" had created the first, moving assembly line in this same Highland Park factory. By 1927, the moving assembly line had been adopted by high-volume carmakers everywhere. After the car had been assembled, Edsel, with his father in the front seat and Sorensen and Martin in the back seat, drove it to the Dearborn Engineering Laboratory. There, before a crowd, it was placed beside the quadricycle Ford had built in his barn at 58 Bagley Avenue, in 1896, and with the first "Model-T" that had been assembled in the Piquette Avenue plant in 1908. One after the other, Henry Ford climbed into the driver's seats of the antique Fords. The machines started promptly and he drove them around the engineering building plaza.

The announcement that the "Model-T" would be suspended brought in enough orders so that the existing high inventory was exhausted and it was necessary to produce almost another half million. The final total on the "Model-T" stands at 15,485,781. The job of replacing the family horse had been completed.

The need to make additional "Model-T" cars and a large supply of parts made it possible to keep key employees over the next nine months. Except at the plant where Lincolns were produced, no cars came from the Ford factories around the world. For six months, Ford refused to approve plans for a new car. He gave ground slowly on the issue of whether his pet features of the old "Model-T" would be carried over into the new car. Ford saw the possibility of improving the old planetary transmission and making it automatic. It would have advanced the general use of automatic transmissions by a decade, but in the end he had to concede and use a standard transmission. All this took time.

Ford dealers agonized. Hundreds of thousands of Americans delayed buying a new car in hopes the new Ford would soon be avail-

In 1925, the New York banking syndicate of Dillon, Read and Company, bought the Dodge Brothers Company. Clarence Dillon wrote the check for $146,000,000 "and no cents." Less than three years later, the bankers sold Dodge to the Chrysler Corporation for $170,000,000.

able. The question of when the new car would go on sale received front page attention across the country for months. At the peak of public concern, the Ford Motor Company posted coast-to-coast billboards whose inscription read, "It won't be long now." But it was a long while. Although Edsel Ford announced that the new "Model-A" was an accomplished fact in August of 1927 and production did begin early the following year, there were so few available in the spring of 1928 that dealers could not promise when delivery could be made. It was 1929 before "Model-A" production could begin to cope with demand.

While the news was being made at Ford, history was being made at Chevrolet and at General Motors. With the collapse of the "Model-T," Chevrolet took over the motorcar production leadership almost by default. Ford production had dropped from 1,368,383 to 356,188 in 1927, while Chevrolet, with its new 1927 model, moved up from 589,000 to 749,998. 1927 total car production in the United States declined to 2,936,533 cars compared with 3,783,987 the year before.

Chevrolet achieved a victory over Ford in 1928 and, at the same time, set the stage for an even greater triumph in the year to follow. Knudsen and Sloan were making it clear that they expected to share in industry leadership in the future. With new models in both passenger cars and trucks, Chevrolet, in 1928, together with Ford, produced more than a million motorized vehicles in a year. Chevrolet car and truck production for 1928 stood at 1,123,995 in comparison with the 750,298 cars and trucks produced by Ford in the first full year of "Model-A" production.

No new model of Chevrolet, before or since, has attracted such public attention as the introduction of the 1929 model. Months before, there were rumors that Chevrolet would change to a six-cylinder motor in 1929. The wheelbase of the 1928 Chevrolet had been lengthened by six inches. Service station mechanics across the country delighted in pointing out that there were many holes bored, for which there was no use. They were placed there, it was said, for some future use, such as mounting a new and larger motor.

In January of 1929, Chevrolet not only announced that its new model would have, as standard equipment a six-cylinder motor, but also that it would sell for approximately the same price as the four-cylinder car of 1928. The new car had one-third more power and became the first low-priced car that could operate, hour after hour, at speeds of 65-to-70 miles an hour.

Walter Chrysler with the first Chrysler car, late in 1923,
in the old Chalmers plant in Detroit where it was built.
The car was first shown to the public in January, 1924,
in the lobby of the Commodore Hotel in New York City.
Less than three years later, Chrysler car production was
exceeded only by Ford and General Motors.

Not since Ford had introduced the moving assembly line before the first world war had any mass production achievement equalled the Chevrolet model change from the four to the new six. Within four months after the 1928 model had been closed out, Chevrolet plants throughout the world were in full production on the new sixes. Knudsen build a special factory at Saginaw, Michigan, where the new motors were made, beginning November 15th, 1928. The special factory was for the sole purpose of teaching workers in regular engine plants the use of the new machines and techniques.

Chevrolet plants were in full production by early February, 1929, and deliveries of the new, spectacular, six-cylinder over-head-valve motorcars and trucks were made promptly during the spring. The feat set the standard for a new kind of service to American car buyers that endures to this day. Henceforth, model changes at Chevrolet and, ultimately, with all firms would be accomplished with little inconvenience to the public. No matter how great model changes might be, new cars would be ready for delivery in volume at the time of the announcement, or soon after.

The decision of the Sloan management at General Motors to include engineering improvements on a new model each year introduced the motorcar as it is known today. Producing annual models to maintain a high volume of sales necessary to hold down the cost of cars is a very complicated and expensive process and explains, perhaps, why there are only four firms producing motorcars in the United States.

The annual model is a massive application of engineering and research. General Motors and the other firms soon found that it was necessary to work for three years to complete each new model.

Since General Motors was the first to increase its engineering and research effort, credit must be given for an imposing list of new developments, including some of the most important: new types of more durable and rapid drying finishes; the introduction of important additives to gasoline; automatic control of water temperature in the engine; silent transmissions; many important body innovations; engine-driven fuel pumps; improvements to reduce motor noise; automatic engine choking devices; individual wheel suspension; automatic transmissions, and many others.

Alfred Sloan, more responsible for the high performance of the modern motorcar than any other one person, made his greatest contribution in organization. It was Sloan who discovered a plan for unifying the efforts of the many divisions of General Motors while preserving an effective flexibility and individual initiative within each. His methods have been adopted by the other carmakers and by large businesses in other industries throughout the world.

It was Sloan who took a production expert cast off by Ford and enabled him to become one of the all-time leaders in the production of fine cars. Henry Ford was once asked how it happened that he permitted Bill Knudsen, an important Ford production expert for so long, to get away to lead the Chevrolet victory over the "Model-T." "I consider Mr. Knudsen the best production man in the United States ... Mr. Knudsen was too strong for me to handle," was the answer. Alfred Sloan, with his new method of management, found it easy to harness the great capacities of strong men. It made the great difference.

Sloan often explained that the new management technique he developed at General Motors involved eight priceless ingredients— facts, an open mind, courage, equity, confidence, loyalty, search for progress and work. On one occasion, he discussed each in these terms:

> Management: The collective effort of intelligence, experience and imagination.
> The Facts: A constant search for the truth.
> The Open Mind: Policy based upon analysis without prejudice.
> Courage: The willingness to take a risk, recognizing that leadership exacts a price.
> Equity: Respect for the rights of others.
> Confidence: The courage of one's convictions.
> Loyalty: The willingness to make a sacrifice for the cause.
> Search for Progress: There must always be a better way.
> Work: The catalysis that energizes all these ingredients so that they may take their respective parts in promoting the common cause.

25

Walter Chrysler Makes it
"The Big Three"

The first week in January, 1924, the motorcar business in the United States had the appearance of being more stabilized than at any time since its birth twenty-five years before. There were no rumors of spectacular new cars being displayed at the 1924 New York Automobile Show, ready to open at the Grand Central Palace. As always, there was Ford, with the "Model-T" accounting for half the car sales made in the United States, just as had been the case for more than a decade. There was General Motors returning to good health and producing in ever greater quantity five of the oldest and best-known cars in the country. There were several, firmly established, independent companies, among them Packard, Hudson, Dodge, Studebaker, REO and Nash. Finally, there was Billy Durant successfully back in the motorcar business with his Durant, Flint and Star cars.

While there had been new cars introduced every year (even during World War I), none had moved into the front ranks of the business. Yet, in the second week of January, an exciting new motorcar was introduced that put the entire industry on the alert within a period of five days. To add to the fanfare (and consternation of competitors), the car was not exhibited at the big automobile show.

Walter Chrysler (left) and Fred Zeder, key figures in the welding together of Chrysler and Dodge into the third largest producer of motorcars and trucks by 1929. Chrysler briefly became president of Dodge and Zeder took charge of Dodge engineering, as well as that of Chrysler.

Instead, it was shown in the lobby of the Commodore Hotel in New York.

In terms of cars made in so short a time, the Chrysler's rise was more rapid than anything either Ford or General Motors had accomplished in their first five years. Walter Chrysler and his henchmen had marched directly into the entrenched, competitive guns of a highly developed motorcar industry. Nothing had taken place before, or has since, to match the daring and sudden success of Chrysler.

The Chrysler car was an outgrowth of the dislocations in the motorcar business caused by the war and its aftermath. Car factories, dealer organizations and financing were available on a scale that had not existed before. The success of General Motors led to constant probing into the possibilities of merging other firms into similar, new corporations that would be large enough to compete more effectively.

After Walter Chrysler left General Motors and retired, most of his friends thought it would be only a matter of time until he came back into the industry. This was a logical assumption. Chrysler was only forty-five years old and had been extremely active all his life. But, Chrysler was not yet ready to organize a new firm. For a time after he left General Motors, he spent months disposing of his General Motors stock, placing his large estate in trusts for his family.

He opened an office in Detroit to which he commuted daily from Flint. There he worked out the arrangements for his family holdings. Although Chrysler seriously considered himself in retirement at this time, the manner in which he arranged his investments was a tipoff to his future plans. He placed his wealth in trusts that could never become involved in any further business undertakings which he might head. Had he not recognized the possibility of his going back into business such arrangements would not have had meaning.

From the time he left General Motors, he began receiving offers. Most of them did not carry salary offers equal to his $600,000 at General Motors. Chrysler enjoyed talking, but he showed little real interest. Meanwhile, the 1920-21 depression struck the industry and within weeks many firms were in serious financial condition. One of the largest was Willys-Overland at Toledo. Another was the Maxwell Motor Company in Detroit .

Willys-Overland was soon staggering under an indebtedness of nearly $50,000,000. The banks that had loaned the money faced fearful losses if Willys-Overland failed. The bankers sent a committee to

In 1928, Plymouth was
introduced to compete
with Chevrolet and Ford
in the low-priced field.
This picture of Chrysler
was used in a special
Plymouth advertisement
in which Chrysler created
the reference to "the
big three."

411

meet with Chrysler and they proposed that Chrysler take over the management of Willys-Overland for a period of two years. On the banker committee that came to Flint to see Chrysler was his longtime friend, Ralph Van Vechten of Continental National Bank of Chicago, the man with whom Chrysler arranged a loan of $4,300 to buy his first motorcar.

With the bankers looking over their shoulders, Willys and Chrysler worked out a plan by which the former head of Buick would take over complete management of Willys-Overland for two years. Chrysler asked a million dollars for each of the two years. The bankers urged Willys to accept the Chrysler terms. At the end of two years, Chrysler was to decide whether he wished to remain with Willys-Overland. If he did, a new arrangement would be worked out. It was agreed that a new car would have to be developed at Willys-Overland. It was understood that if the Flint man made his association with Willys-Overland permanent, the new car would be given the name, "Chrysler."

The Chryslers moved to New York City since the Willys-Overland executive headquarters were there. Except for Ford and General Motors, Willys-Overland's network of factories and subsidiaries was the most extensive in the U. S. Clearly emulating Durant's moves at General Motors, the firm even had farm implement and airplane factories. Chrysler worked furiously at his new job. He cut expenses sharply, even reducing John Willys's salary by 50 percent. Before the end of the two years, Chrysler had trimmed the Willys-Overland debts down to about $18,000,000.

At the time Chrysler became manager of Willys-Overland, the firm had just begun building a large new motorcar factory at Elizabeth, New Jersey. Chrysler turned this into an engineering center. To develop the new car, he maintained a team of motorcar engineers, designers and research consultants. Heading the group was Fred M. Zeder. His two key associates were Owen Skelton and Carl Breer. Until the year before, the trio had been at Studebaker. Chrysler had known them almost from the time he came to Buick. They had left Studebaker to establish their own consultants' firm, and one of their first important jobs was the assignment at Willys-Overland by Chrysler.

Chrysler constructed offices for the engineers in one corner of the new, Elizabeth plant. The association quickly developed into an exciting experience for all four men. With Chrysler's own creative ideas and experience in production, Zeder and his men were soon

The Sloan-Knudsen-Kettering concept of an annual
model with improvements each year, introduced after
World War I, brought to an end the era of the
"Model-T" Ford after almost two decades. This 1927
Knudsen-inspired Chevrolet became the first car
since 1910 to outsell the "Model-T."

probing new possibilities for engines. These ideas were too advanced for the executives of Willys-Overland and the Zeder-Skelton-Breer team was put to work designing a new car. Failure to get the Willys officials to take an interest in a new type of motorcar engine convinced Chrysler that his association would not become permanent.

Herbert R. Lewis visited Chrysler at the plant in behalf of General Motors' Harrison Radiator, which at that time was producing radiators for firms outside of General Motors. Chrysler took Lewis aside and told him, "There's not much here, Herb."

Early in his second year at Willys, the bankers who were holding notes of the Maxwell Motor Company for some $26,000,000 came to Chrysler. They knew that his debt-liquidation efforts at Willys-Overland were making rapid headway. They wanted him to take over the operation of Maxwell, even while working for Willys-Overland. John Willys approved the arrangement, indicating that he, too, realized that Chrysler's association with his firm was not destined to become permanent.

Chrysler's work with Zeder and his engineers on the new car had drastically changed his outlook. Instead of asking Maxwell for an astronomical salary for a short time, Chrysler took the new assignment for $100,000 a year. At the same time, he retained Zeder, Skelton and Breer to begin work on the dream engine they had discussed, but which had not been of interest to John Willys. Chrysler used his earnings from his Willys-Overland contract to support the engineering work on the new engine.

Willys-Overland found it necessary to sell the Elizabeth plant to further reduce its debts. Chrysler and Zeder wanted the plant and the design for the new car which went with it. The property was sold at auction. Chrysler set a bidding limit of $5,000,000 on the big plant that had cost $14,000,000 only two years before. Durant knew the plant was a bargain, also. He saw it as a means of getting not only a new factory but a new car at the same time. His bid for $5,525,000 got the factory. The car which Zeder and his men did design for Willys-Overland soon went into production as Billy Durant's new "Flint."

With the Willys-Overland job done, Chrysler brought the engineering work on the new engine into Maxwell. Zeder, Skelton and Breer were located in the renovated Chalmers plant in Detroit. Soon after, Chrysler came close to losing his control of the new engine, entirely. Studebaker, also seeking a new car, learned of the develop-

In May, 1927, Henry and Edsel Ford rode from the
Highland Park Ford factory to the Henry Ford Museum
in the 15,000,000th "Model-T." Except for minor
changes, such as adding a front door and shifting the
steering wheel from right to left, the car was unchanged.
The production chiefs during the entire "Model-T"
period, Charles E. Sorensen and Peter E. Martin, not yet
arrived, rode in the back seat on the historic, short trip.

ment and almost completed a deal to buy Maxwell and all its properties, including the new, mystery engine.

By this time, Zeder and his men had actually built one of the new engines and had installed it in an old car for highway tests. Chrysler enjoyed riding with his engineers who tested the new engine's remarkable get-away speeds in Detroit traffic. Many a time the shabby, old car would line up at a stop light beside a new, heavy car only to leave the expensive motorcar half a block behind. Drivers of some of the big cars would make a contest of the matter, only to be left behind again and again.

By the fall of 1923, when Chrysler had sharply reduced Maxwell debts, he was able to find the money to complete the design of the new motorcar and produce a few, handbuilt floor models for exhibit. Even in its improved financial condition, Maxwell could not raise the $5,000,000 required to put the new car into production. It would be necessary to rely on the New York Automobile Show to produce enough dealer and customer interest and advance orders to convince bankers that they should loan the money needed to advance the new car to a reality.

The exhibition models and the 1924 Maxwells were shipped to New York City. Chrysler, Zeder, Skelton, Breers and the Maxwell executives were already at their hotel in New York. Then came chilling news. Because the new car was not in production and had not been sold, it could not be shown, along with the 1924 Maxwells, at the New York Automobile Show.

There was much more at stake than the future of the new car. Maxwell's ability to get the credit needed to produce its regular new models was hinged, to some degree, on exhibiting the new car and making it a success. The bad news left everyone silent and grim. Zeder was away from the hotel at the time the news arrived, and Chrysler dreaded having to tell him that their two years of hard work had been for nothing, after all.

Hours passed. Chrysler refused to stir from his hotel. Suddenly an idea and a wave of hope swept over him. He was never able to fully explain it. He just stood up and began yelling through the Maxwell hotel suite for Joe Fields, the sales manager. When Fields came, Chrysler explained something Fields and everyone in the suite knew. The Grand Central Place was where the public paid admission to see the new cars, but the executives of the motorcar industry spent much of their time at the hotel, the show's official headquarters. The headquarters, in 1924, was at the Hotel Commodore.

Five years and five models later, William S. Knudsen
(left), looks over the newest Chevrolet which had taken
on many of the features of today's cars—six cylinder
valve-in-head motor, colorful quick-drying finishes,
extensive use of chrome and a heavy bumper. High
compression V-8 engines, automatic transmission and air
conditioning were the only major features of today's cars
missing from this 8,000,000th Chevrolet built in
August 1932.

"Joe, you've hired plenty of hotel rooms," said Chrysler. "Go and hire the lobby of the Commodore. We'll have a show all right."

In a short time Joe was back waving a piece of Commodore stationery as though it were a small flag. He handed it to Chrysler. On it was written, "Boss, we own the lobby."

The new Maxwell car displaying the name, CHRYSLER, was placed in the Commodore lobby during the night before the Automobile Show opened the next morning. The crowd gathered early that first day, and the new car was never alone day or night for eight days. Chrysler stayed with it almost constantly.

Mr. and Mrs. Herbert Lewis had reservations at the Commodore. They arrived the first day of the Show and were surprised to see the new Chrysler car on display, and even more surprised to see Walter Chrysler with it. They had just begun walking toward the registration desk when Chrysler saw them. He ignored Lewis, but walked over to Mrs. Lewis, the image of an excited man having a wonderful time. "Now I know your old man is a General Motors man, but we've got something over here that I want to show you," he said, as he took her arm and escorted her to the new Chrysler. As she was leaving, and still speaking in a voice that everyone in that part of the lobby could hear, Chrysler said, "This is a great new car and I'm going to sell you a Chrysler."

Shortly after, Chrysler had the opportunity to use his great sales ability in what was the largest sale of his life. Ed Tinker, president of Chase Securities Corporation, came in to see the new car. He knew that Maxwell needed the money to put the car in production. Chrysler got into the car with Tinker, rolled up the windows and locked the doors. They talked for an hour with a ring of faces pressing against the glass. Chrysler explained the new, light, six-cylinder, ultra-high compression engine had more kick than cars costing $5,000. The new, hydraulic four-wheel brakes and some new features, such as, seven bearings on the crankshaft and a replaceable oil filter were also on the car.

Finally, Ed Tinker agreed to make the loan. He said later, in humor, that it was the only way he knew to get away. After he had gone, Chrysler happened to think to himself, "What if he should change his mind?" He had his treasurer go at once to see Tinker. He found him in a barber shop, nearby. Chrysler and his lawyers joined them and the conference went on through the night as the big money contract was worked out down to the last phrase. Other Maxwell and Chase officials joined the group during the night, some

Charles W. Nash kept Nash output at relatively high levels despite the Great Depression of the 1930s. In one depression year, the profits of Nash Motors exceeded those of General Motors. It was a proud moment for Nash in 1934, when the 1,000,000th Nash car rolled off the Kenosha, Wisconsin, assembly line.

of them called away from automobile show parties and still in their gala outfits. Everyone saw the dawn come up out of the east but, before breakfast was served, the money contract was signed. The Chrysler car was a reality.

During 1924 it was possible to produce 32,000 of the new Chryslers. The Maxwell four-cylinder cars sold well, also. Maxwell profits for the year were $4,115,000, almost as much as the $5,000,000 borrowed to put the Chrysler into production. In 1925, Zeder and his men came up with another major feature when they put the motor entirely on rubber mounts that greatly reduced vibration. That year, Maxwell-Chalmers was reorganized and became the Chrysler Corporation. By 1926, the new corporation had produced nearly 200,000 cars. The Maxwell had been discontinued and in its place was the Chrysler "50." There were three other Chryslers, the "60," the "70" and the Chrysler Imperial "80" to compete with Cadillac, Lincoln and the top Packard models.

The model numbers on the new Chryslers had great significance. No such telling use of numbers had been made in the name of a self-propelled vehicle since Henry Ford gave his racer the name, "999," after the famous New York Central train that had set a world speed record. The numbers of those first Chrysler cars indicated to the public the sustained speed the car could maintain on good highways. The small Chrysler "50" that had replaced the Maxwell could travel fifty miles an hour.

The Ford "Model-T," at that time, was the standard with which all cars were compared. The "Model-T" was capable of sustained speeds of thirty-five to forty miles an hour on good roads. A car that could travel fifty miles in an hour and maintain reasonable passenger comfort was a remarkable achievement. The speeds of sixty, seventy and eighty miles an hour had previously been associated only with racing cars running on a carefully built race track. The model numbers were an astute device for letting the public know that a new age in motoring had begun. The numbers were eventually changed to the "62" and "72" to indicate that the latest models were improved.

Chrysler's success proved, once again, that the heart of the motorcar was its engine. Zeder and his engineers, backed by the encouragement and understanding of Walter Chrysler, had followed in the footsteps of Frank Duryea, Ransom Olds, Henry Leland, David Buick and Henry Ford. They had produced a highly superior motor. They had done it by converting the high compression motors of racing cars, in which length of engine life and cost of maintenance

Henry Ford's final
contribution to the
motorcar was an
important factor in the
depression years of the
1930s. In 1932, the Ford
Motor Company
introduced the first V-8
motor in the low-priced
field. Ford had had an
important personal role
in the development of the
V-8 motor which until
then had been available
only in the heavier and
more costly cars. Ford
was nearly eighty years
old

are of little importance, into a power plant that could perform quietly in a family car for tens of thousands of miles with only normal maintenance.

As had always been the case before, the American public was quick to respond. By 1927, the Chrysler Corporation was among the nation's leaders in car production, but Chrysler himself was not satisfied. He knew that his Chrysler Corporation, whose operations (in only three years) already extended around the world, could not become a permanent part of the motorcar industry in the United States unless it was able to enter the low-priced field. Chevrolet was, at the time, cracking Ford's two-year strangle hold in the low-priced field.

Chrysler had most of the resources at his command to enter the low-priced field against Ford and Chevrolet. His company had good men. K. T. Keller, his right-hand production man during Chrysler's last years at Buick, was now in charge of production for the Chrysler Corporation. Management was sound, modeled along the lines Sloan had introduced at General Motors. In Zeder and his engineers, Chrysler had an outstanding research team. Yet Chrysler knew that his company lacked the production capacity that would be needed to force Ford and General Motors to share the low-priced market.

The Chrysler Corporation did not own either a foundry or a forge shop. The company was now making bodies and many components that went into Chrysler cars, but far too much still had to be bought outside. All cast iron parts and all forged parts—the very guts of the all important engines—were being bought from suppliers. Chrysler's men figured again and again how much it would cost to build a foundry, a forge shop and the other new factories. No matter how the figuring was done, the total came to $75,000,000, and that was beyond the reach of the 1927 Chrysler Corporation.

There was one other way. John and Horace Dodge's great Hamtramck factory had the foundry and the forge shops and all the other equipment to support the Chrysler Corporation's entry into the low-priced field. Chrysler had known John and Horace Dodge well and favorably. He had visited Hamtramck many times to see the new shops and equipment added there from year to year. He knew that, as a manufacturing center for motorcars, Hamtramck stood next to Ford's River Rouge factory. Knowing the factory and the business of producing motorcars as he did, a vision of the Dodge plant being acquired by the Chrysler Corporation took shape in Chrysler's mind. It could become the cornerstone of an organization

During the depression years, when buying of new cars dropped to one-third the 5,350,000 cars and trucks marketed in the boom year of 1929, it was general practice to get famous Americans to endorse new models. Amelia Earhart is seen with her 1932 Essex, Lowell Thomas with a 1934 Hudson and baseball's all-time homerun king, Babe Ruth, with the 1937 Nash.

able to compete effectively with General Motors and Ford—a firm that could give the national motorcar business a third giant.

There had been major developments at Dodge. With Frederick Haynes in semi-retirement and the more intense competition that followed World War I, Dodge sales had been receding. As mentioned previously, unable to find capable management for the vast enterprise, the Dodge widows had sold the business and all its assets to the New York banking house of Dillon, Read & Company.

Clarence Dillon had written out a single check in longhand, as the operator of a country store might have done, for the entire $146,000,000. John and Horace would have approved of the check. It had been made out simply to "Dodge Brothers," the second word spelled with a capital B. It was the largest amount of cash ever to change hands in the motorcar business to that time—perhaps at any time, since large transactions of that nature generally involve exchanges of stock, taking over debts or other non-cash considerations.

Dillon, too, knew that the Dodge manufacturing capacity was the greatest in the industry, together with Ford and General Motors. His banking house knew that Dodge factories could become the hub of a third giant in the business. They considered such firms as Packard, Hudson and Nash, with higher-priced cars in their lines as good possibilities for an effective merger with Dodge. Dillon also spoke to Chrysler about the matter soon after his banking house bought Dodge in the spring of 1925. Chrysler was determined not to appear to be too anxious, and nothing developed for two years.

In May of 1927, Chrysler and Dillon agreed to meet for a thorough discussion of the advantages of the Chrysler Corporation acquiring the Dodge car and all its facilities. Dillon came to Chrysler's office for the talk, but Chrysler advised him that, since the talks would be of some duration and they needed to be free from interruptions, he had reserved a suite at the Ritz-Carlton. Chrysler said that he wanted to have some of his associates take part in the talks.

Chrysler and Dillon did not leave the Ritz-Carlton Hotel suite for five days. At the end of the protracted negotiations, the Chrysler Corporation had bought the Dodge car, the Hamtramck factory, the Dodge dealer organization and all manufacturing materials on hand for $225,000,000. No cash changed hands. Chrysler gave Dillon $170,000,000 in Chrysler Corporation stock and assumed all Dodge obligations outstanding, which amounted to about $55,000,000.

Agreement was reached about 5:00 in the afternoon. When daylight swept over the Hamtramck factory the next morning already

On January 11th, 1940, General Motors produced its
25,000,000th motorcar, a Chevrolet made in Flint.
An executive vice-president and three presidents of
General Motors took part in the ceremonies. (Left to
right): M. E. Coyle, head of the Chevrolet Division and
later executive vice-president of General Motors;
William S. Knudsen, General Motors president; Alfred
P. Sloan, Jr., chairman of the board and former
president; and Charles E. Wilson, later president
of General Motors.

in place were huge signs which read, "Chrysler Corporation, Dodge Division." The announcement came exactly one month later. In 1928, the Chrysler Corporation introduced into the low-priced field, the Plymouth, with the Chrysler feature of the high compression motor mounted in rubber.

The announcement of Chrysler's purchase of Dodge found a large part of the nation's financial experts of the opinion that the Chrysler Corporation had made a large, perhaps fatal, mistake. Walter Chrysler had the last laugh, and enjoyed it to the fullest. Despite the Great Depression Chrysler had, by 1935, absorbed Dodge, established Plymouth as the foremost competitor of Ford and Chevrolet in the low-priced field, had enlarged and improved the Dodge line of cars and was completely debt free. The "Big Three" was a reality.

Walter Chrysler had produced magic. He had been confident that he could. He understood the new American formula for magic which had produced the motorcar. He had learned from Durant a man can be as tall as his dreams, and from Leland the importance of one-10,000th of an inch when working with standardized metal parts. From Ford he had learned the magic of the fully mechanized and moving assembly line.

As vice-president of General Motors, he had convinced Kettering that the Ohio wizard should come to General Motors as its first research director. He had found Fred Zeder and his engineers and had helped them design exciting, new cars for Willys-Overland, Maxwell and, finally, the Chrysler Corporation. Chrysler had learned the magic of communication with the public and customers from a Detroit advertising man. Theodore F. MacManus never learned to drive a car but judged a new car by the character and desires of the men behind it. He launched several great motorcars, including the Chrysler.

From Alfred Sloan with whom he had worked at General Motors, Chrysler had learned the magic of helping every man on his team do his best work. He could explain the new formula and what it could do for America and mankind.

"Nowhere in the world," said Chrysler, "is there a people with wealth so widespread as in America; nowhere is there a people who have so much. It seems to me quite obvious that we do not owe this difference to a few outstanding men; we owe it to a scheme of working whereby a lot of varied intelligences in a great business organization pool their most effective parts."

"Nourished by such a mind as that of Kettering of General

Motors," continued Chrysler, "or Fred Zeder of the Chrysler Corporation, a great corporation's departmentalized intelligence becomes still greater; but to support a Kettering there must be other kinds of minds, those of production men, of merchants, of mechanics, of advertising men and countless others. *When all these minds, through organization, are made to function as a single intelligence, each member of which is a special, gifted part, why, then you can expect to produce magic."*

26

Shield of the Republic

The great order went out in the name of the President of the United States. Production stopped the same day on every motorcar assembly line in Detroit, Flint, Lansing and everywhere else across the country. The date was February 9th, 1942. Sixty-three days earlier America had entered World War II.

Americans entered the war in a spirit of high confidence. The confidence was based in large degree on the conviction that the carmakers in Detroit would put their moving assembly lines to work and quickly turn out a flood of weapons. With an ample supply of superior weapons, the outcome of the war could not long remain in doubt. Many incidents occurred in 1940-41 to raise these hopes.

In the spring of 1940, after Italy declared war on already prostrate France, President Franklin D. Roosevelt established a National Defense Council. He appointed William S. Knudsen as its chairman. In May, Knudsen resigned as president of General Motors to take the difficult job without pay, glad to serve his adopted country in an emergency. The month before, his native Denmark had been occupied by the Germans. The Roosevelt action made it plain that the government was looking to the carmakers to produce whatever weapons might be needed.

Here is the last Hudson manufactured until after
World War II. All car production in the country ended
February 9th, 1942, on an executive order by the
U.S. government under its wartime powers. The firm's
facilities were used to produce war materials that
included sections for B-29 bombers, folding wings for
the Helldiver fighter plane, Aircobra cabins, 240,000
Hudson Invader engines and landing boats, mine
anchors and other items for the U. S. air force,
army and navy.

Henry Ford made a statement to reporters in Detroit that greatly added to the confidence of Americans. He created the National Defense Council, and President Roosevelt called for an annual production of 50,000 airplanes until the war emergency was over.

Shortly after, Ford inspected a pre-war military plane and was asked by reporters how many of those planes the Ford Motor Company could produce. The man, considered by most Americans to be the father of the mass production, said that there was nothing complicated about this military plane and that his company could produce 50,000 in a year.

The Ford observation had a tremendous impact on the morale of Americans and those countries looking to the United States for military planes. Actually, the Ford pronouncement, the Knudsen appointment and similar developments in 1940 presented a much too favorable image in the public mind of the capacity of even the motorcar industry to meet the World War II challenge. There were other factors which had to be weighed.

The industry had suffered from the Great Depression of the 1930s and had not fully recovered. In 1929, the motorcar factories of the United States had produced 5,530,000 cars and trucks. By 1932, the depression had whittled that volume down to one-third of the 1929 level. Only 1,370,000 cars and trucks were made in 1932. By 1940, production of motor vehicles had only partially been restored to 4,475,000 units. The industry had experienced another setback in the recession of 1938. Production in 1937 had risen to 4,800,000 units, but almost half the volume was lost in the recession the following year.

Further, the experience of making military goods was entirely lacking. In theory, it should be possible to make modern tanks on the moving assembly lines of the motorcar plants, but none had ever been made. The machine tools and the procedures did not exist. In 1940, with the domestic car and truck business reviving, even the plants to produce tanks did not exist. The case of the tank pointed up a fact hard for other countries, already at war for two years or more, to understand. The United States had no industry for production of specialized weapons of war.

In learning to build weapons, the motormakers did have some important advantages. Trucks for military transport were so nearly like trucks for peacetime use that they could be ordered and delivered, in volume, within sixty days. In the year before the United States entered the war, Knudsen was able to get a record 1,060,820 trucks produced to meet both the domestic and military needs.

The moving assembly line, devised in the motorcar plants, was quickly put to use making U. S. weapons in World War II. In May, 1940, the Chrysler Corporation was urged by the U. S. Army to build tanks. The firm built 25,000 before the end of World War II. Here are three lines of General Grant tanks being made in the Chrysler tank plant at Detroit. Willys-Overland produced 200,000 Jeeps. General Motors produced more war weapons and materials than any other business in the United States.

By the time of World War II, the annual model, and the higher levels of research to support it, were almost universal in the motorcar business. Carmakers had learned to make a model change as an almost routine procedure. In 1940, Buick plants made the model change in only ten days. In 1938, Pontiac moved the gear-stick from the floor, where it had been on all cars from the beginning, up to the steering column, a complicated change. The same year, Chrysler began adjusting front seats up and down as well as forward and back. Ford introduced an entire line of new cars, called the Mercury. Dodge, Ford and Chevrolet all introduced cab-over-engine trucks.

The 1939 models presented the most complicated changes yet; good experience for factories that soon would be faced with day-to-day model changes on war weapons. Sealed beam headlights were introduced. The first push-button radios appeared in cars. Oldsmobile introduced its automatic transmission, and Packard offered air conditioners in its cars. Heaters and defrosters were made standard equipment on several makes. In 1940, the final model changes were made. Nash introduced the first mass-produced, unitized body. Automatic transmissions appeared on Cadillac, Dodge and Chrysler cars. Chrysler introduced the two-speed windshield wiper, also.

Knudsen moved into his job as defense coordinator quickly. Dodge contracted to produce 20,000 U.S. Army trucks. European branches of United States auto firms generally took on war contracts. But, Knudsen encountered problems, too. In June, the British government asked him to secure an American carmaker to build Rolls-Royce motors for Britain's hard-pressed Royal Air Force. Knudsen called Edsel Ford, by that time, president of the Ford Motor Company. Edsel came to Washington and accepted the British contract. When he went back to Detroit the seventy-seven-year-old Henry Ford exercised his authority as owner of the company and refused to permit the British Royal Air Force motors to be made in Ford factories. Knudsen shifted the job to Packard. Ford's pacifist views were blamed for the embarrassing situation. There is no question about his dislike for war, but there probably were other reasons. There were indications that he felt strongly about Roosevelt's appointment of Knudsen from General Motors as National Defense Coordinator. Knudsen and General Motors had toppled the "Model-T." Whatever the reasons were, they apparently disappeared because a few months later he approved the building of Pratt and Whitney airplane engines for military craft.

From the time Knudsen arrived in Washington as the nation's

Most of the tanks produced by Chrysler were Shermans,
as is this one being loaded in Detroit for shipment
to the war fronts.

defense coordinator it was evident that, if the British and the Russians were to stay in the war, tanks and airplanes would have to be produced for them in the United States in large numbers, and as quickly as possible. Knudsen was convinced that standardization of parts, the moving assembly line and precision mass production offered the only solution to the critical shortage of weapons.

So critical was the tank shortage that, in May, 1940, the same month of his appointment as defense coordinator, Knudsen called Detroit on a Sunday morning for K. T. Keller, now president of the Chrysler Corporation. In his Danish accent (that Keller recognized immediately), Knudsen asked, "K. T., do you want to make tanks?"

"Sure," said Keller, "Where can I see one?"

Knudsen arranged for Keller and several of his Chrysler associates to go, the next day, to an island in the Mississippi River where the Army's Rock Island Arsenal has been located since Civil War days. There they studied the army's latest tanks. When Keller left the arsenal, he and his Chrysler team took with them 168 pounds of blueprints for the army's newest tank, one which had not yet been put into service.

Back in Detroit, Keller began harnessing the many energies of the corporation, working out the procedures for mass-producing an army tank. Engineers began the development of the new machine tools. The Chrysler staff located a cornfield just outside Detroit, bought the land and began designing a new factory with a moving assembly line nearly fifteen hundred feet long. Seven months later, completed tanks began coming from the cornfield arsenal of the Chrysler Corporation.

Knudsen's progress was slow during 1940 and 1941. The country was not at war, and the most he could do was to ask firms to undertake the production of weapons. During these two years, the motorcar industry produced a total of 7,500,000 cars. Even so, the 1940-41 record of Knudsen's National Defense Council achievements within the motorcar industry was impressive. Chrysler not only achieved mass production of tanks, but began delivery of its first anti-aircraft guns. Ford agreed to build the heavy bomber, the B-24 Liberator, and was tooling up for the job. Some General Motors Divisions were already producing machine guns. Studebaker had begun work on aircraft engines. Pontiac had begun work on the Oerlikon anti-aircraft guns. Oldsmobile was producing shells for U. S. Army. Graham-Paige was at work on amphibian tanks.

From the time the United States entered the war on December 8th,

The Detroit-built Sherman tanks in combat on the
Western Front in Europe in 1943. Chrysler has continued
to build tanks for use both in Korea and Vietnam.

1941, the government began assuming wartime powers which revealed how indispensable had become the motorcar and truck to the country's ability to produce. The car factories and the men who operated them were important. So also were the cars owned by individuals, which were soon brought under strict government control.

The first important wartime move with respect to the motorcar was the halt of new car production early in February, 1942. Nearly 250,000 cars had been built before the 9th of February. There were assembled from parts on hand a total of only 139 motorcars in 1943 and 610 in 1944. Truck and bus production in 1943 totalled 669,689, and in 1944 the figure was 737,524.

The halting of car production was only the beginning in 1942. On March 2nd, the rationing of new cars began for civilians. The next day, the rationing of civilian trucks took effect. On May 3rd a national speed limit of 40 miles per hour was set by the federal government to conserve gasoline supplies. Later, the speed limit was lowered to 35 miles an hour. Gasoline was urgently needed on the Allied fighting fronts in Europe. On May 15th, the government, without advance notice, simply slashed the supplies of gasoline going to service stations in seventeen eastern seaboard states by 50 percent. On September 10th, President Roosevelt ordered gasoline rationing as a means of conserving both fuel and rubber supplies. The program required every car owner in the United States to be classified according to the importance of his car to the war effort, and ration stamps were issued. That huge task took several weeks and rationing began December 1st, 1942.

The darkest hours of the war occurred in the winter, spring and summer months of 1942. The first dawn of Allied hope came in July. General Rommel's German army was stopped. General Montgomery's Eighth British Army, using American Curtis P-40 fighter planes and Chrysler-built tanks, turned the Germans back and soon began its own offensive. Knudsen's hard work in Detroit and around the country had paid its first dividend.

Once motorcar production had been stopped, the research and engineering staffs of the carmakers had been put to work designing new weapons. General Motors became the nation's largest single producer of weapons and war materials. General Motors engineers designed, all or in part, 72 percent of the items the firm produced under wartime contracts. Other items were adapted from plans furnished General Motors. These included the Wildcat Fighter and

Here is the mile-long moving assembly line at
Ford's Willow Run plant where a soybean farm was
converted into a factory that built 8,685 Liberator
heavy bombers by war's end.

Avenger Torpedo-bomber planes and the 20- and 50-caliber Browning machine guns.

Of the war items produced by General Motors, 20 percent were designed completely by its engineers in cooperation with the United States armed services. These included tanks, armored cars and aircraft engines. General Motors peacetime products, such as trucks and diesel engines modified for military use, amounted to 17 percent, while 13 percent were items made by General Motors in peacetime which did not require adaptation for war use; sparkplugs, for example. Finally, 15 percent of the items were produced from plans provided from outside General Motors. The Pratt & Whitney airplane engine is an example.

The magnitude of Knudsen's remarkable wartime work never will be fully known. The manpower problems encountered were awesome. General Motors alone had more than 113,000 employees taken into the armed services, and had to hire and train 750,000 new workers to meet its government contracts. The number of women workers increased from 10 to 30 percent.

The cooperation Knudsen developed among the carmakers extended to loaning entire plants in order to enable another war contractor to meet his goals. While understandings in the end were recorded properly, many tank and plane programs were begun merely as a spoken agreement between Knudsen and officials of contracting firms.

Some of what Knudsen accomplished—including important services with no pay—has never been recorded.

One such arrangement involved Frank Duryea, the man who had built the first, successful, self-propelled road vehicle in this country. Duryea had retired from public view twenty-six years before World War II. He and Mrs. Duryea lived comfortably in his modest home by the sea in Madison, Connecticut. His only luxury was an elaborate, personal machine shop which he maintained in his home. Nevertheless, as former chief engineer of the Duryea Motor Wagon Company and the Stevens-Duryea Motor Car Company, Duryea kept in touch with the men prominent in early work on the motorcar, including Knudsen.

One early summer morning during the war's darkest days in 1942, Duryea had invited Judge Donald M. Macaulay to accompany him to a conference in Washington, D.C. They were to take the train from nearby New Haven. Macaulay arrived at 9 a.m. Mrs. Duryea met him at the door and explained that Duryea was not ready.

In September, 1945, Henry Ford II was elected president of the Ford Motor Company, succeeding his grandfather, Henry Ford, who lived until 1948. Walter P. Chrysler died in 1940, but K. T. Keller had earlier succeeded him as president of the Chrysler Corporation.

439

"Last evening Bill Knudsen called him from New York and they talked on the phone for an hour and a half," explained Mrs. Duryea. "After Frank put down that phone, he went directly to his shop and has never been out of it since. I took him some breakfast about an hour ago and he told me then that he would finish his work but that he still expected to go to Washington with you—on the noon train. I guess you will just have to be patient."

A half hour or more passed, then seventy-three-year-old Duryea, looking surprisingly fit after his all-night machine shop vigil, greeted Macaulay. He turned to his wife and directed her to call Bill Knudsen and report to him the job was finished. Knudsen thanked Mrs. Duryea for the call and explained to her that he would send a government courier from New York at once to get the mechanism. Before handing the mechanism to his wife to keep until Knudsen's courier arrived, Duryea exhibited it to Macaulay. It had the appearance of an oversized railroad man's watch. Duryea's only explanation was that Knudsen wanted it to improve the steering accuracy of an army tank.

With this new breed of men available, men who had worked out the miracles of the motorcar industry, the United States was able, in a remarkably short time, to equip America and her allies with an overwhelming supply of the most complicated weapons of war. No more dramatic example is to be found in the annals of World War II weapons production that the building of the B-24 Liberator bomber by the Ford Motor Company.

Germany suffered one of her greatest defeats in a single room of the Coronado Hotel in San Diego almost a year before the United States entered the war. This was during the period when Knudsen and his National Defense Council were seeking to get military plane production started under voluntary agreements. In November, Knudsen came to Detroit to meet motorcar executives to discuss possibilities for establishing cooperation between West Coast firms making planes and Detroit firms making cars and trucks.

In December, Dr. George Mead, Knudsen's aviation assistant on the National Defense Council and an engineer for whom Henry Ford had great regard, came twice to Dearborn to discuss the possibility of the Ford Motor Company taking a major responsibility in the production of heavy bombers. On the first visit he was accompanied by Major Jimmy Doolittle. Mead discussed the possibility of Ford producing the Flying Fortress. Before he left, the talk had switched to the B-24 Liberator bomber, used later on the spectacular

In 1954, a fourth of today's American motorcar
producers came into being through a merger of the
Nash-Kelvinator Corporation and the Hudson Motor
Car Company. George Romney (right) became head
of the new American Motors Corporation of Detroit.
George W. Mason (center), last president of Nash, and
A. E. Barit, last president of Hudson, exchange greetings
during the ceremonies launching the new firm.

raids on the Ploesti oil fields in Romania. The military men liked the bomber developed by Consolidated Aircraft in San Diego, but they were able to build only one plane a day, about 350 a year. At that rate, it would take Consolidated three years to build a thousand bombers, and the air force wanted several thousands as quickly as possible. Before Mead left Dearborn it was agreed that Sorensen, Edsel Ford and Mead would meet in San Diego January 8th to visit the B-24 factory. They did. Edsel was accompanied by his two sons, Henry II and Benson.

After spending the day in the plane factory, Sorensen went back to his room at the Coronado Hotel. He spent the night drawing, on hotel stationery, the rough plan of a bomber plant that would produce a B-24 bomber every hour. By four a.m. Sorensen knew the specifications of the new factory and the approximate cost. The building and the moving assembly line would be a mile long. The building, also, would be a quarter of a mile wide—the largest factory of its kind in the world. At breakfast Sorensen showed his plans to Edsel who said that the Ford Company would build such a plant. They met Dr. Mead and the air force officials during the day. They were immediately interested.

Henry Ford approved the idea and agreed with Sorensen that the Ford soybean farm on Willow Run Creek, west of Dearborn, would provide a good site for the bomber factory. The government approved the Willow Run project February 25th, 1941. Ground breaking ceremonies were held April 18th, the first structural steel went into place May 3rd, the first machine tools were installed August 12th. First production work on sub-assemblies began November 15th. By July of 1942, plane components, such as the giant wings, were being trucked to Consolidated Aircraft's new plant in Fort Worth. September saw the first complete bomber produced. Only nineteen months had passed since the government had approved the Willow Run contract, and before the Willow Run plant was closed June 23, 1945, it had produced 8,685 Liberators.

A few days after the Willow Run bomber factory began production, President and Mrs. Roosevelt came to see the only place in the world where a bombing plane was being built in an hour. On September 18th, 1942, a Lincoln parade car slowly travelled the length of the mile-long moving assembly line. Henry Ford was seated between the President and Mrs. Roosevelt in the back seat. Edsel Ford and Sorensen sat in the jump seats so they could describe the production steps for the Roosevelts. Donald Nelson, czar of all U. S. war

Alfred P. Sloan Jr. led the motorcar industry for almost three decades. He developed and applied to General Motors the concept of management by which each of the many divisions could have the research, purchasing, financial and other benefits of General Motors affiliation while maintaining full local division responsibility and flexibility. His management concept has been adopted as widely as the moving assembly line and has become a cornerstone of today's industrial process.

443

production, had come with the President and sat in the front seat. It was the first airplane production the President had seen. He often requested the car to stop so that he might ask questions, and he was greatly encouraged by what he saw.

By the time the great war ended, the motorcar factories had accounted for approximately 20 percent of the total amount of weapons and war materials produced in the United States. General Motors became the country's largest single producer of weapons. This is all the more remarkable considering that two-thirds of the war items produced by the carmakers were entirely new to them.

The motorcar industry produced 5,947,000 guns, 600,000 trucks, 50,000 tanks and 4,131,000 engines. The industry produced 27,000 complete military aircraft. The car factories produced more than 5,000,000 bombs, nearly 3,000,000 rockets, 2,500,000 torpedoes and 12,500,000,000 rounds of ammunition.

The motorcar plants had produced 100 percent of the military trucks, 100 percent of the armored cars, 92 percent of the scout cars and carriers, 87 percent of the aircraft bombs, 85 percent of the army helmets, 57 percent of the tanks, 56 percent of the carbines and 47 percent of the machine guns.

Willow Run produced more than bombers. It became a showcase of American weapons production: a new hope for victory. The airplane became the key to victory. Neither troops on the ground nor ships at sea could prevail unless friendly airplanes controlled the air overhead. President Roosevelt had electrified the free world when, in 1940, he appealed for a production of 50,000 planes a year in the United States.

Considered at first to be unrealistic, the production of 300,000 war planes in less than five years was attained. Knudsen explained the importance of the achievement, saying that America "smothered the enemy in an avalanche of production the like of which he had never seen or even dreamed of."

As Historian Allan Nevins observed: "If we had not developed the mass production techniques and the moving assembly line in our motorcar factories, how would we Americans have defended ourselves in the Second World War?"

Appendix

These Are the Founders

After years of considering the men who worked with those early cars that made possible the ones we drive today, I have been able to list just twenty-seven whose roles in the development of the motorcar were decisive. All were not of the same importance. There were ten giants among them—men who did astounding things that had never been done on this earth before. Listed in chronological order in which they did their most important work, they are: Frank Duryea, Ransom E. Olds, Henry M. Leland, John and Horace Dodge, William C. Durant, Henry Ford, Alfred E. Sloan, Jr., William S. Knudsen and Walter Chrysler.

Those twenty-seven men collectively shaped our lives.

Yet some of them are almost entirely unknown. This is particularly true of one of the most important founders, Henry M. Leland, who is as responsible as any other man for the high performance of today's cars.

Their names in alphabetical order, and a short description of their contributions follow:

DAVID BUICK

1855-1929

Developed the original Buick which was the first to demonstrate and popularize a motorcar powered by a valve-in-head engine. The principle is now universally used in the American motorcar.

Roy D. Chapin
1880-1936

First to drive a motorcar from Detroit to New York. The first sales manager for Oldsmobile. One of the founders and, for twenty years, chief executive of the Hudson Motorcar Company. The Hudson was produced from 1909 to 1957, then merged with Nash to establish today's American Motors Corporation.

Louis Chevrolet
1878-1941

Chief engineer for the first Chevrolet motorcars which were 6-cylinder cars, heavy, beautiful and expensive. The name, Chevrolet, has been stamped into the metal of more transport vehicles than any other, including Ford.

Walter Chrysler
1875-1940

Founder and first president of the Chrysler Corporation. He added Dodge to the Chrysler empire. Trained in railroading, Chrysler was formerly president of Buick and a vice-president of General Motors.

James Couzens
1872-1947

Early business manager of the Ford Motor Company. His uncanny talent for holding Ford's confidence and respect, his ability to hire and hold capable men and his financial sense placed his contribution to the Ford Motor Company close to that of Henry Ford in the decisive years from 1903 to 1916. The "Model-T" Ford was developed and became the foremost motorcar in America during these years.

John and Horace Dodge
1864-1920   1868-1920

After making their own bicycle, they produced parts for the first Oldsmobile. Builders of all Ford motors in the early years of the Ford Motor Company. Developers of the Dodge motorcar, the first vehicles to be used by the United States Army in combat.

William C. Durant
1860-1947

Took over management of the Buick Motor Company in 1904 and made the Buick the outstanding motorcar in the early years of this century. In 1908, Americans bought more Buicks than Fords and Cadillacs combined. Founded General Motors and acquired for the firm Buick, Oldsmobile, Cadillac, Oakland (Pontiac) and Chevrolet.

Charles and Frank Duryea
1861-1938   1868-1967

First Americans to develop, prove, build and market a successful self-propelled road vehicle. Charles had the idea and sketched the first plans. Frank was the first in the United States to build more than one successful motorcar. He was not aware that anyone had built an earlier machine.

Edsel Ford
1893-1943

President of the Ford Motor Company for nearly twenty years. Directed the building of the mile-long Willow Run factory where the B-24 bomber, the Liberator, was mass-produced. It was a decisive development in weapons production during World War II.

Henry Ford
1863-1947

Creator of the "Model-T" Ford that accounted for half the motorcars used in the United States from 1912 until 1924. His Ford Motor Company introduced the moving assembly line and was the builder of the River Rouge Ford plant, one of the world's great industrial complexes.

Norval A. Hawkins
1876-1947

Sales genius behind the "Model-T" Ford. Hawkins devised the branch assembly plant system. Later an executive for General Motors, he served on the executive committee during the 1920-21 financial crisis.

Elwood G. Haynes
1857-1925

Supervised the designing and building of the second successful motorcar in the United States. The car was marketed continuously from 1894 to 1924.

Charles F. Kettering
1876-1958

Builder of the first electrical self-starter now universally used on motorcars. Largely responsible for establishing automotive research as a separate and vital factor ranking with production and marketing of American automobiles.

William S. Knudsen
1879-1948

Danish immigrant who became the builder of Ford assembly plants in the United States and overseas. Later, he led Chevrolet to the position of the most widely used automobile. Resigned as president of General Motors to serve as the United States Defense Coordinator during World War II for which he was awarded the government's Distinguished Service Medal.

Henry M. Leland
1843-1932

Developed the Cadillac and the Lincoln. His machine shop was the first capable of producing a continuous supply of motorcar parts machined to 1/10,000th of an inch. He introduced dependable interchangeable parts into the American motorcar industry. He invented the electric self-starter and the modern electrical system of the motorcar. He received for Cadillac the Dewar Trophy for each achievement, the only man and car to win this international award for advanced automotive engineering two times.

Wilfred C. Leland
1869-1958

Wilfred Leland suggested the V-8 motor perfected by his father and Cadillac engineers and now universally used in motorcars. His greatest contributions to the development of the motorcar were in business management and finance. Leland handled the delicate negotiations through which the Cadillac Motor Car Company was sold to General Motors. In 1910 he saved General Motors from immediate financial collapse. He extended by years the brilliant career of his illustrious father.

Charles W. Nash
1864-1948

An outstanding executive in the Durant-Dort Carriage Company of Flint, he became president of Buick and General Motors. In 1916, he established The Nash Motor Company, one parent of The American Motors Corporation.

Ransom E. Olds
1864-1950

Developed first mass-produced motorcar in the United States, using component suppliers, interchangeable parts, assembly line production, national advertising, nationwide and foreign distribution and customer service standards established by a car manufacturer.

James W. Packard
1863-1928

Designed and introduced the Packard, in 1899, at Warren, Ohio. Sold in 1902 to Henry B. Joy of Detroit, the Packard became America's luxury automobile between the two World Wars and was on the market for fifty-nine years, 1899 to 1958.

Alfred P. Sloan, Jr.
1875-1966

Under his direction, General Motors became America's foremost producer of motorcars and the largest privately owned industrial organization of record. Sloan's decentralized management concepts have become a model for major industries in the western world.

Charles E. Sorensen
1881-1965

Associated with Henry Ford for forty years, he stands as one of the industry's top production wizards. He helped develop the River Rouge factory and managed the vast complex for twenty-five years. He supervised the construction and directed the operation of the Willow Run factory where a bomber an hour was produced during World War II.

451

C. HAROLD WILLS
1878-1940
First engineer and designer to work with Henry Ford. He had a key role in developing motors for early Ford cars, including the "Model-T." He first urged use of new lighter and stronger steel alloys that advanced the usefulness of the motorcar. Created his own car, the Wills-St. Clair, one of the fine motorcars of the 1920s.

JOHN N. WILLYS
1873-1933
Founded, and, for two decades, managed the Willys-Overland Company. The Willys-Overland Company sold more cars in competition with "Model-T" Fords than any other company from 1916 to 1921.

ALEXANDER WINTON
1869-1932
Working independently, he designed and produced for sale the third successful internal combustion motorcar in the United States. America's first luxury car in the period before World War I, the Winton, was produced from 1896 until 1925.

FRED ZEDER
1895-1950
The research genius behind the early Chryslers, Plymouths and Imperials. He made higher compression motors practical, and introduced rubber-mounting of engines and bodies.

References for Further Reading

The classic literature on the motorcar will be found in the three volumes, each about 700 pages, written by Allan Nevins and Frank E. Hill: *Ford: The Times, the Man the Company* (1954); *Ford: Expansion and Challenge 1915-1932* (1957); and *Ford: Decline and Rebirth 1933-1962*.

Alfred Sloan's *Adventures of a White Collar Man* (1941) and *My Years With General Motors* (1964) constitute the best view of the development of General Motors. For an insight into the Sloan management concept, widely adopted by large business enterprises everywhere, *My Years With General Motors* will be especially helpful. Sloan had the help of the staff of *Fortune Magazine* in the preparation of this manuscript whose chapters first appeared as articles in *Fortune*.

The Turning Wheel (1934), by Arthur Pound, provides an excellent review of the events which led to the formation of General Motors and the firm's first twenty-five years.

For a general review of the early years of the motorcar, *The Gasoline Age* (1937), by C. B. Glasscock, is most useful and interesting. Glasscock talked with most of the founders before writing his book.

The American Automobile (1965), by John B. Rae, gives the best report on what the automobile has meant to America and the world.

Also of interest in Rae's *American Automobile Manufacturers: The First Forty Years* (1959).

The Last Billionaire (1948), by William C. Richards, first book to be written on Henry Ford after his death, is entertaining and presents the human side of the man who put America on wheels.

My Forty Years With Ford (1956), by Charles E. Sorensen, is a well-documented, inside view of what made the Ford Motor Company great.

One of the great biographies of motorcar literature is, *Master of Precision—Henry M. Leland* (1966), by Mrs. Wilfred C. Leland and Minnie Dubbs Millbrook. Encouraged by Allan Nevins, this book is important reading for anyone who wonders how we happened to have the modern motorcar and why Detroit turned out to be the Motor City.

The Automotive Career of Ransom E. Olds (1963), by G. A. Niemeyer, tells much of Olds not generally known before. The early pictures of Olds and his famous Curved-Dash Oldsmobile would make this book especially important if for no other reason.

Life of an American Workman (1950), by Walter Chrysler and Boyden Sparks, is interesting, accurate and important to understanding both General Motors and the Chrysler Corporation. The chapters first appeared as articles in the *Saturday Evening Post* in 1937. Chrysler died in 1940. The book was published a decade later, with a special chapter covering the period from 1937 to 1950.

Knudsen: A Biography (1947), by Norman Beasley, is the only book on the gracious man with the heavy accent who served Ford, General Motors and his country so well.

Professional Amateur: The Biography of Charles F. Kettering (1957), by Thomas Alva Boyd, like the Knudsen book, is the only one and hence worthwhile.

The Road Is Yours (1951), by R. M. Cleveland and S. T. Williamson, possesses unusual pictures and the best year-by-year record diary of motorcar achievement to be found in any book.

The Story of the American Automobile (1950), by R. E. Anderson, is exactly what the title says. It contains many interesting anecdotes about the motorcar. Excellent pictures, entertaining and accurate as to fact.

In some respects, I have saved the most important for the last. If you have $1.95 and want the finest dictionary yet published on the

Herbert R. Lewis (left), who knew both Buffalo Bill
Cody and Alfred P. Sloan, Jr., is seen visiting with the
manager of the 1966 Chicago Automobile Show. Lewis
had a wide acquaintance with the men who made
today's motorcars possible. He was personally acquainted
with all of the founders exxcept James W. Packard and
John Maxwell. The Lewis memoirs have provided
valuable first-hand reports for this book.
Lewis lives in Oak Park, Illinois.

motorcar, send your money to Wayne State University Press, Detroit, Michigan, and ask for a copy of *Automobiles of America*. You never will be sorry.

If, for any reason, you would like to examine the taped interviews with persons who were actually on the scene when the horseless carriage and the motorcar were bringing about the great change in America, they will be found along with the Ransom E. Olds collection at the library of Michigan State University at East Lansing, Michigan. They are all interesting and historically significant.

The recorded memoirs of Herbert R. Lewis constitute some of the outstanding new source material to become available in recent years on motorcar developments from 1908 until World War II. Lewis's contribution rests on his universal acquaintance throughout the young industry at the top management level.

Index

461

463

467

Richard Crabb

is the author of two previous books, "The Hybrid Corn Makers" published by Rutgers University Press, and "Empire on the Platte" published by World. His writing craft is solidly based on a long career as a newspaperman with a string of family-published weekly papers in the midwest. As reporter and political writer, he learned early in life the value of research and of digging out the facts, an asset which he has used meticulously in assembling material for "Birth of A Giant."

A native of Indiana with upbringing in the Mormon country of western Illinois, he attended Western Illinois University and now lives in Wheaton, near Chicago, where he is gathering material for his next, and as yet untitled, book.

BIRTH OF A GIANT · THE MEN AN